ANDREA COSTA
AND THE RISE OF
SOCIALISM
IN THE ROMAGNA

Manuel G. Gonzales
Diablo Valley College

University Press
of America™

Library of Congress Catalog Card Number: 79-6771

To the People of Imola

PREFACE

The years from 1871 to 1892 represent a very crucial period in the history of the Italian socialist movement. It is at this time that Italy witnessed the transition from anarchism to socialism, a transition that
culminates in the formation of the Italian Socialist Party
at the Congress of Genoa. Much of the credit for this
development should be given to Andrea Costa, who was widely regarded as the leader of the socialist movement in
his country during these two decades. Unfortunately,
Costa's role as an architect of the Socialist Party, or
the Partito dei Lavoratori Italiani as it was originally christened, has not been fully appreciated. In fact,
Costa has been almost wholly neglected by historians,
and the little that has been written about him rarely
goes beyond the symbolic stature of the man as the "Father of Italian Socialism." Since a scholarly study of
Andrea Costa seems long overdue, particularly one which
focuses on this important period in Italian history, this
task is the one to which I am addressing myself.

In this biography Costa will be seen in the context
of the Italian socialist and working-class movement, but
a major emphasis, as the title of the book indicates, will
be placed on his work and influence in northern Italy,
especially in the Romagna. There are two reasons why the
regional aspect will be stressed: first, because it is
my firm belief that before 1892 (and to some extent afterwards also) socialism on the peninsula was divided re-
gionally and its characteristics differed markedly according to its particular environment; and secondly, because
while Costa's impact on socialism outside of the Romagna
and the surrounding area was rather limited, in that region he clearly dominated the situation. Perhaps, too,
it should be added that in the two decades encompassed by
this study the Romagna was widely acknowledged as the principal citadel of the socialist movement in Italy.

I realize that looking at Costa from a special point
of view, as a Romagnol socialist, will result in a rather
circumscribed perspective from which much will be excluded. This is unfortunate, but apparently unavoidable. Had
I approached Costa from another point of view, other matters would have been stressed. For instance, after 1882,
when he was first elected to the Chamber of Deputies, Costa

could be studied in terms of his activity as socialist
deputy. In this case the emphasis would be on his parliamentary career, hence on a different set of questions:
his role in the Extreme Left, his participation in the
Masonic movement, his view of the African campaign. Inasmuch as there is an obvious relationship between Costa's
activities in and out of Parliament, I will touch on these
various questions; but the scope of my research will limit
the attention I can devote to them.

A second deficiency should also be mentioned: while
I made extensive use of police records contained at the
State Archives in both Forlì and Bologna, those at Ravenna
(and the surrounding province), one of the major urban
centers in the Romagna, were not utilized at all. This
omission is indeed a serious defect in a regional study
such as mine. But here, too, the problem was insurmount-
able--the Archivio di Stato at Ravenna, along with its
records, was totally destroyed during the Second World War.

The book was made possible by generous grants made
available to me in 1973-74 by the American Council of
Learned Societies and the National Endowment for the Hu-
manities. I wish to express my sincere appreciation here
for these monies. My thanks also to Doctor Luigi Arbizzani, Director of the Istituto Antonio Gramsci in Bologna,
upon whose vast knowledge of the Italian socialist and
working-class movements I drew on many occasions; and to
Professor Richard Hostetter of the University of Califor-
nia at Riverside, who offered invaluable advice and on
whose work my own relied so heavily. I am indebted to
Charles Scribner's Sons for permission to quote, in Chapter XI, from A Farewell to Arms by Ernest Hemingway, copy-
right 1929 by Charles Scribner's Sons. Finally, I would
like to acknowledge a special debt of gratitude to my wife,
Cindy, for her able assistance and immeasurable encouragement.

TABLE OF CONTENTS

CHAPTER ONE

THE INTERNATIONAL IN THE ROMAGNA, 1871-1872

Bakunin, the Commune, and the International in Italy

The attempt to create a socialist movement in Italy
began in 1864 with the arrival of Michael Bakunin (1814-
1876) in Florence.[1] His impact in the peninsula during
the next few years, all through the 1870's and even later, would be a profound one.

By the time of his Italian sojourn the aging revolutionary was approaching the twilight of his long and tur-
bulent career.[2] Bakunin's origins were most unlikely;
born into the Russian aristocracy, at the age of fifteen
he embarked on a military career--like so many other
young members of his social class--and served in the imperial guard in Poland. Army life did not agree with him.
He abandoned the military in 1834 and went to Moscow,
where he studied philosophy. During this period he came
to experience a growing awareness of the tyranny of the
Czarist regime and a sensitivity to the social inequali-
ties existing in his country. Disillusioned, he left
Russia after six years and traveled extensively--Germany
Switzerland, Belgium. In the meantime, because he refused
to return to Russia when ordered to do so, his estates
were confiscated by the government.

Bakunin spent the four years from 1844 to 1847 in
Paris, where he frequented the company of a number of
agitators who believed in social revolution, among them
Pierre Joseph Proudhon and Karl Marx. By now the Russian
was an ardent revolutionary himself, and it was his subversive activities that led to his expulsion from France
in December, 1847. He was forced to leave for Belgium,
but he would not remain there long.

The Russian played a very active role in the revolutionary upheavals of 1848-49. He participated in the February Revolution in Paris in 1848, and later in the year
we find him at the Slavic Congress held in Prague, pre-
dicating war against the Germans. Early the following
year he was in Leipzig and Berlin, and in May he helped
lead the insurrection at Dresden. Arrested, Bakunin was

1

condemned to death for his part in the revolt, but the sentence was later commuted to life in prison. After imprisonment in Germany and Austria came extradition to his motherland in 1851, and years of confinement, first in St. Petersburg and six years later in eastern Siberia. His only hope now was escape. Leaving Siberia in mid-1861 he journeyed half way around the globe, via Japan and the United States, and arrived in London by the end of the year. The Panslavic movement now engaged most of his activities. When he arrived in Italy in 1864, though, social rather than national revolution had become his main interest.

Perhaps the most profound influence on Bakunin's thought was that of Proudhon. Like the Frenchman, he was obsessed with the idea of liberty--individual liberty above all. But from this basic need stemmed others. How, Bakunin asked, could the individual be free when he was continually subjected to the oppression of the landlord, the priest, and, most intolerable of all, the government? Freedom, true freedom, he concluded, required the abolition of Private Property, Church, and State.[3]

And the means to achieve this utopia? The liberty which Bakunin demanded would not be easy to obtain. The institutions of authority were strong, and no tyrant, he knew, willingly conceded freedom--Bakunin's reasoning here undoubtedly conditioned by the Russian experience. Hence the need for a violent revolution. This revolt, moreover, must be a popular one; the masses must participate in it, and in fact must initiate it. The only other alternative would be a revolution led by an elite, but this element, he cautioned, would soon form a new ruling class as oppressive as the old one, and the situation would remain essentially unaltered.

By 1864 Bakunin had become the leading exponent of this set of ideas, an ideology known as anarchism. It would be this form of socialism which would take root in Italy at the very outset and which would continue to dominate the movement there until the end of the 1870's.

Bakunin's stay in Italy lasted, with some interruptions, from March, 1864, to August, 1867.[4] During this time the Russian was busy constructing a secret society which came to be known as the Alliance of Socialist Revolutionaries or, more commonly, the International Fraternity. Given its clandestine nature little is known about the association except that it established branches in several European countries and its scope was social

2

revolution.

In 1865 Bakunin moved to Naples where, with a small group of devoted followers which included Carlo Gambuzzi, Alberto Tucci, Saverio Friscia, and Giuseppe Fanelli, he succeeded in winning wider acceptance of his anarchist philosophy and extended the organization of the Fraternity.

In November, 1868, after Bakunin had left Naples to take up residence in Switzerland, he and his friends in the various European countries created a new association, one which would function openly, the International Alliance of Socialist Democracy.[5] Some months previously, in July, the Russian had adhered to the rapidly-expanding International Workingmen's Association (I.W.A.), and by the end of the year the Alliance, following his example, did likewise.

The I.W.A., later to be known as the First International, was founded in London on September 28, 1864, by a group of workers representing the laboring classes throughout Europe. The scope of the newly-formed Association was to unify the working class and improve its social, political, and economic status. The International soon came under the control of Karl Marx and his followers who attempted to organize the Association according to the principles annunciated in the Communist Manifesto of 1848.

As was true of Marx, Bakunin, who would soon become the German's bitterest rival, had not been involved in the creation of the International. Nor was he immediately impressed by the Association; though he was aware of its existence by the end of its first year and in general agreement with its principles, the anarchist leader refused to adhere to the organization for some time. He finally joined its ranks in 1868 when it became apparent that the I.W.A. had begun to make sizeable inroads among the European working class.

Among Bakunin's associates who followed suit were the Italians. The founding of Internationalist sections in Italy in 1869 marked the beginning of the I.W.A. in that country. The first of these nuclei was created in Naples by Gambuzzi and other friends of Bakunin. Naples would remain the foremost center of Internationalist, and Bakuninist, activity there for the next two years.[6] The Association also made some headway in the regions of Apulia and Sicily. In the northern half of the country, on

the other hand, there was little trace of socialist or-
ganization--a situation that would change dramatically
in the aftermath of the Paris Commune.

The French defeat at the hands of the Prussians created the conditions which led to the insurrection of 1871.
On March 18 of that year the citizens of the French capital rose up against the central government, and for the
next two months civil war raged in Paris. The destruction was incredible. Not the least of the consequences
was the loss of lives: it has been estimated that over
20,000 Frenchmen died during the conflict, many of them
victims of the massacres which characterized both sides.
The scars would take years to heal; the Commune conditioned French history into the twentieth century.

The impact of the Paris revolt was also immense outside of France. In Italy the general reaction was the
same as everywhere else--almost universal condemnation.[7]
The Commune, it was widely believed, had threatened not
only order and stability, but private property and religion as well. Equated with anarchy, the Commune inspired
fear and hatred. The same held true for the I.W.A.,which
received the blame for the bloody episode.

The newspapers in Italy which defended the Commun-
ards in 1871 were but a small handful: these included
L'Eguaglianza (Girgenti), Il Gazzettino rosa (Milan),
Il Lavoro (Bologna), La Plebe (Lodi), and Il Romagnolo
(Ravenna). Invariably these papers had an orientation
that was democratic and republican.

On the whole, however, even republican opinion in
Italy was hostile to the Commune. Initially the Allianza
Repubblicana Universale (A.R.U.), the national republican
association founded in 1866, looked on the insurrection
in the French capital with a certain amount of sympathy,[8]
which was natural for a party with a long revolutionary
tradition. The republicans had been among the most active participants in the Risorgimento, the Italian movement for national unification; many of them had fought
under Garibaldi's banner during the wars for independence.
Some of the republicans had also followed the General to
France during the previous year when they had helped the
French in their struggle against the Prussians. But it
was not long before these same republicans turned against
the Commune. Like so many democrats in other countries,
they quickly grew disillusioned with the violence that
soon characterized the uprising. This repulsion was but
one element accounting for the volte-face. More decisive,

perhaps, was the influence exerted on the A.R.U. by Mazzini.

Giuseppe Mazzini (1805-1872), the prophet of the
Risorgimento and at this time still one of the leading
apostles of revolution in Europe, turned against the
Commune almost immediately. Already by April the Genovese had begun a series of articles in La Roma del popolo, a newspaper he had founded with Giuseppe Petroni in
Rome two months before, condemning the insurrection.

Like most of his contemporaries, Mazzini saw the
spector of the I.W.A. behind the events taking place in
Paris. He detested the International and the principles
it represented. This had not always been his attitude.
In its initial stages he had supported and taken an active part in the formation of the Association. As Marx
extended his sway over it, however, Mazzini drew back.
The socialism which Marx predicated was the negation of
everything the Italian revolutionary stood for.

Mazzini was obsessed with the problem of liberty.
In the Republic he found the best means of obtaining and
ensuring this freedom. Marx's insistence on stressing
the social problem, and economics which was at its core,
rather than the political one naturally alienated him.
Not that he was oblivious to the plight of the masses.
Quite the contrary was true.[9] Mazzini recognized the
social question, but he insisted that the political problem, that of the Republic, should take precedence.

The German's class orientation also found little
sympathy in Mazzini, who chose to pin his hopes on humanity rather than on a single social entity, the proletariat. Nor, it follows, could he accept the notion of class
struggle which was so basic to Marxian ideology. The relationship between classes, Mazzini insisted, should be
characterized by cooperation, not perpetual conflict.

And finally, Marx's socialism--and the International which adhered to it--was condemned as materialistic,
a charge the German would certainly not deny. A "scientific" philosophy that reduced man and his world to
mere atoms left little room for that morality so essential to the Italian's "Apostolate." Mazzini, moreover,
felt that this morality had to be based on a concept of
God (hence his motto "Dio e Popolo"), a concept difficult
to reconcile with a materialistic philosophy.

As the founder of the A.R.U., Mazzini was deeply

revered by the republicans in Italy--and to some extent
outside of republican circles as well. His long career
of over forty years as a revolutionary and his blind and
constant devotion to the cause of the Republic had surrounded him with a mystique which has survived to this
very day. The admiration of his followers knew no bounds.
He was made the honorary president of every republican
association. Every article written by a republican paper
at this time seemed to begin and end with a quotation from
the Duties of Man (1860), his most famous work. Given
this adulation, it is not surprising that his party soon
came to endorse his view of the Commune.

But this was not true in every case. Many republicans were becoming dissatisfied with the teachings of the
"Prophet," as he was referred to by his faithful followers. The dissidents were generally men of a younger gen-
eration, men who did not know the Genovese personally
and thus found it easier than their leaders to question
his authority. Intensely anticlerical, these critics began by attacking Mazzini's nebulous notion of God. "When
a new God is preached," one of them lamented, "one should
at least be able to say what God this is."[10] Before long
their attention began to focus on Mazzini's scant concern
with the social question, which had become a blatant reality after unification and could no longer be ignored.
The International started to exert an irresistible attraction. Beginning to embrace socialist ideas, these men
rallied to the defense of the Commune, and instead of
looking to Mazzini they found their inspiration in Garibaldi, the greatest figure of the Risorgimento.

Giuseppe Garibaldi (1807-1882), the "Hero of the Two
Worlds," was the only personality among the Italian Democrats whose reputation could rival that of the Genovese.
The General's deeds on the battlefield captured the popular imagination in a way which the philosopher's ideas
never could. As the Risorgimento drew to a close with
the addition of Rome to the Kingdom in 1870 the condot-
tiere's appeal was at its height.

Given Garibaldi's past--he had always been the champion of the underdog--his reaction to the Commune was
predictable. Although he had taken part in the Franco-
Prussian war (as opposed to Mazzini, whose Francophobia
is proverbial, Garibaldi always felt a profound affection for the French), the General had not participated
in the subsequent insurrection. Still, when he received
news of the revolt in Paris he immediately declared his
solidarity with the Communards. Like Mazzini he believed

GIUSEPPE GARIBALDI
Biblioteca Comunale Aurelio Saffi, Forlì

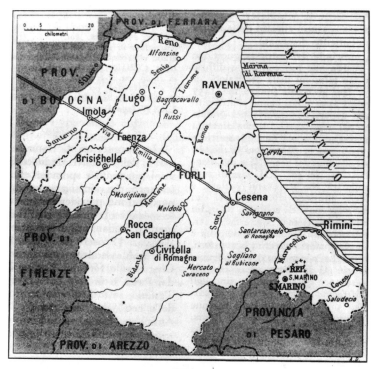

LA ROMAGNA

THE ROMAGNA
(from Enciclopedia Italiana)

8

that the events had been socialist-inspired; unlike his
old colleague, however, he sympathized with socialism,
albeit in a very vague way.[11]

The difference of opinion between Mazzini and Garibaldi over the Commune proved to be irreconcilable. Both
refused to budge in the slightest from the positions they
had taken. The question became one of principle: was
the republican party to continue along its traditional
path or would it now shift its emphasis from the political to the social problem? The A.R.U., which had been
Mazzinian and Garibaldian at the same time, was in a quan-
dry. Mazzini or Garibaldi? Unable to opt completely for
one or the other, the inevitable result would be schism.
Achille Bizzoni, the editor of Il Gazzettino rosa, and
his colleagues on the Milanese paper became the leading
defenders of the Commune among the dissident republicans.
They had supported the revolt from the very outset.[12]
By early July, according to the French consul in Milan,
the division between the local republican party and the
Bizzoni-led faction had become "irrevocable."[13] This
same split between Garibaldians and Mazzinians was soon
evident on a national scale. Probably the most significant repercussions of the schism were to be felt in the
Romagna, then the strongest republican citadel in the
country.

The Origins of Anarchism in the Romagna

Stretching from Imola on the west to the Adriatic
on the east, and from the Po River on the north to the
Republic of San Marino and the crest of the Apennines on
the south, is the Romagna, one of Italy's most beautiful
regions. Primarily an agricultural area, the Romagna
(or le Romagne as this part of the country is sometimes
referred to because historically it had been divided into four papal legations) encompasses seven major cities:
Imola, Faenza, Forlì, Cesena, Rimini, Lugo, and Ravenna.
With the exceptions of the latter two, all "Seven Sisters" lie along Via Emilia, the ancient Roman road built
in the second century B.C. by M. Aemilius Lepidus. This
major artery of commerce runs from west to east, from
Bologna to Rimini, a distance of fifty miles, and divides the mountains on the south from the fertile plains
of the Po Valley on the north.[14]

Provincial and socially conservative, the Romagna
has traditionally tended to isolate itself from the rest
of Italy. A result has been the development of one of

the country's most distinctive types, the Romagnol. Although differing somewhat in character according to their rural or urban background, these people can generally be described as extroverted, verbose, sentimental, and coarse.[15]

Two other outstanding characteristics--and a pair which unfortunately has been stressed to the exclusion of all others--have been their rebelliousness and tendency toward violence. "Over the centuries," one observer has commented (though with a good deal of exaggeration), "the sons of Romagna became violent and proud, accustomed to fighting and quick to revolt against established law. Their hands ran swiftly to a knife or a gun if their passions were aroused, and they did not mind the splash of blood on themselves or others."[16] The passion of the Romagnol has become proverbial: so much so, in fact, that the region was long known as the "Sicily of the North."

Unlike the Sicilians, though, Romagnols found an outlet for such extreme sensitivity in politics--a tradition which continues even today. The obsession with politics has a long history (one has only to remember the violent battles which took place in this region between Guelfs and Ghibellines); yet not until the time of the French Revolution was it translated into political action on a large scale. The vehicles for this activity became the political sects.

From the very beginning the inhabitants of the Romagna "conceived of politics as one of the many hues of red;"[17] that is, these sects that were formed were invariably revolutionary and left-wing. Why did they appear under this guise? The answer is to be found in the history of the region. Continually under the domination of outsiders, the Romagnols have regarded themselves as a conquered people since the Middle Ages. This has been especially true during the last two centuries.[18] The concept of a conquered Romagna, which I will return to later, explains much of the unique Romagnol character, first under papal, then, after 1860, under monarchical rule. To the Romagnol the institutions of Church and State came to epitomize oppression and conservatism. Thus inevitably his response was both radical and violent, and led to sects having a revolutionary and left-wing orientation. Indeed, the Romagna became the breeding ground for a variety of revolutionary and conspiratorial groups, among them the Jacobins, the Carbonari, and the Mazzinian republicans.[19] By 1871 the latter, adhering to the A.R.U., formed the most powerful political party in the region.

The Romagnol republicans' strength derived to a large
extent from the party's capable leadership. The most prestigious of its members was Aurelio Saffi (1819-1890) of
Forlì.[20] Converted to the republican faith after 1848,
Saffi soon became one of Mazzini's chief collaborators.
An ardent revolutionary during the _Risorgimento_, the Forlivese was forced to spend years in exile, first in Switzerland, then in England. When he finally returned to Italy
for good, in 1867, the popular patriot was given a hero's
welcome and immediately became the Romagna's ranking spokesman in the republican party. Other regional leaders included Eugenio Valzania of Cesena and two young Forlivesi
who were destined to leave their mark on the political
life of the country: Antonio Fratti and Alessandro Fortis.[21] All of these men were devoted to Mazzini, especially Saffi, who had been one of the triumvirs of the
Roman Republic of 1849, Mazzini's short-lived creation,
and was now widely-regarded as the Prophet's chief disciple.

No less popular in the region than Mazzini was Garibaldi. The Romagnols, after all, were Garibaldians by
nature. Many of them, moreover, had fought under the General during the wars for unification (1859-60) and again
at Mentana in 1867.[22] The leading Garibaldian in the area
was undoubtedly Valzania (whom the authorities described
at this time as a "person of discrete education, little
culture, and limited intelligence, but endowed with common
sense and great astuteness and excessively ambitious").[23]
He had followed the General in all his major campaigns
and, after Saffi, was the most celebrated of the local
party chieftains.[24]

It was not Valzania, however, who would lead those
Romagnols who were becoming increasingly disaffected with
the orthodox (Mazzinian) interpretation of the Paris revolt. These dissidents would come instead from the ranks
of the younger members of the _Allianza Repubblicana_. It
was these youths who met at Lugo in April, 1871, in what
Germanico Piselli of Forlì, one of the delegates, later
termed the First Italian Internationalist Congress.[25] Almost nothing is known about the deliberations of this
meeting;[26] quite possibly the conferees limited themselves
to a simple declaration of solidarity with the Communards.

In addition to the twenty-one-year-old Piselli, the
only other person whose attendance at the meeting is cer-

tain was Francesco Piccinini of Lugo, one year older than
the Forlivese.[27] Still it is likely that another participant was Lodovico Nabruzzi (1846-1920) from Ravenna.
"Serious of character, closed, tenacious,"[28] Nabruzzi
would soon establish himself as one of the foremost schis-
matics in the party. Concurrently he was becoming the
chief writer for Il Romagnolo, the Ravenna-based organ of
the Romagnol republicans. The paper had been founded in
September, 1868. Its views were those of Mazzini. After
suffering a series of interruptions, caused chiefly by
its precarious financial condition, it resumed publication
late in May, 1871. The management was now in the hands
of the young republicans;[29] aside from Nabuzzi, these included Sesto Montanari, Claudio Zirardini, and the brothers Luca and Giovanni Resta, founders and leading lights
of Ravenna's republican-dominated Società di Mutuo Soccorso, the city's most popular mutual aid society.[30] In early June, almost immediately after gaining control of the
paper, Nabruzzi and his friends expressed their admiration for the Communards and condemned the reaction, "avid
for vendetta and blood," which "brings back the kingdom
of the vilest egoism with death and slaughter on the smok-
ing ruins of heroic Paris; and frantically insults the
vanquished proletariat, which it vainly believes it will
destroy with summary executions on the banks of the
Seine."[31]

These opinions won them little sympathy among their
coreligionists.[32] Dissension began to appear within the
A.R.U. The situation steadily deteriorated as Il Romagnolo went beyond a defense of the Commune and began to
voice approval of the principles of the International.[33]
Nevertheless, criticism of the paper remained rather subdued, as Nabruzzi and his friends still considered themselves republicans and insisted that their views were not
contradictory: "To be materialist or rationalist, spiri-
tualist or idealist, socialist or not, none of this im-
pedes in the slightest that individuals adhering to these
dissimilar scientific opinions belong to the great republican party."[34]

Late in June Il Romagnolo began to meet heavier resistance as its emphasis on the social question and its
neglect of the political problem came increasingly under
attack. Faced by this opposition, Nabruzzi felt a need
to define his program and reaffirm his faith in republican ideals. This was done in the June 25 issue of the
paper. Prophetically, however, in addition to the conciliatory program, which was extremely vague, the first
page of the number also carried an article praising the

International.

The Mazzinians were not reassured in the least. Tension continued to mount and reached a breaking point in July and August. By the end of the latter month it became evident that the direction of the paper had decided to make a clean break with the <u>Allianza</u> <u>Repubblicana</u>.[35] On August 27 the young Ravennati reproduced an article in their weekly taken from <u>Il</u> <u>Proletario</u> <u>italiano</u>, a socialist paper in Turin, in which Carlo Terzaghi, its editor, declared "Mazzinianism divides us, the International unites us."

It was at about this time that Saffi and the older party chieftains of Forlì and Cesena, the major republican strongholds in the Romagna, began to take positive steps to counter the heresy which had appeared in Ravenna. Working behind the scenes they attempted to isolate the rebels. Undoubtedly it was in response to the encouragement of these leaders that the various republican associations of the Romagna began to write in to the paper protesting its views. <u>Il</u> <u>Romagnolo</u>'s comments on this widespread criticism: "This increasingly justifies our suspicion that a ruthless war has been organized against us, and this offends us, because we perceive a lack of civil courage in those who, not daring to raise their voice against us, have others say that which they perhaps find inconvenient on their own lips."[36] The reference to Saffi and the Old Guard was unmistakable.

But by now Nabruzzi was busy doing some organizing of his own. On September 5, five workers' associations from Ravenna and the surrounding area, all apparently affiliated with the <u>A.R.U.</u>, met in the city and formally requested that all the local republican societies adhere to the International.[37] The suggestion, which was more of an ultimatum, was of course rejected, and the renegade associations promptly declared their solidarity with the I.W.A. and organized a local socialist federation.

From April to September, 1871, then, socialism as an organized movement made its appearance in the Romagna, and it did so in the form of the International. Though it is possible that there might have been individuals who sympathized with these new ideas before, I believe it is safe to say that socialist notions had not really penetrated into the area to any measureable extent earlier than this. It has been pointed out that some Romagnols had been active in the creation of the I.W.A. in London in 1864, notably Domenico Lama of Faenza, but these ex-

13

iles do not appear to have had any influence in the Romagna itself.[38] Nor did Bakunin's visit to Italy in 1864-
67 leave any trace in the region.[39]

  The formation of I.W.A.-inspired groups in the middle of the Romagna, the bastion of republican sentiment,
created havoc among the Mazzinians there. Their immediate reponse was the convocation of a regional meeting of
all republican associations. The gathering took place in
Forlì on September 4. Its scope: to discover the extent
to which subversive ideas had made headway among the republican workers' groups in the Romagna. The results were
encouraging. The delegates at Forlì unanimously reaffirmed their belief in Mazzini's teachings[40]--the Ravennati
did not attend the assembly. Still Saffi and his cohorts
could not be completely satisfied with the situation; on
September 24 another workers' association in Ravenna, the
Società di Fratellevole Soccorso, broke away from the A.R.U.
to join the renegades;[41] in October still another followed suit.[42]

  Three weeks after the Forlì meeting a new republican
weekly, La Rivoluzione, appeared in the Romagna. Published by the Forlivesi (Fratti was one of the most prolific
writers), its purpose, though not stated explicitly, was
to counter the influence of the Ravennati. It did not
waste much time; after defining its program ("We work now
for the revolution of ideas, for the transformation of
the life of a people, for the appearance of a New Age
which will prepare us for that end which all Humanity anxiously strives for") the first issue of the paper immediately attacked Il Romagnolo.[43] Every number thereafter
concerned itself with the relationship between republicans and socialists, by now two groups that were more or
less clearly defined. While some of the more moderate
republicans had begun to talk of healing the schism which
had developed, the publishers of the Forlì paper were completely intransigent on the question of reconciliation.[44]

  But republican hostility was not the only concern of
Il Romagnolo. As its political views became clearer the
paper began to attract the attention of the authorities.
The police were determined to keep Italy immune to the
bloody theories of the Communards. Persecution of the paper followed shortly thereafter; on October 6 Nabruzzi
was heavily fined for articles in Il Romagnolo which were
judged subversive.[45] That same day Claudio Zirardini,
next to Nabruzzi the most eminent of the young dissidents
in the city, and several of his comrades were rounded up
by police and brutalized.[46] Burdened by fines and threat-

ened with imprisonment, the direction of Il Romognolo decided to suspend publications. The last issue of the paper appeared on October 29, 1871.

Notwithstanding the loss of their only periodical, the Internationalists in the Romagna had begun to make some notable gains. This progress was not confined exclusively to Ravenna. In September a socialist section had been created in Imola.[47] At the end of October another three sections were in the process of formation in both "the upper and the lower Romagna."[48] During the following month the International made its appearance, thanks to Nabruzzi, in Campiano and the other small villages lying between Ravenna and Forlì.[49]

The result of this rapid proliforation of sections was the regional meeting of Internationalist associations which took place in Forlì on November 19.[50] From an account of the gathering given in L'Eguaglianza on December 10, we learn that the delegates represented the Romagnol sections of "Bologna, Imola, Ravenna, Forlì, Faenza, Lugo, Rimini, etc...."[51] It appears that all the major cities in the Romagna, with the possible exception of Cesena, had now constructed sections. The resolutions included the following: 1. To adhere to a Democratic Congress which would be held in the spring in Bologna, 2. To hold a preparatory meeting in the same city prior to the congress, 3. To try to republish Il Romagnolo, 4. To encourage the publication of additional socialist newspapers and other forms of socialist propaganda, and 5. "To give the greatest impetus to the organization of the working masses which has already been favorably initiated and to hasten the formation of new sections." Undoubtedly this latter determination was the most significant one. It appears too that a provisional Regional Council was formed at this meeting.[52] The conclave of November 19 thus signified the first attempt by the newly-formed socialist associations of the area to cooperate and to create some kind of centralized organization.

It was also in these days that the Romagnols made initial contact with the International movement outside of Italy. Nabruzzi began his correspondence with Friedrich Engels, who had been appointed Corresponding Secretary for Italy by the General Council of the International on August 1, early in October; two months later, on December 1, he wrote Bakunin his first letter. This correspondence was to have momentous consequences for the I.W.A. in Italy during the next decade.

15

Bakunin's entrance into the International in 1868 had signaled the beginning of a titanic struggle within the Association. Already by the Basel Congress of the following year it became apparent that there were two opposing tendencies within the organization, authoritarian and anti-authoritarian, one led by Karl Marx, the other by Bakunin himself. The Russian's ideas, as we have noted, were those of the anarchist: he believed in the complete freedom of the individual and the total abolition of authority. In the I.W.A. he inevitably came into conflict with Marx and his followers, who advocated a dictatorship of the proletariat. For Bakunin any form of coercion, even one imposed by the workingman, was to be despised.

The disagreement between the two revolutionaries was not entirely a doctrinal one. There was a more personal element involved. Marx wanted to control the Association and to impose his ideas on it. Bakunin, who was, it is only fair to add, something of an authoritarian personality too, condemned Marx for his intolerance and called for a greater amount of democracy within the organization. In this way he hoped to gain control of the International himself.

By 1870 Bakunin had begun to make some headway within the I.W.A.--at Marx's expense. During the regional Congress of Chaux-de-Fonds on April 4 of that year, many of the Swiss members of the International rebeled against Marx's authoritarianism and formed a dissident group inspired by Bakuninist sentiments. The following year Marx counterattacked; the Marxians won an overwhelming victory at the Congress of London of September 17-23, after Marx had done all he could to keep his opponents from attending. Between the London Congress of 1871 and the Fifth Congress of the International, held in The Hague one year later, the battle between Bakunin and Marx intensified.

In need of supporters, both men became interested in the Italians after the Paris Commune, when they first saw the possibility of achieving positive results there.[53] Before this time Mazzini, whom they both opposed on principle, stood in their way. But as the Italian's prestige ebbed and the socialist movement grew the General Council of the I.W.A. (i.e., Marx and Engels) and Bakunin began to cultivate the country.

Initially both Bakunin and Engels, who carried on the fight in Italy, concentrated their efforts on the South--especially Naples--that part of the country which

16

had been affected by the socialist movement before 1870, and on the industrial cities of the North, Turin and Milan. Both moved cautiously--Mazzini was still a factor. Unfortunately for the General Council, Engels never acted with much determination in Italy. Being Corresponding Secretary for various countries he perhaps lacked the time to adequately focus his attention there. The Russian, on the other hand, had decided to proceed more vigorously by August, when he initiated his attacks on Mazzini and the latter's condemnation of the Commune by writing a pamphlet, Risposta d'un Internazionale a Giuseppe Mazzini per M. Bakunin, membro dell'Associazione Internazionale dei Lavoratori. The ideas Bakunin expressed here and in his other writings of the period, in Il Gazzettino rosa, "contributed enormously to precipitating the internal crisis of the republican party."[54]

Given the growing strength of the socialist movement in north-central Italy, Bakunin was only too happy to establish direct communication with this area in November and December, 1871. At this time correspondence was initiated not only with Nabruzzi in the Romagna but also with two of the leading Garibaldians of near-by Emilia, Erminio Pescatori, in Bologna, and the Mirandolese, Celso Ceretti.[55]

Professor Aldo Romano goes to great lengths to show that the first contact between Bakunin and the nascent socialist movement in Emilia and Romagna took place at this time. He concludes that before November Bakunin had no influence whatsoever on the events that had been taking place there previously.[56] It is not altogether certain, though, that the exchange of correspondence began in November. On October 10 Terzaghi had written Engels informing him that he, Engels, would soon receive a letter from the Ravennati "via Bakunin."[57] This suggests that the Romagnols might have been in contact with the Russian in October, and perhaps before. But even if Romano is correct in his dating of the initial correspondence, his conclusion that Bakunin's impact before November was nil nevertheless remains unwarranted. Bakunin had been speaking out against Mazzini and in defense of the Commune since August. His pamphlet and articles in Il Gazzettino rosa were well known in Italy after this time. There is little reason to suppose that the Romagna had remained ignorant of these writings. The evidence suggests the contrary. On September 3 Il Romagnolo published a complaint it had received from the Società del Progresso of Cottignolo. The republican circle was critical of Bakunin's views and those who espoused them.

The protest was clearly aimed at Nabruzzi, who had seemingly been propagating the anarchist's ideas during his excursions into the small villages in the province of Ravenna. It is possible that the Russian's influence was felt as early as the first half of 1871. Germanico Piselli later recalled that he and other young republicans had been "inflamed by Bakunin's writings" even prior to the Lugo meeting of April.[58] Though Piselli's assertion is unlikely, it is none the less true that Bakunin must have exerted some pressure on the Romagna before November, 1871.

This is not to say that Bakunin was the only or even the dominant force in convincing the republicans of Emilia-Romagna to espouse the cause of the Association. Undoubtedly a more powerful impetus here came from Garibaldi, who on August 29 had written Nabruzzi and the editors of Il Romagnolo declaring that it was their duty to associate themselves with the International.[59] During the next few months, however, Bakunin's authority would gradually supersede that of the General.

The Fascio Operaio

On November 25 Nabruzzi wrote Engels--the Romagnols were ignorant of the conflict taking place between Marx and Bakunin--informing him that "the International's work in the Romagna is coming along marvelously; every city of any importance already has its own section whose organization is modeled for the most part on the Statutes of that of Bologna...."[60] Already by the end of November, then, the Romagnols were coming under the sway of the socialists in Bologna. In addition to the provinces of Forlì and Ravenna, the Romagna also encompasses Imola and the eastern part of the province of Bologna. The city of Bologna itself lies in Emilia, a region tied to the Romagna administratively but maintaining its own identity. Nevertheless, the city of Saint Petronius has always had a close relationship with the neighboring provinces to the east, a characteristic especially pronounced during this period when the I.W.A. began to take root in Italy. Cooperation between the city and the Romagna was now made possible by an association called the Fascio Operaio.

The Fascio Operaio was founded in Bologna on November 27, 1871.[61] This body replaced the provisional Regional Council created a short time before and represented the first serious attempt by the socialists of northern Italy to construct a regional organization. Its

18

jurisdiction, the "region of Bologna" as it was called, included "all of Emilia and the Romagna: which is the zone from Piacenza, Ferrara, Ravenna, Cattolica, Porretta to Bologna."[62]

Given its location and leading personalities (all Bolognesi), the _Fascio Operaio_ must have been erected primarily through the efforts of the socialist section of Bologna. This nucleus had been represented at the November 19 meeting in Forlì; and, as Nabruzzi's letter of November 25 suggests, its existence, unlike that of many of the Romagnol groups, was real, not theoretical. The origins of the section are vague. Apparently it e-volved as an offshoot of the city's mutual aid society.[63] Perhaps it developed concurrently with those cells which sprang up in September in Ravenna and Imola. There is also a possibility that already at that time the Bolognesi had exerted their ascendancy over these groups. According to prefect reports, Pescatori, the leading light among the republican dissidents in the city, had been in the province of Forlì in early September and had visited Pio Battistini, later a ranking I.W.A. chieftain, at Cesena on the 12th.[64] He may have entered the neighboring province of Ravenna, too. This would suggest that the initiative for the creation of the Romagnol sections came from Bologna. If such was the case then almost certainly it was the Bolognesi who organized the November 19 gathering in Forlì. There is no doubt that Pescatori was among the conferees.[65]

Erminio Pescatori (1836-1905) was to become the chief protagonist in the schism which was now beginning to appear within the _Allianza Repubblicana_. Born in Parma, he had joined the party in his youth and had fought valiantly under Garibaldi during the patriotic wars. After spending two years in Ravenna, he and his family settled down in Bologna in the late 1860's. Pescatori then became active in republican circles, where his distinguished war record won him the admiration of many of the younger members of the party. When the Mazzinians launched an unsuccessful revolt in 1870 he was among the participants.[66] His fiery spirit also made him one of the earliest defenders of the provisional Regional Council set up by the republican dissidents. Upon its foundation he became the "consul," the title given the presiding officer, of the _Fascio Operaio_.[67]

The _Fascio_'s program as it appeared in the first number of _Il Fascio operaio_, its official newspaper, was rather mild. The document was firm but there was no

19

talk of revolution: "We do not want to depose an enemy in order to take his place: instead we would abolish the privilege of birth and monopoly in order to substitute it with the universal right to work, to work to be free, to be free in order to achieve equality for everyone."[68] This platform was inspired by Garibaldi rather than Bakunin (Pescatori only began writing to the Russian, who now lived in Locarno, in the last week of November).[69] On December 5 the General officially joined the Fascio as an honorary member and thereby gave it his blessing.[70] To some extent the program still espoused Mazzinian ideas; in fact, the Fascio would never completely break with Mazzini, not even after his demise in May, 1872.[71]

In December, 1871, the Bologna Fascio began to penetrate into the Romagna.[72] The campaign to encourage affiliation was spearheaded by Pescatori, who carried on an extensive correspondence with the sections scattered throughout the area. At the end of the year we find him traveling through the Romagna, first to Russi, then to Ravenna.[73] Accompanying the Bolognese on this excursion was Piccinini, who in the next few months would attain a prominence in the region rivaling that of Nabruzzi and Pescatori himself. By this time, regardless of increasing resistance from the republicans, socialist ideas had begun to make considerable progress, especially in Ravenna, where Nabruzzi continued to work indefatigably, and in Imola, which because of its location came more directly under the sway of the Bolognesi than did its Romagnol sisters.

Early in 1872 Pescatori's work began to produce tangible results. Endorsements for the regional organization began to come in from every part of the Romagna (and from a few cities in Emilia, notably Mirandola and San Giovanni in Persiceto).[74] The publication of Il Fascio operaio, under Pescatori's direction, and its widespread diffusion throughout the area contributed mightily to the movement.

As the various sections enrolled in the Bologna Fascio they were obligated to change their names (and statutes) to conform to that of the mother organization. Consequently by the end of 1871 there was a Fascio Operaio in Imola,[75] probably the first to be formed after that of Bologna, and during the first three months of the following year they appeared in all the major cities of the Romagna.[76]

Paralleling the diffusion of the Fascio Operaio in

20

the region during early 1872 was another trend: the ascension there of Michael Bakunin. By the end of the preceding year the old revolutionary had come to realize that his dream of creating an Italian Federation based on anarchist principles--an organization which would be used against Marx inside the I.W.A.--hinged on Bologna and the Romagna. It was there that the impact of the Commune and the reaction against Mazzini had been the strongest. The formation of the socialist nuclei which sprang up there, even before the birth of the _Fascio_, seemed to confirm this. Bakunin was now positive that the initiative for a nation-wide socialist organization would come from this area. He was also convinced that the sections there were especially susceptible to his ideas.

The full impact of his authority began to be felt in December, when Bakunin decided to concentrate his attention on the Romagna.[77] The immediate objective was to completely alienate the region's socialists from the republicans. Consequently the Russian's letters to Ceretti, Pescatori, and Nabruzzi at this time concerned themselves almost exclusively with Mazzini's concepts. The duel between Mazzini and Bakunin, which had begun in August, 1871, was rapidly reaching its conclusion. Continuing, as he had done before, to make use of the divergences which had arisen between Mazzini and Garibaldi, Bakunin attacked the first while stressing the socialistic ideas of the second. This tactic brought him sure success. By the end of the year the young Romagnols of the _Fascio Operaio_ had clearly broken away from the orbit of the Genovese.[78]

But a new threat to Bakunin's plans now surfaced-- that represented by the General himself. It had been under the latter's banner that the Romagnols had mustered up enough courage to oppose the republican party. But now that Garibaldi had served his purpose he had to be discredited; his ideas, from the Russian's point of view, were dangerous. The General's thinking was extremely confused; intertwined with his vague socialistic notions were others which were republican and even Masonic in inspiration. By any standard, Garibaldi's Internationalism was a rather superficial one. Certainly he had little regard for anarchist principles. But minimizing the old warrior's weight among the Romagnols of the _Fascio_, now Bakunin's primary concern, would not be a simple matter. Indeed, it seemed impossible--and yet Bakunin prevailed.

There can be no doubt that in the winter of 1871-72 Garibaldi's prestige among the socialists of Emilia and the Romagna far surpassed that of Bakunin; this was eminently true among the leadership--Pescatori and Ceretti had fought under Garibaldi and were totally devoted to him. Indeed, it was the influence of the General, as we mentioned before, and not that of Bakunin, which had been decisive in creating the unbridgeable breach in the ranks of the republican party.

Some measure of the General's popularity can be gained by examining the degree to which the Romagnols supported the proposed Democratic Congress of 1871-72. The plan had originally been the brainchild of Ceretti and his friends in Emilia, who in August, 1871, took the lead in calling for a mass meeting of all the democratic associations on the peninsula.[79] The original scope of the gathering was to heal the division then beginning to plague the republican party. Garibaldi agreed to preside over the meeting and before long the initiative for its convocation passed into his hands (this was the congress which had been endorsed at the Forlì meeting of November 19). For a few months it seemed that the idea might elicit a favorable response. But by the end of 1871 it was obvious that the reunion would not take place; the cause: the intransigence of Mazzini and his followers. These were against any form of reconciliation, except one based on the complete acceptance of Mazzini's principles.

At the beginning of the following year reunification seemed impossible. And yet it was at this time that Garibaldi revived the old idea of a Democratic Congress. For all of his warmth for socialist ideas, the General still considered himself a republican. Thus he continued to press for reconciliation.[80]

But the socialists in the Romagna, while willing to see this _rapprochement_ the previous year, were now opposed to it.[81] This change in attitude was a reaction to the infexibility of the republicans in Bologna and the Romagna. The opposition of the socialists was more pronounced among the rank and file than among the leaders (Ceretti was one of the main instigators of the congress again in 1872). Still the Romagnol socialists reluctantly adhered to the meeting,[82] so great was their respect for the General. Once more, however, the republicans rejected the proposal. Unable to obtain Mazzinian participation, in August the General postponed the gathering anew. Little more was heard about it thereafter.

The movement for the Democratic Congress testifies to the General's appeal among the members of the _Fascio Operaio_ in the Romagna. But it also has a wider significance: undoubtedly its most important result was the gradual estrangement of the socialists from Garibaldi. The proposal for the congress had driven the republicans toward a greater recalcitrance. The _Fascio_, in turn, reacted by moving further to the left, toward a stronger espousal of I.W.A. principles. At the same time the attitude of the republicans forced the General to clarify his own position--he ended up by demonstrating the limitations of his "socialism." The Internationalists in the Romagna now discovered that their ideas no longer coincided with those of the man who had been their inspiration.

Bakunin, of course, did not remain a passive spectator during this crucial period. Taking full advantage of the situation, his correspondence with the socialists of Emilia and the Romagna began to point out the differences which existed between his ideas and those of the General. Although he was dealing with Garibaldians, his opinions of his apparently unsuspecting rival were surprisingly frank. On January 3, 1872, he warned Nabruzzi about the old patriot:

> Dictatorship is his obsession, and nothing poses a greater danger to the social revolution than _dictatorship_. All of his real ideas--and he is too old and obstinate to change them--all of his political habits chain him to the old world, to that which we want to destroy....My friends /the letter was supposed to be shown to Pescatori and Ceretti/, let me speak to you with that frankness which should be displayed between brothers and which I owe to the cause which I serve:--if you have the misfortune of following Garibaldi's political and socialist direction, you will permit yourselves to be led astray in a maze of impossible contradictions--because his politics is an endless contradiction and his socialism, as a rational system, not as instinct, is as inconsistent as that of Mazzini.[83]

Garibaldi was not Bakunin's only concern at this moment; there was also Karl Marx. In order to understand the anarchist's preoccupation with Marx, however, it would be well to review events outside of Italy.

All during 1871 the battle between Bakunin's followers and the General Council of the I.W.A. had been in-

tensifying. Up to September hostilities were confined
below the surface, but after the Congress of London in
that month and Marx's attempt to dominate the Association,
the struggle became overt. The immediate response to the
power play came from the Jura Swiss, who held a Congress
at Sonvilliers on November 12 and created an anti-authoritarian and semi-independent regional organization. Among
the architects of the new Jurassian Federation were Adhé-
mar Schwitzguébel, Auguste Spichiger, James Guillaume,
and the Frenchman, Jules Guesde. Their first official
act was the publication of a manifesto in which the General Council was censured and the dissident members of
the Association were invited to adhere to a new international congress which would be held under their aus-
pices before too long.[84] The unity of the I.W.A. was
now in shambles.

It seems that the action by the Swiss had been taken
without Bakunin's knowledge and that he only received
word of the Sonvilliers deliberations at the end of November. The news probably did not surprise him; a showdown
with the General Council was inevitable sooner or later.
His timetable had to be advanced, though; Bakunin, who
had been careful not to mention his disagreement with
Marx to the Italians before, was now forced to bring it
out into the open. On December 2-8 he wrote Ceretti and
Pescatori a letter introducing the subject and comparing Mazzini (still an issue) with Marx. Both, he concluded, were equally dictatorial.[85] His condemnation of
the German and "the dogmatic...pretensions of the London
General Council"[86] became more pronounced during the
course of the month.

At the beginning of 1872 Bakunin's attention was
equally divided between Garibaldi and Marx. In the letter to Nabruzzi on January 3, where the General was so
severely criticized, Bakunin also attempted to propagate
his particular ideas in opposition to those of the I.W.A.
leader. After explaining his anarchist philosophy ("the
true program of the International") in its general outlines, he asked the socialists of Bologna and the Romagna
if they would adhere to it. If so, "let us give each
other a hand and work together."

Apparently Nabruzzi and his friends were not entirely convinced, for on January 11 Il Gazzettino rosa
published a declaration by the Bologna Fascio ·in which
it defined itself as "an Internationalist society, con-
serving however its own autonomy and liberty." The Romagnols would not, or could not, publicly take sides on

24

the question dividing the Association. But by the middle of the month the sympathies of the _Fascio_'s representatives were clearly with Bakunin rather than with Marx: after receiving Nabruzzi's response on the 18th, the Russian wrote back saying he was happy that "we are thus in agreement and in perfect harmony on all the principal points."[87]

This situation was not bound to change in the last part of January or in February, for Bakunin's correspondence with his friends in Emilia and Romagna remained steady, and he continued to exert his influence. Ties between the _Fascio_ and the General Council, on the other hand, did not exist. Engels had some contacts in Italy, notably Enrico Bignami in Lombardy, but none in either Bologna or Ravenna. Little wonder then that the socialists here were rapidly falling under the complete domination of the Russian. And this was true not only in north-central Italy but throughout the peninsula. Vitale Regis, an emissary sent by the General Council to Italy in mid-February to report on the situation there, wrote back to Engels on March 1 and informed him that the most active elements of the International in the country were increasingly coming under Bakunin's spell.[88] Four days later, writing from Geneva, he was more pessimistic: "The dissidents have completely taken over in Italy."[89]

The extent to which Bakunin's ideas had penetrated into the Romagna and the surrounding territory became manifest at the first Regional Congress of the _Fascio Operaio_. The meeting was held in Bologna on March 17-19 (the organization's statutes called for such convocations in March and September of every year).[90] The list of affiliate societies sending delegates gives an indication of the _Fascio_'s strength by this time. Represented were the sections of Faenza, Forlì, Fusignano, Imola, Lugo, Massignano, Ravenna, Rimini, San Potito, Sant'Arcangelo in the Romagna; and Fano, Montelparo, and Senigallia from the Marches. Also in attendance were emissaries from "adhering" sections (i.e., nuclei from both in and out of the _Fascio_'s territory which wanted to be associated with the organization but insisted on maintaining almost total autonomy): Genoa, Mantua, Mirandola, and Naples. The delegation suggests several conclusions: 1. the _Fascio_'s main source of strength was overwhelmingly in the Romagna, 2. the organization was making some progress in the Marches, 3. Bologna was the only city in the Emilia which completely supported the _Fascio_, apparently Cerretti and the Mirandolesi maintained some reservations about its program, and 4. the _Fascio_ was

already beginning to establish contact with socialist centers outside of its immediate area.[91]

The presiding officers, elected on the first day, were
Camillo Amadio of Forlì, Pescatori, and Nabruzzi, who promp-
ly gave way to Ceretti "for reasons of health and in order
to participate in the discussion more freely." The assembly's initial act was that of eulogizing Mazzini, who had
died on the 10th. The universal esteem for the unyielding
but still respected adversary was expressed in the form of
a resolution, after which the conferees (there were about
twenty of them) got down to the business at hand.[92]

The agenda had been prepared on the basis of twelve
questions submitted by the individual sections. Among the
most important of these was one relating to the Democratic
Congress "proposed by General Garibaldi." The idea, all but
dead now, nevertheless received general support. The representatives who were to attend the future congress, however,
were given specific instructions: they would "adhere strictly to the principles of the International." The Romagnols
had clarified their position. They were determined not to
compromise their socialist principles. It was apparent that
all hope of reconciliation with the republicans had now been
abandoned.

This intransigence in regards to the republicans was
more clearly reflected in two other resolutions. The first
of these was in response to a question, posed by Ceretti,[93]
concerning the socialists' reaction in the event of a republican insurrection, which appeared imminent in the Romagna.
The question was put in rather vague terms, but in essence
Ceretti wanted to know if the socialists would help. The answer was no; the Fascio would only endorse a revolution which
"aimed exclusively at the emancipation of the Proletariat."

The last question regarding the two parties was direct
and to the point. Should the Fascio emphasize the social
problem or limit itself, as "the bourgeois republicans" did,
to the political one? The response: "though recognizing
the importance of the political question, the Congress affirms that the solution of the social question is the necessary and chief objective." The republican sentiments of the
delegates at Bologna had now been superseded--this was one of
the noteworthy aspects of the Congress.

But the most crucial issues resolved at Bologna
were those which called for a definition of socialism as
understood by the Romagnols. Were they Marxians or Ba-

26

kuninites? This was the essence of a query presented during the first session. Would the _Fascio_ recognize and associate itself with the General Council of London, or with the Jura Federation, or would it remain independent of both bodies? The Congress overwhelmingly voted to establish contact with both the London Council and the Jura Swiss but declined to make any further commitments.

It seems that the members of the _Fascio_ still adhered to the position they had formally maintained since January, that of neutrality. Nettlau draws the conclusion, based on this resolution, that despite Marx's charges later on, Bakunin did not exert a real influence on them.[94] But, in fact, we have seen that the anarchist leader had been in direct contact with these men for several months during which time they were persuaded to accept his views "on all the principal points." The motion in question, then, did not really reflect the situation very accurately. Perhaps more significant than this deliberation was the fact that the _Fascio_ did correspond with Bakunin's friends of the Jura Federation, but it never did initiate the intercourse with London which the resolution called for.

Moreover, while this particular deliberation shows little trace of Bakunin's pressure, the rest of the proceedings of the Bologna Congress made it clear that the _Fascio_ was anything but neutral in the Marx-Bakunin controversy. One question, for example, asked the delegates to clarify their attitude toward the unpopular Italian government then in power. The Congress responded that it "does not concern itself with authoritarian governments." Significant here is the word "authoritarian," but more meaningful still is the total rejection of political action which this resolution implies. And what is hinted at here is made overt in the opinion expressed on political elections, a question discussed on the second day. "The Congress," it was resolved, "believes that every authoritarian government is the instrument used by the privileged against the disinherited classes, and in addition to combatting it, it abstains from granting it its means of sustenance." This motion, as Romano justly affirms, was "the explicit acceptance of the Bakuninist concept of political abstention."[95] It was only a matter of time before Bakunin would gain complete ascendance over the socialist movement in the Romagna.

Conclusion

27

The rise of a socialist movement in the Romagna occurred during the year preceding the Bologna Congress of 1872. What accounts for its origins? No doubt the Paris Commune was a factor. The French insurrection aroused considerable sympathy in the region. Identifying the rebels with the I.W.A., the immediate reaction throughout the continent, the Romagnols naturally developed an interest in Internationalist principles. But Andrea Costa was right when he later suggested that socialism in Italy had roots that went beyond the events in Paris.[96]

The form which the socialist movement in the Romagna took was that of anarchism. The history of the region predisposed its inhabitants in this direction. The revolt against authority began under papal rule. The Church, it should be remembered, dominated this part of the Italian peninsula from the thirteenth century. During this time the Pope came to be blamed for all the evils that beset society. In retrospect theocratic rule was less than unbearable. But what made it so odious was that control was being exerted from outside the region, by a "foreign" power residing in Rome. One result of this hostility toward the Church became a pronounced anticlericalism, another was a strengthening of federalist tendencies, and a third was a natural repugnance toward all authority.

These forces gave impetus to the Risorgimento, and helped to create the Italian nation that was born in 1859-60. But liberation and unification did not resolve all the problems; indeed, some of these were aggravated. The reaction against foreign "tyranny" continued. What did it matter that the new masters were politicians instead of priests? The result was the same--Rome continued to drain the Romagna of its resources. The dissatisfaction was especially evident among the Mazzinians (the most numerous political faction in the region), who felt betrayed by the creation of a monarchy rather than the establishment of a republic.[97]

The fact of the matter is that opposition to Rome increased under the monarchy. The popes had controlled the Romagna for so long that their rule had come to acquire a certain legitimacy. But after the revolution-- and the Risorgimento was a revolution, a political one-- even this was gone. Control over the region had been gotten by force; authority had been usurped. Revolt was now justified.

The Paris Commune gave the protest an ideology. The

Romagnols identified with the insurgents in Paris, and they soon came to embrace the Internationalist ideas which they attributed to the Communards. The I.W.A. thus made its appearance in the region, where it took the form of the Fascio Operaio. But the Association offered two alternatives: Marxism and Bakuninism. Why the Fascio chose the latter is obvious enough. In the Romagna there was neither a strong proletariat (this would hold true into the twentieth century) nor pronounced class antagonisms. Marx's socialism found little support. Bakunin, on the other hand, possessed a great advantage: the Romagnols were rebelling against authority, and in the last analysis that was what his anarchism was all about. From the very outset, then, the Romagnols came to identify the I.W.A. with anarchism.[98]

All of this does not mean that Marx was destined to lose out. The General Council could still have cultivated the region and won it over. Instead it was Bakunin who took the initiative. He demonstrated that he knew the area well; stressing the German's authoritarianism above all else, he soon claimed victory over his adversary.[99]

NOTES

[1]Robert Michels, Storia critica del movimento socialista italiano dagli inizi fino al 1911 (Florence:
"La Voce," 1921), p. 17.

[2]The standard biography: Max Nettlau, Michael Bakunin. Eine Biographie (1896-1900; facsimile rpt. 3 vols.
in 2, Milan: Feltrinelli, 1972). The 1st edition is extremely difficult to find, for Nettlau--who had it printed at his own expense--only had 50 mimeographed copies
made. No. 35, which the author originally presented to
Errico Malatesta, is now found at the Biblioteca Comunale dell'Archiginnasio in Bologna.

[3]Some of Bakunin's writings were edited in 1882 by
Carlo Cafiero and Elisée Reclus in Geneva and published
under the title, Dieu et l'Etat. This work contains the
best introduction to the Russian anarchist's ideas on
religion and government.

[4]For Bakunin's activity in Italy, see Max Nettlau,
Bakunin e l'Internazionale in Italia dal 1864 al 1872
(Geneva: Risveglio, 1928).

[5]See James Guillaume's letter to Andrea Costa, May
30, 1876, which is part of the latter's voluminous correspondence found at the Biblioteca Comunale di Imola
(hereafter B.C.I.). This collection has been catalogued
by Fausto Mancini, Le carte di Andrea Costa conservate
nella Biblioteca Comunale di Imola (Rome: Quaderni della rassegna degli "Archivi di Stato," 1964). The cata-
logue number of the letter above is 3.

[6]Already by the following year, however, the movement there had gone into serious decline; on July 4, 1870,
Bakunin wrote Gambuzzi to ask if a section still existed
in Naples. Quoted in Max Nettlau, Errico Malatesta.
Vita e pensieri (New York: "Il Martello," n.d.), p. 53.

[7]For the conservative reaction in Italy, see the
chapter entitled "La libertà e la legge" in Federico Chabod, Storia della politica estera italiana dal 1870 al
1896 (Bari: Laterza, 1951). Aldo Berselli, "Riflessi della comune nella stampa italiana," Rassegna storica toscana,
18 (Jan.-June, 1972), 61-85, describes the reaction of the

30

Italian press in 1871.

[8]Marcella Deambrosis, "Gli echi della Comune in Italia nell'opinione e nella stampa dell'Estrema Sinistra," Rassegna storica toscana, 18 (Jan.-June), 89.

[9]Giuseppe Tramarollo, "Dall'Apostolato Popolare di Londra al congresso operaio di Roma," in L'azione dei mazziniani in Romagna nei primi decenni dopo l'Unità (Ravenna: Girasole, 1973), pp. 25-26.

[10]Mauro Macchi, Almanacco istorico d'Italia di Mauro Macchi: 1873 (Milan: Natale Battezzati, 1873), p. 26.

[11]See Garibaldi's definition of his socialist philosophy in Alessandro Bottero, Dibattimenti nel processo per cospirazione e internazionalismo innanzi alle Assisie di Firenze (Rome: Francesco Capaccini, 1875), p. 265.

[12]See Il Gazzettino rosa, Mar. 23, 1871.

[13]Report to the French Minister of Foreign Affairs, July 5, 1871, Archives de la Préfecture de Police, Paris --hereafter A.P.P.--carton 1475 (more specifically the report is contained in a dossier entitled "Socialisme in Italie de 1871 à 1891").

[14]Excellent geographical and historical studies of the region are provided by Emilio Rosetti, La Romagna (Milan: Hoepli, 1894) and Friedrich Vöchting, Die Romagna. Eine Studie über Halbpacht und Landarbeiterwesen in Italien (Karlsruhe: G. Braun, 1927).

[15]Aurelio Bassi, quoted in Jòmla come Imola, ed. Renzo Renzi (Bologna: Cappelli, 1968), p. 16.

[16]Laura Fermi, Mussolini, 2nd ed. (Chicago: Univ. of Chicago Press, 1961), p. 8.

[17]Ibid.

[18]A fact which helps to explain the existence of social banditry (widespread lawlessness in a society resulting as a reaction to conquest by outsiders) there until late in the 19th century. The most renowned of these brigands was Stefano Pelloni (1824-1851), known as Il Passatore.

[19]This revolutionary tradition has continued into our own century; the Italian Communist Party draws much

of its strength from the region of Emilia-Romagna.

[20]There are no adequate biographies of the Mazzinian leader. Aldo Spallicci and Icilio Missiroli, Aurelio Saffi (Forlì: Valbonesi, 1961), like most republican historians, tend to be general and completely uncritical.

[21]A police report to the prefect of Forlì on Apr. 18, 1872, gives an indication of the function which each republican leader served. As President of the Regional Committee of the Romagna and the Marches, Saffi directed the A.R.U. in that particular area, the prefect was told. "He is assisted," the police official continued, "by Fortis and Fratti: the former as his emissary to the leaders of other regions, and the latter as his secretary and emissary to the dependent subcommittees....Valzania, a man too important to have his activity limited to a subcommittee, is charged with supervising and coordinating, with his immense influence, the minute organization of the party from Bologna to Ancona," in Archivio di Stato, Forlì (hereafter A.S.F.), Gabinetto Prefettura, vol. 48, fasc. 225.

[22]Mentana, a few miles from Rome, was the site of a bloody battle in which Garibaldi and his volunteers were stymied, by papal and French troops, in their attempt to incorporate the ancient imperial capital into the newly-created Kingdom of Italy. According to an undated report by the prefect of Forlì (A.S.F., Gab. Pref., vol. 39, fasc. 144), his province was represented at Mentana by 195 Cesenati, 245 Forlivesi, and 281 Riminesi. Thirty-two of the 150 Garibaldians who fell in the battle were Romagnols, Antonio Mambelli, "La Romagna dal 1865 al 1870," Studi romagnoli, 8 (1957), 483.

[23]"Biografie degli individui appartenenti al Partito sovversivo," 1871, A.S.F., Gab. Pref., vol. 38, fasc. 115.

[24]Sigfrido Sozzi, "L'inizio del socialismo internazionalista nella provincia di Forlì (1871)," Movimento operaio e socialista, 16 (1970), 225.

[25]La Rivendicazione (Forlì), May 19, 1888.

[26]Sigfrido Sozzi, "Documenti riservati, inediti, della prefettura di Forlì sugli inizi del movimento socialista a Lugo ed in Romagna," Studi romagnoli, 21 (1970), 231.

[27]Piselli says that it was at the Lugo gathering that he first met Piccinini (loc. cit.).

[28]According to a report from the prefect of Ravenna on Oct. 29, 1898, "Biografie di 'sovversivi' compilate dai prefetti del Regno d'Italia," ed. Pier Carlo Masini, Rivista storica del socialismo, 4 (1961), 597.

[29]Renato Zangheri, "Il Romagnolo (1868-1874): Un giornale ravennate dal mazzinianesimo al socialismo," Studi romagnoli, 1 (1950), 368.

[30]Massimo Dursi, "Il Terrore a Ravenna," Il Mondo (Rome), Dec. 9, 1950.

[31]Il Romagnolo, June 4, 1871.

[32]Except in Ravenna itself; on June 8 all 18 republican societies there met on the outskirts of the city, where the Parisian insurrection was universally acclaimed. This according to a Lugo correspondence, dated June 15, to a conservative Florentine paper, the Gazzetta d'Italia, rpt. in I Casi delle Romagne, 1871-1874. Lettere di un Romagnolo alla Gazzetta d'Italia (Florence: Gazzetta d'Italia, 1874), p. 5.

[33]See Il Romagnolo, June 11, 1871.

[34]Ibid., June 18, 1871.

[35]Pier Carlo Masini detects the turning point in the Aug. 13 issue of the paper, Storia degli anarchici italiani da Bakunin a Malatesta (1862-1892) (Milan: Rizzoli, 1969), p. 55.

[36]Il Romagnolo, Sept. 3, 1871. The critics did not limit themselves to letter-writing; on Aug. 25, fifteen republican associations met at Lugo and voted to "openly combat the International--an Association foreign to Italian thought--foreign to our memories--foreign to our aspirations." Reported in L'Unità italiana (Milan), Sept. 1, 1871, and quoted by Nello Rosselli, Mazzini e Bakunin: Dodici anni di movimento operaio in Italia (1860-1870), 2nd ed. (Turin: Einaudi, 1967), p. 264.

[37]The deliberation is published in Il Romagnolo, Sept. 9, 1871, and reproduced in Il Proletario italiano, Sept. 14, 1871, and L'Egalité (Geneva), Sept. 23, 1871.

[38]Renato Zangheri, "La prima fame di Marx in Emilia," Emilia, 3 (1954), 78.

[39]Sigfrido Sozzi has written a book which he has called Gli inizi del movimento socialista a Cesena (1866-1870) (Forlì: Coop. Industrie Grafiche, 1969)--a rather strange title, for, as the author himself has shown, the origins of the socialist movement in that city can only be traced back to the year 1871.

[40]The republican declaration was published in Il Satana (Cesena), Sept. 16, 1871, and La Rivoluzione, Sept. 25, 1871. Il Romagnolo, Sept. 17, 1871, was largely critical of this position.

[41]Il Romagnolo, Oct. 1, 1871.

[42]In early October Nabruzzi, Montanari, and Luca Resta wrote the London Council of the I.W.A. and informed Friedrich Engels that seven societies had publicly adhered to the International. See La corrispondenza di Marx e Engels con italiani, 1848-1895, ed. Giuseppe Del Bo (Milan: Feltrinelli, 1964), p. 47.

[43]La Rivoluzione, Sept. 25, 1871.

[44]See issue of Oct. 29, 1871. Il Romagnolo was of the same opinion. Reconciliation, it declared on Oct. 22, was now impossible; the most that could be hoped for was that the two sides could live together without resorting to violence.

[45]See Il Romagnolo, Oct. 9, 1871.

[46]Their protest appeared in Il Romagnolo, Oct. 9, 1871. Among the victims of the attack was Giuseppe Piazza, another member of the paper's staff.

[47]A few years later, in an article entitled "Il socialismo in Italia--cenni storici," Andrea Costa recalls that the Internationalist program had been adopted in this month by the Imolesi. He fails to specify the exact date. See Il Martello (Bologna), Jan. 27, 1877.

[48]Il Romagnolo, Oct. 22, 1871.

[49]Campiano correspondence in L'Alleanza (Bologna), Aug. 31, 1873.

[50]Nettlau mistakenly reports Bologna as the site of

the gathering. See Bakunin e l'Internazionale, p. 285.

[51]Rpt. in La Federazione Italiana dell'Associazione Internazionale dei Lavoratori: Atti ufficiali, 1871-1880, ed. Pier Carlo Masini (Milan: Avanti!, 1963), pp. 11-12. According to a letter which the prefect of Forlì sent to his subordinates in the latter half of November, the International had also made much progress in these towns of his particular province: Cesena, Cesenatico, Campiano, Savignano, Meldola, Civitella, and Forlimpopoli. See Sozzi, "L'inizio del socialismo internazionalista nella provincia di Forlì," p. 229.

[52]Richard Hostetter, Le origini del socialismo italiano, trans. Fabrizio Onofri, rev. and enl. ed. (Milan: Feltrinelli, 1963), p. 360. Nabruzzi mentioned this provisional Regional Council in a letter he wrote to Engels on Nov. 25, 1871. See La corrispondenza di Marx e Engels con italiani, p. 80.

[53]Hostetter, Le origini del socialismo italiano, p. 309.

[54]Ibid., p. 302.

[55]For biographical information on Ceretti (1844-1909), see Renato Zangheri, Celso Ceretti e la crisi della democrazia dopo l'Unità (Ravenna: STER, 1951), and Pier Carlo Masini, "La Prima Internazionale in Italia nelle carte dei fratelli Ceretti," Movimento operaio e socialista, 11 (1965), 41-80. Both Hostetter, Le origini del socialismo, p. 343, and Aldo Romano, Storia del movimento socialista in Italia, Vol. II: L'egemonia borghese e la rivolta libertaria (1871-1882), 2nd ed. (Bari: Laterza, 1966), p. 175, identify Ceretti as a Romagnol, but Mirandola has never been considered part of the Romagna.

[56]Storia, II, 219. Romano generally tends to give the Russian very little credit (see, e.g., Storia, II, 167, 193): this, in my opinion, is the gravest defect of his controversial study. Cf. Romano's view of Bakunin with that of Leo Valiani, "Considerazioni su anarchismo e marxismo in Italia e in Europa dopo la conferenza di Rimini," in Anarchismo e socialismo in Italia, 1872-1892, ed. Liliano Faenza (Rome: Riuniti, 1973), pp. 148-50, and that of Arthur Lehning, "Bakunin e la formazione dell'Internazionale in Italia," in the same work, pp. 153-70.

[57]Nettlau, Bakunin e l'Internazionale, p. 232.

[58] La Rivendicazione, Oct. 1, 1887.

[59] Reproduced in Il Romagnolo, Sept. 9, 1871. Writing on Bakunin and the socialist movement in Romagna ca. January, 1872, Nettlau, an ardent admirer of Bakunin, writes: "the sympathy and praises which Garibaldi then expressed probably still carried greater weight in that environment than socialist thought and Bakunin's words" (Bakunin e l'Internazionale, p. 295).

[60] Nettlau, Bakunin e l'International, pp. 238-39.

[61] See Il Fascio operaio (Bologna), Dec. 27, 1871.

[62] According to Article 91 of the organization's Statutes, in Il Fascio operaio, Jan. 31, 1872.

[63] Some of the leading members of the Fascio Operaio, including Pescatori and Celso Ceretti, had been members of the mutualist society in 1870. See Mario Maragi, Storia della Società Operaia di Bologna (Imola: Galeati, 1970), p. 169.

[64] Sozzi, "L'inizio del socialismo nella provincia di Forlì," p. 226.

[65] The meeting, however, was moderated by Piselli. Among the Ravennati present were Nabruzzi, Lorenzo Spada, and Luca Resta. Ibid., p. 227.

[66] Isabella Zanni Rosiello, "Aspetti del movimento democratico bolognese (1859-1870)," Bollettino del Museo del Risorgimento, 6 (1961), 173. Another participant was Piselli, La Rivendicazione, May 19, 1888. The aborted revolution is treated by Claudio Pavone, "Le bande insurrezionali della primavera del 1870," Movimento operaio, 7 (1956), 42-107.

[67] The other members of the directive committee included Aristide Mastellari, Lodovico Guardigli, Silvio Frigeri, Augusto Errani, Evaristo Poggiolini, Abdon Negri, Alessandro Aquier, and Pilade Campagnoli, Il Fascio operaio, Jan. 7, 1872.

[68] Ibid., Dec. 27, 1871.

[69] Nettlau, Bakunin e l'Internazionale, p. 282. The exact date is Nov. 30, 1871.

[70] *Il Fascio operaio*, Dec. 27, 1871.

[71] Writing in 1879, Costa remembered the *Fascio Operaio* as the "primitive form which the International Association assumed in Italy--a transitory form between Mazzinianism and Garibaldinianism on the one hand and revolutionary Socialism on the other." See *Bagliori di socialismo* (*cenni storici*), 2nd ed. (Florence: Nerbini, 1900), p. 10.

[72] According to *L'Egalité* (Dec. 7, 1871), Imola, Ravenna, Lugo, and Rimini had already adhered to the *Fascio Operaio*.

[73] Prefect of Ravenna to the prefect of Bologna, Jan. 6, 1872, Archivio di Stato, Bologna (hereafter A.S.B.), *Gab. Pref.*, vol. 90. They were met at Ravenna by Giovanni Resta, Claudio Zirardini, and by a third person, possibly Nabruzzi.

[74] Great progress was now being made in the region. On Mar. 10, 1872, Terzaghi writes Engels: "Romagna, the spot in Italy where Mazzinianism is the strongest, is nevertheless the place where sections multiply every day," *La corrispondenza di Marx e Engels con italiani*, p. 168.

[75] According to Costa, during a police interrogation on Mar. 30, 1873, the Imola *Fascio* was formed "toward the end of 1871," A.S.B., *Tribunale Civile e Correzionale, Procedimento contro Costa Andrea ed altri* (1876), vol. 10 (hereafter this set of papers will be designated *Procedimento Costa*). However, Jan. 4, 1872, is the date given in the *Almanacco socialista per l'anno 1873*, ed. Tito Zanardelli (Naples: Stab. Tip. L'Italia, 1873), p. 11.

[76] *Fasci* were formed in Rimini during the first week of 1872 (see Cajo Zavoli's correspondence, dated Jan. 3, in *Il Fascio operaio*, Jan. 7, 1872), in Ravenna and Forlì on Jan. 1 and 19 (*Almanacco socialista per l'anno 1873*, pp. 11, 12), and in Lugo on Feb. 29 (*La Favilla* /Mantua/, Mar. 7, 1872).

[77] Nettlau, *Bakunin e l'Internazionale*, p. 295.

[78] Romano, *Storia*, II, 236.

[79] The Ravennati adhered in early September (*Il Romagnolo*, Sept. 9, 1871).

[80]This was the "implicit aim," according to Hostetter, Gli origini del socialismo italiano, p. 373.

[81]Hostetter disagrees; he says the Internationalists in Romagna still wanted cooperation with the Mazzinians in January and February, 1872 (ibid., p. 379).

[82]Among the Romagnol sections which adhered to the proposal were those of Rimini, Forlì, Faenza, San Potito, Imola, and Bologna, Il Libero pensiero (Florence), Feb. 15, 1872.

[83]Quoted in Nettlau, Bakunin e l'Internazionale, pp. 298-99.

[84]The Sonvilliers Circular was published, among other places, in La Favilla, Jan. 3, 1872.

[85]Quoted in Romano, Storia, II, 221.

[86]Letter to Ceretti, Dec. 15, 1871, quoted in Nettlau, Bakunin e l'Internazionale, p. 288.

[87]Letter from Bakunin to Nabruzzi, Jan. 23-26, 1872, quoted in Nettlau, Bakunin e l'Internazionale, p. 300.

[88]See Rosselli, Mazzini e Bakunin, pp. 340-41.

[89]Quoted in Nettlau, Bakunin e l'Internazionale, p. 314.

[90]The following description of the Congress was taken, unless otherwise specified, from the account given in Il Fascio operaio, Mar. 24, 1872, and contained in La Federazione Italiana, pp. 15-27.

[91]Internationalist nuclei were mushrooming; already on Jan. 13, 1872, La Favilla reported that there were over 100 of them on the peninsula.

[92]The newspaper account of the Congress generally avoided mentioning names, but these can be obtained from two detailed descriptions of the sessions, both documents unsigned and undated, found in the Fascio's own archives, files later captured by the police and now contained in Procedimento Costa, vol. 11. In addition to the delegates previously cited others included Aquier, Costa, Negri, Tucci, Terzaghi, Raffaele Castelli (Senigallia), and Francesco Chiarini (Faenza).

[93]See Ceretti's correspondence in L'Alleanza, May 25, 1872.

[94]Bakunin e l'Internazionale, p. 348. Rosselli, on the other hand, Mazzini e Bakunin, p. 350, concludes that in simply rejecting the authority of the two bodies, "the conferees deliberated to follow Bakunin's anti-authoritarian program."

[95]Storia, II, 283.

[96]Il Martello, Jan. 25, 1877. The Commune is also seen as a catalyst rather than the major cause of Italian socialism by Osvaldo Gnocchi-Viani, Ricordi di un internazionalista (Milan: Ed. Operaia, 1909), p. 120.

[97]The republican point of view, that living under the popes had been better than under the succeeding Savoy monarchy, is forcefully presented in the anonymous work, Divagazioni d'un malfattore di Ravenna (Ravenna: Ugo Leonardi, 1872), p. 37.

[98]The same can be said for Italy in general. See Gastone Manacorda, Il movimento operaio italiano attraverso i suoi congressi, 1853-1892, 2nd ed. (Rome: Riuniti, 1963), p. 106.

[99]That this propaganda was effective is demonstrated in testimony given by Lorenzo Piccioli-Poggiali, an ex-Internationalist, in 1875. "I am not too familiar with Bakunin's ideas," he admitted, "and thus I cannot say if these were accepted by the Italian Federation; that which I can verify is that it rejected Marx's ideas...." Bottero, Dibattimenti, p. 84.

CHAPTER TWO

COSTA AND THE ANARCHIST MOVEMENT, 1872-1873

Andrea Costa

Pietro Costa was a small shopkeeper in Imola. As
a young man he had been a servant of the Orsinis, one of
the town's oldest and wealthiest families. He was employed by Orso Orsini for many years. In 1861 he finally decided to go off on his own; he had a large family
to support and was in need of a more substantial income.
Signor Costa first tried his hand as a grain dealer on
Via Appia, a busy street running through the center of
town, and later opened up a delicatessen nearby. A
hard worker, in time he achieved modest success as part
of Imola's expanding lower middle class.

Apparently Pietro developed a close relationship
with the Orsini family, for the first of his four children was named after Andrea Orsini, his master's brother
(and father of Felice, the would-be assassin of Napoleon
III). Young Andrea, born on November 30, 1851, was a
bright and precocious child.[1] Because he displayed considerable promise, his father, a devout Catholic, determined that the boy should receive the best clerical education possible.

The first school the child attended was that of the
authoritarian Don Moducci.[2] Gaetano Darchini, one of
Andrea's close friends and schoolmates, writing during
the First World War, recalled that the priest's philosophy of education was a rather crude one; lashings were
administered daily. But the stringent discipline encountered at school was good, Darchini claimed, for it
was there that he first learned to tolerate injustice--
his most valuable lesson in life.[3] Andrea undoubtedly
drew different conclusions.[4] It is perhaps in this early experience that the roots to his intense anticlericalism and resentment of authority are to be found.

Andrea's education at home was no more liberal than
it had been in school. An acquaintance described Pietro
as "modest, hardworking, honest, religious though not

bigoted," but "quite severe and rigid with his children."[5]
As a matter of fact, Andrea was nurtured on a steady diet
of beatings.[6] The same was true of Darchini, who recognized that their parents had been strict because "they
could not tolerate their children thinking differently
than they, especially in regards to religion and politics."[7]

But like all childhoods, theirs was filled with happy memories as well. These were exciting times to be a-
live. The wars of the Risorgimento were still raging.
Tales describing the heroic exploits of Garibaldi and the
other patriots abounded. The young Imolesi would sit for
hours enthralled by these sagas. Then they would go off
to play war games. "For us," Darchini reminisced, "games
meant battle, and consequently to risk one's life, to rebel against all authority, to come to blows, to beat each
other up, to get wounded, and, when wounded, to hold one's
tongue swearing vendetta and revenge, all of these things
were completely natural for us, and moreover, if we had
not had them in our blood we would have breathed them in
the air."[8]

Indeed the behavior of these young boys mirrored
that of their fathers. During this period, at the climax of the Risorgimento, Imola, like the other towns of
the Romagna, was in constant ferment. These were years
of conspiracy and revolution. The city, Darchini declared, was full of madmen. "But almost all of them were subject to the same insanity, since almost all of them were
attacked by the microbe of politics....In fact everyone
had his own system, his own particular idea of government
that he wanted to force everybody else to accept."[9]

The most fashionable of these systems was that of
the Republic. The monarchy which was established in
Italy in 1860 was extremely unpopular in many parts of
the peninsula. After Sicily, the most intense opposition came from the Romagna, where centuries of despotic
government based in Rome had created strong federalist
tendencies. "Here in the Romagna," a republican paper
wrote in 1868, "we hate the government: old people and
children, young men and older ones, rich and poor; sal-
aried workers and artisans (the former occultly), small
landowners and farmers, priests and friars, not exclud-
ing from these categories the fairer sex. And if we did
not fear that people would think we were joking, we would
say that even the dogs here hate the government."[10] This
dissatisfaction with the Savoy monarchy contributed im-

measurably to the increasing strength of the <u>A.R.U.</u> in the Romagna.

But not all the Romagnols were Mazzinians. There was also a sizeable conservative, or monarchist, element in Imola and throughout the region. This minority was despised by the republicans. Since many of them were <u>signori</u> (nobles), the conservatives represented the <u>ancien régime</u>. Moreover, they had been discredited during the <u>Risorgimento</u> because they had collaborated with both the popes and the Austrians. Nevertheless, once unity was achieved it was they who had become the real beneficiaries of the revolution: Italy was constituted as a monarchy, not a republic. All of this in spite of the fact that it was the republicans (coming mainly from the artisan and professional classes) who had fought under Garibaldi and had helped to create the new nation.

Bitterness was most pronounced among the Garibaldians, the old conspirators and revolutionaries. Having taken up arms once, they were prepared to do it again. They were sure that a republican revolution was imminent. Imola was full of these fanatics. One of them was described by Darchini in these terms: "Among the <u>Trementi</u>[11] there was poor Bagiulla, who later expired quietly while in confinement on an island prison in the Tyrrhenian. He had married a nice little woman completely devoted to her home, and he would torment her the whole blessed day by preaching the great principles to her. At night he would wake her up by suddenly sitting up in bed, then, while listening intently, he would ask her anxiously: 'Say, Virginia, did you hear someone yell: Long live the Republic?'"[12]

Given this environment, one can understand why Andrea had acquired a reputation as a rebel even as a student in high school. Independence was one of his most pronounced traits. He possessed a tremendous thirst for knowledge, but the ideas he picked up most readily were new and radical ones--like evolution. And already he displayed an almost uncontrollable need to teach these truths to others.[13]

Andrea's future was very uncertain at the time of his graduation from high school. He wanted to continue his studies, but his father insisted that he help operate the family business. Sensitive to his own shortcomings in this regard, Pietro had wanted his children to receive a good education. The problem, though, was

money. Plowing all of his profits back into the store,
Pietro had been unable to provide adequate instruction
for the rest of the children (Battista, Andrea's younger
brother, received but a second grade education), and now
it appeared that his older son's academic career was
destined to come to an abrupt halt, too. But despite his
excessive self-reliance, Andrea had been an outstanding
student in school, and his teachers thought highly of
him. It was one of them who finally prevailed on Pietro
to change his mind.[14] Persuaded that his son would become a lawyer--and make a fortune--the elder Costa agreed
to help the boy through school. Thus Andrea enrolled at
the University of Bologna in November, 1870.

Bologna opened up new vistas for the young Imolese,
hungry as he was for new experiences. Coming from the
provinces the boy was overwhelmed by the flourishing me-
tropolis, then as now among the most renowned centers in
Italy, and intoxicated by the liberty which he discovered
there. Especially impressive was the University, the oldest in Europe. The school attracted students from every
part of the country and gave the city a truly cosmopolitan air, which made its contrast with the near-by Romagna
a sharp one indeed. The faculty was also superior; Bologna attracted the finest professors in the country.
Taking advantage of his opportunities to the fullest the
young Imolese immediately became the favorite of one of
these, Giosuè Carducci, the most acclaimed living poet
in Italy, and something of a rebel himself. The bard
predicted a bright future for the aspiring scholar (who
now decided to major in letters rather than law), but
unfortunately Andrea's academic career came to an end
all too soon.

Coming from a family of modest means, Andrea had
had to make many sacrifices in order to attend classes.
Pietro, given the hard times that the country was experiencing, was not able to provide much assistance. During
the year, the son lived in Bologna, isolated and penni-
less.[15] Badly in need of financial help to continue his
studies, young Costa applied for a scholarship from the
city council of Imola at the end of the academic year
1870-71. The request was denied. During the summer he
took a job as a clerk for an insurance company in Imola.
He hoped to earn enough to return to school.

It was at this time that Costa's main interest began
to shift from education to politics. Given the party
activity characteristic of Imola in those years it was

inevitable, of course, that he should be concerned with political action. But it was at Bologna that this interest became a passion. The atmosphere there was conducive to an exchange of new ideas, and during and after the Paris Commune the popular theories were those of the International. Without abandoning his Mazzinian ideas, which he shared with other young Imolesi, Costa integrated those of the socialists.[16] The amalgamation resulted in some ideological confusion, but he was sure that the two sets of ideas were compatible. The liberal sympathies of the Bologna faculty (e.g., during this period Carducci was an ardent republican) did nothing to discourage him and the other youthful radicals who shared his views.

Costa's socialism was not a purely theoretical one, not solely a product of reading and studying. More persuasive than all the books he read at Bologna was the impact of the Commune. He always insisted that the insurrection in Paris was the single most important factor in converting the republicans into socialists.[17] Undoubtedly he was speaking from personal experience. By the summer of 1871, he too was making the change. In fact, it was because of his radical political views that Costa's request for a scholarship had been rejected a few months before.[18]

In Imola, meanwhile, the political situation had become extremely complex during early 1871. The Commune had had a profound impact on the Imolesi. They were among the first to defend the insurrection and to espouse I.W.A. principles. According to the city's chronicles, Internationalist manifestoes appeared there as early as April.[19] As in the rest of the Romagna, the first socialists were ex-republicans, and thus considered apostates and treated accordingly.[20]

The Mazzinians of Imola were divided into four bands: the Società del Progresso, the largest group; and Società dell'Alleanza ("composed of the most civil and honest part of the young republicans"); the Società del Buon Volere, whose members were mostly laborers rather than artisans, and the Società della Pianta ("the worst of all").[21] The party leaders in the area were two Garibaldians: Epaminonda Farini, forty years old, from Doccia, a small village nearby; and Pietro Landi, thirty-six, Imolese, and president of the Reduci dalle Patrie Battaglie (a supposedly non-partisan fellowship of the veterans of the wars of liberation, in fact dominated by republicans).

The small Internationalist section, originally about

ten individuals, was founded by Paolo Renzi, twenty-five, a bank clerk, and Antonio Venturini, twenty-six, a hospital employee. Like the socialist nuclei in Bologna and Ravenna, it appears that the group sprang from the local mutual aid society.[22] Beginning as an ill-defined tendency sympathizing with the Commune, it evolved slowly during 1871 (the April manifesto was probably the work of individuals rather than an organized cell), until September of that year when, as we mentioned before, it officially dissociated itself from the Mazzinians by becoming an I.W.A. section.[23]

If the political discussions before, when there were only two parties, had been heated, now they verged on chaos. The mood of that period is described by Darchini in his Autobiography:

> Debates, arguments, and brawls would occur in the cafes, in the pubs, and on the streets....One would hear a great deal about the republic, the Commune, the International, the revolution, socialism, anarchism; people would cite contemporary history, ancient history, and even that of the future; Garibaldi, Mazzini, Bakunin; the kings, the popes, the capitalists, and the workers...above all they would yell with flashing, angry eyes and with menacing gestures and would pound the small tables so hard the glasses would jolt....and it would seem as if an earthquake had struck.[24]

Costa joined the nascent socialist group sometime in mid-1871. Anselmo Marabini, one of his later disciples (and a founder of the Italian Communist Party), recounts that its members, especially Antonio Cornacchia, an old Garibaldian,[25] had some reservations about taking in the new recruit; he had the naive aspect of an altar boy.[26]

Once accepted, though, Costa quickly won over his new comrades. The most literate of the fraternity--he was the only non-worker among them--he wrote the section's program after its official creation[27] and was entrusted with the correspondence. It was undoubtedly in his capacity as section secretary that he first established contact with Pescatori and the Bolognesi. By the beginning of 1872 the relationship had been consolidated, and Imola had its own Fascio Operaio.

During the next few months Costa dedicated himself

ANDREA COSTA
Biblioteca Comunale di Imola

to propagating the ideals of the International in Imola
and extending the section's influence at the local level
(he attended the University sporadically, then dropped
out altogether). Venturini, however, was the cell leader, and the ire of the republicans was directed primarily at him. On March 10, Il Fascio operaio published a
protest which was written by Venturini. It was true, he
declared, that he was no longer in accord with Mazzini's
concepts. But why was he accused, behind his back, of
being a traitor, he asked. Had he not done everything
possible for the A.R.U. when he was a member? Was it
his fault that the party was crumbling?

The letter provoked the Mazzinians. The criticism
that they had previously hinted at now became overt. But
they did not stop there. Venturini was challenged to a
duel by Luigi Capra, one of the local republicans. The
combatants chose their seconds. The disagreement, though,
was resolved late in March before any blood was shed,
and a declaration was published stating that the dispute
had been settled honorably.[28] Among the signatories were
Venturini's seconds, Renzi and Costa--this was the first
time the latter's name would appear in print.

It was also at around this time that Costa became
an affiliate of the Fascio Operaio in Bologna. Retain-
ing membership in the Imola nucleus, the young agitator,
as he recalled later, joined the mother association sometime in March.[29] The exact date is unclear; collaboration
on Il Fascio operaio began early during the month,[30] but
admission into the Bolognese society probably occurred
following the Regional Congress (March 17-19).[31]

Costa represented the Imola association at the Congress.[32] He spoke in favor of the complete autonomy of
the individual sections within the regional Fascio and
called for an official protest of the vicious campaign
being waged by the press against I.W.A. principles.[33]
Otherwise the Imolese's role at the meeting was rather
hazy. It is probable, however, that on the question of
reconciliation with the republicans he fully supported
the intransigent position championed by Nabruzzi, who
generally dominated the proceedings, rather than the
more conciliatory one advocated by Ceretti.[34] No doubt
he carried little weight at the time, but immediately
following the Bologna Congress Costa initiated a career
that would rapidly make him the dominant figure in the
Italian International.

Internationalists and Republicans

Costa entered the Bologna <u>Fascio</u> at a very delicate period of its existence. The deterioration of relations between the Internationalists and the republicans in the Romagna would hit rock bottom during the months immediately following the Congress of Bologna.

Before describing the events which led to this sad state of affairs it might be well to take a closer look at the Mazzinians. As was true of the <u>A.R.U.</u> throughout the peninsula, in the Romagna the republicans, following Mazzini, were against participation in the political life of the country. They were determined not to compromise themselves with the monarchy. But the only alternative now open to the republicans was that of revolution, and on this question the Romagnols were badly divided: the more incorrigible of them, led by Valzania, wanted insurrection; but most of the leaders, including Saffi, were set against it. The latter tendency generally dominated following 1870. Unwilling to either compromise with the government or overthrow it, then, the party declined steadily after this date.[35]

Given the <u>A.R.U.</u>'s reluctance to act and the dissension which resulted, the reaction against Mazzini in 1871 was bound to have serious repercussions. As was to be expected, it was among the revolutionary element, composed mainly of Garibaldians, that the new socialist ideas made the most headway. The loss of a good number of these radicals made the party more homogeneous, but at the same time its program became ever more static and the crisis more pronounced.

To meet the challenge of the International, the Mazzinians in Italy were forced to reorganize on a firmer foundation. This attempt began at the Twelfth Congress of the Italian mutual aid societies, which was held in Rome in early November, 1871. Heretofore these assemblies (which began in 1853) had been controlled by conservative elements, and their scope had been strictly economic. At Rome the republicans, led by the Romagnols,[36] defeated the old leadership and succeeded in getting the workers' associations to accept the <u>Patto della Fratellanza</u>, a political program which had been inspired by Mazzini and "responded to all the master's fundamental principles."[37]

After winning the allegiance of the workers' unions
at Rome, the Mazzinians began to effect the merger of these
societies with the party at the regional level. Again
the Romagna led the way. On February 25, 1872, the representatives of about 150 associations gathered in Ravenna,
and after adhering to the Mazzinian Patto, they created
the Consociazione Repubblicana delle Società Popolari
delle Romagne.[38] They met again on April 21 at Cesena
where the structure of the party was determined: the
Consociazione would be governed by an Executive Committee of seven members, and would transmit its directives
to the local bands through District Committees located
in Bologna and in each of the seven major cities in the
Romagna.[39]

The Executive Committee was elected at a third reunion, held in Faenza on May 19. This body included
Saffi, Valzania, and Fratti.[40] The latter was elected
secretary, and the seat of correspondence was established at Forlì, now becoming the ranking republican city in
the region. The members of the District Committees were
chosen by the local sections during the following weeks.

As the republican party reorganized itself the gulf
which separated it from the Internationalists widened.
In fact, by May there was no longer any possibility of
the rapprochement which had been in the air for so many
months. But already at the beginning of the year it was
clear that the situation was worsening instead of im-
proving. Notwithstanding efforts at accommodation, especially on the part of the Mazzinians ("we consider ourselves to be as socialist as any internationalist à la
Garibaldi"),[41] sharp differences of opinion persisted:
on two occasions early in January duels between the staffs
of L'Alleanza and Il Fascio operaio were barely avoided
when representatives of the two papers met and exchanged
apologies.[42]

Thereafter the republicans became increasingly unyielding. They were encouraged to take this stance by
Mazzini's example. On January 10 the A.R.U. leader had
written a letter to La Gazzetta di Milano saying he was
perfectly willing to come to terms with Garibaldi. "But
this agreement, this harmony," he added, "can only be
based on a program. And this program can only be republican."[43] Mazzini was not about to give ground. He would
accept reconciliation on his terms or not at all. But
the situation in the Romagna was encouraging his opponents to hold firm. After the beginning of the year the

AURELIO SAFFI
Biblioteca Comunale Aurelio Saffi, Forlì

12 DICEMBRE 1821 — 13 FEBBRAIO 1889

IN ESILIO GUERRE E PACE
IN OGNI TERRA E FORTUNA
SERBAI UNA LA FEDE
FUI

EUGENIO VALZANIA

BOVIO.

EUGENIO VALZANIA
Biblioteca Comunale Auelio Saffi, Forlì

International started to make phenomenal progress. Sections of the Fascio Operaio were multiplying very rapidly
there. Socialist ideas had begun to win acceptance even
among the inner circles of the Mazzinian party itself:
on January 17 Alfonso Leonesi, the managing editor of
L'Alleanza, quit his post ("for family reasons")[44] and
soon became one of the most powerful members of the
Fascio in Bologna.

Predictably Garibaldi's proposal for a Democratic
Congress, revived in late January, got a cold response
from the republican newspaper. The meeting, it declared,
seemed "inopportune" because although it was true that
the working class was becoming more aware politically,
"a notable part of it has unconsciously accepted certain
erroneous concepts which, we are sure, only time will be
able to clarify and rectify."[45]

The insinuation that they were misguided did not impress the Internationalists favorably. But this insult
did not disturb them as much as the penchant among the
republicans, both leaders and followers, to charge them
with treason.[46] In the face of this treatment, the
Fascio Operaio too was losing sympathy for the idea of
reconciliation.[47] Consequently Garibaldi's proposal was
received without enthusiasm by its members.[48] Like the
Mazzinians of L'Alleanza, however, they wound up endors-
ing the idea, albeit reluctantly.

The acceptance of the Democratic Congress by both
factions was an outward sign of cooperation which gave
rise to real efforts in that direction. Among the rank
and file of both parties the sentiment in favor of a settlement was encouraged. On February 9, workers, mostly
I.W.A. sympathizers, from every part of the Romagnol
plain (the bassa) gathered in Cesena and declared themselves ready to die for the Universal Republic "with
their duci Mazzini and Garibaldi."[49] This and other
appeals possibly had an effect, for there were soon in-
dications that the two powerful rivals were about to set
aside their differences. An understanding seemed imminent.[50]

Actually the apparent pacification in the Romagna
was the lull before the storm. In the last half of February the conflict between the two competing parties ex-
ploded. By the end of the month any hope of an agreement
was irreparably lost.

The Fascio leaders determined to be firm in mid-February. Speaking at the funeral of Torquato Bini, an Internationalist, on the 16th, Pescatori addressed himself to the republicans and accused them of intolerance.[51] That his friends of the Romagna shared Pescatori's sentiments became clear a few days later.

On February 18 the Internationalists of the region held a reunion at Villa Gambellara, one of a cluster of villages (the Ville Unite) centrally located between the cities of Ravenna and Forlì. In Pescatori's absence (for reasons not entirely clear),[52] the meeting was presided over by Nabruzzi. In attendance were "many hundreds of friends" who represented sections from throughout the region: Ravenna, Forlì, Lugo, Madonna dell'Albero, Santo Stefano, San Bartolo, Bastia, Campiano, Carpinello, Coccolia, and San Pancrazio.[53] The deliberations of the delegates took the form of a declaration which was addressed to their "brother workers."[54]

According to the statement, the sole aim of the conferees was to publicly affirm their beliefs, which were those of Truth, Justice, and Morality. But in fact the scope was a wider one. The central concern was the relationship with the republicans. The declaration began by stating that the delegates continued to feel "a profound sentiment" for the "old patriots from which we have divorced ourselves." Consequently during the ensuing separation, the Internationalists continued to display considerable tolerance and fairness with all their opponents, especially "those of our brothers in conspiracy and suffering who did not choose to follow us along the new path of work and sacrifice." But unfortunately, they lamented, this respect had not been reciprocated. Their "detractors" had distorted socialist ideas, and the fight had not been a fair one. They continued to believe, nevertheless, that through mutual respect and the free flow of ideas an understanding was possible. Still they wanted to leave no doubt as to the kind of agreement they were after: "We do not have idols /read Mazzini7, we believe everyone is equal and we do not nourish stupid ideas of intolerance and exclusivism in our breast; consequently we will support any attempt at conciliation among the working class which does not ask the impossible sacrifice of our convictions." They were willing to go anywhere to discuss the issues, but "we will never accept a Program," they declared, "which, inspired by God, obstructs individual liberty, sanctions the principle of authority and maintains many of the privileges of the

landowning classes." The Internationalists were as determined as their antagonists not to give an inch: an
impasse had been reached.

The intransigence of Pescatori and his friends was
undoubtedly conditioned to some extent by the anti-Mazzinian propaganda being aired by Internationalists outside of the Romagna; in places, that is, where the republicans were not as dominant a force and could be censured without fear of retribution. The most vociferous
of these critics were the Neapolitans, led by a young
aristocrat, Carlo Cafiero (1846-1892).[55] Originally from
Apulia, where his family had extensive landholdings, the
ex-seminary student was a zealous supporter of the I.W.A.
Though residing in Naples, the old Bakuninist center, he
tended to favor the General Council in its conflict with
the Russian. By early 1872, however, his primary concern
was not Bakunin but rather the Mazzinians. Convinced
that the Internationalists had to break away completely
from the republican party, he began to attack Garibaldi's
initiative for a Democratic Congress as soon as the idea
was revived in January. He was especially upset that
the Bologna Fascio Operaio, now the foremost socialist
organization in the country, had adhered to the proposed
meeting, and beginning on January 21, in his articles in
La Campana, the I.W.A. organ in Naples, he increasingly
directed his fire at the Bolognesi. Mazzini, he warned
them, was a bourgeois, and consequently no conciliation
was possible with him.

By late February the leaders of the Fascio Operaio
were substantially in accord with the Southerner. If
they adhered to the Democratic Congress it was only because of a desire to improve relations with the republicans, not merge with them. Above all they wanted to
avoid bloodshed. Under the circumstances it would be extremely imprudent to totally disavow the project.

On February 22, a few days after the meeting at Villa
Gambellara, Il Fascio operaio presented its views on the
subject. L'Alleanza had recently attacked Cafiero and
La Campana. Pescatori and his followers were forced to
defend their coreligionists by frankly stating their o-
pinion. It was true, they declared; conciliation was
unrealistic. On principle, the two parties were completely incompatible.[56] What had been suggested at Villa
Gambellara was made explicit now.

But the Mazzinian onslaught continued.[57] Consequently the _Fascio_'s Regional Council met in Bologna on February 24 and issued a protest which reaffirmed its belief in the impossibility of conciliation and condemned the recent attacks.[58] The situation grew ever more tense. The parties exchanged insults and threats. Late in the month Rodolfo Domenico Rossi, _L'Alleanza_'s editor, gave a public speech in which he declared that the only reconciliation he would support was one with bullets.[59]

Both parties were encouraged in their open warfare by the failure of Mazzini and Garibaldi to come to terms. On January 10 the republican high priest declared that he was willing to treat with his rival under the right conditions. Garibaldi's response took the form of a letter to Ceretti on February 20, published in _Il Fascio operaio_ on March 2.[60] Apparently, the General replied, the only way to satisfy Mazzini was by accepting his program. But if this was his idea of reconciliation, the Internationalist champion concluded, an agreement had best be forgotten. This episode ended all hopes of a personal _rapprochement_, for the Prophet died a few days later.

The death of Mazzini appeared to calm the situation a little. During the middle of March the republicans (and to some extent the Internationalists also) paid homage to their leader. _L'Alleanza_ dedicated itself completely to the Genovese and seemed to forget about the socialist opposition. In fact, rancor on both sides continued to grow. On March 17, during the first session of the Bologna Congress, bands of young Internationalists and republicans clashed in Ravenna. Three days of sporadic fighting left two persons dead and over seventy behind bars.[61] Similar incidents threatened to erupt in other towns, and for a few days it looked as if the whole region would become a giant battlefield.

Thanks to efforts by leaders of both parties the general blood bath was avoided, but the Ravenna riot did have important repercussions--in Bologna. On March 24, _Il Fascio operaio_ published a strongly-worded article aimed at the direction of _L'Alleanza_. In it the republicans were condemned in the most uncomplimentary terms: they were called bigots and hypocrites, and the responsibility for the trouble that had arisen in the past, even before Ravenna, was laid entirely at their doorstep. The article concluded by calling on the people to choose, once and for all, between the socialist party and that of the "buffoons of the street."

The pretext for this attack was a correspondence

from Ravenna, written by Pompeo Panciatichi, which had
been published two days before in the republican paper.
According to the Internationalists (the piece was signed
by the Regional Council of the Fascio), the communication had accused them of initiating the disturbance at
Ravenna. Unfortunately, such was not the case. Panciatichi had limited himself to a description of the events,
and, moreover, L'Alleanza had gone out of its way to discourage trouble.[62] The months of tension and the insults,
real and imagined, had forced the Fascio to overreact.
It would pay a high price for its mistake.

The republicans were beside themselves with anger.
Recriminations ensued as tempers boiled. The climax occurred when an enraged Pescatori assaulted Enrico Perdisa, an Alleanza writer, and, as a result, the entire
membership of the Fascio Regional Council was asked to
defend its honor on the field of battle by the direction
of the Mazzinian paper. Negotiations determined that
only two duels were really necessary: one between single
representatives of the republican organ and the socialist association, the other between Perdisa and Pescatori. The first affaire d'honneur was fought on April
1.[63] The second, though, never took place. Pescatori
procrastinated, and in the end refused to fight altogether for reasons which were never explained satisfactori-
ly.[64] Completely humiliated, the socialist chieftain resigned his positions as consul of the Fascio and editor
of its paper. He remained in the organization but never
recovered from the disgrace. His departure from Bologna
about a year later went almost unnoticed. Deserted by
his friends, he left for Trieste where he disappeared
into almost total obscurity.[65] The Fascio Operaio had
lost its founder and most prestigious leader. He deserved a better fate.

A month after Pescatori's humiliation the Fascio
suffered another blow--this time in the Romagna. Francesco Piccinini was one of the earliest adherents of the
I.W.A. in the region; he had been a participant, we will
recall, at the socialist meeting of April, 1871. Intelligent and energetic, the Garibaldian (he had fought at
Mentana) advanced very rapidly in the ranks of the new
party. By the time of the Bologna Congress (March, 1872)
only Pescatori, Nabruzzi, and Ceretti preceded him on
the Fascio's hierarchy. He seemed to have a bright future ahead of him; he was young and well-liked.

Piccinini was less popular with the Mazzinians, most
of all in his native Lugo, where the ex-republican was

severely ostracized. His enemies were intent on perse-
cuting him, he once claimed, because he was a socialist
and had ceased to believe in the religious mystification
of their master, Mazzini.[66]   But the hostility had deeper roots, for it was inspired by fear--the young Lughese
was constantly trying to win new recruits for the International.[67]   In December, 1871, and January of the following year, he was embroiled in a battle against the
A.R.U. chieftains of Lugo and Faenza. He had written
a correspondence to La Plebe in which the Mazzinians in
Italy had been compared with the oppressors of the Paris
Commune, and his outraged opponents now took the opportunity to try to disgrace him. But they failed when Nabruzzi and the Ravennati came to his aid.[68]

Unable to silence him the republicans of Lugo continued to do everything in their power to make his life
difficult. On the day when he had succeeded in creating
a Fascio Operaio in Lugo, February 29, 1872, he and his
companions were followed by an angry mob which insulted
and tried to provoke them.[69]   Piccinini's efforts at reconciliation were to no avail. Early in April he met
some of his enemies in a bar and as a gesture of good
will offered them a drink. They replied that they would
not drink with a coward. Piccinini challenged each man
to a fight, but no one accepted.[70]   Having humbled them,
he knew there would be dire consequences to pay. A few
days later he predicted his death.[71]

As Piccinini was coming out of a cafe facing the
main square in Lugo on the evening of May 2, he was met
by a group of men apparently waiting for him. They called him over, and as he approached, one of them pulled
out a gun and shot him point-blank. Wounded, the socialist chieftain ran screaming "Oh God! Oh God!" The assassins gave chase, overtook him, and stabbed him to death.[72]
He left a wife and two children--and a legacy that would
plague the relationship between the two parties for the
next twenty years.[73]

The Congress of Rimini

The Congress of Bologna in March had resolved that
the Regional Council of the Fascio should take the lead
in convoking a national congress which would create an
Italian Federation of the International. The first concrete attempt in this direction had been made sometime
previously, in January, when Terzaghi and his friends
issued a circular calling for the meeting.[74]   The idea

received an enthusiastic response both in Bologna and in the Romagna.[75] But the project met with difficulties; at first it had to be postponed because it conflicted with Garibaldi's proposed Democratic Congress, which took precedence, and finally it was abandoned altogether as the first suspicions of Terzaghi's treachery discredited him among his colleagues in Turin. Thus the initiative passed into the hands of the Bolognesi at their March meeting.

The situation in Bologna, however, precluded serious preparation for a national congress in the near future. The Piccinini assassination sparked a tremendous ferment and threatened to provoke a final showdown between the Mazzinians and the Fascio.[76] The latter, moreover, was in complete disarray. Its financial condition was disastrous and morale was low; the humiliation at the hands of the republicans had discredited not only Pescatori but the entire Regional Council as well. At a general meeting on June 23 the Fascio's presiding officer lamented that the organization led such a "miserable and shabby existence" that local newspapers were already writing of its demise.[77]

Pescatori's resignation in April had been followed by that of the entire Regional Council. Thereafter chaos reigned at the top as no one seemed to be able to muster enough support to direct the Fascio. The situation remained unstable until the middle of the year, when the power vacuum was finally filled by Nabruzzi and Costa.

Being from the provinces, the two Romagnols were excluded from leadership in Bologna previously and thus immune from the criticism to which the Regional Council had been subjected. Their main strength, however, was a firm determination to separate the Fascio completely and irrevocably from the Mazzinians. Pescatori and Ceretti, the old command, had never gone this far. Both retained sentimental ties with the A.R.U. and were loath to make a clean break. Like Garibaldi, their hero, they espoused the idea of reconciliation; both gave firm support to the General's project of a Democratic Congress (Ceretti was one of its principal instigators in both 1871 and 1872). But not everyone within the Fascio endorsed this position. Provoked by what they considered republican arrogance, some members concluded that no agreement whatsoever was possible. This tendency dominated among the Internationalists after the events of April and May. Given the hatred aroused by the Mazzinians now, especially following the Lugo assassination, it was in-

evitable that the new leaders would be men completely intransigent on the question of reconciliation.

Nabruzzi established himself as the champion of the
anti-Mazzinian faction at the Bologna Congress. Costa,
too, was an outspoken critic of the republicans (never
having been a member of the A.R.U., he had few scruples
about attacking it).[78] A month or two after the March
meeting the Imolese appeared in Neuchâtel, where he spent
the next few weeks. James Guillaume, who was in daily
contact with him, suggests that the young exile had gone
to Switzerland because he feared arrest at home.[79] Since
the future revolutionary had not yet committed an offense
punishable by imprisonment, however, it is more likely
that he had fled Italy (in the aftermath of the Piccinini
murder?) in order to escape the ire of his republican
foes. His estrangement from them was already complete.

In June Costa was back in Italy. Rather than returning to Imola, though, he settled down in Bologna, where
he and Nabruzzi, who had recently transferred his residence from Ravenna, began to revive the local socialist
organization. The most active of the two Romagnols was
the Imolese, who now became secretary of the Fascio. Aided by Alceste Faggioli, a student at the University,[80] he
concentrated on reorganizing the association in Bologna
and strengthening its ties with its sister societies in
the Romagna and the Marches. His central concern, however, was preparing the national congress which would
soon be convoked.[81]

Meanwhile, Bakunin was working toward the same end
in Locarno. He was anxious to see the meeting take place
as soon as possible. He knew that before too long the
I.W.A. would convene its annual reunion (on June 18 the
London Council voted to hold this gathering at The Hague
in September), where his showdown with Marx would finally
take place. It was imperative that the Italians meet
soon, and that they adhere to his views.

By the middle of 1872 Bakunin was making considerable progress toward these goals.[82] The new leadership
of the Fascio was more open to his counsels than the old,
and Nabruzzi now replaced Ceretti as the Russian's main
correspondent in north-central Italy. Anarchist ideas
were also obtaining good results elsewhere. Among the
new converts to Bakunin's views was Carlo Cafiero. The
Pugliese began to desert the London Council late in the
previous year. When the Romagnols came into contact with

him, in the course of the heated debate over Garibaldi's Congress, his conversion to anarchism was almost complete. As a leading advocate of the International Congress he undoubtedly continued to correspond with the Romagnols, and his influence pushed them increasingly to the left. On May 20 Cafiero arrived in Locarno to visit Bakunin. This was the first time the two had ever met. They became fast friends and found that ideologically they were totally in accord.[83] The sojourn lasted almost a month.

On June 23, a few days after Cafiero's departure, the Russian received another visitor from the peninsula--Nabruzzi, who came to meet the man with whom he had been corresponding for some time now. Undoubtedly the subject of Bakunin's conversations in both cases was the Italian Congress.[84] These talks produced immediate results. On June 24 the Regional Council of the Fascio Operaio--composed now of Lodovico Guardigli, Francesco Orsoni, Nabruzzi, and Costa--issued a circular reaffirming its intention to hold the meeting and asking the Italian sections to prepare for it.[85] Early in July invitations were extended to the nuclei throughout the peninsula.[86]

The Congress took place in Rimini, in the Romagna, on August 4-6, 1872.[87] The majority of sections represented were in Emilia, the Marches, and the Romagna, but they also included those of Rome, Naples, Mantua, Siena, Florence, and Sciacca (in Sicily).[88] The official account of the meeting did not give the names of the delegates (there were twenty-five, according to Nettlau),[89] but we know for certain that they included the following individuals: Carlo Cafiero, Celso Ceretti, Andrea Costa, Giuseppe Fanelli, Saverio Friscia, Gaetano Grassi, Errico Malatesta, Lodovico Nabruzzi, Lorenzo Piccioli-Poggiali, Paride Suzzara-Verdi, Carlo Terzaghi, Tito Zanardelli, Teobaldo Buggini, Giuseppe Capacini, Alceste Faggioli, Giuseppe Piccinini, Germanico Piselli, Tommaso Schettino, Cajo Zavoli, Francesco Orsoni, and Carlo Gambuzzi.[90]

The Congress, moderated by Cafiero (Costa served as secretary), accomplished a great deal in three days. The conferees spent most of this time dealing with the primary objective of the meeting, the creation and organization of the Italian Federation. In the end it was determined that the confederation would be composed of autonomous sections and headed by two administrative organs, a Commission of Correspondence and a Commission of Statistics. Elected to the first were Costa, Faggioli,

and another member of the Bologna _Fascio_, probably Pilade
Campagnoli; Ceretti, Nabruzzi, Terzaghi, and Suzzara-Verdi
formed the second body. The Federation's Statutes and Regulations were patterned, with slight modifications, after those of the I.W.A. and the Internationalist section
in Naples respectively.

But the delegates did not stop here; despite their
declaration that they would concern themselves only with
questions of organization rather than those of principle,
they proceeded to deal at length with the conflict taking
place within the I.W.A. between the London Council and
the Bakuninists. They heard "several speeches in which
the representatives all spoke against the great Council,"
and then voted to break every tie with it. Rather than
adhering, moreover, to the Congress of The Hague, which
the Council had scheduled for September 2, they proposed
that an anti-authoritarian congress be held in Neuchâtel
on the very same date. Marx's suspicions that the Italians were being swayed by Bakunin were more than justified. In fact, the Rimini Congress went beyond the Russian. Its resolutions represented the beginning of the
end of the First International.

The Mirandola-Bologna Congress

Bakunin was rather displeased with the results a-
chieved at Rimini. Certainly he was glad to see an anti-
authoritarian Federation constructed. But his strategy
at the moment was to win over the I.W.A., not to detach
his supporters from it. The essential task, as he saw
it, was to get organized and ready for The Hague. Consequently the decision by the Italians to break all ties
with the London Council and to encourage their friends
abroad to do likewise, by adhering to a rival congress,
was not a welcome one. The Russian's attitude was shared
by his followers outside of Italy; as soon as word of the
Rimini declarations was received, the Jura Swiss and the
Spanish requested that their colleagues reconsider.[91]
Would they make peace with the General Council, rescind
their proposal for a Swiss Congress, and send delegates
to The Hague? After some hesitation, Costa and his associates held firm.[92] "That deliberation was so solemn,"
the Romagnol replied from Imola, "the representatives
who approved it felt its need so greatly, that we could
not now revoke it without negating our sentiments."[93]
Still, some concessions were made: the Swiss Congress,
which was eventually held in Saint-Imier rather than
Neuchâtel, was postponed until after that of The Hague;

and while refusing to send official delegates to the latter, Cafiero was allowed to attend the sessions in the
role of an observer.

As Bakunin had expected, the Congress of The Hague
on September 2-7, 1872, witnessed the confrontation between the two dominant factions of the I.W.A.[94] Badly
outnumbered, the anti-authoritarians were forced on the
defensive from the very beginning; and after a heated
debate both Bakunin and Guillaume, his most able ally,
were expelled from the Association. The triumph of the
Marxians over the anarchists seemed to be complete. But
it turned out to be a Pyrrhic victory, for the rift which
resulted meant the effective demise of the I.W.A.; the
Congress voted to transfer the General Council from London to New York, where after a moribund existence it soon
expired.

After their failure in Holland, the Saint-Imier Congress took on much more meaning for the anarchists. The
meeting proposed by the Italians was the only remaining
hope of unifying the anti-authoritarian forces and suc-
cessfully contending with Marx for hegemony of the socialist movement in Europe. The conferees met on September 15.[95] The Italian Federation was well-represented;
Cafiero, Costa, Fanelli, Malatesta, and Nabruzzi were
among the fifteen delegates, which also included French,
Spanish, and Swiss representatives. The Fifth Congress
of the I.W.A.--Bakunin and his followers insisted that
they represented the true International; the authoritarians were the heretics--lasted two days. Its deliberations are summed up in the following declaration: "The
destruction of all political power is the first duty of
the proletariat; every organization of a political power,
/though/ calling itself temporary and revolutionary, and
created to achieve that destruction, can only be one more
deception, and would be very dangerous for the socialist
proletariat; rejecting all compromise in order to achieve
the fulfillment of the social revolution, the workers of
all countries should establish, independently of all bourgeois politics, the solidarity of revolutionary action
on principle."[96] Based on these tenets the delegates at
Saint-Imier succeeded in creating some degree of cohesion
in a movement which by its very nature made unity difficult. The anarchist International which they erected
would be the only European-wide socialist organization
in existence during the next few years.

Saint-Imier marked Costa's first appearance at an
international meeting. Despite his youth and inexperi-

ence, Costa, who had met Bakunin for the first time only
a few days before,[97] was one of the most outspoken delegates at the Swiss Congress. Thoroughly radicalized by
his recent experience in the Romagna, where the A.R.U.
represented the authoritarianism he had come to despise,
the young Imolese was implacable in his criticism of the
London Council.

On September 17, the day after the Saint-Imier Congress concluded its sessions, several of its delegates
met secretly at Neuchâtel. The main scope of this second
gathering was the resurrection of the International Fraternity, Bakunin's old conspiratorial and elitist association.[98] This project had been initiated by the Russian prior to the Saint-Imier Congress, but it was only
now that its details were fully worked out.[99]

Undoubtedly a good deal of discussion was also devoted to the subject of social revolution, the Fraternity's chief objective and a theme that came to preoccupy
anarchist thinking increasingly after Saint-Imier. Since
the insurrection had to be a general one, however, it was
recognized that the immediate problem was that of gaining
popular support. A means of educating the masses was
necessary. Realizing this, the conferees determined to
found a newspaper. Its title, significantly, was to be
La Rivoluzione sociale.

The paper was published in Neuchâtel at the end of
September by Bakunin and Costa.[100] From this moment on,
the Romagnol became the old man's leading Italian collaborator. The Russian had been favorably impressed by
his new associate at Saint-Imier, but he had had his eye
on the youth even before. This interest stemmed from the
fact that Costa had become the key figure in the Italian
Federation--as Secretary of Correspondence, the highest
post in the organization, he was in fact its chief di-
rector--and also from a recognition that the two men
shared almost identical views; by now the Imolese had become a convinced revolutionary and anarchist.[101]

Costa returned to Italy in the last days of September.[102] Inspired by his recent association with Bakunin,
he initiated a feverish activity aimed at establishing
the Federation on a firmer foundation. One of the party's
glaring weaknesses before had been the creation of nuclei
composed of members from different backgrounds and with
diverse interests. The result was a sad lack of cohesion.[103] An organization based on job categories seemed

to make much more sense. Accordingly Costa reconstructed the section of Imola along these lines,[104] and encouraged other cells to do likewise.[105] A steady stream of
letters and circulars emanated from Imola, where the young
activist had his headquarters.[106] Working closely with
Cafiero, who traveled the length of the peninsula creating new sections,[107] the Imolese was indefatigable in his
efforts to expand and strengthen the Italian Federation.

It did not take the authorities long to notice this
unusual movement in the Romagna. The Minister of Interi-
or wanted to know what was happening. The prefect of Bologna, in his reply of November 13, was reassuring:

> Costa has no other position save that of Secretary
> and Representative of the _Fascio Operaio_ of Bologna.
> Up to now he has been in Imola because school is in
> recess, but he is about to return to Bologna in or-
> der to resume his studies at the University. He is
> a youngster without any importance whatsoever; with-
> out influence on the working class, without energy,
> without any of those qualities that are required in
> a party leader.[108]
> I do not believe that he writes letters and cir-
> culars in which he qualifies himself as the head of
> a committee and promotes strikes and revolutions,
> but if he does, this activity should be interpreted
> as nothing more than immature boasting typical of
> his age.
> As for surveillance the Minister can be sure that
> it leaves nothing to be desired on my part. Not
> that I mean to brag by saying this, for up to now he
> has espoused the International with so much frank-
> ness and impudence that it has not been difficult
> to follow, little by little, all of his movements.[109]

Perhaps it was the close surveillance which convinced
Costa to leave Imola and move to Bologna late in 1872.[110]
He continued, however, to encourage and direct the work
of reorganization.[111] Another concern (and another possible reason for his transfer to the Emilian city) was the
preparation of the Second Congress of the Italian Federation.

In December, 1872, it was determined that the gathering would convene in Mirandola--which attests to the influence which Ceretti still exerted--on March 15 of the
following year.[112] The scope of the meeting would be
organization; "we must oppose the monopoly of capital,"

65

Costa announced in January, "...with the formidable organization of labor. But without reaching some agreement we will not be able to organize ourselves; and the
Congress provides a means of coming to an understanding."[113]

The gathering did not take place without some difficulty. The I.W.A., now recognized as a subversive party, was beginning to concern the government. In an effort to impede the meeting, the police arrested Ceretti
and disbanded the section of Mirandola a few days before
it was to convene. But the Commission of Correspondence,
acting swiftly, was able to find a new locale, and on the
scheduled date nearly sixty delegates, representing all
regions of the country, met in Bologna.[114]

The assembly opened with a declaration of war on
the authorities: "Absolute incompatibility exists between us and the State, between us and the bourgeoisie
and its government, between us and their immorality,
their violence, their privileges, their cabals and mono-
polies." The General Council of the I.W.A. and the authoritarian communism it represented were also condemned,
and the deliberations at The Hague and those of the Council, now in New York, were declared void. A statement
of principles followed. The assembly declared itself
atheist and materialist, anarchist and federalist, and
in favor of collective property. A special emphasis was
to be put on the infiltration of socialist ideas into
rural areas. Given the wretched conditions that existed
there, especially in Lombardy and in the South, "the very
first duty of the workers in the city is the promotion
of an active propaganda in the countryside."[115] On the
question of organization it was determined that the most
effective way to unite the workers was through the creation of craft and trade unions. At the executive level
it was decided to add a new body to the two already in
existence, the Commission of Propaganda.

After the Second Italian Congress had concluded its
official business on March 17, a special meeting was held
to decide on the Terzaghi question. During the course
of the previous year it had become evident to all, not
just the members of his own section, that Carlo Terzaghi
was in the employ of the questore of Turin.[116] During
October and November, Cafiero had been in the Piedmon-
tese city, and after a thorough investigation, had found
evidence of foul play. He, Costa, and Ceretti prepared
the case against the accused, and the proof, though not
conclusive, was sufficient to condemn him. Terzaghi was

66

thrown out of the Italian Federation.

None of Terzaghi's principal accusers, though, had the satisfaction of seeing him disgraced. On the night of the 16th, after the second session of the Congress, some of the delegates were surprised by the police at a cafe near the University. Among those arrested were Costa, Cafiero, Malatesta, Chiarini, Negri, Faggioli, Antonio Sajani, and Giuseppe Nabruzzi, Lodovico's brother.[117] On that same night the Fascio Operaio nuclei of Bologna, Imola, and San Giovanni in Persiceto were disbanded by the police.

Regardless of these setbacks, as we noted, the assembly continued to deliberate, and it was not adjourned until its work had been finished. When it ended, the delegates left with a sense of accomplishment. The meeting had achieved a good deal. It was clear that the Federation had made great strides during the short period of its existence. Undoubtedly much of the credit belonged to Costa. The twenty-one-year-old agitator, who had been described as "a youngster without any importance whatsoever" five months before, now came to be recognized as "the directive mind of the Italian International."[118]

Conclusion

Despite the friction which characterized the relationship between the Mazzinians and the socialist dissidents since the previous year, both in the Romagna and throughout the country, it was still possible that the two warring factions might resolve their ideological differences and reunite within the A.R.U. up to March, 1872. But the situation changed dramatically following the Regional Congress of the Fascio Operaio held during that month. It was now that the republicans' uncompromising stance on the question of reconciliation, and the equally unyielding reaction of their socialist rivals, brought the crisis to a full head, resulting in brawls, duels, and eventually assassination.

The impact of this internecine warfare was profound. One of its most fateful results was a strengthening of anti-republican sympathies within the Bologna Fascio and the subsequent rise within the organization of the most intransigent of its members. The new leadership, headed by Costa and Nabruzzi, determined to end all attempts at compromise once and for all.

Having burned their bridges behind them, the young

67

Romagnols were ready to turn their attention to other problems. The most pressing of these was the revival of the
Fascio, now on the verge of total collapse after its recent struggle with the Mazzinians. It was during the
course of this reorganization that the Romagnols consolidated their hold on the Fascio. The operation, however,
was but a prelude to a greater task, that of unifying and
giving direction to the nascent socialist movement throughout the peninsula. This ambitious project was spearheaded by the Fascio, and its efforts culminated in the creation of the Italian Federation at Rimini in August, 1872.[11]

The new association was firmly based on anarchist prin
ciples rather than those of Marx. Indeed, the Italians
immediately became the most extreme of Bakunin's followers.
This direction was largely dictated by Costa and his
friends. Historically conditioned to revolt against authority, the Romagnols were pushed further along this road
by their recent humiliation at the hands of the "intoler-
ant" republicans. Tired of Mazzinian insults and provo-
cations, the young leaders of the Federation were in no
mood to treat with other authoritarians--those in London.
Thus they acted resolutely and responded to the General
Council as they had done earlier to the Mazzinians: they
completely severed all ties. This impulsive act precipi-
tated the schism within the I.W.A. which became definitive at The Hague a month later.

Costa's star rose rapidly after Rimini. Before long
he became the dominant figure within the Italian Federation.[120] Spurred on by Bakunin, the Imolese, now the Russian's protégé, was untiring in his efforts to organize
the anarchist movement. While centering his activities
in the Romagna and the neighboring regions, notably the
Marches, the aspiring revolutionary established contacts
throughout the peninsula. Thanks in large measure to
these efforts, the vast network of I.W.A. sections gradually expanded, and the Federation made steady progress, as
became evident at the Mirandola-Bologna Congress.[121]

NOTES

[1]There are inadequate biographies for most of the leaders of the Italian socialist and workers' movement. Costa is no exception. The most popular study is that of Lilla Lipparini, _Andrea Costa_ (Milan: Longanesi, 1952), which, however, has the serious flaw of neglecting almost completely the decade of the 1880's (she devotes only twelve pages to this period). Moreover, the book tends to be sentimental; in fact, it has been referred to as a romantic novel. See Giuseppe Talamo's review in _Rassegna storica del Risorgimento_, 11 (1953), 295-96. A better life is Alessandro Schiavi's more recent _Andrea Costa_ (Rome: Castaldi, 1956). Because of its small size (123 pp.) this volume, like Lipparini's, is necessarily uneven; yet despite this limitation, Schiavi begins to approach his subject in a more erudite fashion. Paolo Orano's work, _Andrea Costa_ (Rome: Società Libraria, 1910), makes no pretensions of being scholarly. As a biography, it leaves much to be desired. Orano, though, does an outstanding job in describing Costa's Romagnol heritage.

[2]Guido Piani, "Aneddotti e ricordi sulla fanciullezza di Andrea Costa," _La Gazzetta dell'Emilia_ (Bologna), Jan. 20-21, 1910.

[3]"Autobiografia," ed. Amedeo Tabanelli, _Movimento operaio_, 4 (1952), 229.

[4]Andrea did not submit meekly to his teacher's austere methods. On one occasion Don Moducci threw a ruler at him but missed and broke a crucifix. "The Lord protests because you beat us," the young rebel cried, an indiscretion which cost him dearly. See Piani, "Aneddotti e ricordi."

[5]Giuseppe Mazzini, "Notizie su Andrea Costa" (Biblioteca Comunale di Imola TS, 1947), p. 2.

[6]Darchini, "Autobiografia," p. 238.

[7]Ibid., p. 237.

[8]Ibid., p. 233.

[9]Ibid., p. 234.

[10]See Mambelli, "La Romagna dal 1865 al 1870," p. 489.

[11]"Shakers," a fictitious republican club.

[12]"Autobiografia," p. 244.

[13]This according to Darchini, who came under the spell of his older friend and became one of his first students (Ibid., p. 239).

[14]Piani, "Aneddotti e ricordi."

[15]Giuseppe Barbanti-Brodano, Assisie di Bologna. Processo degli internazionalisti. Difese proferite dall'Avvocato Giuseppe Barbanti per Costa Andrea e Matteuzzi Vincenzo, ed. Raffaello Cervone (Bologna: Società Tip. dei Compositori, 1876), p. 4.

[16]On Aug. 14, 1874, Giovanni Codronchi, Imola's mayor, informed the local pretore that it was at the University of Bologna that Costa "was lured to internationalist ideas" (Procedimento Costa, vol. 1). According to his own testimony during the Bologna trial of 1876, Costa had never belonged to the republican party. See the anonymous transcript of this testimony in Biblioteca Comunale di Forlì, Collezione Piancastelli, Raccolta autografi e carte, vol. 29 (hereafter this document will be designated Piancastelli MS.).

[17]Bagliori di socialismo, p. 7.

[18]Lipparini, Andrea Costa, p. 48.

[19]Cronaca Cerchiari, MS, pp. 13-14. Portions of this chronicle, conserved in B.C.I., have been published as "La vita sociale e politica imolese della 'Cronaca Cerchiari', 1865-1901," ed. Amedeo Tabanelli, Movimento operaio, 2 (1950), 149-57, 212-22, 279-84, 325-38, 398-403; 3 (1951) 473-84, 548-69, 673-90; 4 (1952), 93-103, 482-85, 634-39; 5 (1953), 68-73, 616-19.

[20]Nello Rosselli (Mazzini e Bakunin, p. 287) suggests that about two-thirds of the original Internationalists in Italy had been republicans. Given the political complexion of the area at the time, the Romagna must have had an even higher percentage.

[21]Prefect of Bologna report to Minister of Interior, Dec. 4, 1872, A.S.B., Gab. Pref., vol. 90.

[22]Several of the Internationalists, including Venturini, Antonio Cornacchia, and Francesco Poli, were enrolled in the mutual aid society in 1871, B.C.I., _Carte della Società Operaia di Mutuo Soccorso_, Imola, MS. 86.

[23]Romeo Galli ("Cimeli garibaldini raccolti a Imola," _Il Resto del carlino_ /Bologna7, July 18, 1932) suggests that the Imola section had its origins in 1870, something which is to be discounted entirely.

[24]"Autobiografia," p. 227.

[25]For biographical information, see Romeo Galli, "Antonio Cornacchia: 'Bavaresa,'" _Il Resto del carlino_, June 19, 1934.

[26]_Prime lotte socialiste: Lontani ricordi di un vecchio militante_, 2nd ed. (Imola: Galeati, 1968), p. 20. Marabini's book is largely anecdotal, and not surprisingly there are a number of factual errors to be found in it. In this case, for example, Marabini recalls that the name of the association in question was _La Alleanza_ and that the year was 1870. We have already seen that _La Alleanza_ was a republican society and that the year 1870 is too early; there was no I.W.A. section in Imola until after the Commune. Marabini does, however, recall that Costa was employed by an insurance company, which was true only in mid-1871.

[27]This according to Costa's testimony in 1876 (_Piancastelli_ MS.), at which time he also admitted to membership in the socialist section from the time of its foundation in September, 1871.

[28]_L'Alleanza_, Mar. 31, 1872.

[29]Interrogation of Mar. 30, 1873, _Procedimento Costa_, vol. 10.

[30]An unsigned article in the Mar. 2 issue of _Il Fascio operaio_ is attributed to Costa by Romano, _Storia_, II, 277.

[31]According to Carlo Terzaghi, Costa joined the Bologna _Fascio_ immediately after the gathering. Terzaghi, who was one of its delegates, recalls that he and some of the other representatives retired to a restaurant after the session of Mar. 19, and it was there that Costa was presented to him. The young Imolese wanted to know how he would go about joining the International. Terzaghi

urged him to join the _Fascio_. See _Il Tribuno_ (Salerno),
Apr. 23, May 6, 1876 (a similar version appears in _Il
Rabagas_ /Rome-Naples/, Nov. 30-Dec. 1, 1882). This relation, however, should not be taken as absolute truth.
The Turinese wrote these recollections after being expelled from the Italian International in 1873 as a suspected _agent provocateur_. His subsequent articles in
Il Rabagas and other newspapers, both in Italy and later
in Switzerland, were always full of invective and often
libelous when dealing with his estranged ex-companions,
the Internationalists. These, of course, detested their
unscrupulous tormentor. Terzaghi's writings were rarely
full-fledged lies (in which case his opponents would hardly have bothered with him); they were usually distortions.
In this case, for example, it is true that Terzaghi had
been at the Regional Congress. And although it is unlikely that Costa asked about admission into the I.W.A.--
he was already a member by virtue of his association with
the Imola nucleus--it is possible that he was seeking admission into the Bologna _Fascio_ at this time.

[32] According to his testimony of 1876 (_Piancastelli
MS._).

[33] See the anonymous accounts (previously cited) of
the Congress in _Procedimento Costa_, vol. 11.

[34] Ibid.

[35] Mazzini saw the problem very clearly: a choice had
to be made between political participation or revolution.
He was for the latter. On Sept. 12, 1869, he wrote Saffi,
"You make the Party a passive body...I travel along a
path diametrically opposed." Quoted in Mambelli, "La
Romagna dal 1865 al 1870," p. 485.

[36] Giovanni Spadolini, _I repubblicani dopo l'Unità_,
2nd ed. (Florence: Le Monnier, 1963), pp. 18-19. The
Romagnols, led by Ludovico Marini of Sant'Arcangelo and
Pietro Turchi of Cesena, are referred to as "Young Turks"
by Spadolini, because they were more determined than Mazzini himself to force the Congress to declare itself republican.

[37] Ibid., p. 16. The representatives also voted (33-19)
the following declaration: "The Congress solemnly pro-
claims the political and social principles sustained for
40 years by Giuseppe Mazzini as those which will lead most
readily and effectively to the true emancipation of the
worker."

[38]L'Alleanza, Mar. 1, 1872. The paper began to carry the subheading, "Organo quotidiano delle Società Repubblicane Consociate delle Romagne," on Feb. 28.

[39]Ibid., May 2, 1872.

[40]Ibid., May 23, 1872. The other members were Turchi, Leopoldo Malucelli (Faenza), and Rodolfo Domenico Rossi and Aristide Venturini (both from Bologna).

[41]Ibid., Jan. 2, 1872.

[42]Ibid., Jan. 9 and 13, 1872. During this time a duel was also avoided in Forlì, where Piselli, the I.W.A. head, and Pompeo Panciatichi, a prominent republican, had clashed, La Rivoluzione, Jan. 14, 1872. The reconciliation was apparently brought about by the mediation of Pietro Turchi. See prefect of Forlì to the prefect of Bologna, Jan. 9, 1872, A.S.B., Gab. Pref., vol. 90.

[43]Republished in La Rivoluzione, Jan. 28, 1872, and L'Alleanza, Jan. 26, 1872.

[44]L'Alleanza announced his forthcoming resignation on Jan. 7, 1872. For biographical data on Leonesi, who established a reputation as a Garibaldian, see Dizionario del Risorgimento Nazionale, ed. Michele Rosi, III (Milan: Francesco Vallardi, 1933), 359-60.

[45]L'Alleanza, Feb. 1, 1872.

[46]On Jan. 12 a friend (he signed his letter "C") of Rodolfo Domenico Rossi, the chief editor of L'Alleanza, wrote him in defense of the rebels: "I only want," he explained, "to combat the idea that generally prevails among the Mazzinians (though I do not refer to those with your good sense); the idea, that is, that those youngsters who have accepted the principles of the International should be considered turncoats," ibid., Jan. 13, 1872.

[47]On Jan. 29 the Mazzinian chieftains of the cities in the Romagna were called to Forlì by Saffi, where they parleyed with representatives of the Fascio. The object of the meeting was a settlement of their differences. But the negotiations broke down, it was reported, because the Internationalists insisted that no agreement was possible without the approval of Garibaldi. See prefect of Forlì to the prefect of Bologna, Feb. 2, 1872, A.S.B., Gab. Pref., vol. 90.

[48] Questore of Bologna to the prefect of Bologna, Feb. 1, 1872, A.S.B., Gab. Pref., vol. 90.

[49] Il Fascio operaio, Feb. 15, 1872. The meeting, which included Piccinini, also voted to help finance the I.W.A. paper in Bologna.

[50] Minister of Interior to the prefect of Bologna, Feb. 22, 1872, A.S.B., Gab. Pref., vol. 90.

[51] Il Fascio operaio, Feb. 21, 1872. Part of the speech is also quoted in Darchini, "Autobiografia," pp. 254-55.

[52] A few days later Pescatori expressed total agreement with his companions at Villa Gambellara, but regretted that he could not attend the gathering "on account of circumstances beyond our control," Il Fascio operaio, Feb. 21, 1872.

[53] See Nabruzzi's account of the meeting, ibid.

[54] Ibid.

[55] The only scholarly studies of his life now available: Antonio Lucarelli, Carlo Cafiero: Saggio di una storia documentata del socialismo (Trani: Vecchi, 1947), and Pier Carlo Masini, Cafiero (Milan: Rizzoli, 1974).

[56] This idea was also repeated by Costa in an article which appeared in Il Fascio operaio on Mar. 2.

[57] L'Alleanza, Feb. 24, 1872.

[58] Ibid., Feb. 27, 1872.

[59] Darchini, "Autobiografia," p. 253.

[60] Garibaldi also sent a copy of the letter to Luigi Stefanoni, editor of Il Libero pensiero in Florence. This correspondence was reproduced in L'Alleanza, Feb. 25, 1872.

[61] These riots are described in L'Alleanza, Mar. 21 and 22, 1872.

[62] Ibid., Mar. 23, 1872.

[63] Il Fascio operaio, Apr. 7, 1872. The names of the two combatants were not revealed in order to avoid criminal prosecution, but it is almost certain that the re-

publican was Antonio Fratti (who won) and the socialist, Augusto Errani.

[64]Pescatori's apologia (ibid.) is contradictory; it is not clear whether his refusal was motivated by a desire to protect his family (i.e., wife and four children), or whether he was against duels on principle. Charges of cowardice were also current.

[65]Pescatori was still being criticized by the Bolognesi four years later. See his letter to Celso Ceretti, Jan. 8, 1876, Carte Barbanti-Brodano, MS. 432, in Museo Civico del Primo e Secondo Risorgimento, Bologna.

[66]Letter of Dec. 31, 1871, to L'Alleanza, Jan. 4, 1872. On Jan. 7, 1872, La Rivoluzione described Piccinini as "a citizen of Lugo...noted as an initiator of schisms in a city whose patriots...do not have foolish ambitions of deserting the A.R.U."

[67]At his death, Piccinini was recalled as the "founder of many Internationalist sections." See L'Egalité, May 7, 1872.

[68]See La Rivoluzione, Jan. 7, 1872. Piccinini also received moral support from La Favilla, Jan. 9, 1872.

[69]Il Paria (Ancona), May 3, 1885.

[70]Ibid.

[71]Romano, Storia, II, 323.

[72]La Favilla, May 9, 1872. On Mar. 4, L'Alleanza published this terse comment: "Misfortune--we are told that a vile assassin treacherously shot Francesco Piccinini of Lugo on the evening of the...2nd at 9 p.m. in the main square of that city instantly killing him."

[73]Two months later a second socialist, Domenico Pocaterra, was killed by republicans in Ravenna. See L'Internazionale, Sept. 7, 1913 (special supplement to La Lotta, Imola).

[74]The circular, dated Jan. 28, appears in La Favilla, Feb. 3, 1872, and is reproduced in Nettlau, Bakunin e l'Internazionale, p. 303.

[75]On Mar. 10, 1872, Terzaghi informed Engels of his

idea. "The proposal," he wrote, "was received with enthusiasm except by the sections of Milan and Florence." See
La corrispondenza di Marx e Engels con italiani, p. 168.

[76]According to a report from the questore of Naples
to his prefect, July 9, 1872 (quoted in Romano, Storia,
II, 345-46), Cafiero had recently informed his friends
in the city that trouble was brewing in the Romagna, where
the assassination "has stirred up so much hatred between
the two parties that they threaten to slaughter each other
from day to day."

[77]Anonymous relation, June 23, 1872, Procedimento Costa
vol. 11.

[78]"It was the Romagnol element," Costa testified at
his trial in 1876 (Piancastelli MS.), "...which, after
the painful disputes of April, 1872, transformed the Fascio
Operaio, stripping it of all that which was found to be
vague." One of the indeterminate aspects of the Fascio
program was that which dealt with the republicans. On
this question Costa's position was very clear: he would
have nothing to do with Mazzini's followers. See Il Fascio
operaio, Mar. 2, 1872. Costa's anti-republican bias became even more pronounced a few months later. See the
Imolese's correspondence in La Favilla, Sept. 2, 12, Oct.
3, 1872.

[79]Guillaume, L'Internationale. Documents et souvenirs
(1864-1878), II (Paris: Stock, 1907), 280.

[80]A short biography of Faggioli is contained in L'Internazionale, Sept. 7, 1913.

[81]A report from the prefect of Bologna to the Minister
of Interior, Aug. 17, 1872 (A.S.B., Gab. Pref., vol. 90),
has some interesting observations on both Costa and the
Fascio during these months: "The Fascio Operaio in Bologna
and in the Romagna had but two leaders with sufficient
intelligence to keep it going--Pescatori in Bologna and
Piccinini in Lugo. Once Pescatori was expelled it was
inevitable that the society should decline. In fact it
came under the direction of a provisionary committee
which was composed at various times of seven, three, or
eight members--members who would resign almost every
week. The association no longer had headquarters nor a
newspaper nor, above all, money. No one on the committee
had enough education to keep the correspondence, and consequently the functions of secretary were entrusted to a

young student from Imola named Andrea Costa, who went about his work doing and undoing as he pleased and paying no attention to the committee. But then came the school recess and Costa, who had to study for his examinations, returned to his family. Before he left he entrusted the secretaryship, and the Fascio's files, to another youth, and friend, by the name of Alceste Fagioli /sic/ from Bologna. Even today the latter can be considered the one and only representative of the Fascio Operaio."

[82]Regis wrote Engels on May 13, 1872, informing him that the "Bologna Fascio Operaio is completely won over to the cause of the Jurassians." See La corrispondenza di Marx e Engels con italiani, p. 206.

[83]"Perfectly concluded alliance," Bakunin wrote in his diary on May 21. Quoted in Nettlau, Bakunin e l'Internazionale, p. 328.

[84]Ibid., p. 355.

[85]La Favilla, June 26, 1872. This must be the circular mentioned by Romano, Storia, II, 341, although he insists it was only sent out on June 28.

[86]Manacorda, Il movimento socialista italiano, p. 111.

[87]The compte-rendu (published as a leaflet) is contained in La Federazione Italiana, pp. 30-34. Unless otherwise specified, the following description of the gathering will be based on this document.

[88]The sections in Emilia: Bologna, Mirandola, and San Giovanni in Persiceto; in the Marches: Fano, Fermo, and Senigallia; and in the Romagna: Ravenna, Rimini, Imola, Lugo, Fusignano, San Potito, Sant'Arcangelo, and Forlì. Paride Suzzara-Verdi claimed that every region in Italy was represented except for the Veneto (La Favilla, Aug. 13, 1872).

[89]Bakunin e l'Internazionale, p. 357.

[90]The most complete list up to now has been that of Romano, who mentions the first twelve names (Storia, II, 348); the next seven are found in police records contained at the Archivio di Stato in Forlì (Gab. Pref., vol. 47, fasc. 214); the next to the last name is contained in a report from the prefect of Bologna to the Minister of

Interior on Aug. 17, 1872 (A.S.B., Gab. Pref., vol. 90);
and the last individual is indicated in memoirs by Piccioli-Poggiali (La Fieramosca /Florence7, Jan. 22, 1910).

[91]Rafael Fargo-Pellicer, one of the heads of the Ba-
kuninist-dominated I.W.A. in Spain, wrote Terzaghi on
Aug. 19 informing him that on the previous day he had
written Costa asking the Italians to send delegates to
The Hague. Now he wanted Terzaghi's help: "Could you,
dear friend, write to Cafiero, Bernardell /sic7, Gandolfi,
Costa etc. etc. so that they will immediately resolve to
attend the Congress in Holland...." This letter, quoted
in a directive from the Minister of Interior to the prefect of Bologna, Aug. 26, 1872 (A.S.B., Gab. Pref., vol.
90), suggests that both Augusto Bernardello of Ferrara
and Mauro Gandolfi of Milan were at Rimini. The Minister
did not say how he came into possession of this information, but he seemed to have a direct pipeline into Turin,
as his dispatches to the prefects of Bologna and Forlì
in this period indicate. It was never conclusively proved
that Terzaghi was a spy, but this evidence would certainly
tend to substantiate the charge.

[92]At first there was some disagreement among the I-
talians. On Aug. 21 Ceretti had La Favilla publish his
correspondence saying that delegates would be sent to The
Hague. But Cafiero, who had not been consulted, wrote
and ordered him to make a retraction (found in La Favilla,
Aug. 27). Ceretti was so offended by the Pugliese, who
had criticized him severely for making such a crucial decision on his own, that he threatened to quit his post on
the Commission of Statistics.

[93]Letter of Aug. 24, 1872, to the Federal Committee
of the Jura Federation, published in La Favilla, Aug. 27,
1872, and Bulletin de la Fédération Jurassiene de l'Association Internationale des Travailleurs (Sonvilliers),
Sept. 15-Oct. 1, 1872.

[94]Accounts of the meeting are found in the Bulletin
de la Fédération Jurassienne, Sept. 15-Oct. 1, 1872, and
L'Egalité, Nov. 2, 1872.

[95]Its deliberations are found in Guillaume, L'Internationale, III (Paris: Stock, 1909), 6-10. Costa's
account from Saint-Imier, dated Sept. 17, is contained
in La Favilla, Sept. 22, 1872.

[96]Quoted in Romano, Storia, II, 365.

[97]Nettlau, _Bakunin e l'Internazionale_, p. 365. Guillaume (_L'Internationale_, III, 1) declares that Costa arrived in Zurich, where Bakunin had been living for over two weeks, on Sept. 12; the Russian's diary (quoted in Romano, _Storia_, II, 363) says Sept. 11.

[98]Nettlau, _Malatesta_, p. 88.

[99]The only Italian members of the Fraternity were Cafiero, Costa, Fanelli, Malatesta, and Nabruzzi (ibid., 89).

[100]The place of publication, which is not mentioned in the paper, was later verified by Costa (_Piancastelli MS._), who also admitted that only one number was ever issued. A copy of this extremely rare newspaper is contained in _Procedimento_ Costa, vol. 70.

[101]See Costa's correspondence, dated Sept. 30, in _La Favilla_, Oct. 6, 1872.

[102]He returned to Bologna from the "Congress of Lugano" (sic) on Sept. 28. See prefect of Bologna to the Minister of Interior, Sept. 28, 1872, A.S.B., _Gab. Pref._, vol. 90.

[103]More than its war with _L'Alleanza_, it was "the _sentimental_ organization" of the _Fascio Operaio_, Costa claimed, which was responsible for its decline (_La Favilla_, Oct. 31, 1872).

[104]The Imola section was reconstituted in early October. See Costa's letter in _L'Indipendente_ (Ancona), Oct. 24, 1872. The nucleus in Bologna had already been divided into trade categories as early as August, according to a letter from Faggioli to Pietro Magri, Aug. 26, 1872, in Franco Della Peruta, "Documenti sull'Internazionale in Venezia (1872-73)," _Movimento operaio_, 2 (1950), 132.

[105]See Costa's letter to Rodolfo Boenco, a Venetian, Dec. 12, 1872, _Procedimento_ Costa, vol. 15.

[106]On Nov. 14, for example, the Imola section met and voted against sending a representative to a demonstration which was to be held in Rome in favor of universal suffrage. A circular to that effect, dated Nov. 15, was signed by Costa, Renzi, and Albo Albericci. Reproduced in _La Federazione Italiana_, pp. 235-36.

[107]Minister of Interior to the prefect of Bologna, Nov. 5, 1872, A.S.B., Gab. Pref., vol. 90. The Pugliese had also helped Costa in the reconstruction of the Imola section. See Minister of Interior to the prefect of Bologna, Oct. 26, 1872, A.S.B., Gab. Pref., vol. 90.

[108]The subprefect of Imola had a higher opinion of the Imolese (report to the prefect of Bologna, Dec. 18, 1872, A.S.B., Gab. Pref., vol. 90), who was described as possessing "extraordinary intelligence." Although only the secretary of the local section (the titular heads were Venturini, Renzi, and Poli), Costa was its most powerful associate. The nucleus had few members, the subprefect added, and its leaders, including Costa, lacked influence both in the city and in the countryside.

[109]A.S.B., Gab. Pref., vol. 90. The report also contained information on Nabruzzi: "The most important center of the International in this province is still that of Bologna, where Ludovico Nabruzzi keeps himself hidden, but he works assiduously and corresponds with Cafiero in Turin constantly." The prefect claimed he could seize the Ravennate's papers at any time, but wanted to wait until he was sure there was something to be gained by it.

[110]Costa was already in Bologna in early December, 1872; his letter to Boenco on Dec. 12 was dated from that city rather than Imola.

[111]On Jan. 30, 1873, the Minister of Interior complained to the prefect of Bologna that directions for the construction of new sections were continually emanating from Bologna and Imola; on Feb. 26 he informed the prefect that in addition to taking care of matters in Italy, "Costa ...is in frequent contact with foreign centers, and is the intermediary of several sections with the consulate of Jura Bernese;" and on Feb. 27 he told his subordinate that Costa and Chiarini had gone to Modena on the 23rd to organize a workers' nucleus (A.S.B., Gab. Pref., vol. 102).

[112]La Favilla, Dec. 29, 1872.

[113]Manifesto of Jan. 10, in La Plebe, Jan. 19, 1873.

[114]The Romagnols still had a preponderant number. Over a third of the 35 groups at Bologna were from the region. The Romagnol federations represented at Bologna were Ravenna and Rimini; the sections: Forlì, Faenza, Lugo, San Potito, Fusignano, Imola, Sant'Arcangelo, Santo Stefano,

80

San Pierino della Madonna dell'Albero, Carpinello, and
Campiano. An account of the meeting, on which my own
description is based, is found in the booklet, Associazione Internazionale dei Lavoratori: Atti del 6° Congresso
Universale di Ginevra e del 2° Congresso Regionale Italiano di Bologna (n.p., n.d.), and is reproduced in La Federazione Italiana, pp. 55-67. Another relation is contained in Bulletin de la Fédération Jurassienne, Apr. 1,
1873.

[115]During this deliberation, according to the Minister
of Interior, "The well-known Costa proposed the institution of special committees for the propagandizing of the
countryside. He cited the example of the organization
of the associations of the Romagna--he said that the government could arrest at will without being able to destroy that organization, erected as it is on solid foundations. Even if all the leaders were arrested, he ex-
claimed, the existence of the associations would not suffer: their place would be taken by subordinates, and if
these too were arrested, the members themselves would
take over the Direction according to a pre-established
plan." See note to the prefect of Forlì, Mar. 21, 1873,
A.S.F., Gab. Pref., vol. 49, fasc. 21.

[116]The first suspicions of Terzaghi's treachery, outside of Turin, are reported in La Favilla, Oct. 13, 1872.
The Terzaghi affair continued to occupy the Mantuan paper
--the Turinese had been one of its most faithful corres-
pondents--during the remainder of the year. For Costa's
own account of the celebrated affair, see Piancastelli MS.

[117]Other delegates at the Congress were Luigi Magnani,
Paolo Renzi, and Pescatori (Minister of Interior to the
prefect of Forlì, Mar. 21, 1873, A.S.F., Gab. Pref., vol.
49, fasc. 21); and Zanardelli and Piccioli-Poggiali (Minister of Interior to prefect of Bologna, Mar. 21, 1873,
A.S.B., Gab. Pref., vol. 102). On Mar. 18, 1873, the
prefect of Modena sent the prefect of Bologna a list of
people who were supposed to be there; it included Cajo
Zavoli, Gnocchi-Viani, Friscia, and Fanelli (A.S.B., Gab.
Pref., vol. 102).

[118]Questore of Bologna to prefect of that city, Mar.
20, 1873, A.S.B., Gab. Pref., vol. 102.

[119]The main impulse for the creation of the Federation came from the Romagna, according to Nettlau, Bakunin e l'Internazionale, p. 395.

[120]The central figure at the Rimini Congress had been Cafiero, Romano, *Storia*, II, 350. Hostetter, *Le origini del socialismo italiano*, p. 461, describes Costa as the Federation's chief organizer after Saint-Imier.

[121]For the growth of the I.W.A. during these months, see Masini, *Storia degli anarchici italiani*, p. 74.

CHAPTER THREE

REVOLUTION AND REPRESSION, 1873-1876

The Beginning of Conspiracy

The arrests that took place before and during the Mirandola-Bologna Congress began a period of incessant police repression that would enfeeble the Italian Federation and eventually suffocate it altogether.[1] "Addresses were confiscated," recalled Francesco Pezzi, an anarchist from Ravenna. "The most noted socialists were threatened with the loss of their jobs, many of them were placed under surveillance, held, tried, condemned, sent to prison. The fiercest police reaction was unleashed against them."[2] But the campaign was in its initial stages in early 1873; the government did not feel intimidated yet. Consequently it generally failed to press charges. Costa and his comrades arrested in Bologna were released in early May.[3] The papers found on their persons, and in the headquarters of the Bologna Fascio, had not been incriminating. In fact, practically all the Federation's activities had been publicized in the various socialist newspapers, notably in Suzzara-Verdi's Favilla, which served as something of a party organ.

Once out of prison Costa immediately set to work. There was much to be done. The recent setbacks had nullified the progress made during the last few months. Now the gains had to be recovered. The time spent in prison had done nothing to flag the Imolese's enthusiasm.[4] He resumed his efforts as zealously as before. "Costa toils with everything he's got in the Marches and the Romagna," Piccioli-Poggiali wrote a friend on June 14, "and his hard work is rewarded by considerable success."[5] Indeed, these efforts were crowned with good fortune. By the end of that month new sections had been formed in San Bartolo in the Romagna and Camerata Picena, Osimo, Pergola, and Sassoferrato in the Marches, as well as in Fitto di Cecina, Poggibonsi, and Ponte San Giovanni in Tuscany.[6]

The work of reviving the Italian Federation went on throughout the peninsula. The initial step was the founding of new cells and the reconstruction of old ones. Their

association into regional organizations was the next task.
The first regional meeting to be held was that of the Romagnols, which took place in San Pietro in Vincoli, one
of the <u>Ville Unite</u>, on July 20.[7] Costa presided over the
assembly, which included close to seventy delegates from
all over the region.[8] The main resolutions passed were
those dealing with the creation of the Romagnol Federation: it was decided that each group adhering to the
Federation would establish funds for resistance (to help
sustain strikes) and for propaganda; the members of the
nuclei were to pay dues of thirty centimes annually; and
the regional organization was to be headed by a Federal
Commission, which was to have its seat in Ravenna (elected to the body were Giacomo Lega, Pirro Rivalta, Francesco Pezzi, and Claudio Zirardini, all Ravennati). The
Mazzinians continued to be an issue. It was voted that
a manifesto would be sent to the republican workers of
the Romagna warning them against the mystifications of
the <u>Consociazione</u> and exhorting them to enroll in Internationalist sections.[9]

On August 10, less than a month after the Romagnol
Congress, that of the Marches and Umbria was convened.[10]
This too was a product of Costa's activity.[11] The conference was held in Pietra la Croce, a village a few
miles outside of Ancona, the main anarchist center in
the region. The result was the creation of a Federation
for those regions and the establishment of a Federal Commission at Ancona.

In addition to the matter of local organization the
conferees were especially concerned with the international anarchist Congress at Geneva which had been scheduled
for September. The Congress at San Pietro in Vincoli
had also devoted a good deal of attention to the Swiss
meeting. The Romagnols determined that Costa would be
their representative to Geneva. He was granted 300 <u>lire</u>
to cover expenses and given mandatory instructions on
the position he was to sustain there.[12]

The Geneva Congress--the anarchists maintained it
was the Sixth Congress of the I.W.A.--was held on September 1-6, 1873.[13] (The authoritarians also held a convention in the city a few days later, but it was poorly attended and little was accomplished.) The delegates reaffirmed their adherence to anarchist principles, and,
as was becoming traditional, they blasted the authoritarians. Costa, who was one of the presidents, "played
a very important role," according to the Minister of

Interior, "and it can be said that he alone represented 'almost all' the sections of the Italian International. ...During the course of the congressional discussions he spoke many times, in French,...demonstrated a good speaking ability, and earned the applause of the assembly over and over again with the violence of his speech."[14]

The Congress of Geneva did not result in any radical innovations. Much more significant than the meeting itself was what took place afterward. Costa returned with Bakunin, who had also been at the gathering, to Locarno, where the Russian had been living since mid-1873 on the Baronata, an estate purchased with Cafiero money. At Locarno it was resolved to give the Italian Federation a new orientation: it was to go underground and rather than concentrate on propaganda its main objective now would be to prepare the long-awaited revolution. What caused this turn? The sections in Italy were not functioning well: this was one consideration. While it was true that the Federation had grown, its affiliate cells were rather weak. One of their problems was money. More serious still was the lack of numbers.[15] During the previous year the Internationalist groups had attempted to divide their membership according to job categories. Given the size of most nuclei, the experiment had been a complete fiasco.

But there was a more compelling reason for the new direction being proposed--the mounting pressure exerted by the police. The repression had not ebbed in the slightest after the release of Costa and his friends in May. In fact, in that very month a new wave of arrests began. Among its victims were Pietro Magri, the anarchist chieftain from Venice, who was sentenced to a long prison term on May 8; Zanardelli, Gnocchi-Viani, Vincenzo Petrillo, and other anarchists in Rome, arrested on May 15; and Alfonso Leonesi, who was imprisoned on May 17[16] (and who chose to go into Spanish exile in July, when he was released, rather than risk another internment). Given these "incessant persecutions," continuing along the same lines as before had become impossible, and the International "was forced to follow the path of conspiracies and /revolutionary/ attempts...."[17]

When Costa returned to Italy, he began to lay the basis of a clandestine organization which would instigate the revolution. Late in September the tireless conspirator visited the anarchist leaders of Emilia,[18] and during the following month he moved so quickly and surrep-

85

titiously between Imola, Florence, and Rome that the police had trouble keeping track of him. But they did not need to follow his every movement to know what the mercurial youth was up to. The Imolese, the _questore_ of Bologna reported to his prefect on October 31, was busy creating secret revolutionary cells in accordance with the plan formulated at Locarno the month before.[19]

Late in October or early in November the Commission of Correspondence of the Italian Federation was transferred from Bologna to Florence.[20] Thus Costa, who had been nominated to serve on the directive body--together with Nabruzzi and Michele Guglielmi--at the Mirandola-Bologna Congress and had done virtually all the work himself, turned over his duties to Grassi, Piccioli-Poggiali, and Francesco Natta.[21] Apparently he was too involved with his other activities to handle the correspondence.

Indeed, the Romagnol was in perpetual motion. He spent the last part of November in Locarno, consulting with Bakunin,[22] but was back in Italy before long. In December the Minister of Interior warned the prefect of Forlì that according to informants, Costa was busy in the province of Forlì forming sections of "intransigents" as part of a larger plan "to create a secret society within the breast of the association."[23] These suspicions were confirmed a short time later when the subprefect of Rimini reported that Costa had stopped there on December 10-12, bound for Ancona, and had conferred with Giovanni Donati, one of the local chieftains, about the organization of secret revolutionary societies.[24]

Costa's efforts to prepare the Italian Federation for insurrection met with good results, especially in the Romagna, where "even the rocks...are revolutionary."[25] This new direction, however, did not receive universal approval within the organization. Not everyone was willing to go as far as the Imolese. Piccioli-Poggiali, for example, recently appointed to the Commission of Correspondence, resigned from the Federation in mid-November pleading "personal reasons,"[26] but later admitted that the real cause of his estrangement from his comrades was his unwillingness to follow Bakunin; he had not wanted to give up propaganda for action.[27]

The "action" that Piccioli-Poggiali talked about was still very vague in November, 1873. The decision made two months before had called for conspiracy and insurrection, but the actual time and place had not been

discussed. Late in the year the plans began to crystal-
lize when Costa and Bakunin met in Locarno. The conference probably took place in late November or early December (which would explain why Costa failed to attend the
Regional Congress of the Tuscan Federation on December
7). Included in the correspondence later sequestered
from Natta in Florence was an anonymous and undated letter which was sent to the Commission of Correspondence
from Switzerland during this time.[28] As the police correctly surmised, the letter was written by Costa.[29] The
Imolese, who was in Locarno,[30] had compiled the official
Acts of the Congresses held in Bologna and Geneva in March
and September respectively, and he was sending them to
Florence for publication and distribution in Italy. After
giving instructions to that effect, Costa informed his
correspondent (Natta?) that he would return from abroad
in about fifteen days. All of this was to be strictly
confidential; as far as everyone was concerned he was
supposed to be in Italy. He had been summoned, the Imolese confided, "in order to organize a new project."

Costa was still talking about revolution, but this
time it was a concrete, not a theoretical one. Its general outlines were worked out at Locarno. Armed bands
were to be formed by the anarchist sections in every region of Italy. At the appropriate time these groups were
to converge on the major cities, where political prisoners would be released, arms confiscated, and a popular
insurrection aimed at the government initiated. These
activities would be coordinated by a secret executive
organ located in Locarno, the Comitato Italiano per la
Rivoluzione Sociale (Italian Committee for Social Revolution). The ambitious undertaking was scheduled for the
spring of 1874.

It was probably the economic situation in Italy in
the winter of 1873-74 which convinced the two revolutionaries that the time had come to act. Economic difficulties plagued the country during the entire preceding year.
The crops had been bad and prices rose steadily. By winter the cost of living had reached unprecedented heights.
The price of grain, a good index of the general trend,
rose to the highest level since unification, before de-
creasing steadily during the next few years.[31] The economy, which had been shaky before, now threatened to collapse altogether. Discontent among the masses was widespread. In the countryside many peasants lived at a sub-
sistence level; the crisis brought them to the verge of
starvation. Riots and strikes ensued. Bakunin and Costa

saw the beginning of their spontaneous revolution in these
demonstrations of protest. They were convinced that if
ever there were a time for insurrection it was now.[32]

Costa returned to Italy in early December to inform
his comrades of the momentous decision that had been made.[3]
He remained only a short time, though, for he was back at
the Baronata by the middle of the month. In order to prepare the ground for the insurrection it had been decided
that a series of manifestoes would be addressed to the
workers, encouraging them to join in. The bulletins would
be written in Locarno and distributed on the peninsula
at regular intervals during the next few weeks. The Imolese composed the first of these appeals--they were all
signed by the Comitato Italiano--in mid-December.[34] It
was dated January, 1874, and distributed to all anarchist organizations in Italy during the course of that month.

The document left no doubt as to the path the International now meant to follow. Costa began by inveighing
against the violence that the state used to crush its
enemies. Oppression was evident everywhere, he admitted,
but it was time to do something about it: "The reaction
wants to crush us, let us rise; the reaction wants to
disperse us, let us organize; the reaction wants us dead,
let us show that we are alive." We need to declare war,
he continued. "We have the right and we will have the
ability." But our tactics have to change, he said, for
we are convinced "that the peaceful propaganda of revolutionary ideas has outlived its usefulness." What we
need now, the revolutionist concluded, is "the clamorous
and solemn propaganda of insurrection and the barricades."[3]

As the circular was being distributed the Commission
of Correspondence in Florence informed the Central Commission of the anarchist International, located in Brussels, of its determination to prepare an uprising in the
spring and asked for moral and financial assistance.[36]
Meanwhile Costa remained busy.[37] In the next few months
he divided his time between the various rebel centers in
Italy and his base of operations in Switzerland. It is
difficult to trace the young agitator's movements at this
time; he was careful to remain as inconspicuous as possible. Still, his activity is not totally obscure. In
early February he was in Tuscany, traveling first to Florence, where he probably conferred with the members of
the Commission of Correspondence, and then to Leghorn.[38]
In the middle of the month he returned to Locarno, where
he wrote the second Revolutionary Bulletin for the Comi-

tato _Italiano_[39] and further elaborated the plan for insurrection with Bakunin, Natta, and French revolutionaries including Victor Cyrille and Jean-Louis Pindy.[40]

The end of February found the Imolese in the Romagna.[41]
His major concern there was Ravenna, where the recent arrest of Claudio Zirardini, the most capable of the local
heads, had removed one of his most faithful collaborators
and created much confusion among the anarchists. Costa's
intervention achieved the desired results. Not only did
the section reorganize, under the leadership of Pezzi and
Rivalta, but the Ravennati also succeeded in resurrecting
Nabruzzi's old paper, _Il Romagnolo_.

At the beginning of March Costa was in Rimini, Ancona, and Mirandola, where he met with Celso Ceretti.[42]
The Central Commission at Brussels had called for a secret meeting to be held in Locarno on the 18th to study
the Italian plan and determine if money should be spent
on it. The scope of the Romagnol's visit to Mirandola
was the preparation, together with Ceretti, of a project
which would be presented in Switzerland.[43] The Locarno
conference took place as scheduled. Aside from Costa
and two representatives of the Italian Federation, Cafiero
and Grassi,[44] it is not entirely clear who was present
at the meeting; undoubtedly, though, the conferees included Bakunin and delegates of the Brussels Commission.
The Italians argued their case but apparently were not
too convincing for their proposals were turned down.
Still, the defeat was not total; it was decided to reconsider the decision in Brussels.[45]

With or without aid, however, the Italians were determined to act. Costa resumed his work of preparation.
At the end of March he was in the Italian capital.[46] But
a few days later, early in the following month, he was
back in Switzerland again.[47] Why had he returned so quickly? On April 21 the Minister of Interior informed the
prefect of Parma that a plan for insurrection had been
worked out by Costa, Nabruzzi, Ceretti, Bakunin, and Cyri-
le.[48] It appears that the Italian project had been approved in Belgium and this information was communicated
to the Imolese in Locarno.

Meanwhile Costa had re-entered Italy. Stopping first
at Florence, he reached Rome by the end of April.[49] The
plan of insurrection had established the Eternal City as
one of the primary centers of operation; the dynamic organizer returned there in early May and again in the first

days of June.[50] By this time the revolution was entering its final stages of preparation.

The Bologna Insurrection of 1874

The plot hatched by Bakunin and Costa in Locarno
during the previous year had evolved considerably during
the early months of 1874 and, despite some remaining am-
biguities, by mid-year it was complete in all of its es-
sentials. The revolt would be initiated in the Romagna
and the South, the areas judged to be the most revolutionary by the Imolese,[51] but all regions were expected
to participate. The arms, to be purchased with money
provided by the Brussels Commission and what was left of
Cafiero's inheritance (Bakunin had squandered much of
the Pugliese's fortune on the Baronata), would be smug-
gled into the country from Switzerland and Sicily--at
least this is what the police suspected--and once armed,
the anarchist bands would converge on the major cities
of those provinces where the International had its main
strength. Supported by the masses, the insurgents would
erect revolutionary municipal governments patterned after
that of the Paris Commune. The end which was envisioned
was a federation of free city-states. The insurrection
was tentatively set for about the middle of August.[52]

The grandiose project depended on three men: Bakunin, who directed the entire operation from Locarno; Errico
Malatesta (1853-1932), soon to become the most famous of
the Italian anarchists and at the moment the chief organizer of the insurrection in the South;[53] and Costa, who
concentrated his attention on the North but was in charge
of coordinating the movement throughout the peninsula.
This latter responsibility was a heavy one, since it was
generally recognized that the timing had to be perfect
in order for the plan to have any possibility of success.
Thus the Romagnol's frantic activity in July, on the eve
of the revolt. Early in the month he was in Venice, where
he talked to Emilio Castellani, his chief lieutenant
there,[54] and a few days later he went to see Bakunin.[55]
The visitor did not stay in Locarno long; on July 14 he
was in Aquila, under an assumed name, to parley with
Carlo Leoni and other local anarchist leaders. It was
reported that he also left them money.[56] On the following day he left for Pescara (another town in the Abruzzi),
then Naples, where he probably conferred with Malatesta
and left money and instructions, and, after a quick excursion to Tuscany (Arezzo and Pontassieve), the Imolese

returned to Rome.[57] The local section in the Italian capital was led by Northerners who had recently emigrated
there, including his old friend Antonio Cornacchia, and
these were among the conspirator's most faithful followers.[58] After consulting with them, Costa headed for Milan
to see Armand Ross, a Russian anarchist aiding the Italians,
in order to cash some foreign currency to buy arms.[59]
Once the operation was completed Costa transported the
money to Bologna, his headquarters during the last days
of the month.[60] On July 30 he was joined in the city
by Bakunin,[61] who had had a falling out with Cafiero a
few days before (over the Russian's mismanagement of the
Baronata). Bakunin arrived to direct the insurrection
personally. He fully expected to die fighting behind
the barricades.[62]

The Romagna, meanwhile, was alive with activity.
The anarchists there, as we have seen, had been aware of
the plans for insurrection from the beginning of the year.
The idea was widely endorsed. Commenting on rumors of a
proposed socialist gathering in their area, the editors
of Il Romagnolo declared on March 14 that it should not
take place. "We believe instead," they opined, "that the
time for Congresses and words is past, and that the proletariat should organize itself and decide on something
more serious!" ("On that, they added optimistically, "we
are glad to say that we are fully in accord with the majority of the workers in Romagna.")

The details of the insurrection in the region were
revealed a few weeks later. The Imolesi, together with
their comrades from San Giovanni in Persiceto, were to
march on Bologna--because of its size and location a major theater of operations--and in concert with the local
anarchists were to bring the city to its knees. The rest
of the Romagnol nuclei were to converge on Ravenna and
Rimini. The groundwork for this undertaking was entrusted by Costa to the Garibaldians, Pirro Rivalta and Temistocle Silvagni.

In fact it was Silvagni who did most of the work;
the renewed publication of Il Romangolo after February
7 kept Rivalta, one of its editors, tied up in Ravenna
for long periods of time. Silvagni carried on as best
he could. He initiated a steady correspondence by mail
with all of the area's anarchist groups (the regional
Federation included three federations--i.e., municipal
coalitions of two or more nuclei--and over twenty sections)[63] and traveled from one end of the region to the

other encouraging the formation of armed bands.[64] The
Forlivese also established contact with the Marches and
became Costa's chief intermediary with that region.[65]

The process of forming the armed bands began late
in April. At the beginning of the following month the
Minister of Interior informed the prefect of Forlì that
meetings had recently been held in that city and in Rimini, through the initiative of Piselli and Zavoli respectively, to recruit volunteers.[66] These gatherings continued during the next few months.[67] Concurrently, efforts were begun to encourage popular participation in
the future revolt, as anarchist propaganda in the countryside was accelerated.[68] All of this activity naturally
worried the police. The ranks of the Italian International were thoroughly infiltrated by government spies (Giuseppe Campetti, a Tuscan who served on the Italian Federation's Commission of Correspondence in late 1873, was one
of them),[69] and the authorities had been alerted to a
possible uprising for months. Observing the increased
tempo, it became evident that the reports had not been
exaggerated and that the anarchists were indeed getting
ready to move. The police in the Romagna decided to act
immediately. Rivalta, who had returned from Rimini that
very day, was placed under arrest in Ravenna on July 25.
The papers confiscated from his residence incriminated
a number of his colleagues in the city.[70] Wholesale arrests ensued.[71]

The Mazzinians were the government's next victims.
On August 2 the police invaded a republican meeting being held at Villa Ruffi, an estate a few miles outside
of Rimini, and arrested the twenty-eight delegates in
attendance.[72] These included Saffi, who was presiding,
Valzania, Fratti, and all the most prominent members of
the Consociazione Romagnola, which had sponsored the conclave. Though the avowed purpose of the gathering was
to discuss the role of the A.R.U. in the coming national
elections, the authorities guessed that the real aim was
to finalize an alliance with the anarchists and to sanction an uprising by the two parties.

These suspicions were partly justified. During the
middle of 1874 the republicans and the anarchists were
indeed coming together in many parts of the peninsula for
the purpose of staging a joint revolution.[73] Possibly
the initiative had been taken by Garibaldi. At any rate,
it was the Garibaldians in both parties who embraced the
idea. This was certainly the case in the Romagna, where

the prime movers were Valzania on the one hand and Ceretti on the other. The latter had always advocated cooperation of this kind. In March the Mirandolese went to Cesena to see his old comrade in arms, and before long he had won Valzania over to the plan for a combined assault on the government.[74] The idea became extremely popular in both parties, particularly among the republicans.[75] In late July Valzania wrote Ceretti and informed him, according to the Mirandolese, "that everything is going well and that he will convoke the representatives of the Consociazione Romagnola before the 15th in order to submit the agreement and the new Program for their approval."[76] Apparently, then, the Cesenate's proposal was included on the agenda at Villa Ruffi. The fact that the meeting was a clandestine one also suggests as much.

The police were wrong, however, in thinking that an alliance was about to be concluded. Except for Valzania, the republican chieftains in the Romagna never really took the idea seriously. In fact, the great concern at Villa Ruffi was, as the conferees claimed, the approaching election.[77] The party's attitude toward participation had become a crucial issue. Several of the leaders, notably Fortis, were beginning to question the traditional policy of political intransigence. They were of the opinion that the A.R.U. should propose candidates and involve itself to some degree in the parliamentary life of the nation. Saffi wanted to clear the air by bringing the difference of opinion out in the open, though of course he had no intention of deviating in the least from the position that Mazzini himself had established.

As for insurrection, that was a question which no longer concerned the A.R.U. in the Romagna, where Saffi dominated the party. The anti-revolutionary position of the regional Consociazione had been demonstrated only recently. The height of the widespread agitation caused by the economic crisis and particularly by the spiraling of prices had occurred in June and July. This unrest was most pronounced in the Romagna.[78] Yet in the midst of the riots and strikes the Executive Committee of the Consociazione, inspired by Saffi, had issued a manifesto calling on the people to abstain from violence.[79] The Mazzinian attitude toward the discontent was in striking contrast to that of the anarchists, who tried to encourage and profit from it.[80]

The republican chieftains had no interest in revolu-

tion, much less a revolution in concert with the anarchists. The relationship between the two parties had improved only slightly during the past two years. Open
warfare had abated, but tension remained high. Saffi and
his colleagues did not want to have anything to do with
their old antagonists. On principle--the Mazzinians always acted on principle--they completely rejected an
ideology that represented "the obliteration of all moral
consciousness."[81] Then, too, there was a more practical
consideration. The leaders of the Consociazione knew
that substantial sentiment in favor of revolutionary action continued to exist among its rank and file, and
they realized that the party's gradual disavowal of this
alternative made it increasingly vulnerable to anarchist
propaganda. The specter of mass desertions loomed before them.

This fear was not without foundation. Signs of discontent within the party had already appeared, beginning
in Imola. By the middle of the year one of the four republican associations in that city, La Pianta, was pressing for a change of direction: it wanted the regional
Consociazione to put greater emphasis on the social question and to work toward its solution by using revolutionary means. Seemingly the local anarchist nucleus was
making an impact.[82] The Executive Committee tried to be
diplomatic at first, but when La Pianta persisted the
leaders in Forlì acted resolutely. Fearing that the
heresy might spread, they officially disbanded the renagade chapter in early June.[83] The Imolesi would not be
put down so easily. They made entreaties for readmission
but at the same time remained inflexible in their demands. By late July the situation had become embarrassing; the Executive Committee was forced to act again.
On July 26 Rossi and Fratti were sent to Imola to bring
the dissidents back into line, or at least to make sure
that their views did not spread to the other associations.
The speeches made by the Forlivesi were conciliatory but
firm, and they eventually won the overwhelming support
of the 200 persons at the meeting. Only a handful of
hotheads, all probably members of La Pianta, remained re-
calcitrant.[84] The mission was accomplished: schism had
been avoided.

During the meeting in Imola on July 26, Costa attempted to enter the city but was dissuaded from doing
so by Renzi, who warned that the police were everywhere.[85]
Apparently Costa had wanted to speak before the assembly
in order to enlist republican support for the coming in-

94

surrection.

This activity would suggest that Costa was working for the republican alliance which was then the government's chief concern, but such was not the case. The young agitator's attitude toward the A.R.U. was ambivalent. He had the highest regard for the rank and file, which he considered revolutionary; hence his visit to Imola. However, his attitude toward the Mazzinian leadership was less than enthusiastic. Saffi and his cohorts were bourgeois and their ideas reactionary; their sole ambition, Costa warned the workers in the second Revolutionary Bulletin, was to secure "the triumph, government, domination, and the very legal exploitation of the bourgeoisie." On principle, therefore, no compromise was possible with this party. Even a temporary alliance aimed at revolution was out of the question.

Undoubtedly this rigid stance met some opposition among Costa's own comrades, especially from Ceretti, who was as staunchly in favor of interparty cooperation as the Imolese was against it.[86] The ranking anarchists in the Romagna, though, were won over to the anti-republican position. This was demonstrated in the March 14 issue of Il Romagnolo. Why should we get together with the Mazzinians, the paper asked. So we can spend the next ten years doing nothing? No, it concluded, "let us go it alone." On April 4, in an article entitled "Too Late," the Ravenna paper further illustrated the unbridgeable chasm that separated the two parties. "The reaction could not have servants more faithful than you," it told the republicans. "Oh, what difference is there between your God and the God of the Pope? And your Republic, what is it, if not a masked monarchy?" The anarchist rank and file was not entirely persuaded by its heads; by July the Internationalists in the area were deeply divided on the question of alliance, which was "for the most part rejected" by the nuclei in Lugo, Forlì, Cesena, Pescara, and Rimini, and "immediately accepted" by those of Bologna, Imola, Senigallia, and Ravenna.[87]

Costa was in Rome when he received the news of Villa Ruffi. First the anarchists had been arrested, now the republicans. It was obvious that the authorities were on to something; the element of surprise which had been counted on so heavily had now vanished. Still, it was too late to turn back. The arms had been bought, the plans worked out. Accompanied by Cornacchia, the Imolese returned to Bologna on August 3, where he conferred with

Bakunin, Faggioli, Natta, and Serafino Mazzotti, a comrade from Faenza.[88] On the following day he left with Faggioli for Rovigo, in the Veneto.[89] On the fifth the two travelers proceeded to Adria, where they attempted to enlist the support of Francesco Ortone, a member of the directive council of the local republican club.[90] They returned to Bologna later that very day. Their arrival did not go undetected. Toward midnight, as they were entering Giuseppe Nabruzzi's apartment on Via Broccaindosso, the two conspirators were set upon by the police.[91] His friend managed to escape, but Costa was arrested on the spot and after a quick interrogation was sent off to the city's most dreaded prison, the Torrone.[92]

The arrests of Costa and Silvagni, who was apprehended in Bologna on the same day, completely disrupted the plot. To add to the anarchists' woes, all republican and Internationalist associations in the provinces of Forlì, Ravenna, and Bologna were disbanded by the police in the aftermath of Villa Ruffi.[93] Everything seemed to go up in smoke. What to do? A hasty conference was set up in Bologna to examine the situation.[94] Bakunin was reluctant to turn back, and his colleagues agreed. The revolution would go on as planned, except for one modification--the revolt would take place immediately.[95]

On the night of August 7 a band of about 150 Imolesi, composed of both anarchists and republicans, gathered on the outskirts of town.[96] The group was then divided into two columns of roughly the same size. The first squad, led by Cornacchia, was to advance toward Bologna at once; the second, led by Renzi, would follow a few hours later. Their destination, twenty miles away, was a spot called the Prati di Caprara, just outside the walls of the Petronian city. The Bolognesi and a band from San Giovanni in Persiceto would also converge there. Once armed (rifles and ammunition were buried in a meadow), the small army would storm the city's gates.

In order to avoid detection, Cornacchia's men marched along the railroad tracks rather than along Via Emilia, the main road. They stopped at the station of Castel San Pietro, halfway to their destination, where they destroyed the telegraph apparatus and cut the power lines. A few antiquated guns were also collected. Everything seemed to be going according to plan. Near Idice, however, a few miles further, the enthusiastic but tired marchers were met by Alessandro Calanchi and Abdon Negri, who had come from Bologna in a carriage. The whole en-

terprise was off, the Imolesi were told. The turn-out
in the city had been disappointingly low. The best thing
to do was hand in the few guns they had at their disposal
and beat a hasty retreat back to the Romagna.

In the meantime the authorities had gotten wind of
what was happening. The subprefect of Imola, who was
not ignorant of the unusual activity in his town during
the past few days, had been informed that a band of young
men was seen out in the countryside heading for Bologna.
Without a moment of hesitation the alert official dispatched a trainload of carabinieri speeding westward. The revolutionaries from Imola were overtaken by the heavily-
armed convoy just as they had finished depositing the few
weapons in their possession. The lucky ones managed to
escape into the Apennines, but forty-three rebels, including Calanchi and Negri, were arrested in their tracks.

Some Bolognesi did arrive at the Prati di Caprara.
Eventually, though, they grew tired of waiting for their
comrades and led by Leonesi and Mazzotti, they armed themselves and made for the hills above the city, where most
of them were rounded up by the police in the early hours
of the morning.

The Renzi-led group from Imola and the band from San
Giovanni in Persiceto were more fortunate. The latter
arrived at the Prati late, and seeing that the plan had
aborted they returned home undetected. The second Imolese column never left town.

Bakunin, who had been ready to die for the revolution, changed his mind. He remained in hiding in Bologna
for several days. Then, dressed as a priest, he quietly
slipped out of the city on August 12. A few days later
he arrived safely in Switzerland. Plagued by financial
worries and bad health, the Russian anarchist died two
years later.

The insurrection in Bologna ended without a shot
being fired, and it was virtually the same story elsewhere. In Apulia, Malatesta took the field and led a
small band of armed men around the countryside until he
got tired and sent them all home a few days later. In
the Marches, the anarchists of Pergola, Sassoferrato, and
Fabriano started for Tuscany but returned to their homes
when word of the failure in Bologna was received. Even
less than this was accomplished in Rome, Sicily, Calabria,
and Tuscany, other "major" centers of activity, and the

same can be said of the eastern part of the Romagna, where the insurgents decided to wait to see what would happen in Emilia.

It is difficult to see how the revolution could have triumphed. Despite its financial woes the monarchy was firmly established, and the army remained loyal. The authorities also had the advantage of knowing what their enemies were up to. The insurgents, on the other hand, were shamefully weak. They had neither the manpower nor the weapons to wage a successful revolt. Moreover, as it was conceived by Costa and Bakunin, the revolution had been based on the false assumption that once it began the masses would rally enthusiastically to the anarchist banner. In fact the working class in Italy, mostly peasants, knew little about the International, and the few concepts that did filter down to the popular level were anything but attractive. As far as the masses were concerned, the anarchists meant to destroy God, Property, and Family. This program was not one that people died for. But perhaps the failure can be explained much more simply. The revolution never had a chance to demonstrate its theoretical inadequacies; the insurrection was stymied even before it began. It had not been a failure, but a fiasco. The revolt could hardly have turned out otherwise given its incomplete preparation.[97]

The Anarchists: Trials and Tribulations

All Internationalist associations in Italy were dissolved by government decree on August 9, 1874. Concurrently, efforts were begun to eradicate every last trace of subversive ideas. Anyone who was even remotely connected with the attempted insurrection (and this included some republicans) was rounded up; having belonged to an anarchist association was sufficient cause for arrest. Prison terms and ammonizioni were freely meted out.[98] Only those anarchists who fled abroad were able to evade the intense persecution. Living in the Swiss towns along the Italian border, these exiles--including Cafiero, Grassi, and Pezzi--kept in touch with their comrades at home and tried to arouse them from the lethargy which inevitably set in.[99] Especially active was Cafiero, who managed to keep the Comitato Italiano functioning.[100] But despite these efforts the anarchist movement in the country was practically nonexistent during the next year and a half.

Undoubtedly the second stay in the Torrone did not

inspire the same sense of exhilaration in Costa that he had felt there in 1873. The future looked bleak indeed. The prospect of having to spend the major part of his life in confinement loomed up before the twenty-three-year-old prisoner. The situation was depressing, but resignation set in as the months crept along. Much of the time was devoted to study. Books were readily available; the prison authorities had a rather liberal policy in this regard. His favorite subjects were literature and languages: English, Russian, and German.[101] Newspapers were also a source of instruction. Letter-writing provided another diversion. As his correspondence was thoroughly censored before it left the prison, Costa confined himself to love letters, which were at first directed to Vera Karpoff, a Russian revolutionary he had met in Switzerland in 1873, and, when this affair cooled, to Violetta Dall'Alpi, daughter of a Garibaldian from Bologna and a radical in her own right.[102] And so the time passed.

The long-awaited trial finally opened in Bologna in mid-March, 1876. It was held on the eve of national elections, but this did nothing to detract from the attention it received. A multitude of newspapers covered the event. The courtroom overflowed with people as visitors came into the city from miles around. In addition to Costa, the seventy-nine defendants included Silvagni, Leonesi, Buggini, Faggioli and the other anarchists from Imola, San Giovanni in Persiceto, and Bologna who had marched on the Emilian capital; Rivalta and the Ravennati; Matteuzzi and the Marchegiani; and Leoni and his followers in Aquila.[103] They were represented by seventeen lawyers, mostly republicans, headed by Giuseppe Ceneri, a professor at the University of Bologna and one of the leading legal minds in the country. The charge was conspiracy.

The authorities were confident of a favorable verdict. They had every reason to be. They had managed to find the arms which were to be used in the insurrection (the rifles had been bought in Brescia, shipped to Bologna and Ravenna by rail, and had been buried in the surrounding countryside); a number of the accused, the Imolesi, had been caught in the act of rebellion; and, if that were not enough, a multitude of confiscated papers clearly demonstrated that the anarchists had been preparing the revolt for months. These documents also established that Costa was the head of the International in Italy and, as far as the authorities were concerned, the mastermind behind the events of August, 1874.[104]

Thus from the very beginning the Imolese became the special target of the prosecution and the protagonist of the trial. He rose to the occasion. Among the first prisoners to be interrogated, he admitted to being an anarchist but he categorically denied a part in an insurrection, or that one had even been attempted.[105] His companions, in their turn, made statements which paralleled that of their leader. A parade of witnesses was then called up to testify on the moral character of the accused. They survived this portion of the ordeal rather well, especially Costa; on April 24, Carducci, Codronchi, and Saffi all testified to his outstanding character.[106] Things were beginning to look up. But the best was yet to come; on May 18-19 Ceneri concluded the defense of his number-one client. Everyone agree the attorney was brilliant.[107] The first day he expounded on Thomas Hobbes, the French Revolution, Cain and Abel, Victor Hugo--everything under the sun except the Imolese and the insurrection. But on the second day the professor got down to the matter at hand. Some of his arguments were rather weak (How could someone as intelligent as Costa, he asked, have been responsible for something so ridiculous as the fiasco in Bologna?), but he did succeed in taking advantage of the prosecution's incompetency. The government had maintained, for example, that Costa was in Brussels on August 1-2, 1874, preparing the uprising. Ceneri demonstrated that this was physically impossible (something the police's own files indicated).[108]

As the trial neared its conclusion the anarchists became increasingly self-confident and, taking advantage of the opportunity presented them, they boldly propagated their ideals before the large assembly.[109] These efforts were crowned by Costa's final speech on June 16. A zealous defense of Internationalist principles, the oration stressed the humanitarian side of the philosophy: "We want the full and complete development of all human instincts, faculties, passions; we want the humanization of man! Thus it follows that we are after not only the emancipation of the working class, but...the total and complete emancipation of mankind: because if it is true that the working classes have to free themselves from poverty, the privileged classes, in their turn, have to free themselves from a poverty a good deal more serious than that of the proletariat, from profound moral poverty."[110]

The following day the jury rendered its verdict: not guilty. The decision was not unexpected, for it was

100

consistent with those which had been handed down during
the previous year at Florence, Leghorn, Massa, Rome, Perugia, and Trani, trials which also dealt with the 1874
insurrection. Yet it seems impossible that the anarchists in Bologna could have been absolved. The evidence
was heavily against them, and it was almost universally
acknowledged that the defendants had been involved in the
plot. Later they themselves freely admitted it. Professor Hostetter--who emphasizes that there had been a
miscarriage of justice--gives several reasons for the
unusual verdict, among them the influence of the 1875
trials and the eloquence of Ceneri and his colleagues.[111]
I would add that the decision was aided by the incompe-
tence of the prosecution, which was considerable, and
the sympathy which the anarchists had won after spending
over twenty-two months in prison--Italian justice proceeded rather slowly at that time.

Immediately upon his release Costa turned his attention to reviving the shattered socialist movement.[112]
"The work of reorganization...has already begun," he informed the Swiss a few days later. "The federations of
Rome and Naples are already reconstructed; the Imola section has been reconstructed this very day, tomorrow the
federation of Bologna will be reconstructed; and within
a few days we will convoke the second congress of the
Romagnol sections and federations, which will be followed soon after by the 3rd congress of the Italian sections
and federations."[113] Reversing the trend that had been
dominant among the Italian exiles in the last two years,
the Imolese decided to abandon conspiracy and to work out
in the open.[114] He was confident that after the recent
court decisions this approach was reasonably safe. Congresses were again the order of the day.

The first of these took place in Bologna on July 16,
when representatives from Emilia and the Romagna met to
resurrect the regional anarchist movement.[115] Moderated
by Costa, the gathering opened with the official creation of the Federation of the Romagna and Emilia (the
latter was too weak to form an organization of its own).
Costa followed with an eulogy of Bakunin, who had died
in Bern on July 1, and was authorized by the delegates
to write a popular biography of the Russian revolutionary.[116] Thereafter the ideals of anarchy and collectiv-
ism were reaffirmed and the Program and Regulations which
were to govern the existence of the Federation were approved. The executive organ of the reconstructed association continued to be the Federation Commission, but

its headquarters were transferred from Ravenna to Imola, nearer the geographical center of the area it now served.

The Bologna Congress was followed by that of the Tuscans, who met in Florence on July 23 to reorganize their own Federation.[117] It was decided that there would be a Commission of Correspondence and another of Statistics and Propaganda; the first was set up in Siena, the second in Leghorn. Otherwise the structure of the Tuscan Federation resembled that of its sister organization to the north.

Costa had been in Florence early in July.[118] The initiative for the meeting, however, had been taken by the Tuscans themselves. It was quite a different matter in the Marches, where the anarchist movement came under Costa's political direction.[119] Encouraged by the Imolese, the sections of the Marches and Umbria held their reunion at Jesi on August 20.[120] The deliberations mirrored those of Bologna. The Commission of Correspondence of the renovated Federation was composed of Fernando Cardinali, Cesare Picchi, and Guglielmo Zappelli; its seat was established at Jesi.

In the meantime, this extraordinary activity was being observed closely. The police had not been excessively concerned by the initial creation of the Italian Federation, but thereafter their attitude gradually changed. The International began to be viewed as a potential menace. The attempted insurrection in 1874 did nothing to allay their fears. The public at large, though, did not share these sentiments, as the verdicts rendered in the recent trials amply demonstrate. The decisions, needless to say, infuriated the police. Outraged by the courts' leniency, they determined to go after their enemies with greater zeal--and the anarchists, working in the open, made themselves easy targets.

The best way to eliminate the dangerous radicals, it was reasoned, was to move against their heads, foremost among them Costa. On August 24, accordingly, immediately after the Marchegian-Umbrian Congress, the Romagnol leader was arrested at Fabriano (in the Marches), transferred to Imola on the following day and, on the 26th, brought before the local _pretore_, who declared the agitator "irresponsible and vagabond" and placed him under _ammonizione_.[121] Protests were useless. Confined to Imola and subject to close surveillance, he was a virtual prisoner.

The fiery Romagnol's enforced isolation seriously hindered efforts at reorganization,[122] but these were not completely stifled. The initiative was resumed by Natta and Grassi, who sat on the Italian Federation's Commission of Correspondence. Their immediate concern was the convocation of a national congress, slated to be held in Florence on October 22. The police, though, were well aware of the preparations being made in the Tuscan capital and decided to act.[123] Using a recent fight between Mazzinians and anarchists in Jesi as a pretext, they inaugurated a campaign aimed at the Internationalists.[124] Their focus was Florence, where both Grassi and Natta were arrested on October 19. Also apprehended at that time was Costa, who had just arrived in the city after sneaking out of Imola.[125]

Yet in spite of the absence of their leaders the Florentines were able to make new arrangements, and the Third Congress of the Italian Federation met secretly in Tosi, a small village near Pontessieve, on the night of October 20-21. Thirty-eight delegates evaded the police, who searched frantically for them, and attended the meeting. Among them were Cafiero, who presided, Malatesta, Pezzi, and Emilio Covelli (the Romagna was represented by Antonio Castellari of Imola and Silvagni of Forlì).[126] After a report on the condition of the Federation--great progress, it was declared, had been achieved in the last few months--the discussion turned to the most suitable means of bringing about the emancipation of the worker. Sharply affected by the pressure being exerted on them by the government, the delegates reaffirmed their faith in conspiracy and revolution, the only methods now at their disposal. They were convinced, however, that propaganda had to precede action (this was the major lesson they had drawn from the failure of 1874). Consequently, increased efforts were called for in the propagation of anarchist views in the countryside. On the question of organizational structure, it was decided that the Federation should continue along the same lines as before. The new Commission of Correspondence was composed of Cafiero, Grassi, and Pezzi; its seat was transferred from Florence to Naples.

Before the assembly adjourned, several of its braver delegates signed a declaration--published together with the account of the meeting--censuring the government severely for the arbitrary measures it had adopted. The anarchists had hoped that the fall of the moderate Right (Destra) earlier in the year would alleviate their plight somewhat. The triumphant progressive Left (_Sinistra_), after all, was composed in large part of men who had fought during the _Risorgimento_ as conspirators and revolutionaries themselves. Such a man, for example, was the new Minister of Interior, Giovanni Nicotera. By the Congress of Tosi, though, it had become painfully obvious that the new regime would not display more tolerance than the old; indeed, it threatened to combat subversive ideas even more tenaciously. This repression, and the bitter disappointment it brought, accounts for the vehemence with which the anarchists now reacted.

The intransigent point of view was completely shared by Costa, who sat in a Florentine jail, charged with violating his _ammonizione_, as his comrades conferred nearby. Nor did his attitude improve on November 10 when Imola's _pretore_ sentenced him to a month in prison and six more of special surveillance.[127]

The dejected prisoner's personal predicament mirrored that of the International in Italy. By the end of 1876 the Federation, the optimism it had expressed at Tosi notwithstanding, found itself in a very precarious position. Not only did it continue to labor under the strain imposed by its limited resources and the lethargy of the populace, it was now faced by a government intent on waging the uneven war right down to the very end. At best this was a difficult situation, and the Federation's problems did not stop there. By the end of the year there was the added burden of an internal schism within its ranks.

The Italian International had harbored contrasting views from the time of its birth. It was only in early 1873, however, that a well-defined tendency in opposition to the majority of its membership could be discerned. The dissidents, who called themselves Intransigents, or Independents, admitted, like the Bakuninists, that authority was evil and revolution was necessary, but they disagreed with the anarchists' multiclass orientation. Indeed, they took Marx's dictum that the emancipation of the working class should be the product of its own efforts to a logical extreme; only workingmen, they insisted, should be allowed to join the organization. Nor should there be any cooperation whatsoever with the bourgeoisie (hence the name _Intransigenti_). These men were not Marxians, though, for regardless of their espousal of revolution, which they voiced in the most unequivocal terms, they tended in practice to forsake political action and

104

to concentrate completely on winning economic reform
through the creation of workers' unions. In a word, they
were syndicalists.

Their ideas made some headway during the course of
1873,[128] and early in the following year, when the school
reached its maximum strength, several sections of the
Federation had been won over, among them the nuclei of
Genoa, Turin, and Parma.[129] But the center of Intransigent strength was Ferrara, on the periphery of the Romagna,
where the local cell was led by Oreste Vaccari, Vincenzo
Dondi, and Augusto Bernardello. The latter, according
to Carlo Monticelli, "exerted an undisputed authority a-
mong the Internationalists of the area, which derived
from his superior intellect, breeding, and perseverance."[130]
The Ferrara section was formed in January, 1872,[131] and
as is true of most other Intransigent groups, apparently
it had originally leaned toward the ideas of the London
Council rather than those of Bakunin.[132] Its members immediately became among the most active in the Italian Federation, and Dondi, second in command to Bernardello, was
elected to its Commission of Propaganda after the Mirandola-Bologna Congress in 1873. In July of that year, however, Bernardello wrote Costa informing him that a difference of opinion had developed within the local section--
the cause is unclear--and that he and his supporters were
withdrawing from it to form a cell of their own.[133] It
appears that this was the real beginning of the new tendency. Early in 1874 Bernardello and Dondi published a
newspaper, Il Petrolio, which became an Intransigent organ.[134] The Ferraresi's propaganda had a notable effect,
especially in the Veneto.[135] When in November of the
previous year an international syndicalist organization,
the Universal League of Workers'Corporations, was founded in Geneva with a program that approximated their own,
the Ferraresi gave it their support, though not without
some hesitation.[136] Under their leadership the various
Intransigent groups in Italy adhered to the League's
Geneva Congress of August 30-September 2, 1874.[137] During the following year the tendency gained some support
in Sicily and the South,[138] but by then it had begun to
decline.

The Ferraresi and their sympathizers never really
had a profound impact on the Italian Federation. The
Intransigents were hurt most of all by their association
with Carlo Terzaghi, who came to be recognized as the
leader of the dissident minority. Despite the expulsion
of the Turinese from the International, the Intransigents

gave him their full support.[139] Bernardello, his most
ardent admirer, insisted that Terzaghi had been cruci-
fied because he opposed the intellectual approach of the
other party heads (anti-intellectualism was another marked characteristic of the school).[140] The exact relationship between Terzaghi and his followers is not entirely
clear. Did these men endorse the new ideas because of
their respect for Terzaghi, or did they come to his defense because they shared his views already? Were they
"intransigent" because they defended him, or did they
defend him because they were "intransigent"? Costa, who
believed that the difference of opinion between the two
factions in the Federation was motivated solely by questions of personality rather than those of principle,
would say the former was true.[141] But the Imolese underestimated his adversaries, I think; given Terzaghi's
vindictive and malicious personality, it is unlikely that
Bernardello and his group defended him without real conviction of the ideas he represented. What is beyond
question is that the school came to be identified with
the suspected spy, hence its ephemeral success.[142]

If the Terzaghi group posed little threat to the
solidarity of the Italian Federation, it was quite a
different matter with the second schismatic current, the
Legalitarians, or Evolutionists, which arose in 1875.[143]
The failure of the insurrections of the previous year
had thoroughly discredited the conspiratorial method a-
mong a large number of Internationalists on the peninsula, many of whom had not been perfectly in accord with
this approach from the outset. Such was the case with
Tito Zanardelli and Lodovico Nabruzzi.[144] Neither had
participated in the 1874 uprisings, and during the next
few months they dissociated themselves completely from
the views which Cafiero and the Comitato Italiano continued to sustain in exile. In November, 1875, the two
men founded an Italian nucleus at Lugano--the Ceresio
section, which openly rejected conspiracy and emphasized propaganda rather than revolution.[145] During the
course of the following year they attempted from their
base in Switzerland to reconstruct the Italian Federation according to these ideas.[146]

Concurrently a second center of Legalitarian resistance arose, this one in Italy itself. Its initiators,
Enrico Bignami and Osvaldo Gnocchi-Viani, in contrast to
the Ceresio group, had never adopted the anarchist program in its entirety. Bignami, an ex-Mazzinian, had been
one of the staunchest supporters of the General Council

in 1870-71. Once the Bakuninists triumphed he went along, but halfheartedly. In fact, he made a poor anarchist; he ran for Parliament in the political elections of 1874 and his newspaper in Lodi, La Plebe, expressed rather moderate views. When the periodical was transferred to Milan in November, 1875, it became the rallying point for the Legalitarian group which arose in the Lombard capital.

The Milanesi were also impressed by Gnocchi-Viani, who lived in Rome during this period.[147] Born in the province of Mantua, he had been a Mazzinian and a Garibaldian before joining the I.W.A. in the aftermath of the Commune. Like Bignami, a close friend, he flirted with the Marxists before adopting the anarchist program. His conversion was never complete, though; he always insisted, in contrast to the orthodox Bakuninists, that the International should be predominantly proletarian in its composition and leadership. Moreover, he tended to emphasize economic reform rather than political action (i.e., revolution). The Federation should stress workers' solidarity and amelioration, he said, not abstract principles.[148] His views resembled those of the Intransigents (although his syndicalism was avowedly anti-revolutionary), and in truth he was one of the few individuals in Italy outside of this group who supported the Geneva-based Universal League of Workers' Corporations.[149]

The Italian Legalitarians in both Milan and the Ticino were closely associated with Benoît Malon, a French Communard who spent the decade following the Parisian insurrection in Italian and Swiss exile.[150] The Frenchman's influence was decidedly anti-Bakuninist, for Malon was convinced that the aim of the socialist movement should be to win control of the state rather than to annihilate it. His approach was evolutionary rather than revolutionary. He shared these ideas with Marx. But there was a basic difference here, too, for Malon came to believe that revolution could be dismissed altogether--Marx never went that far. Moreover, Malon was firmly opposed to Marx's concept of class warfare and his materialism: "It is not enough," he insisted, "to appeal only to class interests and to disdain the multitude of sentimental and moral forces, which are the most potent of all."[151] Here he approached Bakunin again. Malon's philosophy was clearly eclectic, though there is little question that his views came closest to those of Marx. It was in this watered-down form, in fact, that Marxism entered Italy.

Malon spent most of 1875 in Milan and established firm ties there with Bignami and the <u>Plebe</u> group. When he was expelled from the country early in the following year he went to Lugano, where he worked with Nabruzzi and Zanardelli. A few months later he returned to Italy and took up residence in Palermo. This was the Frenchman's second stay in the Sicilian city; he had been there three years before. An old acquaintance, Salvatore Ingegneros Napolitano, editor of the city's socialist organ, <u>Il Povero</u>, was soon converted to Malonian ideas.[152] By the end of 1876 <u>Il Povero</u> had become more radically anti-Bakuninist than its sister paper in Milan, which moved rather cautiously and not without a certain amount of confusion.

Nevertheless, it was in the Lombard capital that the Legalitarians had their most active center, and it was under the sponsorship of the <u>Plebe</u> group that they began to organize themselves. In mid-October, 1876, Bignami and his colleagues created a Federation of Upper Italy which endorsed their views and refused to adhere to the Italian Federation.[153] Initially the anarchists were not sure what to make of the Milanese initiative, but once the new Federation was formed and its program made clear they directed all their energies to countering its authority. The uncompromising stance which emerged at the Congress of Tosi, and the similar position sustained by Cafiero and Malatesta at the international Congress of Bern in late October,[154] was as much a reaction to this internal threat as it was to government persecution.

Conclusion

When the anarchists turned to conspiracy in 1873 they justified the new course by claiming that, given the oppressive conditions which then existed in Italy, no other alternative was possible.[155] In retrospect it seems that this claim was exaggerated. In that year the government was just beginning to concern itself with the recently-created party. Small and weak, the International did not yet inspire much fear. The authorities were only slightly more alarmed as the movement went underground and increased its activity. But the situation changed abruptly in the middle of 1874. The attempted insurrections which took place at that time demonstrated that the Italian Federation was to be taken seriously. The party was indeed a menace to law and order. It was

this realization more than anything else which explains
the determined opposition it encountered from the police
after the Left assumed power in 1876. By now the anarchists had replaced the republicans as the country's most
determined subversives and the government's foremost
enemy. An ever-increasing repression was thus the most
pronounced theme in the history of the Italian International from 1873-1876.

This policy had far-reaching consequences. One effect of the numerous arrests and ammonizioni was the radicalization of the anarchist movement. As its least
committed members were forced to drop out, the Federation came to be dominated by uncompromising extremists.
This hardcore element grew more and more fanatical as
the police applied pressure. Conspiracy became a way
of life. Despite the failure of 1874 and the ensuing in-
carcerations, then, revolutionary activity had intensified rather than ebbed two years later.

This trend was perfectly illustrated in the person
of Costa. The experience in prison left a lasting impression. The injustice which had perhaps been little
more than a theoretical abstraction before, became a
profound reality thereafter. By the end of 1876 the
angry young man had reaffirmed his belief in the necessity
of violence. Indeed, he was among the most adamant of
the revolutionaries. The vehemence of this reaction no
doubt reflected a profound disillusionment. His acquittal in Bologna had led him to believe that the anarchists would at last be allowed to abandon conspiracy and
return to the propagation of their ideas among the masses, that the International would become a party instead
of a mere sect. The events of late 1876 dissipated these
hopes.

Another momentous consequence of the government's
repressive policies was the intensification of dissension within the Italian Federation. The schismatic
trend most invigorated was that of the Legalitarians,
which had arisen in opposition to the Bakuninist majority in the aftermath of the 1874 episode. The insurrection, despite misgivings from many quarters, had been
attempted and failed miserably. The moderate elements
within the International ranks drew the conclusion that
the time for violence was past. A return to the people
was in order, and if this meant struggling for economic
and political reforms they were prepared to follow this
"legalitarian" path. Reaction fortified this determin-

ation. As the police offensive continued it was inevitable that the radical revolutionaries would lose their ascendancy within the socialist movement to the moderates--those willing to work within the system.

NOTES

[1] Costa, _Bagliori di socialismo_, p. 13.

[2] _Un errore giudiziario ovvero un po'di luce sul processo della bomba di via Nazionale_ (Florence: Birindelli, 1882), p. 16.

[3] Less fortunate was Ceretti who, together with Luigi Castellazzo and Luigi Bramante, remained in prison for five months, charged with conspiracy, before he was released for lack of evidence.

[4] The time spent in jail at Bologna was something of an exhilarating experience. See Costa, "Prime carceri," _I Maggio_ (Rome: Tip. Piazza Apollinare, 1902).

[5] Letter to Victor Cyrille, June, 14, 1873, in Marc Vuilleumier, "La Correspondance d'un internationaliste: Victor Cyrille (1871-1874)," _Movimento operaio e socialista_, 12 (1966), 259.

[6] Italian correspondence, dated June 26, _Bulletin de la Fédération Jurassienne_, July 20, 1873. Other nuclei were in the process of formation, the letter continued, in Lavino near Bologna; Castelfidardo, Chiaravalle, Filotrana, Jesi, Treia, and Offagna in the Marches; Budrio in the Romagna; and Colle and Cortona in Tuscany.

[7] It is generally assumed that this meeting took place on July 26 (see Hostetter, _Le origini del socialismo italiano_, p. 467, and Manacorda, _Il movimento operaio italiano_, p. 121). Apparently the source of this misinformation is to be found in a pamphlet published by the anarchists of Emilia and the Romagna after their Bologna Congress of 1876 (contained in _La Federazione Italiana_, pp. 105-20) which gives this date. Writing in 1879, Costa, who may have been the author of the pamphlet in question, also recalls July 26 (_Bagliori di socialismo_, p. 14). Much closer to the event, however, _La Favilla_, July 27, 1873, reports that the meeting was held on July 20, a date confirmed by police reports at the Archivio di Stato in Forlì.

[8] _Questore_ of Bologna to the prefect of Bologna, July

111

21, 1873, A.S.B., <u>Gab</u>. <u>Pref</u>., vol. 102 (my account of the meeting is based on this report). A letter a few days later gives a list of some of the participants: Claudio Zirardini, Giacomo Lega, Pio (sic) Rivalta, and Francesco Pezzi (Ravenna); Temistocle Silvagni, Michele Silvegni, Cimbro Bucchi, and Raffaele Sacchetti (Forlì); Luigi and Giovanni Caravita (San Potito); Domenico Baldini (Campiano); Domenico Pianetti (Lugo); Carlo De Lorenzi (San Pierino); Angelo Scudellari (Fusignano); Giovanni Donati and Augusto Aducci (Rimini); Paolo Renzi (Imola); and "a Liverani" (probably Gaetano) from Faenza. See prefect of Ravenna to the prefect of Forlì, July 30, 1873, A.S.F., <u>Gab</u>. <u>Pref</u>., vol. 49, fasc. 39.

[9]An anonymous correspondence, dated July 4, in <u>Bulletin de la Fédération Jurassienne</u>, July 13, 1873, had reported that the republican party was in complete dissolution after Mazzini's death, and declared that the anarchists now had a chance to make inroads into the <u>A.R.U.</u>, especially in the Romagna. Costa, who had written the correspondence (Guillaume, <u>L'Internationale</u>, III, 96), probably formulated the anti-republican manifesto also. <u>L'Alleanza</u>, Aug. 31, 1873, covering the Congress, was critical of the extremism represented by Costa, the Imolesi, and the International (moreover, Pezzi, who had tried to defend the latter earlier in the year, was asked to go read the <u>Duties</u> <u>of</u> <u>Man</u>).

[10]For its deliberations, see <u>La Federazione Italiana</u>, pp. 79-84.

[11]On June 26, 1873, Emilio Borghetti, the section leader in Ancona, wrote Costa informing him that following the Imolese's recommendation they were promoting the Regional Congress. He wanted further instructions. See <u>Procedimento Costa</u>, vol. 7. Costa's biographer, Lilla Lipparini, suggests that the Imolese attended the Marchegian-Umbrian Congress, in "Cronologia della vita di A. Costa," <u>Movimento operaio</u>, 6 (1952), 185. This seems unlikely, as Costa wrote a letter to his "dear friends" (?) on Aug. 9, the day before the gathering, from Geneva (found in <u>Procedimento Costa</u>, vol. 70).

[12]<u>Questore</u> of Bologna to the prefect of Bologna, July 21, 1873, A.S.B., <u>Gab</u>. <u>Pref</u>., vol. 102.

[13]See <u>Bulletin de la Fédération Jurassienne</u>, Sept. 7, 1873.

[14]Letter to the prefect of Bologna, Oct. 28, 1873,

A.S.B., Gab. Pref., vol. 102. Part of Costa's speech at Geneva is quoted in Bottero, Dibattimenti, p. 316, and Nettlau, Malatesta, p. 111.

[15]According to statistics compiled prior to the Romagnol Congress in July, the regional Federation, perhaps the biggest in Italy at that time, had only a little over 2,000 members. The document presented at San Pietro in Vincoli broke down the membership according to sections: Bologna, 329; Ravenna, 252; Forlì, 198; Rimini, 261; Lugo, 107; San Potito, 65; Fursignano, 88; Faenza, 184; Imola, 139; Campiano, 105; San Bartolo, 41; San Pierino, 56; Santo Stefano, 38; Madonna dell'Albero, 68; Carpinello, 81; and Coccolia, 28. See report from the questore of Bologna to the prefect of Bologna, July 21, 1873.

[16]The persecutions at this time were "tremendous," according to a letter from Piccioli-Poggiali to Cyrille, May 25, 1873, in Vuilleumier, "La Correspondance d'un internationaliste," p. 257.

[17]Costa, Bagliori di socialismo, p. 11.

[18]He was in Modena on Sept. 23, Bottero, Dibattimenti, p. 325; and in Parma at around the same time, Giuseppe Berti, "Gli inizi del socialismo Parmense-Piacentino (1870-1875)," Rassegna storica del Risorgimento, 51 (1964), 387. Costa himself claimed that he only returned to Italy from Switzerland in mid-October. See Piancastelli MS.

[19]A.S.B., Gab. Pref., vol. 102.

[20]On Nov. 19, 1873, the questore of Bologna informed the prefect there that the Commission had recently been transferred, and that it had held a meeting in Florence on Nov. 7; Grassi had been elected to conduct the Federation's internal correspondence, he added, and Costa was to continue the correspondence with foreign sections (A.S.B., Gab. Pref., vol. 102).

[21]These men composed the new Commission, according to Costa, Piancastelli MS.

[22]The Bulletin de la Fédération Jurassienne, Dec. 7, 1873, carries a Costa correspondence from Bologna, dated Nov. 28, but Guillaume (L'Internationale, III, 159), one of the paper's editors, says that the Imolese had written the piece at the Baronata and had purposely indicated the

Italian city in order to mislead the police.

[23] Report of Dec. 3, 1873, A.S.F., Gab. Pref., vol. 58, fasc. 25.

[24] Report to prefect of Forlì, Jan. 11, 1874, A.S.F., Gab. Pref., vol. 58, fasc. 25.

[25] Piccioli-Poggiali to Cyrille, Aug. 3, 1873, in Vuilleumier, "La Correspondance d'un internationaliste," p. 264.

[26] Letter to the members of the Internationalist section in Florence, Nov. 21, 1873. This document is part of the official correspondence kept by the Italian Federation and sequestered from Natta's home in November, 1874. Copies of all of these papers are to be found in vol. 7, Procedimento Costa (the correspondence is also reproduced in the 1956 ed. of Romano, Storia, III, 383-477).

[27] Fieramosca, Jan. 22, 1910. For Costa's relationship with the Florentine during the early 1870's, see Pier Carlo Masini, "Andrea Costa e Lorenzo Piccioli-Poggiali," Movimento operaio e socialista, 15 (1969), 69-76.

[28] Found in Procedimento Costa, vol. 7. Romano, Storia III, 467, dates the letter November or December, 1873.

[29] Bottero, Dibattimenti, p. 337.

[30] In the letter Costa made it clear that he could be reached at "A. Rossi, Locarno." Rossi could be Michail P. Sazin, a Russian revolutionary who used the alias Armand Ross and was staying at the Baronata during this period.

[31] Elio Conti, Le origini del socialismo a Firenze (1860-1880) (Rome: Rinascita, 1950), p. 169.

[32] See Costa's correspondence, Bulletin de la Fédération Jurassienne, Dec. 7, 1873.

[33] Costa went to Rimini and Ancona. See subprefect of Rimini to the prefect of Forlì, Jan. 11, 1874, A.S.F., Gab. Pref., vol. 58, fasc. 25. In an undated letter sequestered in 1874 from the home of Stanislao Alberici Giannini, of Rotella (Marches), Costa informed the anarchist chieftain that there would soon be a meeting in Ancona where they would talk of "very important things."

If Giannini could attend the meeting, he was told, it would be greatly appreciated by Costa, Borghetti (now in prison), and the "old man." See Procedimento Costa, vol. 29. The letter was probably written in early December, and the "old man" could refer to Bakunin.

[34]"Dearest ones," Costa wrote to the members of the Commission of Correspondence at this time, "here is the 1st number of our Revolutionary Bulletin, which should be published in January and in such a way, as we have already agreed, that no one will ever know where it came from. I beg you to follow the same procedure in its expedition as you did for the expedition of the acts of the Congress; that is, the Bulletin should appear first in those areas farthest, then, gradually, in the areas closest to Florence. I trust, moreover, in your prudence." See Procedimento Costa, vol. 7. This letter was unsigned and undated, but the police say it was written by Costa "at the end of 1873." See Bottero, Dibattimenti, p. 340.

[35]Comitato Italiano per la Rivoluzione Sociale N. 1 (January, 1874). Costa admitted that he wrote the first and second Revolutionary Bulletins during his trial in 1876. See Piancastelli MS.

[36]Conti, Le origini del socialismo, p. 173. The Central Commission replied that it would decide after determining the strength of the Italian Federation. The statistics subsequently prepared for the Central Commission soon came into the possession of the police. They revealed that the Federation was composed of ten regional Federations with 26,704 members. The largest Federation was now that of Tuscany, which had its seat in Leghorn and was composed of 31 sections with 6,941 members. The Neapolitan Federation, centering in Barletta, had 18 sections and 4,265 members. The Romagnol Federation was third. It had its headquarters in Ravenna, and its 3,765 members were divided into 21 sections. See Franco Della Peruta, "La consistenza numerica dell'Internazionale in Italia nel 1874," Movimento operaio, 2 (1950), 105. Given the occasion for the compilation of these statistics the numbers are probably inflated.

[37]Costa spent a good part of January in Locarno. See Guillaume, L'Internationale, III, 169.

[38]Conti, Le origini del socialismo, says Costa was in Florence on Feb. 2 (p. 174) and in Leghorn on the 10th (p. 173). Leghorn was the seat of the Commission of Cor-

115

respondence of the Tuscan Federation.

[39]The manifesto was similar to that of January: "The people are tired of words: it is time to organize ourselves for the struggle." Al Popolo Italiano: Manifesto del Comitato Italiano per la Rivoluzione Sociale (Mar., 1874).

[40]This according to a letter from Costa to Grassi, in Conti, Le origini del socialismo, p. 174.

[41]His first stop was Rimini, where he arrived on Feb. 24 and visited with Aducci and Donati. An informant reported that Costa talked of an insurrection, said he was on his way to Ravenna, and told his friends he would return to Rimini in 15 or 20 days. See subprefect of Rimini to the prefect of Forlì, Feb. 25, 1874, A.S.F. Tribunale Civile e Correzionale, Procedimento contro Saffi Aurelio ed altri (1874) (hereafter this set of papers will be designated Procedimento Saffi).

[42]Questore of Ravenna to the prefect of Ravenna, Mar. 12, 1874, A.S.F., Gab. Pref., vol. 58, fasc. 25. The report also indicated that Natta and Costa had recently returned from Belgium. Actually they had only been to Locarno.

[43]Conti, Le origini del socialismo, p. 174.

[44]Ibid. According to a report from the questore of Ravenna to the prefect of Ravenna (Mar. 12, 1874, A.S.F., Gab. Pref., vol. 58, fasc. 25), the Italian representatives to Locarno were supposed to be Cafiero, Nabruzzi, and Costa, and the object of the meeting would be to sanction the formation of armed bands in the Romagna. Costa's trip to Rimini and Ancona had had something to do with these bands, the questore added.

[45]Conti, Le origini del socialismo, p. 174.

[46]He was in Rome on Mar. 31. See Franco Della Peruta, "L'Internazionale a Roma dal 1872 al 1877," Movimento operaio, 4 (1952), 26.

[47]Berti, "Gli inizi del socialismo Parmense-Piacentino" p. 394.

[48]Ibid.

[49]Costa was in the Tuscan capital on Apr. 16 (Conti,

Le origini del socialismo, p. 174), and in Rome on Apr.
24 (Carlo Monticelli, Avanti! /Rome7, Jan. 20, 1910).

[50]See Della Peruta, "L'Internazionale a Roma...," p.
26; Hostetter, Le origini del socialismo italiano, p. 495.

[51]See Costa's correspondence in Bulletin de la Fédération Jurassienne, Feb. 15, 1874. Surprisingly, the Imolese found that the Southerners were even more revolutionary than his own people. The Romagnols, he declared in
comparing them with the Neapolitans, were plagued by "too
much hero worship, respect for traditions, patriotic prejudices, too much sentimentality." The inhabitants of
Naples did not share these defects, he concluded, and
thus they were, "by virtue of their economic conditions,
instincts and way of life, the most capable of making a
social revolution." As an afterthought, he added that
the same could be said of the people of the Abruzzi,
Apulia, and Calabria.

[52]Police report to prefect of Forlì, Aug. 5, 1874,
A.S.F., Gab. Pref., vol. 58, fasc. 25.

[53]Guillaume, L'Internationale, III, 169. Nettlau
(Malatesta, p. 111), however, disagrees; he tends to minimize Malatesta's role, insisting that the young anarchist was not as active in the preparation as either Pezzi
or Ceretti.

[54]Letterio Briguglio, "Gli internazionalisti di Monselice e di Padova (Carlo Monticelli)," Movimento operaio,
7 (1955), 729. The exact date of his visit was July 3.

[55]Lipparini, "Cronologia," p. 186.

[56]Report from the ufficio d'istruzione in Aquila to
giudice istruttore of that city, Sept. 15, 1874, Procedimento Costa, vol. 67. In an interrogation on Sept.
25, Costa admitted he was in Aquila in July "without a
special objective, but only to see someone...who was thinking of becoming a socialist," Procedimento Costa, vol. 67.

[57]Lipparini, "Cronologia," p. 186.

[58]Della Peruta, "L'Internazionale a Roma...," p. 24.

[59]Romano, Storia, II, 407.

[60]He was reported to be in Castelbolognese, near Imola,

on July 23. See subprefect of Imola to the giudice istruttore of Ravenna, Aug. 4, 1874, Procedimento Costa, vol. 18.

[61] Romano, Storia, II, 422.

[62] His own testimony, ibid., p. 406.

[63] See Costa correspondence, dated Jan. 12, Bulletin de la Fédération Jurassienne, Jan. 18, 1874. The three federations were probably those of Bologna, Ravenna, and Rimini.

[64] Reports from the subprefect of Rimini to the prefect of Forlì, Apr. 5 and July 28, 1874, A.S.F., Gab. Pref., vol. 58, fasc. 25.

[65] On May 13, 1874, Vincenzo Matteuzzi of Ancona wrote Silvagni requesting 100 copies of Costa's second Revolutionary Bulletin. The letter, which was later found on Matteuzzi by the police, made it clear that all the manifestoes that entered the Marches came by way of Forlì. See Procedimento Costa, vol. 21. Later the Forlivese admitted that he was in close touch with Matteuzzi, as well as with Costa and Rivalta, on the "organization of the Internationalist Association." See interrogation of Jan. 28, 1875, Procedimento Costa, vol. 4.

[66] Report of May 1, 1874, A.S.F., Gab. Pref., vol. 58, fasc. 25.

[67] Two of them, for example, occurred in Forlì on May 24 and June 22. See police reports to prefect of Forlì, May 25 and June 23, 1874, A.S.F., Gab. Pref., vol. 58, fasc. 25.

[68] Minister of Interior to prefect of Forlì, July 24, 1874, A.S.F., Gab. Pref., vol. 58, fasc. 25. This was verified by the subprefect of Cesena, who confirmed that the subversives had increased their efforts for some time now. It was generally felt, he added, that the peasants in his territory would listen to the propaganda. See report to prefect of Forlì, Aug. 6, 1874, A.S.F., Gab Pref., vol. 58, fasc. 25.

[69] Conti, Le origini del socialismo, p. 159.

[70] Among these papers was a list, apparently compiled by Rivalta, which gave the names of all 82 members of the

local federation. It also made it clear who the leaders were. Rivalta and Pezzi headed the group. Orders were transmitted through seven squad leaders: Romeo Destefani, Romeo Suzzi, Appollinare Monti, Giuseppe Santandrea, Giovanni Montanari, Ulisse Miccoli, and Luigi Raffoni. See *Procedimento* Costa, vol. 18.

[71]Pezzi, *Un errore giudiziario*, p. 18. Pezzi evaded the police and fled to Bologna where he helped prepare the insurrection of August 7-8. Many arrests were also made in the Marches at about this time. Among those apprehended was Marino Mazzetti of Macerata, on July 17. Vincenzo Matteuzzi, who had succeeded Borghetti as the region's ranking anarchist leader, managed to escape, but letters confiscated at his home on July 27 made it clear that he was supposed to play an important role in the insurrection. One letter sent to Matteuzzi from Bologna, but unsigned and undated (found in *Procedimento* Costa, vol. 26), had contained 500 *lire* "for your needs and those of the friends" in Sassoferrato and Pergola. Matteuzzi was also informed that the "things" he wanted were supposed to arrive in Bologna in a day or two. Costa later admitted that he wrote this document. See Barbanti-Brodano, *Assisie di Bologna*, p. 78.

[72]For this episode, see Aldo Berselli, *Gli arresti di Villa Ruffi. Contributo alla storia del mazzinianesimo* (Milan: Intelisano, 1956), and Liliano Faenza, *La Retata. Il Convegno di Villa Ruffi. Tra repubblica e anarchia (2 agosto 1874)* (Rimini: Guaraldi, 1974).

[73]Romano, *Storia*, II, 414-17.

[74]According to Ceretti's own testimony, *La Libertà* (Bologna), Feb. 6, 1898. Ceretti claims he was sent on the mission by Castellazzo and Garibaldi.

[75]Subprefect of Rimini to prefect of Forlì, Aug. 24, 1874, *Procedimento* Saffi.

[76]Letter to Pietro Artioli of Reggio Emilia, Aug. 1, 1874, *Procedimento* Saffi.

[77]Among the papers confiscated from the delegates at Villa Ruffi was a memorandum of the meeting written by Alfredo Comandini. According to the document, Saffi opened the session by stating "that the scope of the reunion is that of determining the peaceful and legal conduct of the democratic republican party in Italy before the poli-

tical and administrative questions of the day." Rossi and Fortis spoke in favor of having the A.R.U. participate in the coming elections, and Ludovico Marini of Sant'Arcangelo spoke against. Saffi refused to commit himself one way or the other. This is as far as the meeting went. The note is contained in Procedimento Saffi.

[78]Angelo Bertolini, "Il socialismo contemporaneo in Italia," in Giovanni Rae, Il socialismo contemporaneo, 2nd It. ed. (Florence: Le Monnier, 1895), p. cviii.

[79]The manifesto is found in La Consociazione Romagnola e gli arresti di Villa Ruffi: Lettere di Aurelio Saffi ad Alberto Mario (Forlì: Tip. Sociale Democratica, 1875), pp.104-11.

[80]Hostetter, Le origini del socialismo italiano, p. 483.

[81]See Maurizio Quadrio's letter to Raffaele Pepe, June 28, 1874, in "Internazionalisti e mazziniani in un autografo di Maurizio Quadrio," ed. Antonio Lucarelli, Movimento operaio, 1 (1949), 9.

[82]According to testimony given by Count Codronchi, the anarchists had worked on La Pianta through Carlo Marocchi, its president. They also tried to infiltrate a second republican association in the city, L'Alleanza. See interrogation of Nov. 12, 1874, Procedimento Costa, vol. 8.

[83]All of this was done with the utmost secrecy, but testimony given by Pietro Landi, a member of Imola's District Committee, on Aug. 12, 1874, tends to substantiate these facts. The Società della Pianta, he declared, had been expelled because it refused to accept the views of the District Committee. "The differences between that Society's opinions and those of the Committee consisted in that the former tended...toward a radical amelioration of the working class...; while, on the other hand, those of the Committee meant to obtain that improvement through time and education...." The local Committee, he concluded, had expelled the Pianta "not wanting to assume any responsibility whatsoever for any imprudent act which members of the Society might have succeeded in committing." See Procedimento Costa, vol. 4.

[84]According to Codronchi, who stated that the main

scope of the meeting was to prevent more defections, the session was extremely unruly, as a few members of La Pianta refused to compromise and insisted on dominating the proceedings. Fratti was forced to call them to order on several occasions. The dissidents wanted action, but the Forlivese wanted to "impede untimely rebellions." See interrogation of Nov. 12, 1874.

[85] Ibid.

[86] In his second Revolutionary Bulletin, in February, Costa had attacked a "new party, self-styled socialist and revolutionary...which calling itself Garibaldian seeks to divide the strength of the workers, sowing discord and misunderstandings, and thus, intentionally or not, allies itself with the Italian bourgeoisie" (views echoed in Il Romagnolo, Mar. 7, 1874). The allusion to Ceretti and the Garibaldians who wanted the republican alliance is unmistakable. This group had already been alienated from Costa during the previous year, when the Imolese initiated a campaign against Garibaldi himself. The General, his critic insisted, was even more dangerous than Mazzini, for the latter's ideas were too abstract to be generally appreciated but the military dictatorship represented by the soldier was "a terrible reality" which exerted an irresistible attraction on the masses. See Piancastelli MS.

[87] Subprefect of Rimini to prefect of Forlì, Aug. 24, 1874, Procedimento Saffi.

[88] According to Bakunin's diary (Romano, Storia, II, 422).

[89] Ibid.

[90] Testimony of Pio Colla of Adria, Sept. 22, 1874, Procedimento Costa, vol. 12. It seems that Faggioli and Carlo Penso of Chioggia had been in Adria and Rovigo a few days before, at the end of July. See testimony of Pietro Pegolini of Adria, Aug. 31, 1874, Procedimento Costa, vol. 12.

[91] Questore of Bologna to prefect of Bologna, Aug. 7, 1874, A.S.B., Gab. Pref., vol. 107. The police had been after Costa for about a year, according to Il Monitore di Bologna, Aug. 7, 1874. This information was perhaps exaggerated, but we know from a questore's report in late April, 1874, that already by that time a warrant had been

issued for the Imolese's arrest. See Lipparini, Andrea Costa, p. 71.

[92]Francesca Barbanti-Brodano, Un uomo un tempo: Bologna, 1870-1900. Inizi del socialismo. (Bologna: Ponte Nuovo, 1967), p. 108, claims that Costa had deliberately gotten himself arrested. By now he had little faith in the revolution, she says, and he chose prison over the humiliation which an attempted insurrection was bound to bring. The thesis is not a bad one. Certainly after the arrests of several of the key figures in the Romagna and the Marches, and the repression of the republicans, the future did not look too bright. On the other hand, it might be argued that the prospects had never been good. I rather suspect that Costa would have preferred to avoid arrest. The fact that he had a gun--later on discovered to be part of a shipment which was to be used in the revolt--and some incriminating documents in his possession when he was picked up tends to support this conclusion. One of these papers was an unsigned letter (found in Procedimento Costa, vol. 21) which informed Costa that the writer had not yet received the money and the "crystal boxes." Another was a note written by Costa (it was unsigned, but he admitted it was his in the cited interrogation of Sept. 25, 1874) to the anarchist section in Genoa. In it he declared: "the times, dear comrades, are grave; in a few days we will have made the choice: either we will have crushed privilege forever and inaugurated the new era of liberty and equality or we will all be sacrificed to the triumphant reaction: either we return to the middle ages or we finish that which was begun by the French Revolution and Commune." Quoted in a court report by the Procuratore del Re, Bologna, Feb. 3, 1875, Procedimento Costa, vol. 66.

[93]Cronaca Cerchiari, Aug. 5, 1874.

[94]Pezzi, Un errore giudiziario, p. 19.

[95]Ibid. According to Costa (Bagliori di socialismo, p. 15), prior to this time the date of the insurrection had not been "definitively set."

[96]The following account of the insurrection is taken from the relation of the Procuratore del Re on Feb. 3, 1875 (cited above). A description given by Costa's friends in Bologna 1874-Bologna 1897, Sept. 19, 1897--a special issue published by Imola's socialist paper Il Momento-- is in substantial agreement with the prosecuting attorney's

122

report.

[97] Letter from Giuseppe Barbanti-Brodano to Adamo Mancini, in La Rivolta (Milan), Feb. 19, 1910.

[98] Ammonizione, a special police surveillance, is defined in detail in Hostetter, Le origini del socialismo italiano, p. 519. The reaction was especially fierce in the Romagna. See the Italian correspondence in Bulletin de la Fédération Jurassienne, Oct. 25, 1874.

[99] Pezzi, Un errore giudiziario, pp. 22-23.

[100] By early 1876 the Comitato Italiano was composed of Cafiero, Borghetti, Grassi, Malatesta, and Mazzotti. See Minister of Interior to the prefect of Forlì, Apr. 22, 1876, A.S.F., Gab. Pref., vol. 73, fasc. 116.

[101] Monticelli, Avanti!, Jan. 20, 1910.

[102] Early in 1873 the women's anarchist section in Bologna was composed of 14 members and headed by Violetta (or Violante) Dall'Alpi, then only 15 years old. See anonymous relation, n.d., Procedimento Costa, vol. 11.

[103] Nine anarchists, including Pezzi and Poggiolini, were tried in absentia. A huge number of Imolesi were arrested after Aug. 8, 1874, including the leading republicans in the city (e.g., Farini, Landi, Sassi, etc.) and the anarchists who were suspected of participating in the uprising but had evaded the police before (among them Venturini and Renzi). Anarchists were also arrested throughout the Romagna at this time, especially in Ravenna and Forlì. Virtually all of these prisoners had been released before the trial, the republicans in November, 1874, and the anarchists, 83 of them, in February, 1875.

[104] "The rapid formation and development of the Italian International," the Attorney General charged in the Florentine trial of 1875, "is in fact the work...of Andrea Costa of Imola: an intelligent, cunning, ambitious, and extremely hardworking youth, he devoted his life to it; we see him undefatigable in organizing sections and local and regional federations, in persuading indifferent workers' societies to adhere to its principles, and in eliminating doubts and difficulties, in stirring the uncertain, in provoking the timid, in skillfully combatting the resistant and intractable: the papers of the Italian

Federation's Commission of Correspondence...are a precious monument which reveal his prodigious activity, the predominant influence he exerted and how he succeeded in giving the federation a vigorous and promising organization in a short time." Quoted in Bottero, _Dibattimenti_, p. 319.

[105]Costa spoke with "frankness and elegance. The very large audience lent him the greatest attention," _La Democrazia_ (Forlì), Mar. 18-19, 1876. His three-day interrogation is described in a Bologna correspondence in _Bulletin de la Fédération Jurassienne_, Apr. 2, 1876.

[106]Carducci "judged him his best student," _La Democrazia_, Apr. 29-30, 1876.

[107]"The famous Orator has never been as splendid in his eloquence," ibid., May 20-21, 1876.

[108]See _Difesa proferita per Andrea Costa nel processo degli internationalisti alle Assise di Bologna dal prof. avv. Giuseppe Ceneri_ (Bologna: Zanichelli, 1876), p. 60.

[109]Even Giuseppe Barbanti-Brodano, Costa's friend and another one of his lawyers, publicly declared his adherence to Internationalist principles. See _Bulletin de la Fédération Jurassienne_, June 4, 1876.

[110]_Parole di A. Costa ai giurati della Corte d'Assise di Bologna, nell'udienza del 16 giugno 1876_ (Bologna: Monti, 1876).

[111]_Le origini del socialismo italiano_, p. 514.

[112]On June 17, the day of his acquittal, Costa wrote the Swiss informing them that his efforts had already begun. See _Bulletin de la Fédération Jurassienne_, June 25, 1876. On the latter date, the Imola section sent a circular to all the anarchists on the peninsula inviting them to reorganize their sections and contact each other in order to build up their regional and eventually their national Federation. Signing for the nucleus were Cornacchia, Antonio Castellari, and Vito Solieri, all defendants in the recent Bologna trial. The appeal was published, among other places, in _Bulletin de la Fédération Jurassienne_, July 9, 1876, and reproduced in _La Federazione Italiana_, pp. 248-49.

[113]_Bulletin de la Fédération Jurassienne_, July 2, 1876.

[114]Hostetter, *Le origini del socialismo italiano*, p. 515.

[115]The compte-rendu was published as a booklet, *Associazione Internazionale dei Lavoratori: Regione italiana. Atti del Congresso delle sezioni e federazioni delle Romagne e dell'Emilia, tenuto a Bologna il 16 di luglio del 1876* (Bologna: Azzoguidi, 1876), and is reproduced in *La Federazione Italiana*, pp. 105-20. Represented at the meeting were sections from Bologna, Reggio Emilia, Modena, Budrio and San Giovanni in Persiceto, all in Emilia; and Forlì, Forlimpopoli, San Leonardo, Sant'Andrea, Carpinello, San Pierino in Campiano, Campiano, San Zaccaria, Santo Stefano, Coccolia, Sant'Arcangelo, Imola, Faenza, Ravenna, and Rimini in the Romagna.

[116]Costa was unable to finish the biography; he carried it only up to 1869. A copy of the rare *Vita di Michele Bacunin* (Bologna: Azzoguidi, 1877) can be found at the Istituto Giangiacomo Feltrinelli, Milan.

[117]Account in *La Plebe*, July 30, 1876.

[118]On July 10 the *questore* of Florence informed his prefect that Costa had been in the city and had told the Tuscans that the Romagnol sections were almost completely reorganized. He assured them, moreover, that he was busy trying to get the same results in various other provinces. See Conti, *Le origini del socialismo*, p. 191.

[119]Romano, *Storia*, II, 546.

[120]The official account of the Jesi Congress is in *Il Martello* (Fabriano), Aug. 23, 1876.

[121]For once, the Imolese quipped, justice was prompt. See letter to *La Ragione* (Milan), reproduced in *La Democrazia*, Sept. 2-3, 1876. According to *Il Martello*, Aug. 26, 1876, Costa had been in Fabriano preparing the publication of the recent congressional deliberations. (*Il Martello* was the official organ of the Marchegian-Umbrian Federation.)

[122]Costa's arrest put a stop to the steady progress which the International had been making in the Romagna after the Bologna Congress. See subprefect of Rimini to the prefect of Forlì, Oct. 7, 1876, A.S.F., *Gab. Pref.*, vol. 75, fasc. 259/bis.

[123]On July 1, 1876, Natta and Grassi had issued a circular declaring their intention to hold a national congress. On Sept. 13 a second circular, signed by Natta, announced the date.

[124]Alfredo Angiolini, Socialismo e socialisti in Italia, 3rd ed. (Rome: Riuniti, 1966), p. 112. The persecution of the anarchists, however, had never really been relaxed. See Bulletin de la Fédération Jurassienne, July 16, Oct. 8, 1876.

[125]Monticelli, Avanti!, Jan. 20, 1910, suggests that Costa had been living in Florence rather than Imola at this time. The Imolese, he contends, hid in the house of Guido Corsi, a republican who was later suspected of being a spy, for "several months" preparing the congress. I have not found any evidence to substantiate Monticelli's claim, however.

[126]Accounts of the meeting are found in Il Risveglio (Siena), Nov. 5, 1876, and Il Martello, Nov. 19, 1876. Covelli was a student in a Molfetta seminary with Calfiero. He comes into his own as an anarchist chieftain after Tosi. Biographical information on Covelli is found in Lucarelli, Carlo Cafiero.

[127]Il Martello, Nov. 19, 1876. Costa later appealed the sentence in Bologna, and on Nov. 22 he was absolved of the ammonizione, Lipparini, "Cronologia," p. 188.

[128]On June 21, 1873, N. Pucci of Siena wrote Costa asking him what he thought of the new "independent sections." See Procedimento Costa, vol. 12. This is the first concrete reference to these nuclei I have been able to find.

[129]There was also an Intransigent section in Florence in mid-1873. The group was led by Giuseppe Mazzini (not The Prophet) and was not affiliated with the local Fascio Operaio. Apparently it returned to the orthodox camp before too long. See letter from Piccioli-Poggiali to Costa n.d. /but mid-1873/, Procedimento Costa, vol. 12. The defection of the Parma section is surprising in that Guido Ravazzoni and Aristo Isola, its leaders, had been among Costa's most faithful followers. Both of them, however, were reported to have endorsed Intransigent ideals by March, 1874. See prefect of Parma to the Minister of Interior, Mar. 31, 1874, in Berti, "Gli inizi del socialismo Parmense-Piacentino," p. 394.

[130]"Pagine di storia socialista: Augusto Bernardello, Igninio Vincenzo Dondi e Oreste Vaccari," Avanti!, Jan. 8, 1911.

[131]L'Alleanza, Jan. 29, 1872, reported that the newly-formed society in Ferrara had adhered to the International.

[132]The same holds true for the Parma section which was in correspondence with Engels both before and after the Rimini Congress of 1872. See Stefano Merli, "Alle origini del socialismo a Parma: il 'Comitato per l'emancipazione delle classi lavoratorici,'" Movimento operaio, 6 (1954), 728-29.

[133]Letter of July 3, 1873, Procedimento Costa, vol. 12.

[134]The paper was published from Jan. 5 to Mar. 18, 1874. It made many enemies, among them the republicans; at one point Bernardello fought a duel with Pescatori's old adversary, Enrico Perdisa, now editor of Bologna's La Voce del popolo. See Il Petrolio, Mar. 2, 1874. The editors' biggest worry, however, was the government. Both Dondi and Bernardello were arrested in March, 1874, the former for an incendiary speech on the 16th, the latter for subversive articles in Il Petrolio. See letter from Terzaghi to Sebastiano Baldrati, Mar. 20, 1874, Procedimento Costa, vol. 69. Apparently police repression was the chief cause of the paper's premature death.

[135]Briguglio, "Gli internazionalisti di Monselice e di Padova," p. 730. Dondi, in particular, seemed to cultivate this region. Monticelli recalls that beginning in 1875 the young agitator propagandized Rovigo, Adria, and Monselice. See Avanti!, Jan. 8, 1911. Dondi died prematurely at the end of 1877.

[136]The Ferraresi's initial reaction to the League Statute: "We radical socialists have some due reservations in regard to it because, to speak truthfully and frankly, it smells too much like a mutual aid constitution, and there is very little revolutionary about it." See Il Petrolio, Jan. 12, 1874. The Mar. 18 issue carried the section's adherence to the Geneva Congress.

[137]The Italian groups which were represented at the Geneva Congress were Treia (the Marches), Genoa, Parma, Turin, and Ferrara. Della Peruta suggests that only the latter three were Intransigent sections ("L'Internazionale a Roma dal 1872 al 1877," p. 30), but I suspect they

all were. The Treia section was led by Gaetano Didimi,
a well-known Intransigent. Ravazzoni probably attended
the Congress and represented his section as well as that
of Ferrara. See Berti, "Gli inizi del socialismo Parmense-
Piacentino," p. 392.

[138]Hostetter, Le origini del socialismo italiano, p.
465. Intransigent influence, however, was never very
strong here, at least in Sicily, according to Gino Cer-
rito, "La stampa periodica internazionalista edita in
Sicilia fino al 1880," Volontà, 25 (1972), 520, 529.

[139]Bernardello and Dondi wrote the Commission of Correspondence in Bologna a letter on Mar. 10, 1873, in
which they declared that they were behind Terzaghi. See
Procedimento Costa, vol. 12. This was probably the source
of the quarrel which divided the section four months later

[140]Monticelli, Avanti!, Jan. 8, 1911.

[141]Bagliori di socialismo, p. 19.

[142]The influence of the Intransigents on the Romagna,
despite Ferrara's proximity, was slight. No renagade
nuclei were created there, and the only city where personal adherences seem to have been made was Ravenna, where
at least two of the local chieftains appear to have been
Intransigents: Primo Gironi, who was the Ravenna correspondent for Terzaghi's paper, Il Proletario (prefect of
Ravenna to the local Procuratore del Re, Aug. 7, 1874,
Procedimento Costa, vol. 18), and Baldrati, who was the
Turinese's main defender in the city (anonymous letter
from Ravenna to Terzaghi, n.d., Procedimento Costa, vol.
57) and who carried on a steady correspondence with him
(see Baldrati's interrogation of Aug. 16, 1874, Procedimento Costa, vol. 18). Claudio Zirardini was on good
terms with Dondi (La Laterna /Ferrara/, Feb. 23, 1875),
but his ideas were strictly orthodox.

[143]Franco Della Peruta, "La banda del Matese e la
teoria anarchica della moderna 'Jacquerie' in Italia,"
Democrazia e socialismo nel Risorgimento (Rome: Riuniti,
1973), p. 248.

[144]Guillaume, however, suggests that Nabruzzi failed
to participate in the insurrection because of a personal
vendetta with Bakunin rather than for ideological reasons,
L'Internationale, III, 181.

[145]The section was founded on Nov. 20, 1875, according

to Romano Broggini, "Un gruppo internazionalista dissidente: la sezione del Ceresio," Anarchismo e socialismo in Italia, p. 193.

[146]Della Peruta, "La banda del Matese...," p. 258.

[147]Ibid., p. 254.

[148]Letter to Celso Ceretti, Mar. 13, 1873, in Masini, "La Prima Internazionale in Italia...," p. 59.

[149]Gnocchi-Viani had great hopes for this movement, which he considered a Third International equal to those headed by Marx and Bakunin. See his Le tre internazionali (Lodi: La Plebe, 1875).

[150]Della Peruta, "La banda del Matese...," pp. 252-58. Bertolini, "Il socialismo contemporaneo in Italia," p. cxv, suggests that the socialist movement in his country was little affected by foreign influences. This is a gross exaggeration. Bakunin of course comes to mind immediately. More diffuse than the influence of the Russian, however, was that of the French socialists. Malon is but one example.

[151]Il socialismo. Compendio storico, teorico, pratico, 2nd ed. (Milan: Biblioteca Socialista, 1895), p. 139.

[152]It seems that Ingegneros had previously endorsed some Intransigent views; Il Petrolio (Mar. 18, 1874) considered Il Povero a kindred organ. The Ceresio group, too, had ties with Terzaghi's followers. See Lodovico Nabruzzi's letter, dated Feb. 3, in Il Tribuno (an Intransigent paper), Feb. 13, 1876.

[153]The account of the founding congress, which met in Milan on Oct. 15, and the Federation's Statute and Regulations were published in late 1876, and reproduced in La Federazione Italiana, pp. 144-47.

[154]See Bulletin de la Fédération Jurassienne, Nov. 5, 12, 1876, for the Bern Congress.

[155]See Costa's correspondence, dated Jan. 13, L'Egalité (Lagny, France), Jan. 20, 1878.

CHAPTER FOUR

FROM ANARCHISM TO SOCIALISM, 1877-1879

The Insurrection of San Lupo

During the Jesi Congress the Marchegian-Umbrian Federation had adopted Il Martello, a newspaper published
in Fabriano by Napoleone Papini, as its official journal.
Inspired by Costa, the paper achieved a fair degree of
success and within a short time its influence extended
well beyond the confines of the Marches and Umbria.[1] Unfortunately, it was plagued, like all socialist publications at this time, by financial difficulties which forced
it to transfer its seat of operations to Jesi in November,
1876, then threatened to terminate its existence altogether. By now, however, the anarchist party in Italy
was in desperate need of an organ that would defend its
interests. Consequently the paper was taken over by Costa,
who continued its publication, aided by Faggioli, beginning on January 6, 1877, in Bologna.[2] During the next
few months practically the sole concerns of the Bolognese
paper became its chief enemies: the Legalitarians and
the government.

The latter's treatment of the anarchists, as we have
seen, was not any milder under the Left than it had been
under the Right. On the contrary, as Minister of Interior
Nicotera pursued a policy which was more repressive than
that of Cantelli, his predecessor. The new appointee was
determined to demolish the International completely, using any means possible. He justified his extraordinary
vigor by insisting that the subversive organization constituted a gang of criminals rather than a political body.
This was the essence of his speech before the Chamber of
Deputies on December 13, 1876, when he appeared to request
secret funds for his police force and charged that the
anarchists were nothing less than camorristi in Naples,
mafiosi in Sicily, and accoltellatori in the Romagna.
The latter reference was to a mafia-like sect, the Banda
degli Accoltellatori ("Band of Knifers"), which terrorized
Ravenna in the late 1860's and the early 1870's with a
long series of assassinations. Some of the city's first
Internationalists, notably the brothers Luca and Giovanni

131

Resta, had been members of the dreaded ring.[3]

The Minister's allegations incensed the accused, who realized that a general acceptance of his definition of the International as a criminal association would spell the virtual end of the organization. Their response took the form of a letter addressed to Nicotera which appeared in Il Martello on January 25, 1877.[4] Signed by "some Internationalists," the document, as its style demonstrates, was almost certainly written by Costa.

The Minister's plea for secret funds was the Imolese's initial concern, for it was clear that these monies were earmarked for the anti-anarchist campaign. How strange it was, Costa pointed out, that this petition should be made now when ten years earlier, as a republican deputy, Nicotera had spoken out vehemently in the Chamber against this very kind of expenditure. Here, it was implied, was just one more example of the anarchist thesis that power corrupts.

Then the letter turned to the Minister's speech of the previous month. Nicotera had suggested that the government did not have to worry about violating the legitimate rights of the International, since this body was not a political party, like that of the clericals or the republicans, but rather a conglomeration of illiterate men attempting to confiscate honest people's wealth; in a word, the anarchists were nothing more than a band of thieves. Costa dealt with the charges one by one. That the International was not political in nature was readily acknowledged. Politics was the art of governing well, he explained, but the anarchists, like Proudhon, were against any form of government; thus they were apolitical. Was this a crime, the Imolese queried; had not Nicotera himself gone to great lengths to insure that workers' associations not concern themselves with politics? That the International was made up of men who were mostly ignorant and uneducated was also true, he conceded, but irrelevant. Even illiterate workers were capable of deciding their own destinies: "Their speech may be coarse and unpolished, their style might not be parliamentary; it really does not matter; nevertheless they will be able to express their desires better than any bourgeois philosopher or thinker." Moreover, he argued, the anarchists were no more ignorant than the republicans or the clericals. Costa completely denied his opponent's last assertion, that the anarchists were thieves and hence criminals. In fact, it was their contention

132

that wealth should benefit those who produce it. Nothing could be more just than this. The real thieves, he countered, were "the people that govern all the states of the world." Would the Minister please read the Statutes of the International? Was this the program of a criminal association, the Romagnol asked.

Costa succeeded admirably in explaining the nature of the International and demonstrating that it was "a vast, serious, and impressive party," rather than the motley crew which the Minister of Interior had described. But he did not stop there. His letter did not confine itself to a rebuttal of Nicotera's charges; it also expressed a deep moral indignation over the government's policies with respect to the International. The Imolese's condemnation of this repression was less convincing than his defense of the Federation. The fact remains that the anarchists were advocating and attempting the violent overthrow of the state, and the latter had as much right to defend itself as they did to attack it. Given the circumstances, though, Costa's failure to appreciate this argument at the time is perfectly understandable.

A different threat to the International, but one no less dangerous, was that posed by the Legalitarians, who had gained sufficient strength by early 1877 to force a confrontation with the anarchists. During the previous year, as they were beginning to organize among themselves, their ideas were rather vague; and so the divergence of opinion within the Italian Federation was not at all clear-cut. Unable to discover the extent of the disagreement, Costa and his associates had necessarily moved with caution. Their criticism tended to be indirect. On November 19, 1876, for example, Il Martello, then in Jesi, published an article entitled "Little by Little."5 The immediate danger to the cause of anarchy, the anonymous article began, was not the bourgeoisie ("the fat people"), but rather those socialists who extoll social science and permit themselves to be "guided completely by cold and dispassionate reason." It continued: "Calling themselves socialists, they are more dangerous than the declared enemies of the popular cause. The Government, which attacks and persecutes us, drives us ever more resolutely toward revolution--while they with their little by little seek to lull us to sleep in misery and degradation."

The creation of the Federation of Upper Italy and its refusal to join the anarchist-dominated Italian Federation demonstrated the unmistakable existence of two separate

schools within the socialist movement. Warfare was inevitable. Hostilities were well under way by the beginning
of 1877, when Costa, champion of anarchist orthodoxy,
found himself engaged in a fierce battle with the Legalitarians of Il Povero and La Plebe.[6]

The most violent attacks on the anarchist position
came from Palermo, where Ingegneros Napolitano waged a
savage campaign which oftentimes dwelt on personalities
rather than issues. He was especially disparaging of the
1874 revolts, which he condemned as ineffective as well
as ridiculous. At first Costa tried to ignore the revil-
ing criticism being leveled by the Southerner, but the remarks directed at the Bologna insurrection, which were
taken personally, proved to be too much. In early February the Imolese lashed out at the "cowards" of Il Povero
in terms which they could understand.[7] "Our stroll from
Imola to Bologna," he retorted sarcastically, did more
for the cause of socialism than all of his opponents' useless appeals for organization. Compare the meager results
achieved in Sicily, he boasted, with the much more substantial ones in the Romagna. Apparently the irate anarchist was determined not to be outdone in vindictiveness.
The rest of his article was one long tirade against his
detractors, culminated by a terse summation: "We hate
all of you profoundly." He and his friends, Costa concluded, would no longer have anything whatsoever to do
with Il Povero. "We will not defend ourselves against
the insinuations of Jesuits, nor attempt to disprove fal-
sified assertions."

A week later the Romagnol was forced to apologize for
his derogatory comments made regarding Sicily. He admitted that he had been unreasonable and conceded that the
islanders were the most potentially revolutionary of all
the Italians.[8] Nothing was said of Il Povero. In the
meantime, Il Martello began to publish the declarations
which it received from anarchist circles throughout the
peninsula expressing solidarity with the Bolognesi in
their clash with Ingegneros. During these weeks, however,
Costa refused to mention the Sicilian paper in any of his
articles. Ingegneros and his collaborators, on the other
hand, continued their vituperation in an effort to provoke the Imolese. "Prostitute yourselves as much as you
want," Costa warned his tormentors in the last number of
his paper, "but do not try to prostitute others. We are
telling you: enough."[9]

Refusing to treat with the Sicilian paper, Costa and

the Bolognesi turned their attention instead to La Plebe. The Milanese paper was less vociferous than its ally in the South but represented an even greater danger: through its initiative efforts were being made to reconstruct the Italian International on an anti-Bakuninist foundation. The creation of the Federation of Upper Italy during the previous year was only a beginning. The Legalitarians' Second Congress was scheduled to be held in the Lombard capital on February 17-18, 1877. As this date approached, the anarchists started to focus their attention on it.

Fearing charges of intolerance, Costa was careful to avoid any direct criticism. His attitude, however, was expressed in a letter, dated February 11, sent by his Romagnol followers to the delegates of the meeting on the eve of its convocation.[10] Writing on behalf of the Federal Commission of the Romagnol and Emilian Federation, Vito Solieri and Antonio Castellari extended their best wishes to the Congress and expressed the hope that the Milan-based Federation would adhere to those same principles which animated their own organization. While not wishing to dictate their ideas, the two anarchists felt duty-bound to make these clear. The Romagnols were against middle-class alliances and political and economic reform. The only way of emancipating the worker, the sole means warranted by conditions in Italy, was revolution. Hopefully the delegates at Milan were in accord. It had been rumored, the Romagnols concluded, that the workers of the North were supporters of "non-violent methods"; this was their chance to disprove the slander.

The tone of the letter was not too optimistic. In fact, on the eve of the meeting it was already clear that the Bakuninists were fighting a losing battle in Northern Italy, something which was confirmed completely at Milan. The assembly, presided over by Bignami, was virtually unanimous in voting to pursue the emancipation of the working class with all the means at its disposal, not just revolutionary ones, and in proclaiming the autonomy of its Federation vis-à-vis the anarchist organizations in other regions of the country.[11] The Milan Congress of 1877 thus signaled the definitive break between the two contending schools.

Costa's comments on the meeting were predictable. The delegates at Milan had tried to minimize the rift with their rivals by insisting that even though they differed slightly on the question of methods, they were in complete agreement on that of goals: they too wanted the abolition of authority and the emancipation of the worker. This explanation was unsatisfactory to the Imolese, who objected that "the relationship between end and means is intimate and reciprocal." The eclectic approach which the Milanesi advocated, he warned, would only result in contradictions. Such was the case, he suggested, in _La Plebe_, which would publish an article by Marx, then follow it up with one by Bakunin. The result, he concluded, was bound to be ideological confusion.[12]

Despite his bitter disappointment with the recent defeat in Lombardy, Costa's response was surprisingly subdued; by this time the Romagnol's attention was being directed elsewhere. Police repression and Legalitarian progress were leading to the rapid disintegration of the anarchist International by early 1877. Threatened with total annihilation, the Bakuninists were driven to take desperate measures: it was decided to attempt a second insurrection. The idea had originated during the previous year, at the October Congresses in Tosi and Bern, where it was determined that action was necessary at all costs.[13] Though the chances of a successful revolt were remote, the anarchists generally felt that the publicity of their ideas would more than justify the attempt. This notion, the "Propaganda of the Idea," traced its roots in Italy--as Franco Della Peruta, Romano, and others have shown--back to the time of the _Risorgimento_, when it was espoused by both Mazzini and Carlo Pisacane.[14] The most powerful and recent model, though, was that of the aborted revolution in 1874.[15] The propagandistic value of the uprising and the trials that resulted had been considerable. Faced with complete destruction unless they acted, the anarchists, led by Cafiero and Malatesta, initiated the preparation.

The ideas which now reigned among the conspirators were expressed in an anonymous article entitled "Legal Socialism and Revolutionary Socialism," which appeared in _Il Martello_ in late February.[16] Della Peruta attributes the authorship to Costa, which is probably correct.[17] Beginning with the premise that there can be no liberty without equality and no equality without liberty, the Imolese concluded that both goals had to be conquered simultaneously and that the only way the feat could be accomplished was through revolution, a "popular, violent, destructive, terrible" process. This idea was consistent with his earlier beliefs, but while he had previously emphasized that the insurrection, in order to be popular,

had to follow a period of propaganda and organization,
now he insisted that the upheaval occur immediately, before the "organized forces" (i.e., Legalitarians) of the
proletariat could convince the workers of a "peaceful"
emancipation. The material revolution, he determined,
must precede the moral revolution.

As in most anarchist tracts, there is considerable
confusion here. Costa's concept of popular insurrection
displays traces of brilliance but also betrays a good
deal of contradiction. He continued to insist that the
revolt had to be a popular one; otherwise the elite that
carried it out would have to impose a dictatorship on
the ignorant masses to insure their adherence. The revolution would thus be corrupted, for the use of force
was the negation of freedom. That this elite would be
proletarian made little difference, he observed. "The
workers are neither better nor worse than anyone else,
and, if they were to find themselves in an identical position to that of the bourgeoisie of /17/89, they would
do as the bourgeoisie did." As proof of this assertion
he cited the "exclusivist and mean spirit" of the English
trade-unions. There is little to quarrel with here, but
how could Costa's popular revolt develop without organization and propaganda? Even assuming, as the Romagnol
does, that "the principles of modern socialism...are the
profound sentiment, though unconscious, of the people,"
it would seem that some degree of education would be
necessary to draw out this revolutionary potential.

By this time, however, the anarchists were more intent on action than on thought. The result was the rebellion which broke out on April 5, 1877, north of Naples.[1]
The plan called for leading anarchists from throughout the
peninsula to converge at San Lupo, an isolated village in
the mountains of the Matese. Once armed, they would march
through the countryside arousing the agrarian populace
and instigating a general uprising. Bakunin had maintained that the peasants were the most revolutionary element
in society. This thesis was now to be tested. As Pier
Carlo Masini aptly comments, whereas the insurrection of
1874 was inspired by the Paris Commune, this one looked
instead to the French Jacqueries.[19] The "Band of the Matese," as the armed brigade came to be called, was composed of twenty-six men and led by Cafiero, Malatesta,
and Pietro Cesare Ceccarelli, a Romagnol from Savignano.[20]

The uprising lasted six days. The insurgents roamed
through the province of Benevento in the Matese and suc-

ceeded in "liberating" two hamlets. The peasants were
sympathetic enough, especially when the anarchists set
fire to the local archives (which contained tax records),
but they refused to join the expedition. The revolutionaries were finally encircled by the police and arrested
near the village of Letino on April 11.

The peasants' apathy, no doubt, goes a long way in
explaining the failure of the insurrection of San Lupo.
But there were other factors, also. The revolt had begun before preparations had been completed. Scheduled
to begin in May, it was anticipated on April 5 when some
of the members of the band were surprised by a police
patrol near San Lupo, where the group was to assemble,
and gunfire was exchanged. One consequence of the upset
timetable was that the phalanx never reached its intended
strength. In addition, the armed column was forced to
take to the Matese at a time when the mountains were still
snow-covered and the weather bad, obstacles unforeseen
by the inexperienced rebels. Still more directly responsible for the failure was the government's efficient spy
network. It was not by chance that the anarchists had
stumbled across the patrol on April 5. In fact, the area
was thoroughly saturated with police. An informer who
took part in the preparation of the uprising had kept
them abreast of every detail of the operation. Quick
action by the authorities prevented what could have been
a major insurrection.

Costa himself admitted later that he had not endorsed
the San Lupo revolt.[21] The views expressed in Il Martello
in late February would suggest that he saw eye to eye with
his colleagues on the need for an immediate armed revolt,
but in his letter to Nicotera, written a month before,
he expressed a different opinion:

By means of conspiracy one can achieve a change in
the form of government; one can depose or assassinate a prince and replace him with someone else; but
it is impossible /with these means/ to perform the
social revolution, as the International understands
and wants it. To achieve this, it is necessary to
widely disseminate the new principles among the
masses, or more properly speaking to make these conscious, since they already possess them instinctive-
ly, and organize the workers of all the world so
that the revolution fulfills itself; from the bottom
to the top and not vice versa, by means of laws and
decrees, or by force. And this necessarily implies

138

publicity, since it is impossible to reconcile the
idea of such a vast propaganda with the necessarily
restricted circle of a conspiracy.

The discrepancy between these views and those expressed in the Martello article in February, which in-
directly sanctioned the revolutionary enterprise, is
difficult to explain. The possibility remains that the
latter endorsement, which was unsigned, was someone else's
work. More likely, though, is that the Romagnol, despite his opposition to the venture, had written the piece.
By now he had no other choice. Cafiero and Malatesta were
determined to act; the preparations were well under way.
To oppose the insurrection at this late hour was tantamount to treachery. Not wanting to be put in the same
category as Ingegneros and the Milanesi, his despised
enemies, the reluctant revolutionary chose to second his
friends' efforts.

Given Costa's reservations, it is understandable that
he did not participate in the San Lupo expedition. His
support, however, was not only vocal. He also agreed to
organize armed bands in the Romagna and in the surrounding regions and to await developments there; if the initiative in the South fared well he and his followers would
join in.[22] During the first months of 1877 he was faithful to his word. He divided his time between the newspaper in Bologna and trips into the surrounding countryside to enlist support for the auxiliary battalions.[23]
During one of these excursions, in early March, he was
in Monselice (Veneto), where he met Carlo Monticelli for
the first time. The insurrection, Costa confided, was being prepared in Tuscany, Romagna, Latium, Sicily, and
other places. Would the Venetians help? "We asked him,"
Monticelli recalls, "if the chances were good, and he
simply answered: we'll see!"[24]

The Romagnols were ready to move when the revolt
broke out in the Matese.[25] Only quick action by the authorities prevented the rebellion from spreading. News
of San Lupo was followed almost immediately by the government's dissolution of the International and the beginning
of a nation-wide drive to put the anarchists behind bars.
The police acted with the greatest dispatch in the Romagna
where Costa just barely evaded arrest. From Forlì, where
he had been awaiting word from the South, the would-be
revolutionary fled first to Imola and then to Bologna.[26]
Hiding out in an apartment on Via Cavaliera,[27] he remained
in the city until the end of April, when he escaped into

Switzerland via Milan.[28] The Italian exile would not
return home for over two and a half years.

Exile and Imprisonment

After the failure of San Lupo complete confusion
reigned in the ranks of the Italian anarchists. This
was due in part to the condemnation of the insurrection
by the Legalitarians;[29] primarily, though, it was a result of the most intense repression the movement had yet
experienced. Costa described this pressure in a correspondence, dated April 21, published in the Bulletin de
la Fédération Jurassienne:

> As an example of the measures taken by the ter-
> rorized bourgeoisie I can tell you that in Imola
> the soldiers no longer sleep in their barracks but
> bivouac on the public roads as if the city were in
> a state of seige: patrols of carabinieri, police-
> men, /and/ soldiers incessantly move through the
> streets of the town and the surrounding area, at
> times pushing as far as Dozza, a small village seven
> miles from here, in the mountains.
> Fearing that the armed bands penetrate from Roma-
> gna into Tuscany, or vice versa, troops have been
> sent from Forlì to San Casciano. A large number of
> socialists have been arrested in Bologna: some were
> detained, others released after having been placed
> under ammonizione. Many have been able to escape
> the investigations. Thursday evening, the 19th,
> searches were made at the homes of many other so-
> cialists; and the local authorities, believing that
> a home visit of this kind sufficed to frighten our
> comrades, asked them to sign a declaration asserting
> that they had never been part of the International
> or else obliging them not to be part of it any longer!
> The newspapers publish a decree which declares
> all the Association's federations, sections, circles,
> and groups disbanded, /and/ orders the closing of
> their meeting places and the confiscation of all
> which is found there. The newspapers have also been
> entrusted with informing /the public/ that the Min-
> isters were unanimous in approving this decree (some-
> thing we never doubted). Here we are, then, outlawed
> again.[30]

The Imolese himself did not remain immune to the state's
vengeance. On April 21 the Perugia Court of Appeals sustain-

ed a government petition and ruled that the _ammonizione_
imposed on Costa in November was in fact valid, and on
July 27 the _pretore_ of Imola sentenced him to three months
in prison and six more of special surveillance for violating the recently confirmed sentence.[31]

All of this was done _in absentia_, since Costa was
safely in Switzerland by this time. He established his
residence in Bern at the beginning of May and in the following weeks became very close friends with Paul Brousse,
the French activist who now published an anarchist paper,
the _Arbeiter-Zeitung_, in the city.[32] Costa was also kept
busy earning a living as a house-painter and exhorting
his comrades in Italy to reconstruct their sections and
federations.[33] His main efforts, however, went into the
creation of Italian sections of the International in
Switzerland. The first of these nuclei of Italian-speaking workers he formed was in Bern in early June.[34] A
second cell appeared in Geneva on June 11, two days after
Costa gave a speech in that city.[35] The responsibility
for this group, as well as for a third one which arose
soon after in Saint-Imier, was probably his.[36]

Dissatisfied with his job as a menial laborer, the
busy agitator was forced to move from the Swiss capital
in the first days of August and leave for Geneva, where
he made a living giving Italian lessons.[37] In this month
he also spent some time in Lugano visiting the large col-
ony of anarchist exiles which had taken up residence in
the Ticinese city after the recent persecutions in Italy.
Among the expatriates was a group of Romagnols which included Mazzotti and his wife Marietta Focaccia, and Pezzi
and his consort Luigia Minguzzi. The sojourn proved to
be a fateful one for the Imolese: it was at the home of
the latter couple that he first made the acquaintance of
Anna Kuliscioff (1857-1925).[38]

When Costa met her, the Russian woman, despite her
youth, was already a veteran of years of revolutionary
experience. Born in Moskaja, in the Russian province of
Kerson, Anna came from a family with a Jewish background.
Her father--who had changed his name from Rosenstein to
Kuliscioff--was a moderately successful merchant able to
provide her with a good education. She took advantage of
the opportunity given her, for she was intelligent and
hardworking. Unable to continue her studies in Russia
(where women were denied entrance into the universities),
she was sent to Switzerland and enrolled at the University
of Zurich at the age of sixteen. It was here that she

first came into contact with the radical theories current among the Russian exiles then so numerous in the
Swiss cities. These ideas left a profound impression on
the sensitive girl. She was especially affected by the
views of Peter Lavrov, a Russian populist. Under his
inspiration she decided to leave the University and return home, where she became a member of the "Back to
the People" movement.39 Like many of her colleagues
she soon grew disillusioned with propaganda, which the
populists stressed, and determined that only revolution
would solve the problems of the Russian peasantry. She
became a full-fledged Bakuninist, and during the next
few years, working primarily in the area around Kiev,
she became a devoted conspirator. (Among her collaborators during this period was Vera Zasulic, who attempted to assassinate General Trepov, the notorious
prefect of police, at St. Petersburg in 1878.) On April
14, 1877, Kuliscioff, the police at her heels, was forced
into exile. She would never see her homeland again.
She fled to Zurich, then Bern, where she had visited Bakunin the year before as he lay on his deathbed, before
reaching the Ticino.

Costa and Kuliscioff fell in love at first sight.
It is easy to see what attracted the impressionable
young man to the Slavic exile. An acquaintance later
described her as possessing "an extraordinary beauty and
a very sensitive character."40 Undoubtedly, too, the
similarity of their political views was a factor. During the next few months the couple shared a life of intense party activity together.

Meanwhile, preparations had begun for the two international socialist meetings which were to be held in
September. The first was the annual anarchist congress,
at Verviers. The second and more important of the two
was an extraordinary congress which would meet at Ghent
in hopes of resurrecting the old I.W.A. of 1864 by re-
uniting its dissident factions, the Marxian socialists
and the Bakuninist anarchists. The latter began to get
ready on August 4-6, when members of the anti-authoritarian Jura Federation met at Saint-Imier and led by
Brousse and Costa voted to remain faithful to anarchist
principles and not make any concessions at Ghent.41

Apparently, however, the decisions made at the Swiss
meeting encountered some opposition; by the Congress of
Verviers, on September 6-8, a clear difference of opinion had developed between Guillaume and the Jura Swiss

142

on the one hand, and Costa and Brousse on the other.[42]
The two expatriates sponsored a resolution to be maintained by the anarchist delegates to Ghent declaring
that the only means of emancipating the worker were revolutionary ones. The Swiss wanted to temper this tough
stand, which would obviously be unacceptable to the Marxists, and make reconciliation impossible, but the resolution passed.

Costa, as his co-sponsorship of the uncompromising
measure suggests, had become the champion of a strictly
orthodox anarchist position. This orientation probably
stemmed from his reevaluation of the San Lupo insurrection. During the Verviers Congress the Romagnol spoke
at length on the recent venture and justified it completely.[43] Even if it had failed miserably, he explained, the revolt had popularized socialist ideas and
hence served a useful purpose.[44] During the preceding
months the revolutionary enterprise had been loudly condemned both at home, especially by the Legalitarian organs, and abroad, where the campaign was led by Jules
Guesde in Le Radical, a Parisian newspaper.[45] Costa's
intemperance in defending Cafiero and the other members
of the San Lupo expedition was almost certainly conditioned by this severe criticism.[46]

It has been suggested that the fiery radical was
completely rigid and uncompromising on the question
of revolution at Verviers.[47] This is something of an
exaggeration. Certainly he was a zealous advocate of
insurrection; speaking before the Congress he declared
that "only action can give the people a consciousness
of its own strength."[48] Still he had not entirely superseded his earlier convictions. "We await action,"
he added in the next breath, "without however neglecting those means of propaganda that are at our disposal."
Despite his support of the revolutionary resolution, it
would appear that the Romagnol was sustaining a thesis
he did not fully endorse.

This confusion was also evident at the Congress of
Ghent on September 9-15. Surrounded by his enemies (the
anarchists were heavily outnumbered), Costa felt compelled to accentuate his differences with them. He emphasized his intransigence on the question of conciliation and the desirability of revolution. But now he
was even more equivocal on the latter issue: "Although
we do not neglect the other methods, we believe that
action is the best means of propaganda."[49]

The reconciliation which had been hoped for at Ghent proved to be impossible. The anarchists refused to compromise their program, but they were too weak to impose it on their opponents. As a matter of fact, legalitarian and reformist ideas had made even greater progress among the socialists outside of Italy than within the country. Led by the Germans, the socialist movement was rapidly moving in a Marxian direction. The Ghent Congress revealed the extent to which this process had gone. The meeting represented the end of the anarchist International in Europe.

Once the Ghent Congress was over Costa decided against returning to Switzerland; instead he left for Paris, where he proposed to spend the remainder of his forced exile. On September 18, 1877, he wrote Kuliscioff from the French capital and informed her of the situation there on the eve of the political elections which were to be held the following month. "As for us," he added, "there is little to hope for; an agitation would be exploited by the radicals. Those that think as we do are not numerous....We are no longer understood. It is necessary to start from the beginning; we need an immense propaganda. A government which would permit us to meet, unite and publish something, that is what would be of use to us at this moment. Certainly we would find allies in the people...."50

When Costa had admitted that revolution was but one of many means of emancipating the worker he had begun to approach the position endorsed by the Italian Legalitarians. This letter suggests that he was going further along this same path. Rather than emphasizing revolution, the Romagnol was stressing propaganda. Still, he had not gone as far as his French comrades. Having to choose between Brousse's anarchism and Guesde's Marxism, they preferred the latter. The French International had been eradicated in the aftermath of the Commune, and now, after years of repression, the socialists were content to settle for what they could get. The reformist tendency represented by Guesde became even more popular after November 18, when he began publication of L'Egalité in Lagny (Paris).

Guesde's efforts to revitalize the socialist movement had also received a boost during the previous month. The October elections were among the most significant in French history. Marshal MacMahon, then the head of state, had little sympathy for republican institutions.

144

It was clear that a royalist victory under MacMahon
would mean the abolition of the republic and the re-
establishment of a more conservative government. The
results of the elections spoiled the General's plans;
the Third Republic was saved. But it was not only republicans who benefited from the victory. Under the
old regime all attempts to revive the working-class
movement had been futile. Greater political freedom
was necessary, as Costa had written, before anything
serious could be accomplished. Thus the victory at the
polls was met with enormous enthusiasm among the socialists, both anarchists and Marxists, who now began to
reconstruct the French International in earnest.

Among the most active of these agitators were Costa
and Kuliscioff, who joined her lover in Paris on November 11, 1877.[51] They were aided in their work of reorganization by another expatriate, Prince Peter Kropotkin. The Romagnol was especially zealous in his
efforts. He spent every day, the police were informed, "making assiduous propaganda for the International."[52] His activities were not confined to the French
capital. He was in Lyon in November, 1877,[53] and again
in January, 1878. The scope of his second visit was to
speak before a French Workers' Congress (January 28-
February 8). On his way back to Paris he also stopped
to make speeches at Montluçon, Commentry, and Grannat.[54]
Arrested in the latter city for lack of proper identification on February 10, Costa was released on the
24th and imperturbably resumed his activities.[55] On
February 28 he presided at a Paris gathering of about
fifty anarchists and Marxians.[56] During these months
both factions of the International had set aside their
ideological differences in an attempt to organize the
French working-class movement and channel it in a socialist direction. It was hoped that this could be accomplished at a national congress which would be held
in Paris in the near future. The preparation of this
assembly was the objective of the February 28 meeting.
The results of all of this work, however, were disappointing, as Kropotkin later recalled.[57] Disillusioned, Costa decided to return to Italy.[58] It was
precisely on the eve of his departure, on March 22, that
the youth was arrested in Paris together with Kuliscioff,
Zanardelli, Nabruzzi, and several French anarchists.
Only he and Hippolyte Pédoussant, another of the chief
advocates of the ill-fated congress, were brought to
trial; Kuliscioff and Costa's Italian comrades were expelled from the country after spending a few days in

jail, and the others were released at once. The two unfortunate prisoners were tried on May 3-4 and found guilty of belonging to an outlawed association, the International.[59] The Frenchman was sentenced to thirteen months behind bars and fined five hundred francs; the Romagnol received two years and was levied the same sum. To his dismay, Costa discovered that the French republic was no more liberal than the Italian monarchy had been.

The svolta

Costa's imprisonment in 1878-79 came at a time when the reaction against the socialists was reaching its zenith throughout Europe. The communistic movement was widely viewed as a vast international conspiracy to overthrow existing institutions, and the fear it inspired was immense. It was determined to end the threat once and for all. These efforts were especially zealous in Italy, where the police were irked by the leniency with which the subversives had been treated by the courts. Among the regions hardest hit was the Romagna, which shared the distinction with Tuscany of being the chief bastion of the Italian International. As developments there paralleled those throughout the peninsula, it might be well to take a closer look at the area.

The reaction in the Romagna, as in the rest of the country, was a continuation of that which had begun in April, 1877, in the aftermath of the San Lupo affair, when the International was all but destroyed. The gains that had been made under Costa's direction in late 1876 and early 1877 were entirely wiped out.[60] But it was not long before attempts were begun to reconstruct the sections. Costa, from his base in Switzerland, provided encouragement.[61] His chief agent in the Romagna was Faggioli, who traveled throughout the region setting up meetings with the major anarchist heads in each town:[62] Ferdinando Valducci and the Battistini brothers, Epaminonda and Pio, in Cesena; Secondo Cappellini, Sesto Fortuzzi, and Silvagni in Forlì; Vittorino Valbonesi and Clemente Gramiacci in Forlimpopoli; Castellari and Solieri in Imola; Ferdinando Mazzanti and Claudio Zirardini in Ravenna; Natale Giannini and the Zavoli brothers, Cajo and Bruto, in Rimini; and the Squadrani brothers, Giovanni Enrico and Francesco, in Savignano. A good deal of headway was made in the second half of 1877. This progress was described in a letter from Imola which was read at an Internationalist meeting in Geneva on September 22. In the Romagna, the Imolesi declared, the anarchists made gains every day, at the expense of the republicans.[63] Among the sections that Costa represented at the Congresses of Verviers and Ghent earlier in the month were those of Cesena, Forlì, Forlimpopoli, Rimini, and Sant'Arcangelo, which suggests that reorganization was indeed meeting some success in the Romagnol provinces.[64]

The last months of 1877 witnessed an ever-increasing agitation among the various groups that had been formed. Late in the year a clandestine manifesto was circulated throughout the Romagna calling for reconstruction of the regional federation and asking the sections there to send delegates to a gathering for this purpose (inspired by Costa, and the anarchists in Rome), which would meet in Forlì on January 6 of the new year.[65] The authorities had intercepted the appeal and were on the spot to impede the reunion. A carabiniere report to the Forlì prefect on the 7th assured him that police efforts had been successful.[66] Late in the month, though, Il Nettuno, a newspaper in Rimini which had recently espoused the cause of the International, gave an account of the meeting, which had taken place as scheduled.[67] Thirty-two nuclei had been represented. The Romagnol Federation (minus the Emilians this time) was formally re-established. Each adhering society was to be headed by a commission and governed by statutes modeled on those voted at Bologna in July, 1876. As before, a Federal Commission would act as the directive organ for the confederation.[68] The delegates at Forlì also established a second body, which was charged with the preparation of a national congress. The Romagna would take the initiative in resurrecting the Italian Federation.

After the Forlì meeting, Faggioli was replaced as the chief anarchist agitator in the Romagna by Domenico Francolini (1850-1902).[69] In 1873, when he helped found Il Nettuno, the local organ of the A.R.U., the Riminese was already a highly-regarded Mazzinian, and since his city lacked a charismatic personality comparable to Valzania in Cesena or Saffi in Forlì the young activist promised to become the ranking member in the local party before too long. Francolini had everything going for him: he was socially prominent (his family was one of the oldest in the city), extremely popular, and, by general consensus, the handsomest man in Rimini.[70] Later he married a countess and became a banker. By 1874, however, when he was arrested at Villa Ruffi with the other directors of the Romagnol Consociazione, he had begun to sympathize with socialist ideas.[71] Gradually he dissociated himself from the republicans and joined their weaker rivals. The first real evidence of his conversion came in March, 1877, when he signed (and apparently wrote) a manifesto issued by the Internationalists of Rimini in commemoration of the Paris Commune.[72] When Il Nettuno, now under Francolini's full control, began to publish again on July 25, 1877, after an interruption of almost three years, its program was clearly socialist rather than republican. By the beginning of the following year the ex-Mazzinian had become "one of the most influential members" of the International and was busy trying to win the republicans in Rimini over to his point of view.[73] "But he is only listened to by a few members of the lowest class," the city's subprefect noted in February, "...while he has been unsuccessful thus far in seducing those...who belong to the most civil part of the population with his radical principles."[74] His luck changed for the better before too long, though, for during the course of the year he was joined by two other young men highly regarded in Mazzinian circles, Pellegrino Bagli and Lodovico Lettimi.[75]

Francolini was busy outside of Rimini as well. He traveled extensively throughout the Romagna encouraging the formation and strengthening of anarchist sections. Such, for instance, was the scope of his visits to Cesena on June 15 (where he declared that great strides had been made in Rimini and wondered why so little had been done by the Cesenati)[76] and to Imola in early November.[77] Settling differences of opinion that had arisen within the ranks of these nuclei was another major responsibility. He and Lettimi were in Cesena in August 27 to settle a rift which had developed between the Battistini brothers and a number of their followers. "The Battistinis," explained the subprefect of that city, "do not seem to employ all the zeal which is expected from leaders, and some members seek to get rid of them /by/ attacking their private lives."[78]

Francolini's efforts and those of his colleagues were not without effect. Socialist propaganda increased many times over during early 1878. Il Nettuno achieved a wider circulation (before its demise in April). A number of manifestoes were also published and distributed

148

throughout the region, especially around March 18, when the Paris Commune was traditionally commemorated.[79] The Romagnol sections multiplied and the number of their affiliates grew steadily.[80]

Unfortunately the reinvigoration of the anarchist nuclei occurred at the expense of the Consociazione. The inevitable result was a deterioration of relations. While the two parties never got along well, a truce had been called in August, 1874, when both were attacked by a common enemy, the police. The peace was maintained through the Bologna trial two years later. At the trial itself the republicans were supportive; by defending Costa and his co-conspirators the Mazzinians hoped to discredit the government. But the situation returned to normal after the anarchists were acquitted and resumed their propaganda. Animosity in 1876 was directed especially at Costa, who waged a fierce anti-Mazzinian campaign in Il Martello and vehemently opposed a republican-supported expedition against the Turks in Serbia. The upshot was a duel between the Imolese and Luigi Lodi, a Mazzinian from Saraceno.[81] The A.R.U. was clearly losing out to its more dynamic rivals. ("Why do they laugh at the mention of the republic," Fratti lamented after the San Lupo insurrection, "and die for the International?"[82]) The reaction following the San Lupo revolt momentarily calmed the situation as the anarchist menace subsided and the Consociazione made a little progress. By 1878 open conflict flared up again, as Francolini's work threatened to wipe out the recent Mazzinian gains.

The first sign of trouble appeared in Cesena. On August 31 of the previous year the local subprefect observed that no Internationalist section existed in his city,[83] but by the beginning of 1878 the nucleus had been reconstructed. Moreover, the local anarchists now outnumbered the republicans.[84] The Mazzinian reaction was quick in coming. On March 24, members of the two parties clashed in the streets. Among the participants were the anarchists Francesco Bellavista and Gallo Galli (the secretary of the local section), who were arrested shortly afterwards.[85] The tumult "kept the city in a state of agitation for several days," and it was only at the end of April that the situation improved noticeably.[86]

Another trouble spot was Forlimpopoli, where the section was led by twenty-two-year-old Vittorino Valbonesi.[87] though thoroughly bourgeois in background (his father was a doctor), the young student was a rabid disseminator of anarchist principles. His zeal earned him the hatred of the local republicans, who because of their superior numbers tended to ride roughshod over the small anarchist nucleus,[88] and on the night of September 4 they made an attempt on his life. Valbonesi was shot and came very close to death but he managed to return the fire and wound one of his would-be assassins.[89]

Two days later Emilio Biggi, the capo-squadra in Morciano, a small village near Rimini, was on the verge of fighting a duel with his republican counterpart, who felt that the anarchist had gone too far in his recruiting efforts. Only the intervention of Cajo Zavoli and other party notables from the surrounding area prevented bloodshed.[90] In the following month the Republic of San Marino was the site of a duel between Bellavista and a Mazzinian opponent.[91] But by this time the Internationalists were faced with a far greater menace than interparty strife --that posed by the government.

In fact, the repression which had been initiated throughout the country after the failure of San Lupo had abated only slightly during the course of 1878. The police were spurred on in their efforts by the fear that another insurrection was imminent. These suspicions were fully justified. Despite the absence of their leaders, who were in exile or in prison (Malatesta and Cafiero were not released until August 25 of that year), the anarchists were determined to try again. The instigator of the new attempt, according to the police, was Costa, who began to encourage preparations for the uprising immediately after San Lupo.[92] The insurrection was originally scheduled to take place in February, 1878.[93] But the reorganization of the Italian sections, which was to precede the rebellion, took place more slowly than expected. The result was postponement. Apparently this project was one of the topics of discussion at the Forlì reunion in January. Returning to Imola from the meeting, Castellari informed his comrades that the revolt would take place in the spring, not February, and that Costa had promised that the sections in Imola, Rimini, Jesi, and Tuscany would be well-armed with bombs, revolvers, and good carbines.[94]

During the weeks following the Forlì gathering a great deal of activity was noted in the Romagna. What Castellari had related seemed to be confirmed. When a cache of bombs was found in Leghorn on February 18,[95]

150

the police were sure that something was up and acted
without hesitation. Arrests were made throughout the
country and increased after March 18, when revolutionary proclamations were posted in all the major anarchist centers. Among those taken into custody were
Valducci, who was caught putting up manifestoes in Cesena on the 17th,[96] and Giuseppe Santandrea from Ravenna,
who had been hard at work throughout the Romagna during the two preceding months.[97] It was also in March
that Costa was arrested in Paris--as he was about to
return to Italy.[98]

The plans for revolution were not totally abandoned. On April 11-12 the Fourth Congress of the Italian
Federation was convened secretly at Pisa. Among the
thirteen representatives were Covelli, Natta, and Pezzi,
now directors of the party in the absence of Costa, Cafiero, and Malatesta. There were no Romagnols present.[99]
The most important decision made at Pisa, though for obvious reasons official accounts of the meeting failed
to mention it, was to carry through with the revolt.[100]
The date set, according to the authorities, was May 1,
when armed bands would converge on Bologna, Carrara,
Perugia, and Pisa.[101]

The anarchist movement was thoroughly infiltrated
with informers; the authorities were aware of the conspirators' plan almost at once. The police offensive
that followed insured that the International would remain inert during the next few months. The victims
during this period included some of the Federation's
most illustrious members, among them Arturo Ceretti,
brother of Celso and editor of L'Avvenire (Modena),
and two members of the association's Commission of Correspondence (which had been transferred from Florence to
Genoa at the Pisa Congress), Covelli and Matteucci.[102]
So intense was the persecution that when the leaders of
the San Lupo expedition were released in August (they
had been granted amnesty for their political offenses
earlier in the year but were then tried as common criminals and found not guilty), they chose to go abroad
rather than remain in the country. Malatesta left for
Egypt, Cafiero for France.

The progress that had been made in the Romagna
earlier in the year was also obliterated during these
months. One of the first casualties of the new drive
was Il Nettuno, which published its last number on
April 14. A multitude of arrests followed. The victims

included Galli, Epaminonda Battistini, Pompeo Brunelli, and Cajo Zavoli.[103] Only Francolini's prominence in the community saved him from a similar fate.

By September the Internationalists throughout the peninsula were desperate. On the verge of being completely liquidated they determined to make one last attempt to break out of their impotence. "We absolutely have to rise," Matteucci wrote Kuliscioff at this time, "because if we do not comply with this deliberation of the Pisa Congress the results will be discouragement and loss of respect, as has happened to the republican party which always promised to make a revolution but has never done anything."[104]

Beginning late in the month the police noticed an unusual amount of activity in the Romagna.[105] This movement within and between cities continued all through October. The apparent scope of this agitation was the convocation of a secret Internationalist reunion held in Forlì on November 6. The delegates included all the Romagnol chieftains who had managed to evade prison and a few representatives, like Vincenzo Matteuzzi of Ancona, from outside the region as well.[106] Similar meetings were being held concurrently at Naples, Trani, and Foggia. All had the same objective--the preparation of a revolution which would break out simultaneously throughout the country.[107] The insurrection was scheduled for the spring of 1879.[108]

The enterprise did not get very far, however. On November 17, a few days after the Forlì reunion, King Umberto I was attacked by a deranged fanatic, Giovanni Passanante, while on a royal tour in Naples. The assassination failed, but the impression it made on the country was prodigious. Public opinion was further outraged the following day when a Florentine demonstration on behalf of the monarch was disrupted by a bomb explosion.[109] These two incidents, the attempt on the king's life and the bombing of Via Nazionale, initiated a campaign which completely destroyed the International in Italy.

The police had been waiting for an excuse to move against the anarchists in a decisive way. Now they had it. Prior to this time, it is true, their campaign against the subversives had encountered considerable success. The inability of the anarchists to take the field demonstrated this. But the courts had not backed these efforts up. Almost all the trials against the anarchists up to now had resulted in acquittals. That of the San Lupo insurgents in August was only the latest and most clamorous example. Unable to depend on the judiciary, the police felt that only an all-out offensive against the anarchists could deal effectively with them. The problem was public opinion. Would martial law, even against a tiny minority, be tolerated? The police doubted it.

But now, in November, 1878, the situation changed drastically. Although Passanante was not a member of the Federation and the bomb thrown in Florence had not been its work, the International was blamed for both deeds. In order to appreciate this reaction it is important to understand what was happening to the socialist movement in Europe during this time. By 1878 many socialists, unable to obtain their ends in any other way, had turned to terrorism. This was particularly true in Russia, where the frustration was most evident. A recent case in point there had been Zasulic's attempt on General Trepov in January. But assassination also became a weapon to fight social injustice elsewhere. During the year efforts had already been made to execute Kaiser Wilhelm I, on May 11 and June 2, and the Spanish King, on October 25. Under these circumstances it is easy to see why the middle-class reaction to Passassante's attempt was directed towards the International, which represented the socialist movement in the country, and why--encouraged by the authorities--that reaction became so intense.

The drive which began in November, immediately after the threat to King Umberto's life, was entirely unprecedented. Wholesale arrests took place in every region of the peninsula. Little attention was paid to civil liberties. Given a free hand, the police were intent on taking full advantage of it. The operation was a huge success. When in January, 1879, the Minister of Interior issued a secret circular to all the prefects of the realm instructing them to wipe out the International, the operation was virtually completed. The Italian Federation was in shambles, and its leadership was either in jail or exile. The region hardest hit was Tuscany, now the major stronghold of the Italian International, where the reactionary wave had been anticipated in October. Among the first victims were Kuliscioff (recently arrived from Lugano), Natta, and Luigia Minguzzi, who were taken into custody in the Tuscan capital on the

153

ANDREA COSTA
Biblioteca Comunale di Imola

third. They were joined in prison a week later by Pezzi.
Florence and the other anarchist centers of Tuscany were
the scenes of scores of other arrests during the following weeks. By the end of the year the anarchist movement in the region was almost nonexistent.[110] Close behind was the Romagna, where the party was destroyed in
a matter of days. In November Imola alone witnessed
forty arrests.[111] Nearly every anarchist head in Bologna and the Romagna (save Ravenna, where the authorities
were inexplicably lenient) was put behind bars between
then and May of the following year.

The spiritual crisis Costa had been experiencing
since the time of the San Lupo insurrection matured
completely during his incarceration in Paris in early
1879. Prison weighed heavily on him, and he became increasingly discouraged as the time passed slowly by.[112]
His depression was understandable. Looking around he
saw the anarchist movement in total disarray. Its directors were in prison--as was his beloved Anna--or in
exile. Inevitably he began to examine the results with
a critical eye. The product of this soul-searching was
the confirmation of a suspicion that the path to the
creation of a better world lay in working through the
system, with all of its defects, instead of destroying
it. The old attitude of all or nothing, so characteristic of the anarchist, had been superseded. This train
of thought was clearly expressed in a letter written in
late May to Serafino Mazzotti, who continued to reside
in Lugano under the alias Filippo Boschiero. Once this
period of reaction ended and the monarchy in Italy weakened, Costa observed in the letter, it would be possible
for the party to do something constructive. But he
feared that the Bakuninists would not be able to take
advantage of the opportunity "because of our contempt for
everyday affairs, because of our self-imposed isolation
..., because of our practical incapacity, and finally
because no one knows us...." These shortcomings had to
be corrected. "You can be sure of it, dear Filippo,"
he concluded, "...I want to remedy this /situation/ however I can, and I propose to begin as soon as I come
out. Perhaps I will be at odds with some of our friends,
but what can be done about it? In any case, willing or
not, we will move toward the same goal."[113] Here, then,
was the first clear indication of Costa's famous svolta
("turn"). A public announcement of this change would
not be long in coming.

In June, 1879, Jules Grévy, who had recently suc-

ceeded MacMahon as President of the French Republic,
declared a general political amnesty. One of the beneficiaries was Costa, who was released on the fifth and
left immediately for Switzerland. He traveled to Geneva,
then to Lugano, where he remained, hosted by the Mazzot-
tis, until December. On July 13, the date of his arrival
in the Ticinese city, the Imolese was honored at a banquet
given by his numerous friends there.[114] Among the participants, significantly, were Costa's old opponents, Bignami and Malon, who had been given advance notice of his
new point of view.

The next few days were spent composing an open letter addressed "To my Friends of the Romagna," in which
Costa's conversion to a legalitarian and reformist position was formally proclaimed. The declaration, signed
on July 27 and published in La Plebe on August 3, 1879,
is one of the most famous documents in the history of
the Italian socialist movement. It is in order to examine this letter in some detail.[115]

Costa began by explaining that although he did not
want to deny the past, he was not altogether satisfied
with the results which the International had obtained
in Italy up to that time. While the anarchists had accomplished much, there was also much that they had left
undone. The experience of the last few years had made
it apparent that socialist activity must branch out in
different directions. The movement needed reorientation.
"When one does not move forward," the Romagnol warned,
"one necessarily falls back...."

Why had the Federation not prevailed? Because,
Costa argued, its members had been too dependent on
conspiratorial and insurrectional methods; they had not
relied sufficiently on the common people. Divorcing
themselves from the masses, they had lost sight of reality. "We isolated ourselves excessively," he said, "and
we preoccupied ourselves much more with the logic of our
own ideas and the formation of a revolutionary program
which we endeavored to carry out without delay, rather
than with the study of the economic and moral conditions
of the people and their heartfelt and immediate needs.
Thus we inevitably overlooked many manifestations of
life. We did not become involved with the people...."
Not realizing that "the narrow program of some of us
could not be the program of all of us," Internationalists had plotted insurrection, he continued in a pointed
reference to the San Lupo fiasco, without adequately cul-

tivating popular support. They had forgotten that revolution was a serious matter, "not an affair of a day or a year."

Having diagnosed the illness, Costa proposed the cure, which he was convinced was to be found in a return to the masses. "Let us profit from the lessons of experience," he urged. "Let us now accomplish that which was left incomplete. Let us go back to the people and draw our strength from them once more...."

Re-establishing contact with the common man would enable the socialists to reach him with their ideas. At the base of this education would be the program of the old International. But the Romagnol agitator went on to say that it was its means rather than its end which had to be emphasized. The ultimate goal--which he characterized as "anarchic communism"--was too uncertain, too far in the future to stir the masses effectively. The next steps, he insisted, should be the collectivization of property in the economic sphere and the federation of autonomous communes in the political one.

Costa's program as outlined in this letter hardly appears to be a radical departure from the past. Nevertheless a significant change had occurred in his thinking. In fact, one senses this in the very tone of the appeal. In contrast to his earlier writings, Costa now seemed conciliatory. Nowhere in this communication, for example, does one find the strong anti-statist declarations so typical of anarchism, as well as of the Romagnol theretofore. Certainly Costa was leaning toward reform rather than revolution. While careful not to mention immediate reforms in his letter, he strongly implied that he was more than ready to accept at least some of them. Reforms, he affirmed, were wanted by "a great part of the Italian people." Costa's demand that the socialists rededicate their energies to meeting the people's needs made quite clear, of course, his acceptance of these measures.[116]

The cause of the svolta, an event which had a weighty impact on the working-class movement in Italy, has been the topic of a good deal of historical controversy though even now, almost a hundred years later, its roots remain a matter of pure conjecture. Perhaps the most popular explanation of Costa's conversion, and one which all his biographers accept, is the influence exerted by Anna Kuliscioff.[117] This view, however, is highly problematical. Unfortunately the Russian woman's ideas during the eventful years 1877-78 are not documented at all.[118] On what, then, is this theory based? Eduard Bernstein later recounted that he had been in Lugano in 1879 when news of Costa's svolta arrived, and on that occasion he heard Cafiero attribute the transformation to Kuliscioff.[119] This is the only concrete evidence that has been found to support the thesis. It should be remembered, though, that Bernstein reported the event to Gustavo Sacerdote in 1901, and he in turn wrote it down twenty-five years later. Under these circumstances it is entirely possible that the anecdote might not be completely reliable.[120] Even accepting the story in all its particulars, moreover, it must still be admitted that the conclusion was only Cafiero's opinion. On the other hand, as we will see later, it is clear that in many respects Costa's thinking was more advanced than that of his Slavic companion, a fact which suggests, as Kropotkin contended, that rather than being swayed by Kuliscioff, it was the Romagnol who moved her.[121]

The sources of Costa's inspiration must be found elsewhere, in his intercourse with the legalitarians in Italy and abroad perhaps. Guesde, the founder of the French Socialist Party later but already a staunch Marxist during the mid-1870's, is one distinct possibility. Both Costa and Kropotkin later recalled that while in Paris they had worked with the French leader, who, as the Russian remembered, was much less inflexible then than he was later to become.[122] It should also be noted that at the time of his arrest Costa was found with Nabruzzi and Zanardelli, both of whom would soon return to the anarchist fold but in 1878 were still avowed enemies of the Bakuninists.[123] Once in prison, moreover, the Imolese established relations through Mazzotti, who apparently leaned toward a reformist position himself, with Malon.[124] All of these contacts provided the opportunity for a reconciliation of views.

Still, the determining factor in Costa's svolta was not the pressure exerted by people, as important as that may have been, but rather events. The socialist leader's ideas must be seen in relation to the environment. Every attempt at insurrection had been a farce. Why? Because the bourgeois regimes were too powerful to be toppled. This had become abundantly clear by 1879. In the throes of a conservative backlash, the International had been rendered impotent. His own imprisonment epitomized the

158

fate of the entire organization. To continue along the same paths, it became evident to Costa in the solitude of his cell, was tantamount to suicide. Later he admitted as much: "...the meager success which we achieved with our attempts at insurrection forced us to abandon our revolutionary absolutism."[125] Necessity (not people) dictated a new direction. The Imolese became the instrument of this change.

Conclusion

How profound was Costa's _svolta_? To what extent did his thinking really change in 1879? The answer, I think, is that the Romagnol's "conversion" did not represent a complete _volte-face_. He did not begin as a convinced apostle of revolution, nor did he arrive at conclusions which were typically legalitarian.

Some historians have viewed the _svolta_ as a sudden turn taken only after imprisonment in France. "When Costa entered jail to serve his sentence," one of them has written, "...there was still no sign whatsoever of an orientation toward new positions."[126] On the surface this would appear to be true.[127] But the anarchist leader's initial failure to endorse the San Lupo affair suggests that he was not totally sold on the idea of insurrection even then. Moreover, if the essence of Costa's conversion lay in his rejection of violence as the _only_ means of emancipating the worker, the change had certainly begun by early 1877, judging from the communication written to Nicotera. The posture adopted two years later, then, was not entirely original.

How far did Costa go in accepting the reformist thesis? The letter "To my Friends of the Romagna" provides an answer, though not a complete one. In this declaration Costa rejected conspiracy but not revolution. Like the Legalitarians, he maintained that all means, reformist and revolutionary, were to be employed in creating an anarchist utopia. Unlike Malon and his group, however, the Romagnol stressed revolution; reforms, he insisted, created a revolutionary mentality. Disillusioned with small gains the worker would turn to insurrection--ultimately the only effective means of changing society. His position consequently differed notably from that of his new comrades, who emphasized reform and considered it an end in itself.

Most Italian historians take Costa at his word and see him as eminently revolutionary.[128] This point of view is untenable. The Imolese's position, as Professor Hostetter has aptly pointed out, was theoretically inconsistent.[129] To expect to ameliorate the lot of the workers and to make them insurrectionaries at the same time was absurd. A choice had to be made: either revolution or reform, but not both. I think Costa realized this too, and in practice opted for the latter, as his subsequent career amply demonstrates.

But why then did Costa champion revolt in his letter? Very likely he had no choice in the matter. He was not interested in writing a theoretical tract on socialism; his aim was to rally his comrades in the Romagna and to create a strong movement there based on his new ideas.[130] He had to move cautiously. The anarchist experience was too recent and too deeply entrenched, especially in that region, to be abandoned with ease. Costa's own propaganda had made sure of that. Still his espousal of violence was not dictated entirely by expediency. In fact, he would continue to voice revolutionary slogans throughout his life, at times when he had more to lose than to gain by it. The revolution had become a necessary myth in Costa's eyes.[131] The inevitable result of an exclusive reliance on reform would be crass materialism and stagnation. "You will admit," Costa had once argued with Bignami, "that there has to be someone who holds the flag of idealism high in an absolute and most intransigent way. Arrangements, conciliations, if possible, if necessary, will come. They will be made by history: the logical, natural development of things. Indeed, in order to give rise to this step forward, there has to be someone who wants all, demands all, pretends all."[132] Exploiting the threat of violence, he chose to play this role.

A final observation should be made at this point. The death of anarchism as the dominant socialist ideology in Italy did not arise from Costa's _svolta_. This development, as we have seen, began some time previously. By 1879 virtually all the Internationalists in both Lombardy and Sicily, and a good many nuclei in other regions as well, had been won over to the anti-Bakuninist position. The real pioneers of this trend were the Legalitarians. Costa's conversion came at the end rather than at the beginning of this evolutionary process.

And yet, despite the qualification, the significance

of the _svolta_ should not be underestimated. Neither
Bignami nor Gnocchi-Viani had been included in the inner
councils of the Italian Federation. The Romagnol, on
the other hand, was one of its most prestigious members,
and possibly its dominant figure. His defection had a
much greater impact than those of his predecessors.
Furthermore, it is necessary to remember that despite
their progress the Legalitarians continued to be in the
minority. The strength of Costa's later opposition
from his ex-comrades demonstrates the vast extent to
which anarchist notions had penetrated the peninsula.
Only in 1879, when Costa made his new views known, did
the balance begin to tip in the Marxists' favor. It
was only then that reformist ideas began to make an impression in the citadels of the old International, the
Romagna and Tuscany. Costa's _svolta_ represented the
turning point in the evolution from anarchism to socialism in Italy.

NOTES

[1]The paper during this early period is the subject
of Enzo Santarelli, "Una fonte per la storia del movimento operaio marchegiano: Il Martello di Fabriano-Jesi,"
Movimento operaio, 5 (1953), 817-24.

[2]Several authors (e.g., Lipparini and Orano) have
written that Costa edited a paper called Il Martello
in early 1874. Apparently they got this information
from Romeo Galli's biography of Costa in Andrea Costa:
episodi e ricordi (Milan: Sassu, 1910), p. 17. I have
not been able to verify this fact; I suspect it was an
error on Galli's part.

[3]The band came to an end in 1874 when Giovanni Resta turned state's evidence and a Bologna court gave ten
accoltellatori life sentences. Resta, who was paid well
for his service, left immediately for France and never
returned to the Romagna. The whole episode is covered
in Dursi, "Il Terrore a Ravenna." Nicotera's identification of the Romagnol anarchists with the accoltellatori
was obviously unfair. Still, it must be admitted that
the International in the region had its share of criminal
elements. A prime example is Cajo Zavoli, the most renowned of the section leaders in Rimini, who was arrested
in mid-1874 for beating his mistress (subprefect of Rimini to the prefect of Forlì, June 13, 1874, A.S.F., Gab.
Pref., vol. 59, fasc. 83), and a few years before had
run the risk of being beaten by his own coreligionists
for "indelicacies" he had committed (police report to
the prefect of Forlì, Nov. 28, 1874, A.S.F., Gab. Pref.,
vol. 64, fasc. 37). It seems his reputation was no better among the anarchists outside of Rimini; according to
Monticelli, Cajo Zavoli "counted for little politically
and morally." See La Tribuna (Rome), Jan. 22, 1910.
His brother Bruto, another head of the Rimini nucleus,
was described by the subprefect of that city in late
1873 as "ignorant, evil, lazy, and vain," and judged to
be even worse than Cajo--who was only "lazy and vagrant."
See "biografie di individui appartenenti ai partiti os-
tili al governo," n.d., A.S.F., Gab. Pref., vol. 55,
fasc. 243.

[4]Reproduced in Romano, Storia, III, 371-88.

[5]The article made a big impression on the Jura Swiss, who translated and reproduced it in Bulletin de la Fédération Jurassienne, Dec. 10, 1876.

[6]By this time the Ceresio section had disintegrated almost completely. On Nov. 26, 1876, Il Martello had reported that its existence "has become problematical by this time."

[7]Ibid., Feb. 10, 1877.

[8]Ibid., Feb. 17, 1877.

[9]Ibid., Mar. 18, 1877.

[10]Ibid., Feb. 17, 1877.

[11]Compte-rendu in La Federazione Italiana, pp. 152-94. Il Martello, Feb. 24, 1877, contains a short account written by Florido Matteucci, who was a delegate to the Congress and championed the orthodox anarchist postion but withdrew in protest after the first day when it became clear that the meeting was thoroughly Legalitarian in its sympathies. See also Bulletin de la Fédération Jurassienne, Mar. 11, 1877.

[12]Il Martello, Mar. 3, 1877.

[13]Masini, Storia degli anarchici italiani, p. 108.

[14]See Della Peruta, "La banda del Matese...," pp. 265-79; Romano, Storia, III, 601-02.

[15]Perhaps Costa was thinking of this influence when he later wrote that the Bologna revolt had been "superficial in fact; profound in its significance." See letter of Sept. 17, 1897, Bologna 1874-Bologna 1897.

[16]Issues of Feb. 17 and 24, 1877.

[17]"Il socialismo italiano dall'anarchismo alla socialdemocrazia (1875-1882)," Democrazia e socialismo, p. 301.

[18]See Pier Carlo Masini, Gli internazionalisti: La Banda del Matese (1876-1878) (Milan: Avanti!, 1958).

[19]Storia degli anarchici italiani, p. 109.

[20]The Romagnols played a prominent role in the insurrection. Among the members of the expedition were Giuseppe Bennati, Luigi Castellari, Sante Celoni, Ugo Conti, Antonio Cornacchia, Francesco Ginnasi, and the Poggi brothers, Luigi and Domenico, all from Imola; Carlo Gualandi from Dozza (near Imola); Domenico Bezzi from Ravenna; Giovanni Bianchini from Rimini; and Domenico Ceccarelli, Pietro's brother, from Savignano. Two Bolognesi also participated, Ariodante Facchini and Uberto Lazzari. Another Bolognese, Silvio Frugieri, and a Romagnol, Pietro Gagliardi of Imola, were arrested before they could reach San Lupo. Bennati, Castellari, Conti, Cornacchi, Gagliardi, Facchini, and Frugieri had all been defendants at the trials stemming from the 1874 revolt.

[21]See his open letter, published as a pamphlet, Ai miei amici ed ai miei avversari (Cesena: Tip. Nazionale, 1881).

[22]Ibid.

[23]Armed bands were being formed in Faenza, Forlì, Imola, and Lugo, according to the Minister of Interior on Mar. 6, 1877, and these were to converge on Bologna during the coming insurrection. See note to prefect of Forlì, A.S.F., Gab. Pref., vol. 79, fasc. 357/6.

[24]Avanti!, Jan. 20, 1910.

[25]Costa, Bagliori di socialismo, p. 26.

[26]Lipparini, "Cronologia," p. 188.

[27]Costa had been hiding out at this address for months, according to Angelo Berardi, an anarchist who had been active in the 1874 insurrection. Berardi also recalled that during this period he would receive his friend's mail and, being a shoemaker, would have it delivered to the Imolese inside a pair of boots every day, right under the police's nose. These recollections are quoted in Rino Alessi, "Un internazionalista," Avanti!, Jan. 30, 1910.

[28]Monticelli, Avanti!, Jan. 20, 1910.

[29]See Il Povero, Aug. 26, 1877.

[30]Issue of Apr. 29, 1877. The previous number of the

paper, Apr. 22, carries an unsigned correspondence, dated Apr. 14, which describes the San Lupo insurrection. This too belongs to Costa. See Guillaume, **L'Internationale**, IV (Paris: Stock, 1910), 184.

[31]Lipparini, "Cronologia," p. 188.

[32]Guillaume, **L'Internationale**, IV, 190. For Brousse, whose career closely paralleled that of Costa, see Marc Vuilleumier, "Paul Brousse et son passage de l'anarchisme au socialisme," **Cahiers Vilfredo Pareto**, Nos. 7-8 (1965), pp. 63-80; David Stafford, **From Anarchism to Reformism: A Study of the Political Activities of Paul Brousse within the First International and the French Socialist Movement, 1870-90** (Toronto: Univ. of Toronto Press, 1971).

[33]See letters from Celso Ceretti to Costa, July 23, 1877, and Costa to Paolo Valera, Sept. 15, 1902, B.C.I. nos. 18, 3068. Ceretti's correspondence is quoted in Schiavi, **Andrea Costa**, p. 99, and reproduced--as "previously unpublished"--in Masini, **Storia degli anarchici italiani**, pp. 302-04.

[34]Guillaume, **L'Internationale**, IV, 209. Guillaume (IV, 85) reports that an Italian-speaking group had been formed in Neuchâtel on Sept. 28, 1876.

[35]**Bulletin de la Fédération Jurassienne**, June 17, 1877.

[36]Raffaele Pilota to Costa, Aug. 27, 1877, B.C.I., no. 29.

[37]A letter from Malatesta to Costa, June 22, 1877, B.C.I., no. 16, contains a minute of a note from Costa (to Malatesta?) in which he offers this information. The minute was undated, but in it Costa informs his correspondent that Violetta Dall'Alpi had just made him, Costa, a father. The baby boy, also named Andrea, was born in Bologna on Aug. 5, so the minute was written in mid-August.

[38]Lipparini, **Andrea Costa**, p. 115. Costa's biographer, however, may be mistaken in citing this place or date, or both. On May 21, 1878, while in prison in France, Costa wrote Mazzotti, still living in Lugano, asking him to accept Kuliscioff into his home (B.C.I., no. 34). From the letter it is clear that the Faentino had never met the Russian woman before. Apparently she

had not been in the Swiss city at the same time as Mazzotti. This leads me to believe that Costa did not meet Kuliscioff at Lugano after all, at least not in August, 1877. The most recent biography of the woman revolutionary is that of Antonio Pala, Anna Kuliscioff (Milan: Librimarket, 1973), which is rather superficial and contains a multitude of mistakes. A better work, though uneven, is Alessandro Schiavi, Anna Kuliscioff (Rome: Opere Nuove, 1955). See also Claire LaVigna, "Anna Kuliscioff: From Russian Populism to Italian Reformism (1873-1913)," Diss. Univ. of Rochester 1971.

[39]For Kuliscioff's life in her native country, see Franco Venturi, "Anna Kuliscioff e la sua attività rivoluzionaria in Russia," Movimento operaio, 4 (1952), 277-86. Other information is contained in the same author's Il popolismo russo, 2nd ed., 3 vols. (Turin: Einaudi, 1972).

[40]Alessandro Schiavi, "Anna Kuliscioff e Andrea Costa (da lettere inedite)," Nuova antologia, 82 (Oct., 1947), 109.

[41]See the Bulletin de la Fédération Jurassienne, Aug. 12, 1877.

[42]Accounts of the Congresses of Verviers and Ghent are given in Bulletin de la Fédération Jurassienne, Sept. 23, 1877. Guillaume, one of the participants, describes the conflict at Verviers in L'Internationale, IV, 260-61.

[43]For Costa's speech, see L'Anarchia (Naples), Oct. 6, 1877; reproduced in Romano, Storia, III, 421-31.

[44]It appears that he had been won over to this view for several months. "Propaganda of the Idea" had been the theme of his speech in Geneva on June 9. See anonymous correspondence /but Jules Montels/ to Bulletin de la Fédération Jurassienne, June 17, 1877.

[45]Other Marxist-oriented papers abroad which supported Guesde were Vorwärts in Leipzig and Herman Greulich's Tagwacht in Zurich.

[46]And also by the fact that Costa had been delegated to represent the San Lupo insurgents, then in prison, at both Verviers and Ghent. See their letter in Bulletin de la Fédération Jurassienne, Sept. 9, 1877.

[47] Romano, _Storia_, II, 610; Masini, _Storia degli anarchici italiani_, p. 130.

[48] _L'Anarchia_, Oct. 6, 1877.

[49] Costa's speech at Ghent in _L'Anarchia_ (now in Florence), Oct. 28, 1877; reproduced in Romano, _Storia_, III, 433-40.

[50] This letter was quoted at Costa's trial in Paris in 1878, an account of which appears in _L'Egalité_, May 12, 1878, and is reproduced in Gianni Bosio and Franco Della Peruta, "La 'svolta' di A. Costa, con documenti sul soggiorno in Francia," _Movimento operaio_, 4 (1952), 298-307.

[51] Lipparini, "Cronologia," p. 189.

[52] _Questore_ of Bologna to his prefect, Dec. 4, 1877, A.S.B., _Gab. Pref._, vol. 125. This information had been obtained from an informer who kept the police abreast of the contents of Costa's letters to Violetta dall'Alpi. Costa was thoroughly disgusted with the French socialists when he first arrived; as far as he was concerned their efforts at organization were not energetic enough. See his correspondence to _L'Anarchia_, Oct. 21, 1877; quoted, in part, in Della Peruta, "Il socialismo italiano...," pp. 319-20.

[53] _Questore_ of Bologna to his prefect, Nov. 29, 1877, A.S.B., _Gab. Pref._, vol. 125.

[54] Lipparini, "Cronologia," p. 189.

[55] _La Stella d'Italia_ (Bologna), Mar. 1, 1878.

[56] Note from the prefect of Paris to the French Minister of Interior, July 17, 1878, A.P.P.P., carton 29.

[57] _Memoirs of a Revolutionist_ (1899; rpt. Boston: Houghton Mifflin, 1930), p. 406.

[58] Costa letter to Mazzotti, Apr. 14, 1878, B.C.I., no. 31. Upon his return to Italy Costa intended to publish a socialist newspaper which would have national circulation. See anonymous letter from Naples to Costa, n.d. /but Mar., 1878/, A.P.P.P., carton 1475.

[59] _L'Egalité_, May 12, 1878. Costa's version of the trial is contained in a letter he wrote on June 7 to

Aristide Venturini, one of the republican lawyers who had defended him two years before. The correspondence is published in La Stella d'Italia, June 15, 1878, and L'Avvenire (Modena), June 29, 1878.

[60]It should be said, however, that the reorganization that had taken place was not very far along. According to Costa, in a report he submitted at Neuchâtel in June, 1877, there were 1342 Internationalists in the Romagna and Emilia on the eve of the San Lupo insurrection (Minister of Interior to the prefect of Forlì, June 15, 1877, A.S.F., Gab. Pref., vol. 79, fasc. 357/6). The breakdown by section: Bologna, 120; Imola, 200; Forlì, 250; Ravenna, 450; Cesena, 80; Rimini 50; Forlimpopoli, 70; Faenza, 22; Meldola, 10; Sant'Arcangelo, 20; Mirandola, 30; Reggio Emilia, 30; and Modena, 25. Two years before there had been over 2000 members in the Romagna alone!

[61]On Aug. 13, 1877, the prefect of Ravenna informed the prefect of Forlì that Costa had recently sent Claudio Zirardini and other leaders in the Romagna a letter urging them to organize and hold a regional congress (A.S.F., Gab. Pref., vol. 78, fasc. 357/3).

[62]Faggioli was at one such meeting at Rimini on July 30, 1877. See Minister of Interior to the prefect of Forlì, A.S.F., Gab. Pref., vol. 78, fasc. 357/3.

[63]The letter was read by Augusto Ghetti, a Bolognese. See Minister of Interior to the prefect of Forlì, Oct. 1, 1877, A.S.F., Gab. Pref., vol. 78, fasc. 357/3. Asked to verify this information, the subprefect of Cesena said that the anarchists did indeed gain in his city, though not at the republicans' expense. See report to the prefect of Forlì, Oct. 20, 1877, A.S.F., Gab. Pref., vol. 78, 357/3. The subprefect of Rimini, on the other hand, admitted that the International did make gains in other Romagnol cities, especially Imola, but he opined that this was improbable in Rimini. See report to the prefect of Forlì, Oct. 10, 1877, A.S.F., Gab. Pref., vol. 78, fasc. 357/3.

[64]Minister of Interior to the prefect of Forlì, Oct. 20, 1877, A.S.F., Gab. Pref., vol. 78, fasc. 357/5. Altogether the Imolese represented 35 different Italian sections at Verviers. See Minister of Interior to the prefect of Forlì, Oct. 6, 1877, A.S.F., Gab. Pref., vol. 78, fasc. 357/5.

[65]Minister of Interior to the prefect of Forlì, Jan. 3, 1878, A.S.F., Gab. Pref., vol. 78, fasc. 357/3. The organizers of the reunion were Cappellini, Fortuzzi, Silvagni, and Napoleone Ugolini, according to the Minister. See note to the prefect of Forlì, Dec. 30, 1877, A.S.F., Gab. Pref., vol. 78, fasc. 357/3. The Minister was well-informed; his estimate that there would be about 30 sections represented at Forlì was very accurate.

[66]A.S.F., Gab. Pref., vol. 78, fasc. 357/3. The prefect was told that Aristide Bezzi of Cesena had been arrested and the meeting broken up before it began. Among other delegates there, according to the note, were Epaminonda Battistini and Carlo Aventi of Cesena, Castellari ("ex-secretary of the well-known Andrea Costa") and Angelo Negri of Imola, and Domenico Francolini of Rimini.

[67]Issue of Jan. 15, 1878. The account is reproduced in La Federazione Italiana, pp. 197-99.

[68]Castellari and Solieri formed the Commission of Correspondence, which remained in Imola. See Minister of Interior to the prefect of Forlì, Jan. 24, 1878, A.S.F., Gab. Pref., vol. 78, fasc. 357/3.

[69]Valuable biographical information is contained in Renato Zangheri, "Il Nettuno (1873-1877) e il suo direttore Domenico Francolini," Studi riminesi e bibliografici in onore di Carlo Lucchesi (Faenza: Fratelli Lega, 1952), pp. 227-56.

[70]Antonio Baldini, Italia di buonincontro (Florence: Sansoni, 1940), p. 30.

[71]Zangheri, "Il Nettuno...e il suo direttore," p. 236. Among the papers confiscated at Francolini's house immediately after his arrest in August, 1874, was a copy of Costa's first Revolutionary Bulletin. See Procedimento Saffi.

[72]A copy of this manifesto was sent to the Minister of Interior by the prefect of Forlì on Mar. 19, 1877 (A.S.F., Gab. Pref., vol. 79, fasc. 357/6).

[73]Subprefect of Rimini to the prefect of Forlì, Jan. 4, 1878, A.S.F., Gab. Pref., vol. 72, fasc. 99.

[74]Note to prefect of Forlì, Feb. 22, 1878, A.S.F.,

Gab. Pref., vol. 78, fasc. 357/3.

[75]Bagli, as well as Francolini, was included in a list of the most influential republicans in Rimini compiled by the city's subprefect on Feb. 15, 1876 (A.S.F., Gab. Pref., vol. 72, fasc. 97).

[76]Subprefect of Cesena to the prefect of Forlì, June 16, 1878, A.S.F., Gab. Pref., vol. 78, fasc. 357/4.

[77]Subprefect of Rimini to the prefect of Forlì, Nov. 11, 1878, A.S.F., Gab. Pref., vol. 78, fasc. 357/2.

[78]Report to prefect of Forlì, Aug. 28, 1878, A.S.F., Gab. Pref., vol. 77, fasc. 357/1.

[79]These manifestoes appeared throughout the year. Among the proclamations published for March 18 was one that the federation in Ravenna had posted throughout the Romagna. Vehemently anti-legalitarian and anti-republican, it is reproduced in La Federazione Italiana, pp. 289-92. A similar manifesto was printed in Rimini on June 2 (Romano, Storia, II, 636). In August the Commission of Correspondence of the Romagnol Federation, which had now transferred its seat from Imola to Forlì (Minister of Interior to the prefect of Forlì, Mar. 6, 1878, A.S.F., Gab. Pref., vol. 78, fasc. 357/3), issued a revolutionary circular (found in La Federazione Italiana, pp. 316-20), as did the anarchist nuclei in Ravenna, on Aug. 4 and 28 (see La Federazione Italiana, pp. 312-14, 320-32), Cesena (La Federazione Italiana, pp. 314-15), and Rimini (subprefect of Cesena to the prefect of Forlì, Aug. 30, 1878, A.S.F., Gab. Pref., vol. 77, fasc. 357/1). Another wave of pronouncements occurred in October. Among these was one addressed "To our Comrades in Italy" from the socialists of Cesena (a copy of which is included in a note from the subprefect of Cesena to the prefect of Forlì, Oct. 5, 1878, A.S.F., Gab. Pref., vol. 77, fasc. 357/1) and others which appeared in the streets of Imola on Oct. 28-29 (Minister of Interior to the prefect of Forlì, Nov. 2, 1878, A.S.F., Gab. Pref., vol. 78, fasc. 357/2). The Imolese federation also sent out a declaration on Nov. 17 (La Federazione Italiana, pp. 328-31) and the section at Savignano did the same a few days later (a copy was sent to the prefect of Forlì from the prefect of Naples on Nov. 25, 1878, A.S.F., Gab. Pref., vol. 78, fasc. 357/2).

[80]A Valbonesi correspondence, dated June 12, to an

anarchist paper in Modena, L'Avvenire, no. 8, reported that new sections had just been founded in Forlimpopoli, San Leonardo, and Sant'Andrea. See Minister of Interior to the prefect of Forlì, July 3, 1878, A.S.F., Gab. Pref., vol. 78, fasc. 357/4.

[81] Adamo Mancini, La Gazzetta dell'Emilia, Jan. 21-22, 1910.

[82] La Democrazia, Apr. 14-15, 1877.

[83] Note to prefect of Forlì, A.S.F., Gab. Pref., vol. 78, fasc. 357/3.

[84] Subprefect of Cesena to prefect of Forlì, Jan. 2, 1878, A.S.F., Gab. Pref., vol. 73, fasc. 130. According to the subprefect, the anarchists were "much more numerous and bold /than the republicans/, but most of them are young and count for little."

[85] Minister of Interior to the prefect of Forlì, Apr. 3, 1878, A.S.F., Gab. Pref., vol. 78, fasc. 357/5. Galli, then only 22, joined the group in mid-1877 (subprefect of Cesena to the prefect of Forlì, July 1, 1877, A.S.F., Gab. Pref., vol. 72, fasc. 99). By the end of the year he had replaced Valducci as secretary (subprefect of Cesena to the prefect of Forlì, Dec. 17, 1877, A.S.F., Gab. Pref., vol. 78, fasc. 357/5).

[86] Subprefect of Cesena to the prefect of Forlì, July 2, 1878, A.S.F., Gab. Pref., vol. 73, fasc. 130.

[87] Gramiacci, who had been section leader before Valbonesi, was thrown out of the party in April because of his authoritarian character. See Forlimpopoli police to the prefect of Forlì, Apr. 24, 1878, A.S.F., Gab. Pref., vol. 78, fasc. 357/4. Apparently Gramiacci had caused the dissension which split the nucleus late during the preceding year, when Valbonesi and his followers threatened to break away, as Valbonesi explained, on account of the dishonest individuals in the group who had disgraced the party in the past. He refused to give names, but the local police reported that Gramiacci was part of the opposing faction (note to the prefect of Forlì, Jan. 2, 1878, A.S.F., Gab. Pref., vol. 74, fasc. 208).

[88] Forlimpopoli police to the prefect of Forlì, Jan. 2, 1878, A.S.F., Gab. Pref., vol. 78, fasc. 357/4.

[89]Forlimpopoli police to the prefect of Forlì, Jan. 28, 1879, A.S.F., Gab. Pref., vol. 84, fasc. 11.

[90]Carabinieri of Forlì to the prefect of Forlì, Sept. 12, 1878, Gab. Pref., vol. 77, fasc. 357/1.

[91]Subprefect of Cesena to the prefect of Forlì, Nov. 14, 1877, A.S.F., Gab. Pref., vol. 78, fasc. 357/3.

[92]On May 1, 1877, the Minister of Interior notified the prefect of Forlì that Costa was preparing the insurrection and had already recruited 300 men in the Romagna (A.S.F., Gab. Pref., vol. 79, fasc. 357/6).

[93]Minister of Interior to the prefect of Forlì, Nov. 17, 1877, A.S.F., Gab. Pref., vol. 78, fasc. 357/5. According to the Minister, Romeo Giulici, an anarchist from Perugia, had recently received a letter from Cesena to this effect.

[94]Prefect of Bologna to the prefect of Forlì, Jan. 14, 1878, A.S.F., Gab. Pref., vol. 78, fasc. 357/3. This information was probably correct; on June 23, 1878, Matteucci, writing from Genoa, informed Kuliscioff that they had planned an insurrection for May but had had to postpone it for a few months (he did not explain why). The letter is reproduced in Conti, Le origini del socialismo, p. 272.

[95]Bertolini, "Il socialismo contemporaneo in Italia," p. lx.

[96]Subprefect of Cesena to the prefect of Forlì, Mar. 17, 1878, A.S.F., Gab. Pref., vol. 78, fasc. 357/3.

[97]Santandrea had been in Bologna, Imola, Forlì, and Cesena "to make revolutionary propaganda" in early January. See Minister of Interior to the prefect of Forlì, Jan. 28, 1878, A.S.F., Gab. Pref., vol. 78, fasc. 357/4.

[98]According to Conti, Le origini del socialismo, p. 208, there was much talk of revolution in Tuscany in early 1878, but the news of Costa's arrest in Paris killed the project.

[99]The account contained in Il Nettuno, Apr. 14, 1878, however, indicates that among the sections represented at the meeting were those of Forlì, Faenza, Forlimpopoli,

172

Cesena, Rimini, Lugo, Imola, Sant'Arcangelo, and others which were left unnamed.

[100] Romano, Storia, II, 620. According to Angiolini, Socialismo e socialisti in Italia, p. 130, the Romagnols ratified the Pisa decisions at a meeting held in Forlì on July 14, but I have not been able to verify this fact.

[101] Minister of Interior to the prefect of Forlì, Apr. 20, 1878, A.S.F., Gab. Pref., vol. 78, fasc. 357/5.

[102] Both Covelli and Matteucci were arrested in July. See Angiolini, Socialismo e socialisti in Italia, p. 132, for other arrests made around this time.

[103] See reports from the prefect of Forlì to the prefect of Modena, Sept. 30 and Oct. 6, 1878; and the subprefect of Rimini to the prefect of Forlì, Sept. 9, 1878 (A.S.F., Gab. Pref., vol. 77, fasc. 357/2).

[104] Undated letter /but the police guessed September, 1878/, reproduced in Conti, Le origini del socialismo, p. 273.

[105] See reports to the prefect of Forlì from the police at Meldola and the subprefect of Cesena, both on Oct. 1, 1878; and from the subprefect of Rimini, Oct. 11, 1878 (A.S.F., Gab. Pref., vol. 72, fasc. 99).

[106] Prefect of Forlì to the Minister of Interior, Nov. 1878, A.S.F., Gab. Pref., vol. 78, fasc. 357/2. The gathering was evidently organized by the capi-squadra in Forlì: Fortuzzi, Cappellini, and Antonio Patrignani.

[107] Ibid. Ruggero Moravelli, an anarchist from Perugia, visited Francolini for two days in early September (carabiniere report to prefect of Forlì, Sept. 5, 1878, A.S.F., Gab. Pref., vol. 77, fasc. 357/1), and the Riminese, in turn, toured Emilia, Tuscany, and Umbria from Sept. 27 to Oct. 18 (subprefect of Rimini to prefect of Forlì, Oct. 23, 1878, A.S.F., Gab. Pref., vol. 78, fasc. 357/2). These trips were undoubtedly connected with the preparation of the regional meetings and the uprising that would follow.

[108] This schedule is confirmed in Matteucci's undated letter to Kuliscioff cited above. A report from the prefect of Forlì to the Minister of Interior in late November elaborated on the anarchist plot. Both Cafiero and

Malatesta had recently written Francolini about the insurrection. From this correspondence it appeared that the insurgents in the Romagna would move on Bologna after picking up their arms in Ravenna and Cesenatico (presumably the guns were to come in by ship). In Bologna the leading organizer of the revolt, according to the prefect, was "a certain Pascoli, a student assistant to Professor Carducci and an intimate friend of Costa." See report of Nov. 25, 1878, A.S.F., Gab. Pref., vol. 78, fasc. 357/2. Giovanni Pascoli, who succeeded Giosuè Carducci as Italy's premier poet, was indeed a friend of the Imolese and an ardent anarchist during this period.

[109]See Angiolini, Socialismo e socialisti in Italia, pp. 132-33.

[110]Conti, Le origini del socialismo, p. 228.

[111]La Stella d'Italia, Sept. 7, 1879. Among those arrested were some republicans (Luigi Xella, Decio Fantini, Pietro Mariani, and Elviro Lunati) who had published a manifesto on Nov. 21 protesting the extraordinary measures taken against the International.

[112]See his letter to Mazzotti, Apr. 7, 1879, B.C.I., no. 60; quoted in Lipparini, Andrea Costa, pp. 127-28.

[113]Letter of May 24, 1879, B.C.I., no. 63; reproduced in Bosio and Della Peruta, "La 'svolta' di A. Costa," p.310-12.

[114]Minister of Interior to the prefect of Bologna, July 18, 1879, A.S.B., Gab. Pref., vol. 125; quoted in Bosio and Della Peruta, "La 'svolta' di A. Costa," p. 293.

[115]Parts of the letter have been quoted on many occasions. The entire document is reproduced in Manacorda, Il movimento operaio italiano, pp. 357-61; Le origini del movimento operaio e contadino in Italia, ed. Alberto Pozzolini (Bologna: Zanichelli, 1971), pp. 49-54; and Gabriele De Rosa, I partiti politici in Italia (Bergamo: Minerva Italica, 1972), pp. 51-55.

[116]Something made even more explicit by Costa in La Plebe, Nov. 16, 1879.

[117]See, for example, Lipparini, Andrea Costa, p. 120.

[118]Regrettably Pala's book, <u>Anna Kuliscioff</u>, has little to say on this period.

[119]Gustavo Sacerdote, <u>Anna Kuliscioff in memoria</u>: <u>A Lei</u>, <u>agli intimi</u>, <u>a me</u>, ed. Filippo Turati (Milan: Lazzari, 1926), p. 74.

[120]In fact, another account of the same incident suggests that Bernstein had indicated Mazzotti, rather than Cafiero, in his story. See Masini, <u>Storia degli anarchici italiani</u>, p. 130.

[121]According to Leo Valiani, "Dalla prima alla seconda Internazionale (1872-1889)," <u>Movimento operaio</u>, 6 (1954), 242, who tends to accept this view himself.

[122]See <u>L'Egalité</u>, Feb. 4, 1880; <u>Memoirs of a Revolutionist</u>, p. 406. Clovis Hugues, another French socialist, once described Guesde as "Torquemada in pince-nez." See Daniel Ligou, <u>Histoire du socialisme en France (1871-1961</u>) (Paris: Presses Universitaires de France, 1962), pp. 64-65.

[123]It seems strange that Costa would frequent Zanardelli's company; only a few months before at Ghent, where the Venetian defended the legalitarian thesis, they had been on the verge of a fist fight, according to Terzaghi, <u>Il Rabagas</u>, Nov. 30-Dec. 1, 1882.

[124]Della Peruta, "Il socialismo italiano...," p. 326.

[125]Letter to G.H. Vollmar, Apr. 12, 1880, in Della Peruta, <u>Democrazia e socialismo</u>, p. 412. Adamo Mancini, an anarchist from Imola and an uncompromising critic of Costa's new ideas, was substantially in agreement; the <u>svolta</u>, he explained, was not made because of ambition or self-interest, but "simply to escape the persecutions of the police." See <u>La Gazzetta dell'Emilia</u>, Jan. 21-22, 1910.

[126]Della Peruta, "Il socialismo italiano...," p. 323.

[127]In a Paris meeting on Mar. 16, 1878, less than a week before his arrest, Costa had declared that what was needed was not a revolution of ideas, "but instead a violent revolution with the use of arms...." See anonymous report to the prefect of police in Paris, Mar. 18, 1878, A.P.P.P., carton 29.

[128]See, for example, Della Peruta, "Il socialismo italiano...," p. 327; Romano, Storia, II, p. 672.

[129]Le origini del socialismo italiano, pp. 586-87. This criticism has been made before, by Leo Valiani, Storia del movimento socialista, I (Florence: La Nuova Italia, 1951), 233. Valiani sees in Costa's position the beginning of the maximalist tendency (i.e., irresponsible revolutionists à la Mussolini) within the Italian socialist movement.

[130]Given this necessity, I think Hostetter's charges of hypocrisy, Le origini del socialismo italiano, p. 589, are too severe. Cf. Valiani, Storia, I, 232.

[131]Hostetter, Le origini del socialismo italiano, p. 587.

[132]"Annotazioni autobiografiche per servire alle 'Memorie della mia vita,'" ed. Gioietta Dallò, Movimento operaio, 4 (1952), 322.

176

CHAPTER FIVE

THE FORMATION OF THE ROMAGNOL REVOLUTIONARY
SOCIALIST PARTY, 1880-1881

The Aborted Congress of 1880

The reception Costa's letter received in the Romagna was generally an enthusiastic one. The time was
right for a change of direction. Indeed, the region
had not been altogether immune to legalitarian concepts
even before. Among those who sympathized with these i-
deas was Domenico Francolini. This was made clear in
Il Nettuno. What course of action should the party a-
dopt, the Riminese asked in his paper on September 23,
1877. His answer: We should "fight with all means, as
long as they are honest, from a newspaper article to a
vote at the polls, from individual propaganda to the
more effective one of the barricades, as soon as it becomes possible; accept the struggle on all fronts, not
reject the means of improvement...which can be had, as
/for example/ mutual aid, resistance funds, strikes,
cooperative associations, though without ever concealing
the end...toward which our efforts should lead."[1] As
editor of the only socialist paper in the Romagnol provinces, and the leading organizer there in Costa's absence, it is likely that his views made some headway in
the region.[2] Then too it should be noted that the Internationalists in the Romagna had not been above participating in political elections--a clear violation of anarchist principles--even before Francolini's ascendancy.[3]

But this tendency toward acceptance of reform was
not alone responsible for Costa's success in winning support for his program. Another consideration was the Imolese's immense personal prestige. "Above all else, the
Romagnols are personalisti," wrote Guglielmo Ferrero in
1893. "They become interested in ideas through men; because, that is, those ideas were spread among them by
some impressive and attractive personality. Behind the
diffusion of an idea or a political party, here in the
Romagna you will always find the popularity of a man."[4]
In these surroundings Costa found himself at a considerable advantage. As the unquestioned head of the In-

ternational in the Romagnol provinces, the charismatic youth had won the esteem of his followers and establish-ed sturdy bonds of friendship with them.[5] His eminence in the region was further enhenced by the incessant per-secution he suffered at the hands of the police.

Another factor working in Costa's favor, and one even more telling than the previous introduction of re-formist tendencies and his own personal prestige, was the party's sad state of affairs in 1879. When news of the svolta was received there in early August virtually every major anarchist in Bologna and the Romagna was be-hind bars. In fact, as early as April 7 Pier Luigi Pra-delli, one of the few leaders still at large, had to ad-mit before a meeting of the Bologna section that the re-gional Federation was "almost dead."[6] The capo-squadra was stating the obvious: only four members were there to listen to his presentation!

And finally it should be pointed out that Costa had not presented the Romagnols with a clear-cut alter-native: reform or revolution. While leaning toward the former himself, he attempted to stress the revolutionary character of his ideas. Indeed, he insisted that there was no essential difference between his program now and that of the old Romagnol Federation. "It is not a mat-ter of rejecting our past," he affirmed in his letter, "...nor of ceasing to be that which we were: it is only a matter of doing more and doing it better." Though ambiguous, the proclamation was effective in rallying support; not knowing what to make of Costa's recent or-ientation, many ardent insurrectionaries followed his lead nonetheless. Later, when the divergence between their principles and his became apparent, some would inevitably move into the camp of the opposition. For the moment, however, the ploy was a success: the vast majority of the Internationalists in the Romagna rallied to the new banner.[7]

As we have seen, Costa's open letter to his friends in the Romagna was far from specific. Although it urged a fresh course of action, it did not spell out what the revised program should be. Yet Costa did make one con-crete proposal: he called for the reorganization of the old Italian International. In effect, this plan of ac-tion meant the formation of a new socialist party, for without a doubt the International was to be based on new principles. Thus, even though he had been unable to translate these tenets into a concrete platform, the

178

Imolese had at least provided a vehicle capable of performing this difficult operation.

In his letter Costa stated that the party should
be created at a general socialist congress. He did not
specify when such a meeting should convene. He needed
time to develop support for his new ideas.[8] The immediate order of the day therefore was the convocation of
a regional gathering in the Romagna. The Romagnols
would then take the initiative for the national assembly.

In fact, efforts to hold the regional reunion pre-
dated the announcement of the svolta.[9] After August,
though, its preparation proceeded at an accelerated
pace. Costa was unable to return to Italy because he
faced a jail term there for violation of the ammonizione,
but he worked assiduously in Lugano, where he received
emissaries from the Romagna and directed the process of
reorganization.[10]

Regardless of the many efforts expended during the
remainder of the year, though, the convocation of a regional gathering proved to be impossible. The problem
was a lack of leadership. Nearly every anarchist chieftain in the Romagna was in prison at this time. During
the course of 1879 the Internationalists in Italy suffered through several major trials. The Romagnols were
protagonists in two of these. The first involved twelve
anarchists and six republicans (predominantly Imolesi)
who were tried at Bologna and found guilty on September
7 of belonging to a criminal association and making subversive propaganda.[11] Among the condemned were three
young men who had played a relatively minor role up to
now, but who soon became prominent in socialist circles:
Gaetano Zirardini of Ravenna--Claudio's younger brother
--and the two Imolesi, Franco Baldi and Angelo Negri.
The sentences varied from the three months in prison
given the republicans Decio Fantini and Elviro Lunati
to the eighteen months received by Baldi, Negri, and
several others.[12]

The second Romagnol trial opened at Forlì on September 27.[13] The twenty-five defendants included just about
every head of the Internationalist movement in the region: Domenico Francolini, Rimini; Attilio Tosi, Rimini;
Cajo Zavoli, Rimini; Ferdinando Bigi, Morciano; Secondo
Cappellini, Forlì ; Vittorino Valbonesi, Forlimpopoli;
Gallo Galli, Cesena; Ferdinando Valducci, Cesena; Pompeo Brunelli, Cesena; Filippo Cecchini, Cesena; Alfeo

Amati, Savignano; Enrico Squadrani, Savignano; Alceste
Cipriani, Rimini; Sesto Fortuzzi, Forlì; Giuseppe Pedriz-
zi, Rimini; Pellegrino Bagli, Rimini; Giovan Battista
Lolli, Bologna; Alfonso Leonesi, Bologna; Alceste Faggioli, Bologna; Alfonso Danesi, Bologna; Giovanni Arlotti,
Rimini; Vittorio Grazia, Rimini; Pilade Rossi, Rimini;
Pompeo Fantini, Cesena; and Giovanni Maroncelli, Cesena.[14]
The accused, all members of the Romagnol Federation,
were tried on a variety of counts, the most serious that
of belonging to a criminal association. After a hard-
fought and lengthy battle, the defense--which included
Barbanti-Brodano and Ceneri--was able to gain a largely
favorable verdict on October 7. An appeal by the government, however, resulted in drawn-out legal proceedings
during which the defendants maintained their freedom
but were subjected to continual and tight surveillance.
A Bologna court finally ruled in their favor on December 29, 1880.

But the most famous anarchist trial in the period
began in Florence on November 9, 1879, with the principal
defendants Natta, Pezzi, and Anna Kuliscioff. Charged
with conspiracy, the accused put up a good defense, especially the twenty-two-year-old Russian, who was absolutely brilliant as she dazzled the audience with her
poise and intelligence.[15] It was probably this performance more than anything else which was responsible for
the verdict of not guilty rendered on January 5, 1880.[16]

One of the witnesses for the defense at Florence
was Costa, who was granted safe conduct from Switzerland
in order to testify on his lover's behalf. Leaving Lugano on December 12, he had first gone to Imola, then
to the Tuscan capital, where he was permitted to see
Anna on the 15th.[17] Once the trial was over Costa and
Kuliscioff, closely watched by the police, made their
way across the border and settled in Lugano.[18] There
for the next two months they spent some of the happiest
days of their life together.[19]

During these few weeks the Italian exile was extremely busy making preparations for the long-awaited regional
congress.[20] He was in frequent correspondence with his
comrades in the Romagna, notably Balducci and Valducci,[21]
who in turn were constantly conferring with each other.[22]
With this stepped-up activity, as the Minister of Interior warned, the International was clearly being revived.[23]

The regional congress took place in Bologna on March

180

14, 1880.[24] It was presided over by Costa, who had left
Lugano in Kuliscioff's company two days before. About
thirty representatives of the various cities in Emilia
and the Romagna participated. According to a letter
written by Costa and later published in La Stella d'
Italia, the delegates sanctioned the formation of a
new Italian socialist party "which would include socialists of every color and would attempt to unite the
dispersed working class under a common program...."[25]
They stressed their conviction that the new social order could come about only after a violent struggle,
Costa's letter continued, and resolved that they would
not miss any occasion to initiate or support this struggle; however, they intended in the meantime to avail
themselves of every opportunity to bring about reforms
which would facilitate the fulfillment of the socialist
idea, or provoke the struggle between "the old and the
new order of things," or at least "begin an agitation
from which the socialists will be able to profit in
order to spread and fulfill...all or part of their program." They also declared, wrote Costa, that every individual group within the party would be free to exercise its prerogatives in whatever way it saw fit. The
federation would not impede this freedom, since all socialists had a common end which could be attained through
different means, depending on local conditions.[26]

     Apparently the Imolese tried to reconcile the two
principal factions of the socialist movement, the anarchists and the reformists, by proposing the widest
program possible. For the moment he succeeded very well;
the idea of a national socialist party was approved by
unanimous vote and he met little opposition even from
those present who would later attack him in the vilest
terms.

     After the Bologna reunion Costa took Kuliscioff
to meet his family in Imola. By now, the local subprefect related, the two fugitives were determined to
remain in Italy at all costs.[27] The couple had projected the publication of a socialist newspaper called La
Lotta in Bologna.[28] But first they decided to establish
their residence in Milan, the designated site of the national congress which Costa had proposed the year before
and which was slated to take place in late April.[29] The
preparation of the gathering was not the sole reason for
the transfer to the Lombard capital. In addition to the
Bologna paper Costa intended to found a second periodical, one that would emphasize theory and would link the

socialist movement in Italy with those of the more advanced nations of Europe.[30] The publication was to be
called La Rivista internazionale del socialismo. Its
headquarters would have to be Milan, already the industrial center of the country and undoubtedly a more
cosmopolitan city than either Imola or Bologna.

The preparation of the national congress met with
unexpected difficulties and had to be postponed. The
first number of the Rivista internazionale del socialismo, however, appeared on May 15, 1880, with an international cast of writers including Cesar De Paepe, Malon
and Kuliscioff.

The initial issue also contained an article written
by Costa which provides a valuable key to the Romagnol's
thinking during this crucial period. Once again Costa
emphasized reform. What was needed, he stated, was the
adoption of practical reform measures like the abolition
of indirect taxation, the shortening of working hours,
and the establishment of technical schools. Still, he
continued to justify these gains by insisting that the
disillusion they created would ultimately serve the cause
of revolution. All of this had been said before; what
was new was Costa's suggestion that for purposes of agitation the socialists might do well to enter city councils
and even the Chamber of Deputies.[31] This was much further
than he had gone before. Now the party was asked not
only to accept the state but also to support its institutions, albeit for revolutionary purposes.

For the first time too we have an indication that
Costa nurtured ambitions of becoming a parliamentary
deputy himself. Later the anarchists would charge that
their ex-comrade had intended to enter politics from the
time of his open letter to the Romagnols.[32] To believe,
though, that Costa's entrance into the Chamber of Deputies three years later was a product of a plan which had
been conceived as early as 1879 does not adequately take
into account the confusion which characterized his thought
at that time. Indeed the electoral laws as they existed
then made it impossible for the Romagnol to run for office.
By 1880 the situation was changing. The electoral law
remained in effect but there was talk of expanding the
franchise. It is probable that Costa was now prepared
to achieve for the socialists what Fortis would accomplish that very year for the republicans: enter Parliament.

The first number of the _Rivista internazionale del socialismo_ published under Costa's direction was unfortunately also the last. Both he and Kuliscioff were arrested in Milan on April 22.[33] Police records show that the authorities had been keeping close tabs on the Romagnol from the time of his French exile. Costa was widely viewed as a fanatic apostle of violence, and his _svolta_ had done nothing to change this opinion.[34] By late 1879 the government had become cognizant of the growing difference of opinion between Costa and his old companions in the International;[35] still he continued to be regarded as dangerous.[36] This fear of Costa as an irrepressible revolutionary explains the relentless efforts made by the government in 1880 to put him behind bars and to keep him there.

The attempt began on March 27, when Costa was condemned by a Bologna tribunal for violation of the _ammonizione_ imposed upon him four years earlier.[37] The following month a reward of one thousand _lire_ was placed on his head, and a week later it was trebled.[38] Costa's arrest in Milan, however, stemmed from his violation of the censorship laws.[39] Held responsible for a seditious article in the _Rivista internazionale del socialismo_, he was sentenced by a Milanese court on June 15 to one month in prison and fined one hundred _lire_. Three days later he was transferred to Bologna to await trial on the original charge of violation of the _ammonizione_.[40] When the Bologna Court of Appeals declared on August 3 that no legal action could be brought against Costa for this alleged offense, he and Kuliscioff were charged with a new crime: conspiracy. The verdict of August 19 was again favorable to the accused, and his Russian companion was quickly released. But the Romagnol, though found not guilty, remained in prison, for he was still unable to pay the fine imposed at Milan. It was only on September 17 that Costa was set free. Rather than remaining in Italy, as the authorities had expected,[41] he left for Swizerland.

This freedom was short-lived. On October 6 the August 3 ruling was nullified and Costa's case was sent before the Perugia section of the Ancona Court of Appeals. This tribunal ruled on October 30 that the Romagnol had in fact violated the provisions of the _ammonizione_. Unaware of these proceedings, Costa, who had been living in Lugano with Kuliscioff, returned to Italy and on November 1, while attending a Bologna conference which met to discuss the question of universal suffrage, was ar-

rested once more and sent to Perugia to await trial.[42]
The persecution of the last few months now began to
weigh on him. "Boredom," he wrote Anna, "oppresses me
more and more--Oh! What a life! What a life! And why
all this?"[43] As the days passed his depression deep-
ened. On December 13 he wrote, "You know, *fanciulla
mia*, I have served almost five years in prison; and I
am only twenty-nine! If we continue like this, who
knows where it will all end."[44] The Umbrian court finally rendered its verdict on January 15, 1881: Costa was
found guilty and sentenced to four months in prison.
But because he had already served this term, he was lib-
erated that same day.[45]

     After months of harassment Costa was free at last.
What would he do now? He was tired of fighting, he had
written Kuliscioff shortly before his release. "I have
no intention of remaining in Italy," he declared, "but
propose to spend a few years abroad, working and studying with you."[46] Preferably they would live in Paris
or, if the French authorities denied them permission to
stay, they would go on to London. All of these plans
went up in smoke, though, when Costa was refused permission to leave the country.[47]

The Rimini Congress of 1881

     Confined to Italy, the Romagnol decided to make the
best of the situation. The idea of a socialist party
had never been entirely forgotten; now he returned to it
in earnest. The previous initiative had not gone well.
While Costa had been in prison Bignami spearheaded a
movement to convoke the national congress in Milan on
May 10, 1880,[48] but these efforts were abandoned due to
a lack of response.[49] One of the problems, Costa recognized, was that the Italians had not been adequately
exposed to the new socialist principles which were to
form the basis of the meeting and the party it was intended to create. Popular support had to be encouraged.
What was needed more than anything else at the moment
was a newspaper. Costa decided to dedicate himself to
this necessity.

     That the socialist organ was about to appear was
made public in mid-April. The subprefect of Imola immediately informed his superior in Bologna and apparently had no doubt as to the consequence of the publication:

     I believe it is superfluous to point out the

184

grave danger which so threatens the social order...
and how important it is to prevent the sowing of
this bad seed which tends to subvert public and
private morality, to corrupt even the agrarian
classes which up to now, fortunately, have been
immune to the poisonous socialist maxims; to foment,
in a word, the deadly subversive principles which
constitute the wretched program of the apostles of
socialism.[50]

Nevertheless, the first number of _Avanti!_ was distributed on the streets of Imola on April 30, 1881. The
title of the paper is significant. Discarding the old
idea of _La Lotta_, Costa had chosen to name his publication after _Vorwärts_, the organ of the German Social Democratic Party.[51] Despite his statements to the contrary,
it was clear that Costa's program was far removed from
that of the anarchists.

The main concern of _Avanti!_ was the creation of a
socialist party. By 1881, though, the plans had been
altered considerably from the previous year. Rather than
calling for a national congress, Costa now thought it
wiser to limit himself to the convocation of a Romagnol
meeting and to begin by forming a regional party which
would eventually expand throughout the peninsula. This
revision was motivated partly by the failure of the proposed Italian congress in 1880, but principally by Costa's
recognition that outside of Bologna and the Romagna he
could count on very few followers.[52]

The famous Rimini Congress was finally convoked on
July 24, 1881.[53] About forty delegates were in attendance. From the very beginning it became evident that
they supported Costa overwhelmingly. The "reconstruction" of the party, the main scope of the meeting, was
approved almost unanimously (there were only two dissenting votes).[54]

More divided was the discussion concerning a name for
the new political organization, with Costa insisting on
"Revolutionary Socialist Party." Some old members of the
defunct Romagnol Federation demanded that the word "anarchist" be incorporated in the title, insisting that
the emphasis should be on the final objective of socialism. Though accepting anarchy in principle, Costa wanted
to de-emphasize this aspect of the program; he wished to
distinguish his party clearly from the old International.
He thus chose a name which would encompass _all_ degrees

of socialism--from anarchism to legalitarianism. The
final count gave Costa's choice thirty-two votes and
only six to the anarchists'.

For the moment the touchy question of the party
program was avoided. Its formulation, together with the
party Statute and Regulations, was entrusted to a committee of five. The results of the committee's deliberations were published on August 28 in a special issue of
Avanti!.55

The program began with a call for the economic,
political, and moral emancipation of the individual and
the establishment of a new order in which "a man would
be able to exercise freely all his rights and feel himself a man in the company of other men." This condition
could be realized only through revolution. The upheaval
was defined as, "above all, a violent material insurrection of the multitudes against the obstacles which the
existing institutions place in the way of the affirma-
tion and fulfillment of the popular will." The revolution was seen as inevitable, since no ruling class had
ever surrendered its privileges voluntarily. Its immediate result would be a temporary dictatorship by the
proletariat.

Prior to this despotic stage, the chief instrument
of revolution would be the party. This organization
would have two objectives: (1) awakening the masses
"with speeches, with writings, with examples, and if
necessary with other means"; and (2) turning the masses
against the existing order by taking advantage of any
favorable opportunity to "inspire and direct them in the
struggle and making every effort so that the revolution
will bring those results which the people expect from
it."

The program then dealt at length with reform. The
party must, "in order to live, to progress, to keep in
contact with the people and gain inspiration from them,"
support and where possible provoke all those reforms
which would hasten the revolution by cultivating in the
people a spirit of opposition and a will to revolt.

The program concluded with the following ten proposals for concrete action, specifying that each affiliate association would be free to implement only those
which it saw fit:

186

1. To propagate socialist ideas widely and continually through lectures, newspapers, pamphlets, meetings, and public demonstrations, the propagation of these ideas varying according to the different segments of society to which they are addressed....
2. To organize all socialist and revolutionary elements of the city and countryside effectively into sections of the party, circles of social studies, workers' associations, societies for education and popular instruction, and so on.
3. To organize the working class...to the greatest extent possible, especially into trade unions, in order that it may be convinced, in a practical way, of the advantages of association....
4. To support and, if necessary, to provoke the struggle against capital through strikes, demands for higher salaries, the reduction of working hours, and so on.
5. To support and, from time to time, provoke all those political and economic reforms which offer an opportunity to propagate socialism..., which tend toward the abolition of a privilege..., which favor the organization of labor and popular culture, and which may break down the resistance of the government, render us personally more free, hasten the exhaustion of established political and economic institutions, and favor the socialistic reorganization of society.
6. To take possession of city governments through strong participation in administrative elections, and to transform...the present administrative structure....
7. To submit socialist and working-class candidacies, be they of a positive or protest nature, to Parliament and to give the individual provincial associations the freedom to determine the conduct of those comrades who may be elected deputies.
8. To abet, and, if necessary, to provoke popular demonstrations against economic and political privilege, and to maintain them, if necessary, to the very end.
9. To combat ruthlessly those religious prejudices which plague such a large part of the working class.
10. In sum, to fight every day, every moment, with every means until that time when we feel we are able to engage in the final struggle.

The program was obviously intended to unite all factions within the socialist movement. While it laid down general principles, it specified that the application of these tenets would depend on the "circumstances surrounding the struggle in which the party might find itself engaged." Moreover, it stressed that the action of the party would be "manifold," thereby granting much latitude to the individual associations.

Yet despite its stress on multiple action, the program definitely favored reform rather than violence. Though it accepted revolution in principle, revolutionary action as a practical tactic was discouraged. While in some instances conspiracy and insurrection would admittedly be necessary, members were counseled that "these very means, which should be left to individual initiative, cannot and should not be elevated to a general principle for everyone; they cannot and should not be the systematic conduct of a great party, a party which should be able to make use of much better methods of action and should be able to operate in the open /alla luce del sole/."

Instead, the party was encouraged to seek concrete material gains not only because this line of action would provide a means "to remain in contact with the people," who wanted an amelioration of their condition, but also because a reform program inevitably led to revolt. As the program declared: "The little that is obtained will incite the people to claim and obtain much more." In fact, all ten recommendations were of a reform character. This was especially true of the proposal which urged socialist participation in municipal elections and the sponsorship of socialist candidacies for parliamentary seats.

All the ideas expressed here are familiar. The real author of the program, as Professor Gastone Manacorda suggests, was Costa.[56] The party which was constructed at Rimini was almost entirely his own creation.

The Romagnol Revolutionary Socialist Party

One of the early chroniclers of the Italian socialist movement, Alfredo Angiolini, has interpreted its history in the 1880's almost exclusively in terms of the Partito Operaio Italiano (P.O.I.).[57] This interpretation is unfortunate, since it implies that socialist activity in this decade was limited to Lombardy and particularly Milan, where the headquarters of the P.O.I. were located. As a matter of fact the movement established firm roots in several regions, among the most important the Romagna, where socialism came to be identified with Andrea Costa and his party, the Partito Socialista Rivoluzionario di Romagna (P.S.R.R.). During the early eighties, the P.S. R.R. was to serve Costa as the vehicle for translating his ideas into action. The role it played was a significant one, and yet very little is known about the association.

The organization of the P.S.R.R. can best be understood on the basis of the Statute and Regulations which were formulated along with the program described above. The party was composed of "all those societies and individuals who accept the general principles of modern revolutionary socialism, and endeavor, according to their strength and means, to propagate and put them into effect." In keeping with its aim of unifying all socialist factions, the association took the form of a federation. This structure was imposed not only by tradition (the old International had been organized on the same basis), but also by necessity: a federative arrangement was the best means of uniting antagonistic elements.

The individual associations themselves could be of various types. While the Statute recommended that where possible such bodies take the form of trade unions, other kinds of societies to cope with the local situation were permitted (for example, regional federations and circles of social studies). As we have seen, the associations were allowed much freedom and flexibility insofar as methods of realizing the common goals of the federation were concerned. The Statute did stipulate, however, that all affiliates must accept the party's general program.

A Federal Commission of seven members would serve as the P.S.R.R.'s executive organ. Three of these members would reside within the same city and constitute a Commission of Correspondence to administer the ongoing activities of the party. The purpose of this latter Commission was spelled out as follows: "To give the various associations and members that request them all the information it can; it will also promote the creation of new societies and the adherence of established societies to the party; it will collect federal taxes, look after party publications, convoke congresses, and so on." Should the Commission of Correspondence be disbanded for any reason, the remaining four members of the

Federal Commission were empowered to call a congress for the purpose of electing a new directing body.

Party congresses were to be of two types, regular and special. The purposes of the first, to convene semi-annually, were to discuss and resolve issues proposed by individual associations in the form of orders-of-the-day, elect the Federal Commission and representatives to national and international gatherings, determine the site of the next congress, and decide on both the general and specific policies of the party. Extraordinary congresses could be convoked at any time by the Federal Commission--either on its own initiative or through the petition of ten member associations--to make decisions on special issues.

The P.S.R.R. was to be financed through dues, with each member paying five centimes monthly to the Federal Commission and individual associations being responsible for their collection. This money was to defray the cost of correspondence and propaganda and to aid P.S.R.R. members forced to go into hiding or exile.

This, then, was the way in which Il Partito Socialista Rivoluzionario di Romagna was to be organized in theory. The success of the party, however, would depend on the extent to which this organization could be achieved in fact--which is where the local party leader came in. To appreciate his role, one must realize the degree to which regionalism permeated Italian life during the nineteenth century. As in most agricultural societies, the individual's allegiance to his region was mightier than to his country; one thought of himself not as Italian but as Romagnol, Tuscan, or Venetian. Moreover, not only did the individual have a strong sense of belonging to a particular region, but also to a town within that region; in fact, only his loyalty to his family was more inviolable. Thus, within the Romagna the people took extreme pride in referring to themselves as Forlivesi, or Riminesi, or Imolesi. Reinforcing this identification was the use of the dialect. In the nineteenth century, notably in the countryside, dialects were more significant than Italian, especially since the official language itself also varied from region to region and town to town.[58] In this environment the role of the local chieftain was a powerful one, and at the municipal level he personified the party.

The directors of the P.S.R.R., with few exceptions,

had participated in the First International. Since most of them had been born after 1850 they were too young to have taken part in the struggles of the Risorgimento; hence they had been removed from the direct influence of Mazzini and Garibaldi. They turned instead to the ideas of Bakunin. Most were artisans, but some were middle-class students who had been converted to anarchism in the revolutionary atmosphere of the Italian universities (the University of Bologna being the most popular among Romagnols then as now). Because of their superior intelligence and energy they rose rapidly within the ranks of the Romagnol Federation, where they came into contact with Costa, who won their admiration and friendship. Among these men were Ferdinando Valducci, Secondo Cappellini, Rito Balducci, Franco Baldi, Angelo Negri, Nullo Baldini, and Gaetano Zirardini. In the 1880's they would constitute the leadership of the P.S.R.R.

In Cesena, perhaps the most typical of Romagnol cities, Costa's principal representatives were the Battistini brothers, Pio and Epaminonda, and Valducci.[59] The most "dangerous" of the three, as far as the authorities were concerned, was Valducci.[60] One of the first Romagnols to join the old International, the young agitator had been placed under ammonizione in 1871, at the age of eighteen, and again in 1877.[61] Perhaps the continual police harassment was an inducement to his ready acceptance of Costa's revised program. Here again he was a pioneer: "I am a socialist," he declared before the subprefect of Cesena in December, 1879, "but I have nothing in common with the Internationalists, and I have never shared their theories on the radical methods which they would use to bring about the triumph of their objectives. In Cesena...there may be Internationalists properly speaking, who should fear repression by the government. Neither myself, nor my few friends, wish to be confused with them."[62]

A few miles west of Cesena, on Via Emilia, lies Forlì, a town with a small socialist nucleus but a plethora of chiefs (in direct contrast to Rimini, which had the numbers but not the leaders). Of these, the most faithful servants of the party were Balducci and Cappellini.[63] Both men were Costa's intimate friends and had served with him in the 1870's. Cappellini was extremely active at that time, having partcipated in the San Lupo revolt in 1877.[64] By 1880 he and Balducci had responded to Costa's plea for a new orientation and were devoting their energies to the formation of the party. Their ascendancy among the socialists of Forlì was paramount

at this time. Over the next few years, though, they gradually gave way to two other individuals whose backgrounds
and outlooks differed markedly one from the other: Germanico Piselli and Alessandro Balducci (no relation to Rito).[65]

But the focal point of Costa's strength was not to
be found in either Cesena or Forlì, cities predominantly
republican in sympathy; it was at Imola and Ravenna that
the socialist standard-bearer enjoyed his widest popularity. This was especially true in Imola, his native city.[66]
Also contributing to the advancement of his ideas there,
however, was the work of Baldi and Negri, both of whom
had been supporting Costa since the mid-1870's.[67] During
his exile and imprisonment in France they had assumed the
responsibility, together with Paolo Renzi, of resurrecting the city's anarchist organization. As Imolesi they
shared a special bond with Costa, one which no doubt facilitated their espousal of his revised program.[68] By
1880, Negri, at the age of twenty-five, had become the
acknowledged head of the section in Imola[69] and Baldi
was being described by the local subprefect as one of its
"main leaders" and "one of the strongest supporters of
the Internationalist party" in the region.[70] In that
same year they were instrumental, along with Odoardo Facchini and Adamo Mancini, in founding the Circolo Socialista of Imola, the purpose of which was to propagate
Costa's views throughout the area.[71] Baldi and Negri also did much to attract Imola's republican majority to the
banner of socialism, working for the most part through
the city's A.R.U. chieftains. In fact, they and Renzi
assisted the republican leaders Sassi and Fantini in founding Il Moto in 1880, the newspaper which represented the
democratic party in Imola for the next ten years.[72]

In Ravenna activities were under the direction of
Costa's two most dynamic followers, Baldini and Gaetano
Zirardini. Younger than most of Costa's lieutenants,
Baldini, as Antonio Graziadei recalls, always treated the
Imolese "with the timidity and the fondness of a new
disciple."[73] It was not until 1883 that the youthful caposquadra managed to assert himself. In that year he and
Federico Ceroni helped Armando Armuzzi organize the Associazione Generale degli Operai Braccianti in Ravenna, the
first cooperative of braccianti (agricultural laborers)
in Italy. Unfortunately, Baldini is known only for his
contribution to the Italian cooperative movement; yet few
men did as much as he in organizing the nascent socialist
movement. Indeed, as a result of his work among the braccianti, the P.S.R.R. grew into something of a mass party
in Ravenna.

192

Gaetano Zirardini, Baldini's close friend and fellow townsman, was not only head of the party in Ravenna but probably the ranking socialist in the Romagna after Costa himself. Zirardini had joined the International in 1874 at the age of seventeen.[74] He attended the University of Florence, where he studied sculpture and helped publish La Riscossa, an anarchist paper. His subversive activities led to his imprisonment in 1878. The following year he and his brother Claudio abandoned the old International to join Costa.[75] Gaetano was totally in agreement with the Imolese. "There may be those who believe in God," the Ravennate declared before a Bologna court in December, 1879. "I believe in Social Revolution; in fact I place all my hopes on it. By Social Revolution I mean: the development and application of socialist ideas, which I believe to be the most liberal, the most just, the most humanitarian /and/ which will come together through evolution or revolution to form a social order catering to the legitimate needs and the legitimate aspirations of the community."[76] In the 1880's the socialists in Ravenna were able to hold their own against the long-established republicans largely because of the leadership provided by Gaetano Zirardini. He was a master at organization and his efforts enabled Costa, time and again, to win elections in the ancient Byzantine capital.[77]

Besides the men mentioned above, others who filled a significant role in the development of the P.S.R.R. were Antonio Lanzoni in Lugo, publisher of the Rivista italiana del socialismo, an influential Marxist-oriented magazine after 1886, and Giuseppe Barbanti-Brodano, whose views were not in complete agreement with Costa's,[78] but who was undoubtedly the outstanding socialist leader in Bologna during the early 1880's.[79] Lesser figures, though they carried much weight locally, were Enrico and Francesco Squadrani of Savignano and Alessandro Mussolini, capo-squadra of the socialists in Predappio and father of the Duce.[80]

Almost without exception the P.S.R.R. leaders hailed from the Romagna (or Bologna, which was much the same thing),[81] suggesting something about the party's geographical composition. Even though the federation's Regulations had called for its transformation from a regional to a national organization, and attempts were made after 1881 to achieve this goal, the P.S.R.R. remained confined to the Romagnol provinces. There were some exceptions, the major one being the Marches, where the anarch-

193

ist movement had established solid bonds with the Romagna in the 1870's. Nor were the neighboring regions of the Veneto and Emilia (where Romagnol authority was transmitted via the city of Bologna) totally immune to the party's propaganda. Beyond these areas, however, it is doubtful that the P.S.R.R. was ever much of a factor. In Tuscany its impact was effectively countered by the anarchists, who retained something of their old might there throughout the 1880's. Costa's propaganda also had scant results in the northern regions, which after 1882 inevitably came under the jurisdiction of the Partito Operaio Italiano. In the South, socialist influence of any kind was limited to isolated pockets of individuals until the last decade of the century.

The P.S.R.R., then, was almost exclusively limited to the Romagna, yet even there its strength was concentrated in certain areas while hardly noticeable in others. Generally speaking, the party was more effective in the cities than in the countryside. Robert Michels perhaps oversimplifies the matter when he states that socialism in Italy in the 1880's was urban;[82] nevertheless, it is true that its main support was drawn from the cities and primarily from their artisan and lower middle classes. The P.S.R.R.'s leaders came almost without exception from the Romagnol towns and cities. In the countryside, where the moderate, or liberal-conservative, party held the upper hand, socialist notions met stiff resistance from the conservative and superstitious peasants. Strongly swayed by the country priest, the peasant was naturally repelled by the subversive parties, the socialists and republicans--especially by their anticlericalism. But even beyond the peasant's fear of new ideas was his identification with the local padrone. Economically dependent on the large landowning families, most of whom were moderates (for example, the Pasolinis, the Farinis, and the Rasponis), the peasant was more than ready to acquiesce to his employer's wishes in political matters.

The influence of the P.S.R.R. was more telling in the northern part of the Romagna, the lowland plain known as the bassa, than in the south, much of which was located in the Appennines and therefore known as the montagna. The party's weakness in the south was to some extent due to the fact that the major cities in the Romagna are either in the foothills--along Via Emilia--or on the plain; there are no major urban centers in the highlands. But a more convincing reason for the P.S.R.R.'s weakness here was the type of landholding system prevalent in the area.

194

In the montagna the peasant usually leased a small farm
under the sharecropping system known as the mezzadria,
though sometimes he owned a small parcel of land himself. In either case, he thought of himself as a land-
owner and was naturally suspicious of fellow Romagnols
who advocated the destruction of private property. Hence,
as the power of the moderates declined--something which
occurred steadily after 1870--these mezzadri turned to
the republicans rather than the socialists.

In attempting to evaluate the significance of the
P.S.R.R. in the Romagna one must realize that throughout and particularly at the beginning of the 1880's the
socialists constituted only a very small minority there.
"The Internationalists in Romagna have never amounted
to much," wrote Alfredo Comandini, a republican, in 1881;
"they are called: the Cesena section, the Imola section,
the Faenza section, the section of this and the section
of that; but in substance they are only a small number
of kids."[83]

Exactly how big was the P.S.R.R.? This is difficult to say, as the party's records have been lost or
destroyed. Moreover, if an estimate were to be made,
how would membership be determined? Payment of dues is
not a good criterion, for only a handful of individuals
ever paid, judging by the party's chronic financial problems. Acceptance of the party program? But this platform was so nebulous that it would have been difficult
to decide whether one agreed with it or not. Still, it
is probable that the size of the P.S.R.R. approximated
that of its parent association, the Romagnol Federation.

Fortunately the anarchists did keep statistics. On
July 17, 1881, only a week before the Rimini Congress,
there was an Internationalist meeting in Cesena, presided
by Gallo Galli, "in which a...plan of reform formulated
by Andrea Costa was read, and the register of the organization of the socialist party in the entire kingdom was
communicated."[84] The latter document divided the country
into twenty regional subdivisions (capitanate) and provided the number of socialists in each of these sub-
groups.[85] The total membership of the party in Italy
turned out to be 16,739. The area which later encompassed the jurisdiction of the P.S.R.R. was represented
by three capitante: the fifteenth, which corresponded
with the city of Bologna; the nineteenth, Castelbolognese,
Faenza, Imola, and Lugo; and the twentieth, Cesena, Forlì,
Ravenna, and Rimini. The three capitanate had memberships

195

respectively, of 833, 1310, and 1918, for a grand total of 4061 individuals.

At its peak--ca. 1884--the P.S.R.R. probably attained an enrollment comparable to this figure, an enrollment of 4000-5000 members. Some may object that this estimate is inflated, pointing out that by this time quite a few of the old Internationalists, perhaps as many as half, had abandoned the party after realizing how moderate Costa's program really was. Additionally, it could be argued, and rightly so, that the figure given at Cesena had been too optimistic in the first place. But, on the other hand, compensating for these factors were new recruits and a P.S.R.R. membership that extended beyond the confines of Bologna and the Romagna, though not by much. In any event, it is true that lack of numbers constituted the party's central problem. The anarchist International in Italy has been described as "microscopic."[86] How much more microscopic was the P.S.R.R.!

Conclusion

Costa's open letter "To my Friends of the Romagna" in 1879 signaled the end of anarchism as an effective force in Italian life. The Imolese had the foresight to comprehend that a new direction was sorely needed and he was determined to help bring it about. The creation of a vital socialist party became his immediate goal. He directed his efforts toward this end for the next two years. The preparation of a general congress which would organize the party proved to be a time-consuming undertaking, for this meeting could be convoked only after reorganization had been accomplished at the local level. Then, too, Costa was hampered in his efforts at organization by the various criminal proceedings which were brought against him in 1880. Notwithstanding these obstacles, preparations for the congress were finally completed and it assembled in Rimini on July 24, 1881.

The most productive outcome of the Congress of Rimini was the creation of the Partito Socialista Rivoluzionario di Romagna. Inasmuch as Costa created and led the party, the P.S.R.R. has always been identified with him--an identification, unfortunately, which partly accounts for its incapacity to project its organization beyond the borders of the Romagna and thus become a national party. Yet despite its limited success, the P.S.R.R. represents a milestone in the history of the socialist movement in

Italy because it marks an important step in the transition from anarchism to socialism.

This transformation never ran its full course. Anarchist influence persisted in the new party. In fact, it permeated its very organization: like the Romagnol Federation, the P.S.R.R. was directed by a corresponding commission and its structure was federative. It was inevitable, of course, that the party would reflect anarchist tendencies; it had evolved from the old International and a clean break with the past was impossible. Furthermore, the pressure exerted by the anarchists was not confined to the past, for in the 1880's they continued to be very active in the Romagna.

More specifically, the sway of anarchism within the P.S.R.R. was to a degree a projection of its hold on Costa From the very beginning the Imolese insisted that his party would be a reincarnation of the International. Undoubtedly he took pains to establish this link in order to attract the old Internationalists to his banner. Perhaps, too, he wished to maintain this continuity to avoid being regarded as an apostate. Yet it would be a mistake to interpret Costa's identification with the anarchist past solely in terms of opportunism. It was out of conviction that the Romagnol leader persevered in his support of anarchist notions--a political posture that was evident even after 1892, at a time when the Italian Socialist Party was demonstrating little interest in its anarchist origins.[87]

NOTES

[1]Needless to say, the article did not make a great impression on Costa. See his letter to Francolini, Oct. 1, 1877, published in Il Nettuno, Oct. 7, 1877, and reproduced in Zangheri, "Il Nettuno...e il suo direttore Domenico Francolini," pp. 254-56.

[2]Francolini was jailed in Rimini on Dec. 7, 1878. The following month, speaking before other anarchists in Geneva, Malatesta lamented the arrest, explaining that the Riminese "represented the central figure in the Romagna and in a few months...succeeded, thanks to an energetic propaganda, in making hundreds of converts." See Minister of Interior to the prefect of Forlì, Jan. 31, 1879, A.S.F., Gab. Pref., vol. 93, fasc. 247.

[3]On Nov. 6, 1876, the Forlì police reported that some Internationalists would vote for Fortis in the coming political election. See note to the prefect of Forlì, A.S.F., Gab. Pref., vol. 75, fasc. 259/bis. A few days later the subprefect of Rimini verified this information. During the elections, he wrote the prefect of Forlì on Nov. 15, several "noted" Internationalists in his city "were active and passionate supporters of the candidate backed by the republican party" (A.S.F., Gab. Pref., vol. 75, fasc. 259/bis).

[4]Ferrero, A.G. Bianchi, and Scipio Sighele, Il mondo criminale italiano (Milan: L. Omodei Zorini, 1893), p. 13.

[5]Friendship,too, takes on a special significance in the Romagna. "It seems to me," Orano wrote in 1910, "that in Romagna friendship is even more profound than love." Comradeship there, he continued, is the "creator of a sincere, amorous, sacrificial, passionate brotherhood which I doubt can be found in any other country in the world." See Andrea Costa, p. 14.

[6]Questore of Bologna to the prefect of Bologna, Apr. 10, 1879, A.S.B., Gab. Pref., category VII, 1879 (after ca. 1880 volume numbers are unavailable and so I am forced to use this more general classification). On July 21 the prefect of Forlì reported that in his province the International was practically nonexistent in Cesena and Forlì;

only in Rimini, the third major city in the province, was there any trace of it left. Led by Lettimi, the Riminesi were attempting to weather the storm by allying with the republicans. See report to the Minister of Interior, A.S.F Gab. Pref., vol. 93, fasc. 247.

[7]This does not mean there was no opposition at all in the region. Cesare Ceccarelli and Giovanni Bianchini, both Romagnols living in Naples, met with some of the local lea· ers in Rimini on Aug. 18, 1879, to try to get them to reject the new program. According to Ceccarelli, his efforts were successful there, as well as in Cesena, Cesenatico, Ravenna, Forlì, Russi, and Lugo. He admitted, however, tha· "Costa has more than a few personal friends in the Romagna who support him, or, at the most, remain undecided." This information was uncovered by a spy who talked to Ceccarell in Naples soon afterward and relayed the information to th· local prefect. See Minister of Interior to the prefect of Forlì, Sept. 10, 1879, A.S.F., Gab. Pref., vol. 93, fasc. 247. There is some question on the authenticity of the above account. According to the subprefect of Rimini, the meeting did indeed take place in his city on the date mentioned, but its scope was altogether different. Ceccarelli he insisted, had been sent to Rimini by Costa to see if ev· erything was ready for an insurrection which was to take place in November. Two of his spies confirmed this story, the local prefect said (report to the prefect of Forlì, Sept. 15, 1879, A.S.F., Gab. Pref., vol. 93, fasc. 247). Given Costa's svolta, though, this version appears unlikely.

[8]Costa wanted to hold the congress before November. See his letter to the Venetians, Aug. 25, 1879, in Briguglio, "Gli internazionalisti di Monselice e di Padova," p. 760.

[9]Already by mid-May, 1879, the Ravenna federation had called for the regional congress (questore of Bologna to the prefect of Bologna, May 18, 1879, A.S.B., Gab. Pref., cat. VII, 1879). On June 19, 1879, the questore reported that the Ravennati had postponed the congress, despite the opposition of the Riminesi, on account of the continuing trials (note to the prefect of Bologna, A.S.B., Gab. Pref. cat. VII, 1879).

[10]According to Gaetano Grassi, who also resided in Lugano in late 1879, during this period Costa called on and was visited by comrades from Ravenna, Rimini, Imola, and Bologna. See Della Peruta, "Il socialismo italiano...," p.

326.

[11]An account of the trial is contained in La Stella d' Italia, Sept. 6,7, and 8, 1879. See also Aristide Venturini, Due opposte decisioni sull'Internazionale (Bologna: Azzoguidi, 1879). The list of defendants, according to Venturini (pp. 3-7): Angelo Negri, Imola; Francesco (Franco) Baldi, Imola; Enrico Musa, Imola; Vincenzo Marchi, Imola; Romeo Fava, Ravenna; Battista Caroli, Imola; Ferdinando Zappi, Imola; Giuseppe Sangiorgi, Imola; Enrico Guatteri, Imola; Luigi Renzi, Imola; Romeo Renzi, Imola; Pietro Maiani, Imola; Gaetano Zirardini, Ravenna; Antonio Borghesi, Castelbolognese; Decio Fantini, Imola; Luigi Zini, Imola; Elviro Lunati, Imola; and Luigi Xella, Imola.

[12]Venturini, Due opposte decisioni, pp. 23-25. Twelve of the condemned prisoners (all socialists except Fantini) appealed the sentence and won a favorable verdict on Dec. 13. See La Stella d'Italia, Dec. 11, 12, 13, and 14, 1879. This decision, however, was annulled by a Roman court early during the following year (Franco Baldi and Angelo Negri, Ai nostri concittadini /Imola: Lega, 1880/, p. 1), and it was only in May, 1880, that the accused were completely absolved.

[13]See the account in La Stella d'Italia, Sept. 30, Oct. 1, 2, 3, 4, 5, 6, and 9, 1879; La Plebe, Oct. 5, 12, 1879.

[14]A copy of the sentence of the court, including the defendants' names, is found in A.S.F., Gab. Pref., vol. 93, fasc. 247. See also Venturini, Due opposte decisioni.

[15]Part of her testimony is quoted in Angiolini, Socialismo e socialisti in Italia, pp. 139-40.

[16]Pala, Anna Kuliscioff, p. 41.

[17]Lipparini, "Cronologia," p. 190. Costa was accompanied to Florence from the Romagna by Valducci. See Minister of Interior to the prefect of Bologna, Dec. 30, 1879, A.S.B., Gab. Pref., vol. 125.

[18]The two travelers stopped in Bologna and Modena before continuing on to Switzerland. See questore of Bologna to his prefect, Jan. 7, 1880, A.S.B., Gab. Pref., vol. 125.

[19]See Kuliscioff letter to Costa, Nov. 18, 1880, B.C.I., no. 93.

[20] By the end of 1879 the authorities were already aware that the Imolese had taken the initiative for this regional congress and that it was imminent. They knew that the purpose of the meeting would be the creation of a new party which would be "operaio-socialista-rivoluzionario," but they were under the mistaken impression that the congress would take place in January and would be a reunion of socialists from the Romagna and the Marches. See prefect of Bologna to the prefect of Forlì, Dec. 29, 1879, A.S.F., Gab. Pref., vol. 94, fasc. 262.

[21] Prefect of Forlì to the prefect of Ravenna, Feb. 14, 1880, and to the various subprefects in the province, Mar. 4, 1880, A.S.F., Gab. Pref., vol. 94, fasc. 247/b.

[22] The Battistini brothers, for example, were in Cesena in mid-January (subprefect of Rimini to the prefect of Forlì, Feb. 28, 1880, A.S.F., Gab. Pref., vol. 94, fasc. 262) and Gaetano Zirardini visited Baldi and Negri in Imola in early February (subprefect of Imola to the prefect of Bologna, Feb. 12, 1880, A.S.F., Gab. Pref., vol. 95, fasc. 282).

[23] Note to the prefect of Forlì, Feb. 17, 1880, A.S.F., Gab. Pref., vol. 94, fasc. 279.

[24] An account is given in La Plebe, Mar. 18, 1880, and reproduced in La Stella d'Italia, Mar. 21, 1880. A correspondence describing the congress is also found in L'Egalité, Mar. 23, 1880.

[25] The letter, dated Mar. 21, appears in the Mar. 23, 1880 issue of the paper.

[26] The meeting was clandestine, and the authorities had trouble discovering exactly what happened there. On Mar. 18 the Minister of Interior informed the prefect of Forlì that the Italians had met with French and Belgian Communists "in order to organize armed bands" (A.S.F., Gab. Pref., vol. 94 fasc. 247/b). The prefect, on the other hand, had heard that the reason for the meeting was the need of the Italian leaders now exiled in Switzerland to calm down some of the hotheads, mainly the Florentines, who were bent on revolutionary action (letter to the Minister of Interior, Mar. 10 1880, A.S.F., Gab. Pref., fasc. 247/b).

[27] Note to the prefect of Bologna, Mar. 17, 1880, A.S.B Gab. Pref., vol. 125. According to the subprefect, Costa had told his father that he was willing to risk jail and that

the only thing he really feared, though he was sure there were no grounds for such action, was being placed under domicilio coatto (confinement to an island prison).

[28]Costa letter to Vollmar, Mar. 27, 1880, in Della Peruta, Democrazia e socialismo, p. 412.

[29]Writing on Apr. 12, Costa informed Vollmar that the Milan Congress was to be held on May 10-12. See Della Peruta, Democrazia e socialismo, p. 413.

[30]Apparently the publication of this review had been on Costa's mind since the beginning of the year. See his letter to Vollmar, Jan. 11, 1880, in Della Peruta, Democrazia e socialismo, p. 410.

[31]Della Peruta, "Il socialismo italiano...," p. 333.

[32]A point of view sustained by Nettlau, Malatesta, pp. 170-71.

[33]La Stella d'Italia, Apr. 25, 1880. Costa, the paper commented, had gone to Milan to publish a magazine "and some say to organize a socialist congress."

[34]The Minister of Interior's initial reaction to Costa's letter "To my Friends of the Romagna" was that the Imolese simply wanted to strengthen an alliance with the reformists in order to prepare a revolt. See the Minister's note to the prefect of Forlì, Aug. 16, 1879, A.S.F., Gab. Pref., vol. 93, fasc. 247.

[35]Writing to the prefect of Forlì on Oct. 14, 1879, the Minister of Interior assured him he was confident that had the disagreement not arisen among Costa, Cafiero, and Malatesta, the International would already have taken action, especially in the Romagna (A.S.F., Gab. Pref., vol. 83, fasc. 1).

[36]On Jan. 8, 1880, the Minister of Interior informed the prefect of Forlì that the socialists, under the leadership of Merlino and Costa, were planning revolutionary movements in the Romagna to take place during March (A.S.F., Gab. Pref., vol. 94, fasc. 262).

[37]The dates of the various court proceedings in this period are taken from Lipparini's "Cronologia," pp. 190-91.

[38]See notes from the Minister of Interior to the pre-

fect of Bologna of Apr. 12 and 18, 1880 (A.S.B., Gab. Pref. vol. 125).

[39] This latest imprisonment won Costa and his cause a good deal of sympathy from unexpected quarters: "But is this persecution of the socialists not impolitic," asked Il Secolo, Milan's radical newspaper, "when they declare their desire to abandon conspiracies...and limit themselves to the public discussion permitted by law?" Quoted in La Stella d'Italia, May 10, 1880.

[40] He had been preceded by Kuliscioff, who was sent to the Emilian city in early June. See letter from Costa to Vollmar, June 8, 1880, in Della Peruta, Democrazia e socialismo, p. 414. While in the Bolognese prison Costa spent his time reading newspapers. Among those he received were La Rivista internazionale del socialismo, which continued to be published into the following year by Bignami and his friends, La Plebe, Il Satana (Cesena), and the French periodicals, L'Egalité and L'Intransigeant. See note from the prison warden to the prefect of Bologna, July 24, 1880, A.S.B., Gab. Pref., vol. 125.

[41] The Minister of Interior wrote the prefect of Bologna on Aug. 27, 1880, "We have been informed that the famous Andrea Costa was supposed to have written Enrico Bignami on the 17th of this month informing him that he would soon be released from prison and that after a short stop of a few days at Bologna he would leave for Milan where he intends to settle down and assume command of the party" (A.S.B., Gab. Pref., vol. 125).

[42] Costa arrived in Bologna from Switzerland on Oct. 13 questore to the prefect of Bologna, Oct. 13, 1880, A.S.B., Gab. Pref., vol. 125.

[43] Letter of Nov. 16, 1880, B.C.I., no. 91.

[44] Letter to Kuliscioff, B.C.I., no. 118.

[45] Il Moto (Imola), Jan. 29-30, 1881.

[46] Letter of Dec. 30, 1880, B.C.I., no. 134.

[47] Minister of Interior to the prefect of Bologna, Jan. 21, 1881, A.S.B., Gab. Pref., vol. 125.

[48] See La Plebe, Apr. 4, 1880.

[49]The congress was abandoned in a rather devious way. See Gnocchi-Viani, _Ricordi di un internazionalista_, p. 129.

[50]Apr. 25, 1881, A.S.B., _Gab. Pref._, vol. 125.

[51]Pala, _Anna Kuliscioff_, p. 64.

[52]Masini, _Storia degli anarchici italiani_, p. 178.

[53]Historians of the Italian socialist movement, including Lipparini ("Cronologia," p. 191), have written that the meeting took place in August. No specific dates are ever mentioned. On Aug. 19, 1881, however, _Il Grido del popolo_ (Naples) reported that the Romagnol Congress took place on July 24. All evidence tends to verify this. During this period Costa's movements were well known to the authorities; since he was under _ammonizione_, Costa was under constant surveillance. Moreover, every time he wanted to leave the city of Imola he was required to ask permission from the prefect's office. The police records show only one instance during this period of Costa's presence in Rimini: on Aug. 16, 1881, the subprefect of Cesena (report to the prefect of Forlì, A. S.F., _Gab. Pref._, vol. 96, fasc. 323) related that Costa had been at Rimini late in July. Apparently he had received permission to go to the seaside resort in order to visit the beach (prefect of Rimini to the prefect of Forlì, Oct. 15, 1881, A.S.F., _Gab. Pref._, vol. 106, fasc. 151). That this was the only time Costa was in Rimini in this period is confirmed by a later report from the subprefect of Rimini to the prefect of Forlì (Sept. 3, 1881, A.S.F., _Gab. Pref._, vol. 96, fasc. 323). In his note of Aug. 16, moreover, the subprefect of Cesena stated that there had been a reunion of 42 Internationalists in Rimini in late July; at the time, that is, when Costa was there. These reports, then, all tend to establish that the Congress of Rimini did in fact take place, as _Il Grido del popolo_ had stated, on July 24, not in August.

[54]According to the account in _Catilina_ (Cesena), Aug. 7, 1881.

[55]The program and the Statute and Regulations are reproduced in Manacorda, _Il movimento operaio italiano_, pp. 362-71.

[56]Ibid., p. 164.

[57]Socialismo e socialisti in Italia, pp. 146 ff.

[58]Ca. 1880 the illiteracy rate in Ravenna was close to 70% and in Forlì close to 80% (Luciano Casali, "Il movimento mazziniano in Romagna dall'astensione alla partecipazione alla lotta elettorale," L'azione dei mazziniani in Romagna, p. 52). This suggests that the vast majority of Romagnols had not attended school, where Italian was taught, and hence continued to communicate in dialect.

[59]The relationship of Valducci and the two brothers was not always cordial. See, for example, the report of the subprefect of Cesena to the prefect of Forlì, May 1, 1880, A.S.F., Gab. Pref., vol. 97, fasc. 339.

[60]In a note to the prefect of Forlì a police informant reported, "At this moment, Valducci, with his bold activity and his close relations with Costa, may be the most dangerous of the socialist leaders" (Mar. 19, 1880, A.S.F., Gab. Pref., vol. 94, fasc. 247/b).

[61]Sozzi describes Ferdinando and his brother Giacomo as "the first Internationalists in Cesena." See Gli inizi del movimento socialista a Cesena, p. 199.

[62]Subprefect of Cesena to the prefect of Forlì, Dec. 25, 1879, A.S.F., Gab. Pref., vol. 94, fasc. 1.

[63]An undated /but 1881/ and unsigned report on Forlì's two socialist sections (A.S.F., Gab. Pref., vol. 93, fasc. 228) listed five major leaders: Balducci, Cappellini, Sesto Fortuzzi, Antonio Petrignani, and Temistocle Silvagni. Little was heard from the latter two individuals thereafter, though, and Fortuzzi was very skeptical, at least in the beginning, about Costa's new program. See the report from the prefect of Forlì to the Minister of Interior, Dec. 8, 1880, A.S.F., Gab. Pref., vol. 97, fasc. 339.

[64]Forlì carabinieri to local prefect, n.d. /but 1879/, A.S.F., Gab. Pref., vol. 84, fasc. 11.

[65]Balducci was an extremely important figure. His authority was felt only after 1884, however, when he moved to Forlì. Moreover, he always remained somewhat outside Costa's orbit of influence. His son, Rolando Balducci, has written an interesting biography, Alessandro Balducci

e gli albori del socialismo nel forlivese, 1880-1904 (Milan: Garzanti, 1954).

[66]In a report to the prefect of Bologna, dated Aug. 29, 1890, the subprefect of Imola writes: "The high Pontiff of the socialist and democratic party in Imola is Andrea Costa, and the Imolesi take an interest in him alone" (A.S.B., Gab. Pref., cat. VII, 1890).

[67]Baldi was a socialist as early as January, 1877, when he was refused a job by the city of Imola because of his revolutionary ideas. See La Democrazia, Jan. 20-21, 1877.

[68]Their political views in 1880 were identical with Costa's. See Baldi and Negri, Ai nostri concittadini, pp. 5 ff.

[69]Subprefect of Imola to the prefect of Forlì, Feb. 12, 1880, A.S.F., Gab. Pref., vol. 95, fasc. 282.

[70]Report to the prefect of Forlì, Nov. 24, 1880, A.S.F., Gab. Pref., vol. 95, fasc. 282.

[71]On Nov. 14, according to a report from the subprefect of Imola to the prefect of Bologna, Oct. 15, 1881, A.S.B., Gab. Pref., cat. VII, 1883.

[72]Angelo Negri, Il Comune d'Imola dalla costituzione del Regno alla fine del secolo XIX (1859-1900) (Imola: Galeati, 1907), p. liii.

[73]Memorie di trent'anni, 1890-1920 (Rome: Rinascita, 1950), p. 29. For the most complete treatment of Baldini, see Nullo Baldini nella storia della cooperazione (Milan: Giuffrè, 1966).

[74]Piero D'Attore, "Ricordando Gaetano Zirardini," Cooperazione ravennate, 1 (June, 1952), 15.

[75]Claudio Zirardini, who was so active in the early 1870's, spent three years in prison for violating an ammonizione and after he was released in mid-1876 went into semi-retirement. He played an important role again in the 1880's but was definitely eclipsed by Gaetano. The Zirardini family included three other brothers: Edoardo, Giovanni, and Antonio--all prominent in local socialist and anarchist circles.

[76]La Stella d'Italia, Dec. 13, 1879.

[77]D'Attore, "Ricordando Gaetano Zirardini," p. 16.

[78]Barbanti-Brodano, an exponent of a very moderate socialism, claims that it was only in 1890 that he and Costa established complete rapport. See La Rivolta, Feb. 19, 1910. For the life of Barbanti-Brodano, see Un uomo, un tempo, the biography--very apologetic-- written by his daughter, Francesca Barbanti-Brodano.

[79]Prefect of Bologna to the prefect of Forlì, Mar. 22, 1880, A.S.F., Gab. Pref., vol. 95, fasc. 288. Alceste Faggioli, who might have become Costa's most valuable assistant in Bologna, died in March, 1881, at the age of thirty.

[80]Some historians during the Fascist period--for example, Francisco Bonavita, Il padre del duce (Rome: Ind. Tip. Romana, 1933)--have attempted to portray Alessandro as one of the leading protagonists in the history of Romagnol socialism. The picture presented by these historians is vastly exaggerated. Nevertheless, it is true that Alessandro Mussolini and Costa were on very good terms (carabiniere report to the prefect of Forlì, Sept. 10, 1883, A.S.F., Gab. Pref., vol. 101, fasc. 30).

[81]"Bologna," commented Giuseppe Barbanti-Brodano, "for a great number of Italians, is the capital of the Romagna." See letter to Felice Cavallotti /1889/, quoted in L'Italia radicale, carteggio di Felice Cavallotti: 1867-1898, ed. Liliana Dalle Nogare and Stefano Merli (Milan: Feltrinelli, 1959), p. 15.

[82]Proletariato e borghesia nel movimento socialista italiano (Turin: Rocca, 1908), p. 183.

[83]Adige (Verona), Jan. 31, 1881.

[84]Prefect of Forlì to the Minister of Interior, July 21, 1881, A.S.F., Gab. Pref., vol. 96, fasc. 321.

[85]A copy of this list, procured by a police informer, accompanies a note from the subprefect of Cesena to the prefect of Forlì, July 19, 1881, A.S.F., Gab. Pref., vol. 96, fasc. 321. The statistics which follow are taken from this copy.

[86]Tullio Martello, Storia della Internazionale della

sua origine al congress dell'Aja (Padua: Fratelli Sal-
min, 1873), p. 475.

[87]Filippo Turati, who was the dominant figure in
the party after its foundation in 1892, was notoriously
anti-anarchist. Nor did he have a great deal of sympathy
for the period of the International, which he relegated
to the "prehistory of socialism" (see Turati's letter
in Bologna 1874-Bologna 1897). Cf. Costa's view ("Annotazioni autobiografiche...," p. 324): "It was a necessary
and fertile period...it was inevitable; it corresponded
to our...temperament, culture, traditions, economic conditions....For good or for bad it could not have been
otherwise."

CHAPTER SIX

THE SOCIALISTS, THE REPUBLICANS, AND
THE ELECTIONS OF 1882

The Socialists and the Republicans

After 1870 the most serious challenge to the Savoy monarchy was provided by the republicans. Strong opposition also came from the extreme right, it is true, from the Catholics, who were upset over the loss of papal territories and shocked by the violence and anticlericalism which characterized the liberal Risorgimento. Still the only practical result of the conflict between Church and State was the abstention of the Catholics from political life: in 1874 Pope Pius IX issued his famous non expedit which called on the faithful to refrain from participation in political elections. This policy was also endorsed by the republicans, but their opposition to the government was not entirely passive; they continued to threaten the use of violence. Moreover, while the Catholics were held together in the loosest kind of way—through their common allegiance to the pope—the republicans were able to combine into a party.

Unfortunately for the republicans, they were never able to fully exploit their potential. Part of the trouble stemmed from the internal dissension plaguing the A.R.U. throughout the seventies and eighties. This discord was evident by the mid-1870's, when several tendencies within the party's ranks could already be distinguished.[1] After 1876, when the Left gained power, the main cleavage was between the Mazzinians and the non-Mazzinians.[2]

Most republicans were Mazzinians. Called either mazziniani puri or intransigenti, this sizable wing adhered strictly to the Prophet's teachings. Consequently they were absolutely uncompromising on the matter of political participation. They also called for the violent overthrow of the monarchical system. After the death of Mazzini in 1872, a triumvirate composed of Saffi, Maurizio Quadrio, and Federico Campanella, all ardent Mazzinians, controlled the fortunes of the party.

A minority of republicans, led by Gabriele Rosa, Alberto Mario, and Arcangelo Ghisleri, wanted to update Mazzini's teachings. Looking to Carlo Cattaneo rather than Mazzini, they preferred a republic based on the federal rather than the unitary principle and were convinced that this form of government could be achieved through an evolutionary process. These evoluzionisti, as they were sometimes called, were not so intransigent as the Mazzinians, for although they too refused to enter Parliament--a stand, incidentally, which set them apart from the radicals--they were at least willing to vote in the elections in order to achieve certain reforms.

According to S. Massimo Ganci, the Mazzinian current was centered in Rome and that of the evoluzionisti in Milan.[3] Neither city, however, had a large number of republicans. Rather, it was in the central provinces of Italy that the A.R.U. had its real strength, and nowhere was it more potent than in the Romagna. While the movement rapidly declined throughout the peninsula as the century waned--due to the inertia that set in after the party's failure to accept either a constitutional or a revolutionary course of action--the Romagnol republicans remained active even into the twentieth century.[4] In that region the movement was overwhelmingly Mazzinian until about 1890, the date of Saffi's death. Indeed, it was Saffi who insured Mazzini a wide following there, especially through his vast influence on the Consociazione Romagnola, the most robust of the party's regional federations.[5] Centered in Forlì, Saffi's native city, the Consociazione had active sections in all the major cities of the Romagna.[6]

Concurrent with his svolta, Costa came to view the republicans in a more positive light. If the socialists were to resist the government effectively and guarantee their freedom of movement, they needed allies, and in the Romagna only the Mazzinians were available. Also, if the socialists were to gain strength there, as Costa hoped, their new adherents would have to be drawn in large part from the Consociazione. Through an alliance with the republicans, then, Costa hoped to absorb their membership into the ranks of his own party.

The Mazzinians were aware, of course, of the danger of losing their followers to their more ambitious adversaries. Hence, when Costa began to press for better relations between the two parties in 1879, the Consociazione

210

heads were extremely reluctant to come to an agreement.
Not only were they afraid of losing their own identity,
but they also feared that the alliance would eventually
force them to enter politics, something which the intransigents in the party were loath to see happen.

Efforts to bring the socialists and the republicans
together in the Romagna began in late 1879. As the authorities suspected, it was through Costa's initiative
that this plan of action was formulated.[7] With the Imolese still in Swiss exile the practical work of reconciliation was left to Cappellini, Valducci, Negri, and the
other Romagnol chiefs who now realized that the old International was dead and that the socialist movement des-
perately needed a new direction.

Conditions in the Romagna were conducive to an en-
tente between the two subversive parties at this time.
During the year the Internationalists had not been the
sole target of police repression; republicans had also
been among its victims. For this reason some of the
members of the Consociazione, though by no means the majority, were amenable to the first socialist overtures.
By October, hardly three months after publication of his
open letter, several Romagnol republicans had journeyed
to Lugano to confer with Costa.[8]

Among the visitors was Antonio Fratti.[9] While he
had been one of the International's most resolute critics
some years before, Fratti had recently experienced a
change of heart. Speaking before a republican meeting
in the Romagna on July 7, 1878, the Forlivese "proclaimed
the necessity of a sincere pact between Internationalists and Mazzinians aimed at bringing down the monarchy."[1]
Undoubtedly Fratti went to see the socialist leader to
prepare such an agreement.[11] Apparently, too, his mission
was a success, for republicans and socialists began working together in Forlì--albeit not too smoothly--in late
1879.[12]

Progress was also made in Cesena, where Valzania favored the alliance. As the most incendiary of the A.R.U.
leaders in the Romagna, the old warrior had been urging
closer cooperation throughout the seventies with the objective of generating a meaningful revolution. By late
1879 most of the Cesenati were behind him.[13] Interparty
cooperation was even more productive, however, in Romagnol
cities where republicanism was less entrenched than in
Forlì and Cesena.

At Rimini cooperation was facilitated by the fact that all the local socialist party leaders were former republicans.[14] These men, especially Francolini and Bagli, were still in good standing with their ex-comrades.[15] Moreover, while Mazzinianism was more pervasive in Rimini than socialism, its leadership was weak; hence it was more vulnerable to socialist persuasion. The parties began to draw together late in 1879[16] and by the early part of the following year they were cooperating effectively.[17] Indeed, the alliance made such rapid progress that on July 5, 1880, the subprefect of the city reported that "although essentially separate and distinct, the local republican party conducts itself in the same way as does the Internationalist sect. It appears, in fact, to tag along behind the latter (though superior to it in both numbers and intelligence)."[18]

In Imola a close bond between the two parties manifested itself late in 1879.[19] This cooperation was made possible by the work of Negri and Baldi as well as by Costa's considerable prestige in the city. But another factor which contributed immeasurably to effecting the accord was Costa's personal friendship with Luigi Sassi, the most prominent of the local republicans.[20]

Sassi was universally respected in Imola. Antonio Graziadei, a fellow townsman, describes the republican capo-squadra as "the man of the people par excellence."[21] Another contemporary confirms this opinion of the man: "If there was ever anyone among us who deserved the epithet of citizen...as that which signifies the true, the best and the most popular representative of the town, who dedicated himself to that activity, mind and soul, it had to be Gigino Sassi."[22]

Sassi had become a republican of repute at a very early age. After the assassination of Piccinini in 1872, the young Imolese, then only nineteen years old, had been one of the main peacemakers within the Consociazione.[23] In the following decade, while still in his twenties, he gradually displaced Pietro Landi as the ranking A.R.U. chieftain in the city. Led by Sassi, the republicans in Imola during this period developed able resistance to the dominant moderates, headed by Count Codronchi.[24] One reason for the effectiveness of this opposition was Costa's support. Through the civilizing joint effort of Sassi and Costa, the city was spared those bloody confrontations between Internationalists and Mazzinians which took place in other parts of the Romagna.[25] Clearly, then, the po-

litical cooperation which we find between the two parties
in Imola in 1879 was deeply rooted in the past.

By 1880 the two parties had begun working together
not only in Imola but throughout the Romagna. As the
Minister of Interior put it early that year: "The moral
reconciliation of these two parties....is a fact which
has now been demonstrated on many occasions."[26]

Actually interparty cooperation still left much to
be desired.[27] The Mazzinians remained hesitant to commit themselves. Troubling them most was Costa's persever-
ing espousal of revolutionary action. During the conference on universal suffrage held in Bologna in late
1880, Saffi, angered by a Costa speech calling for popular rebellion, interrupted the socialist leader, object-
ing that violence was not the answer. In response, the
Imolese was quick to remind the A.R.U. head of his own
revolutionary past: "The president /Saffi/ has declared
that violence is always wrong; but let him, the friend
of Mazzini, now tell me whether Italy was created by
moral means."[28] Then, early in 1881, the embryonic socialist-republican alliance suddenly seemed to go up in
smoke. On January 2 members of both parties clashed at
Cesena and Forli[29] and the old Romagnol conflict gave
signs of erupting once again. The work of pacification
began almost immediately, however,[30] and despite stead-
fast opposition in some cities, notably Cesena, the two
parties gradually patched up their differences.[31] By the
middle of the year the accord was re-established.[32] The
effort put forth by both factions during this period was
due in no small measure to their common realization that
a coalition at this time could produce tangible benefits
for both of them in the political elections of 1882.

The Elections of 1882

Prior to 1882 only two percent of the Italian population was eligible to vote in national elections. With
the victory of the Left in 1876, revision of the electoral
law and subsequent expansion of the electorate had been
expected. But once in power the Left proved to be as re-
miss as the Right in extending the franchise. As a result, dissatisfaction with the government was rampant,
expressing itself in widespread agitation for electoral
reform. Spearheading the campaign was the radical party,
demanding nothing less than universal manhood suffrage.

213

One manifestation of this effort was the Bologna conference in late October and early November, 1880, which gathered to promote national suffrage. Presided over by Saffi, the meeting united the radical, republican, and socialist forces. The latter were led by Costa. Addressing the assembly on November 1, the Imolese defined his position on universal suffrage, asserting that socialists had little faith in it as an end in itself:

> We believe that there is a question of more import than that of suffrage, the economic question. The problem is knowing if, given the present relationship between capital and labor, there can be real improvement among the working classes. I declare that I do not believe it possible. We trust, however, in time, and we know enough history to recognize that not all conquests are made at one time. It is necessary to ask for a little in order to eventually gain a lot....It is necessary that... people agitate and begin to discuss their rights: it is natural that we begin with appearances... but then we will get to the substance: then the right to universal suffrage will bring those fruits which it cannot provide today....I say therefore that suffrage is not enough; for the moment it will serve as a beginning of the struggle against the established order....[33]

Costa, then, was saying that he supported the agitation for universal suffrage because he saw it as a means of educating the masses. Once the people learned to fight for one right they would not be satisfied until they had acquired all their rights. He saw the agitation for reform as desirable because of its propagandistic value.[34]

Actually Costa's support of universal suffrage was based on more immediate considerations. By the time of the Bologna conference in late 1880 he had determined that the socialists needed to enter Parliament, which would be possible only with a broader franchise.[35] He himself would be the party's candidate. The problem was that most of his comrades were not willing to endorse this position. They had accepted the need for reform, many of them reluctantly, but the entrance of party members into the government was entirely incompatible with Internationalist principles. As far as they were concerned the situation did not warrant this extreme step which represented almost a total abandonment of their traditional ideas. Costa disagreed. His task during the

214

next few months was to convert the party to his point of view. Given the continuing popularity of anarchist notions, though, this would be a difficult operation at best. The socialist leader was forced to move slowly, and to rely on subterfuge.

At their Bologna meeting of March 14, 1880, the Romagnol socialists had decided on political participation (though at the same time insisting they were revolutionaries). The extent of their involvement had not been specified. Was it to be limited to administrative (city) elections, or would it extend to political (national) elections as well? If the latter, would socialist candidacies to Parliament be protest or positive candidacies? That is, would the candidate only exploit the situation to propagandize his views and if elected refuse to accept the giuramento--the oath to uphold monarchic institutions--and hence not enter the Chamber of Deputies, or would he swear alliance and assume his place in the parliamentary life of the nation? The March gathering did not undertake clarification of these points but merely agreed to political participation in principle--probably because of a desire to appease anarchist sentiment at this time.[36]

Following the Congress of Rimini on July 24, 1881, however, the party's position was defined explicitly. According to the P.S.R.R. program, not only could the socialists participate in municipal elections, they would also "submit socialist and working-class candidacies, be they of a positive or protest nature, to Parliament and give the individual provincial associations the freedom to determine the conduct of those comrades which may be elected deputies."[37] In other words, socialists would be allowed to enter the Chamber of Deputies, their electors permitting.

These views did not correspond very well with Costa's public utterances. During the past few months, the Imolese had been limiting his support to protest candidacies only,[38] a position he reaffirmed on the eve of the Rimini conclave.[39] Still, the recent decision on political participation did not displease him. His comment on the controversial resolution concerning socialist candidacies to the Chamber of Deputies reveals his developing pragmatism: "For now, given...the present political atmosphere we do not believe that the party should send representatives to Parliament....Should the political atmosphere change, our political action could also change."[40]

215

It was becoming apparent that in order to keep the
support of his more revolutionary followers Costa had
adopted a dangerous tactic: while working covertly to
insure general support of positive socialist candidacies,
in public he either endorsed negative candidacies or, at
best, took an ambivalent stand on the issue.[41] After
the Rimini Congress, consequently, anarchist suspicions
that Costa was playing a double game became widespread.

Such suspicion grew during the following months
when it became clearer that Costa was not opposed to
having socialists in Parliament but only to the giuramento. In late October he defined his position. After
the Milanesi of La Plebe had called for the entrance of
the socialists into Parliament, Costa replied:

> We have nothing, certainly, to object to in what
> you say.
> But, how can 'the socialist agent' do all which
> you would have him do, if he does not take the oath?
> Refusing the oath, he will not be able to open his
> mouth and will have to leave, after having, at most,
> protested: something which we recognize to be use-
> ful.
> Because of that, because we believe, that is,
> that a self-respecting socialist should not lend
> himself to the comedy of the oath, for that very
> reason we limited ourselves to 'protest candidacies,'
> adding, moreover, that 'should the political atmos-
> phere change, our political action could also change';
> which is the same as saying, for example, that should
> the oath be abolished and a new political order es-
> tablished, the socialists could go from 'negative
> protest candidacies' all the way to 'positive candi-
> dacies of action.'
> At the moment, such a thing is not possible, ex-
> cept by isolated persons who have no scruples about
> lending themselves to the parliamentary comedy.[42]

Angered and alarmed, the anarchists tended to withdraw their support from Costa. Increasingly, the current
within their ranks demanding complete abstention from the
electoral process began to gain an audience. The Imolese
responded forcefully to this trend. The socialist movement should not count on any of its candidates who might
be elected, he stated, since in the present state of affairs they were powerless to ameliorate the people's
plight. "Nor should we permit," he continued, "our men
to recite the comedy of the oath; but let us accept the

electoral law and the coming election for what they are worth: as means of protest and agitation; and let us prepare ourselves to profit from them."[43] Costa's main concern now was convincing the **P.S.R.R.**'s anarchist element to participate in the elections--a concern which justifies the intransigent stand he himself took at the socialist assembly at Imola in February, 1882.

On January 22, 1882, a revised electoral law which stopped short of universal manhood suffrage but greatly expanded the franchise (from half a million to something over two million voters) went into effect. It was time to begin serious preparation for the national elections slated for the following October. Toward this end, forty-two socialists met at Imola on February 26, 1882.[44] The local subprefect reported that Costa, Mancini, Castellari, and Bennati headed the Imolese delegation; a sizeable contingent, including Valducci, Pradelli, and Rito Balducci, represented the other major cities of the Romagna and also the city of Bologna.[45]

The first matter to be considered was participation in the elections.[46] Surprisingly, the proposals favoring it met with little resistance. Involvement in administrative elections was unanimously recommended and only one dissenting vote was cast against engagement in political elections. While Costa's fear of general electoral abstention therefore appears to have been exaggerated, the fact of the matter is that the most uncompromising anarchists had boycotted the Imola meeting;[47] for example, the city of Rimini, a hotbed of anarchist activity, was virtually unrepresented.[48] Hence this vote against abstention hardly reflects the degree to which this current found favor throughout the Romagna.

The next question was that of electoral alliances: specifically, should the socialists ally with other democratic parties in the coming elections. Even though the intransigent anarchists were not present to express their feelings on the matter, the fear of fusion--in contrast to a simple alliance--with the republicans was so deep-seated even among those socialists in attendance that the delegates were unable to arrive at a clear-cut answer; it was decided that the question should be resolved at the local level. Each association was left free to determine whether or not to ally with other democratic parties in its own electoral district--under one condition, however: in the event of a local alliance the name of at least one socialist must be included on the list

217

of candidates.

The last question on the agenda was the most controversial: how should a socialist candidate conduct
himself if elected to Parliament. A decision was finally reached--with three dissenting votes and one absten-
tion--that the successful candidate should refuse the
giuramento; in a word, socialist candidacies must be
negative. Among those voting against the giuramento
was Costa.

Adamo Mancini later recalled that at the Imola meeting Giusto Goldini, the lone representative from Rimini,
had submitted an alternate proposal: namely, that the
socialist candidate himself be allowed to determine whether
or not to swear loyalty to the monarchy. But according
to Mancini, Costa had been quick to challenge Goldini's
proposal:

> Let us not forget, comrades, that above all we
> should seek to transform society and that those who
> are in Parliament are either lost or almost lost to
> the people. Let us not forget that if parliaments
> accomplish anything, they do it because the people
> want it; and, unfortunately, the energy and initia-
> tive of the people, given the present social condi-
> tions, are in large part lost or exploited when the
> people lack initiators. These incessant initiators
> should be the socialists and we cannot permit our-
> selves the luxury of giving a certain number of our
> members to parliamentary struggles, which are for
> the most part sterile.[49]

In stressing not only his unwillingness to accept
the giuramento but also the uselessness of having socialist deputies in Parliament, Costa had taken a giant step
backwards. Yet this intransigence was probably not a
true reflection of his beliefs at this time, but instead
was dictated by the situation. By adopting this strong
stand he reassured many of his wavering anarchist followers, thereby encouraging their involvement in the coming
election. That the P.S.R.R. leader had not really altered his ideas was made plain the next month when he wrote
and assured his friends of the Don Chisciotte, a democratic newspaper in Bologna:[50] "I do not mean to say that
the presence of one or more socialists in Parliament is
useless. No, certainly not. Nor would I despise that
socialist who, convinced he is doing the right thing,
would enter it today. Let him enter, and we will support

218

him to the best of our ability."[51]

After the Imola meeting of February 26, socialist ferment in the Romagna accelerated noticeably. The authorities construed this stepped-up activity as preparation for an insurrection,[52] whereas the P.S.R.R. was in fact getting ready for the next elections. There was a second gathering in Imola on March 26, attended by party representatives from throughout the Romagna including Arturo Mazzanti of Ravenna and Cappellini, the Forlivese.[53] Although the scope of this meeting remains unknown, apparently it was here that agreement was reached to propose Costa as the socialist candidate in the Romagna.[54]

By March Costa had gained a measure of unity within his own party. Having appeased the anarchists (though only temporarily) he was able to focus his attention once more on solidifying his shaky alliance with the republicans--an indispensable one with the elections not far away.

Cooperation posed no problem in Imola, where socialists and republicans were on the best of terms. Earlier that year the town's Mazzinians had reorganized their party under Sassi and created a new association called Istruzione-Libertà-Benessere.[55] This club was nurtured along by Costa until all the differences between the two subversive factions in Imola had practically vanished. In fact, as early as March 5, 1882, the carabinieri were referring to the local "republican-socialist party,"[56] and a few months later the union became so complete that Negri and Baldi, who were socialists, were included in a list of A.R.U. leaders compiled by the local subprefect.[57]

Outside of Imola the story was not quite the same. Socialists and republicans had worked together during the preceding year, 1881, but cooperation had been very uneasy. Within the Mazzinian movement, adamant resistance to the socialist alliance came from the militant wing, which absolutely rejected electoral participation. This group had swelled enormously after 1880, when Alessandro Fortis ran for Parliament, was elected as a representative from the province of Forlì (that he was able to win even with a restricted suffrage is a tribute to republican strength in and around the city of Forlì) and, to the A.R.U.'s surprise, accepted the oath (to the monarchy!), taking his seat in the Chamber of Deputies--the first step in a political career which was to culminate in 1905 when he was elected Prime Minister. Fortis' "betrayal" necessarily fortified the position of his detractors within the party.

Now, in 1882, the republican intransigents were led by Antonio Fratti. While the Mazzinian chieftain had been a champion of the socialist alliance in years past, he had been an even more zealous exponent of electoral abstention.[58] When the Forlivese realized that the proposed interparty agreement was electoral in scope, he would have none of it.

Perhaps most members of the Romagnol Consociazione, though, were willing to participate in the elections. Like most socialists, they called for negative candidacies. Yet even this majority was disinclined to establish the accord, for two long-standing reasons: revulsion toward the socialist emphasis on revolution and fear that the alliance would mean their party's dissolution.

Still, at the beginning of 1882 the relations between the two parties improved and they slowly came together. As Costa wrote in Avanti! early in January: "Let it not be said that this alliance is brought about by one or the other /party/, because it occurs, instead, spontaneously throughout: in Romagna, in Turin, in the southern provinces and even in Sicily--provoked not by you or me, but by the very nature of things." Continuing, he affirmed the relative ease in advancing political cohesion in the Romagna: "/here/ we do not have... that profound class division which makes a coalition between the people and a part of the bourgeoisie...impossible." And if the two parties did come together and were victorious in the end, what then? "We do not know; but we are firmly convinced that if the republic is established in Italy, this republic...can only be a social one."[59]

To gain republican support Costa was forced to adjust his arguments to the situation. Still, he could not overwork this technique, since he could not afford to alienate the members of his own party. On principle, moreover, there was a point beyond which Costa would not go. He was unyielding concerning his belief in the inevitability of the revolution, for instance, regardless of the fact that it was anathema to the republicans. This was illustrated early in the year, when Gabriele Rosa, one of Italy's foremost A.R.U. leaders, wrote an

article in L'Avamposta (Brescia) condemning the socialists
for wanting to bring about revolution, to which Costa
replied: "It is not a question of wanting revolution but
of being able to carry it out. And now let us ask Gabriele Rosa, who has studied so much history, if a new
social idea can be achieved in this world without a...vio-
lent revolution....Historical experience answers: no;
the revolution is inevitable: and we are powerless to do
anything about it."[60]

Nor did Costa leave any doubt about the degree of
alliance he was working to achieve. Since on principle
socialists could never unite with a middle-class element,
actual fusion was out of the question; thus both factions
should only cooperate. Furthermore, the republicans were
a party of the past, whereas the socialists were a party
of the future. Speaking before the association Istruzione
Libertà-Benessere Costa made this point very clear: "In
his age, Giuseppe Mazzini was that which we are today:
a revolutionary. It would have been too early in...Maz-
zini's time to have been a socialist; at the present time
it would be too late to be a Mazzinian."[61]

Despite the disinclination of the Consociazione
leadership--Saffi as well as Fratti--Costa seemed to be
making some progress toward the alliance.[62] Then his
efforts were dealt a near-fatal blow. At the national
Congress of Genoa on June 22, 1882, the A.R.U. voted in
favor of non-participation in the coming elections. Although party members were left free to vote as individuals
the mazziniani puri had scored a big victory. Costa was
infuriated: "They have not learned anything in ten years
....Despite their good intentions, they remain bourgeoisie
....We may be able to come to an understanding with them
against the common enemy; but to get along well with
them is impossible."[63]

But almost immediately new developments were set in
motion to restore the rapprochement. On June 25 the first
comizio (demonstration) against the government's recourse
to exceptional laws--including the ammonizione and domicilio coatto--took place in Imola. This issue was one
on which all democratic parties could unite; hence the
protests were supported by radicals, republicans, and
socialists alike.[64] The agitation proved to be popular,
for the Imola comizio was followed by similar demonstrations in Ravenna on September 3 and Faenza on September
17. Socialists and republicans were actively involved in
all of them.

When Luigi Lodi and Roberto Landini of the Don Chisciotte came to Imola to confer with Costa on July 24, Francesco Palomba, the local subprefect, reported: "I believe that this movement of people and their meeting at Imola constitute the first concerted efforts to reach agreement on the position to be taken in regard to the electoral question."[65] His calculation, as usual, was correct. The authorities had known that the P.S.R.R. leader was planning to run for a seat in Parliament as early as April.[66] Now Costa was getting his campaign under way. The first step was to reach an agreement with the publishers of the Don Chisciotte, a paper which represented the more flexible republicans of Bologna. Costa wanted to run as a candidate in the second electoral college of the province of Bologna, a college centering in Imola but covering over half of the province including three other major cities: Molinella, Budrio, and Medicina. An agreement with the Bolognesi was essential in view of the immense influence they wielded in the surrounding area.

Costa had little trouble, of course, in reaching agreement with Imola's republicans. On August 12, Sassi's republican Istruzione-Libertà-Benessere voted to participate in the elections.[67] The next day Imola's republicans and socialists formed an electoral alliance called Il Fascio Elettorale della Democrazia.[68]

Two weeks later Costa's venture looked even more promising. On August 27, representatives of the three democratic parties from throughout the region arrived in Imola for the purpose of "establishing in all of Romagna the same agreement among socialists, republicans, and radicals which had already been established at Imola and Bologna."[69] The meeting was a success: the delegates voted to propose a common slate and organized themselves into the Unione Elettorale Democratica Romagnola.

But Saffi and most of the Consociazione chiefs in the Romagna did not approve of the electoral alliance. They saw the Unione as the negation of the decisions they had helped to ratify at the Congress of Genoa. On the other hand, they refused to criticize the alliance openly; instead, they limited themselves to reaffirming that the individual party member was free to vote or not to vote. The closest Saffi came to encouraging the republican vote was in his statement made in September: "Participation in elections...is not, in my opinion, contradictory to the mission of the republican party, under

222

the present conditions in Italy, nor does it clash with the duties of our apostolate...."[70] Outside of the Romagna, however, most republicans were not quite so diplomatic: both La Lega della democrazia in Rome and La Democrazia in Bologna expressed their unconditional opposition to the electoral alliance.[71]

On September 24 the democratic parties of the second electoral college of Bologna met at Imola, the principal city in that district, and selected their candidates. Costa would represent the socialists; Venturini, the republicans; and Quirico Filopanti, the radicals.[72] Il Moto now bearing the subtitle, The Organ of the Democratic Electoral Committee of the Second College of Bologna, enthusiastically endorsed the slate, tried to dispel any doubts which might persist as to the advisability of an alliance with the socialists, and declared: "If the socialists support impossible things, if their economic and political theories are fantastic, in the course of events these ideas...will be subjected to analysis and discussion, and we will see what kind of resistance and force of application they may possess."[73]

The elections were held on October 29. The radical-democratic slate, headed by Costa, was opposed by that of the moderates, headed by Count Giovanni Codronchi. One of the most respected citizens in Imola, Codronchi had already served several terms in Parliament.[74] It was generally recognized that he and Costa would be the main protagonists of the elections. As a correspondent for La Rassegna, the organ of the moderates in Rome, observed: "Of the various colleges in Italy, the one which presents the clearest and most logical electoral situation is that of Imola: it is here that the two old rivals Costa and Codronchi--two names that say it all--finally find themselves face to face. The whole question will revolve around them, and around the slates they represent."[75]

The democratic parties hoped to capitalize on the extension of the franchise,[76] but they were in for a disappointment. While Costa defeated Codronchi in Imola and the larger cities of the college, the moderate candidate fared well in the countryside.[77] The result was a victory for Codronchi and his slate. The votes were distributed as follows: Venturini, 2,690; Costa, 2,843; and Filopanti, 3,467 for the radicals; Berti, 3,627; Codronchi 4,304; and Inviti, 4,587 for the moderates.[78]

The defeat of the democratic parties was attributable in part ot the dissension which weakened their ranks. Filopanti had always been uneasy about being included on the radical-democratic slate--an attitude he had made plain to the voters.[79] More significant in the defeat, though, was the poor showing by the leftist parties outside the cities. The countryside was dominated by rich clerical families who because of their fear of the democrats were able to deliver the vote to the moderates.[80]

Although the democratic parties in Imola were embittered by their defeat,[81] their disappointment was mitigated somewhat by the results at Ravenna: in addition to Alfredo Baccarini, a progressive, and Luigi Farini, a moderate, the Ravennati had elected socialist Costa and Agostino Bertani, a radical, to Parliament.[82]

In Ravenna Costa had overcome extremely difficult odds. The architect of his victory was Gaetano Zirardini, who henceforth would be regarded as the most effectual young socialist in the region. Earlier in the year Zirardini had been living in Florence.[83] A few months later he was back in the Romagna, where he helped organize the Ravenna comizio of September 3.[84] On the very day of the antigovernment rally he also commenced publication of Il Sole dell'avvenire.[85] The Ravenna paper's editorial staff included Gaetano's brother Giovanni, Ugo Ginanni Corradini, Carlo Traversi, Giuseppe Piazza, Romeo Destefani, Aristide Trerè, Giovanni Bissi, Lodovico Nabruzzi, Baldini, Armuzzi, and Ceroni.[86] Costa described succinctly the program of the new weekly: "In theory, it will support socialism; in practice, the union of the democratic forces against the common enemy."[87] Apparently the paper was intended to prepare the ground for Costa's candidacy in Ravenna.

The ideas expressed by Il Sole were very close to Costa's. In the first issue Zirardini and his staff proclaimed themselves "revolutionary socialists," but at the same time they made clear their willingness to accept a reform program: "These reforms which we will endeavor to introduce, especially in the commune, will be sustained in our newspaper and will be extremely radical in that they will be the cause of a moral and material improvement of the working classes...."[88]

Also in September, Zirardini and his comrades began to press for an electoral alliance with the republicans in Ravenna,[89] but by the end of the month they had made little or no progress. The correspondent for Il Sole from Imola (possibly Costa) informed the paper of the accord reached in that city on September 24, and admonished the Ravennati: "The uncertainty which still dominates in your province disturbs us. You too should decide on which parties you can work with....Why can you not accomplish there what we have done here?"[90]

This was easier said than done. In fact, the conditions for an alliance in Ravenna were far less favorable than in Imola. Here the republicans were not nearly so accommodating as Sassi and his friends had been, and they made their position crystal clear in a letter sent to Il Sole by the Consociazione Repubblicana Ravennate: "Yes: our party is abstentionist and it will continue to be so until it has obtained universal suffrage based on popular /rather than monarchical/ sovereignty...."[91]

Yet while such abstentionists dominated the movement in Ravenna, not all republicans espoused their point of view. Allying themselves with these more transigent elements, the socialists, led by Gaetano Zirardini and Tullo Ginanni Corradini, were able to create an Associazione Elettorale Democratica Ravennate patterned after Imola's.

Within this organization, however, not everything went smoothly. One week before the election the Associazione announced its candidates: Gino Vendemini, Venturini, Costa, and Gnocchi-Viani.[92] But the republicans resented the inclusion of two socialists--Costa and Gnocchi-Viani--on the slate; by the date of the election Gnocchi-Viani had been replaced by Bertani, who as a radical was closer to the republicans ideologically.[93]

A Costa victory at Ravenna seemed highly improbable. It was expected, of course, that the socialist candidate would have a harder fight there than in Imola. Not only was he an outsider, but Ravenna's leftist parties were weaker than those of his own city. Also, he was faced with republican abstention. Yet despite these disadvantages Costa would provide the main competition to the upholders of the status quo. As the conservative newspaper Il Ravennate[94] admitted: "After our four,...the name which will receive the most votes will be that of Andrea Costa."[95]

The conservatives' fears were more than justified:

only two of their candidates, Farini and Baccarini, were elected. The radical slate received over 3,500 votes; the moderate slate, which included Farini, 2,500; and the progressive slate, that of Baccarini, only 1,800.[96] What accounted for the triumph of the democratic parties in Ravenna? Certainly the socialist leadership--particularly Zirardini--had much to do with that victory. Also contributing thereto was the dissension among their conservative opponents. Since 500 republicans abstained from the elections,[97] the democrats were not completely united, but the conservatives did not do much better. The progressives and the moderates, traditional enemies in Ravenna, tried to muster a single front against the democratic parties. For a moment it seemed that they would succeed. But the ancient rivalries kept surfacing, and instead of proposing a common slate they managed only to agree to cooperate with each other. Such qualified unity was not enough; hence the democratic victory in Ravenna.

Il Giuramento

The day after the elections Gaetano Zirardini wrote to Costa in Imola congratulating him on his victory. Zirardini was ecstatic over his friend's election, but he was also disturbed. As he put it to Costa, point-blank: "Let me ask you a question. Do you intend to take the oath and thereafter enter Parliament and provoke a scene over the question of the giuramento?"[98]

What was Costa's position on the parliamentary oath now? Even Zirardini, by now one of the Imolese's most trusted lieutenants, was unsure. Costa, of course, knew exactly what he wanted by this time: he was prepared to take his seat in the Chamber of Deputies. But he found himself in an embarrassing position. Most members of the P.S.R.R., socialists as well as anarchists, opposed the taking of the oath, and Costa himself had encouraged this position before his election--this was the only way he could muster up enough votes among his comrades to win in the first place. Could he now persuade the party to sanction the new step forward, or would he have to abandon his political ambitions?

Fortunately, the recently elected representative had some valuable allies. Both La Plebe and La Favilla, two of the most prominent socialist papers in the country, recommended that the obstacle of the giuramento be removed.[99]

Closer to home, Sassi and his friends in Imola concurred
with this advice. On November 18, Il Moto declared that
a socialist deputy--an obvious reference to Costa--should
take the oath of allegiance and enter Parliament. "We
have always thought that to do otherwise," the paper continued, "would constitute...a sterile protest, sterile
because it would be isolated...." The Imolesi were not
the only Romagnols to take this accommodating stance.
Pellegrino Bagli and the Riminesi of L'Alfabeto also
counseled Costa to swear and accept his elected position;
only thus, they argued, would the people's will be val-
idated.[100]

Would this support be enough to permit the P.S.R.R.
leader to do as he wanted? The subprefect of Imola, for
one, believed it would suffice and on November 16 he predicted that Costa was about to follow in the footsteps
of Bertani, Fortis, and Aventi by taking the oath.[101] All
doubts were soon dispelled. At a meeting in Ravenna four
days later, the local socialists determined that Costa
should take the oath, though with the reservation that he
go on record as opposing the institution of the giuramento
in his first parliamentary speech.[102]

On the surface, consequently, it would seem that
Costa had bowed to the wishes of his socialist electors,
as required by the P.S.R.R. program. In reality it is
doubtful that the Ravennati made the momentous decision
themselves. In the first place, the socialists in Ravenna had never looked favorably on the giuramento. As late
as September of that very year Il Sole had stated their
position: "What reasons can possibly militate in favor
of sending revolutionary socialist deputies to a monarch-
istic and conservative Chamber? Who has ever proved...
that an honest man in Parliament can do something useful for the moral and material welfare of the people?
No one! ...If useful improvements and reforms can be obtained under the present state of affairs, it is elsewhere that it is necessary to seek and promote them."[103]
Nor is it likely that they had changed their minds in the
few intervening weeks. Their leader, Gaetano Zirardini,
had demonstrated in his letter to Costa of October 30
that he, for one, was of the same mind. Acceptance of
the giuramento, he declared, "is not compatible with our
ideas or yours." Thus he strongly suggested that Costa
refuse to take the oath. Instead, the Imolese should
make use of the occasion by speaking out against the parliamentary oath in the Chamber of Deputies. Costa must
sacrifice himself, Zirardini concluded, in order to ad-

vance the cause of socialism. Nor was there anything to suggest that the Ravennati disagreed with their __capo-squadra__ on this matter.

It appears, then, that the choice made at the November 19 meeting was Costa's, not that of his followers in Ravenna.[104] This suspicion was confirmed in a __questore__'s report which stated that prior to the meeting Costa had individually contacted all of Ravenna's ranking socialists to insure that their judgement would be in accord with his.[105]

A few days later, __Il Sole__ was urging Costa to take the oath: "Costa should not protest and retire, but should swear __knowing that he swears falsely__, should protest, and should remain /in the Chamber/ in order to provoke there...principles never before heard and in order to take advantage of the /parliamentary/ privileges of __inviolability and of free transit throughout Italy__, which he will use for the exclusive interest of our party and of the people's cause."[106] On November 25, 1882, Costa took the oath of allegiance and entered Parliament, where he would serve almost without interruption until his death in 1910.

Conclusion

By mid-1880, as the first number of the __Rivista internazionale del socialismo__ tends to suggest, Costa had determined that he would enter Parliament, a logical corollary to the essentially legalitarian stance taken during the previous year. Working within the governing body, the ex-Bakuninist reasoned, provided the most effective means of bringing about the sadly needed reforms which had only been implied in the open letter to the Romagnols in 1879 but would be made specific in the __P.S. R.R.__ program two years later.

The fulfillment of his ambitions, though, depended upon how well Costa could perform two related tasks: the establishment of a socialist-republican alliance in the Romagna and the overcoming of the natural sentiment in favor of electoral abstention which persisted in the two subversive parties. The latter mission was the more difficult of the two. Both republicans and socialists were dead set against electing representatives to the Chamber of Deputies. Among the socialists the abstentionist trend was centered in the anarchist wing, those party members who wished to remain faithful to the old Internationalist program and avoid any unnecessary compromise with the state. But sympathy for the anarchist stance on elections could be found, to a greater or lesser extent, throughout the socialist ranks. Likewise, this attitude permeated the A.R.U. in the Romagna. The republicans were as intent on avoiding collaboration with the government as were the anarchists (though Saffi and his friends objected not to the state per se, but rather to the monarchy, the form the state took). This position of extreme intransigence was gradually being superseded, as Fortis' election demonstrates; yet even those members of the Consociazione who managed to overcome the prejudice against elections balked before the giuramento, the oath to uphold the institutions of the monarchy. No republican could accept this requirement in good conscience.

The unwillingness of the socialists and the republicans to engage in politics had an adverse effect, of course, on Costa's efforts to achieve his second goal, the interparty alliance. Agreement, which had been sought by the Imolese since 1879, had always encountered keen opposition from elements in both parties who feared that cooperation would lead to fusion--that is, absorption by their allies. After 1880, when it became increasingly evident that the alliance was intended to be an electoral coalition, the resistance grew more intense. But Costa needed the alliance; he knew that without the aid of the republicans, the biggest party in the region, he would have no chance at all of winning against the conservative candidates.[107]

The obstacles Costa faced in attempting to get the socialists and the republicans to cooperate on the eve of the election were overwhelming; he was shrewd enough, however, not to compound the difficulties by publicly admitting that he fully intended to accept the giuramento and enter the Chamber of Deputies.[108] Indeed, he did everything he could to discourage this impression. Campaign strategy was based largely on deception: working diligently behind the scenes to achieve his political ends one step at a time, Costa made it appear that he was following his party rather than leading it. This subtle Machiavellian approach required all the skill at his disposal, but in the end Costa reaped its benefits-- a seat in Parliament.

NOTES

[1]Franco Catalano, Storia dei partiti politici italiani, 2nd ed. (Turin: Radiotelevisione Italiana, 1968), p. 75.

[2]L'Italia antimoderata: radicali, repubblicani, socialisti, autonomisti dall'Unità a oggi (Parma: Guanda, 1968), p. 122.

[3]Ibid., p. 111.

[4]An excellent study of the Romagnol republicans at the turn of the century is that of Luigi Lotti, I repubblicani in Romagna dal 1894 al 1915 (Faenza: Fratelli Lega, 1957).

[5]Giovanni Spadolini, I repubblicani dopo l'Unità, p. 60.

[6]In 1879 the police estimated that almost two-thirds of the city of Forlì belonged to the Circolo Mazzini, the local republican organization. See "Elenco delle società repubblicane, Forlì," Jan. 6, 1879, A.S.F., Gab. Pref., vol. 83, fasc. 2.

[7]Subprefect of Rimini to the prefect of Forlì, Dec. 5, 1879, A.S.F., Gab. Pref., vol. 83, fasc. 1.

[8]Police inspector of Forlì to the prefect of Forlì, Oct. 27, 1879, A.S.F., Gab. Pref., vol. 83, fasc. 1.

[9]The best biography of the republican leader: Aldo Spallicci, Antonio Fratti (Milan: Garzanti, 1965).

[10]Prefect of Naples to his questore, July 18, 1878, quoted in Romano, Storia, II, 633.

[11]A few years previously Fratti had described Costa in this way: "He is an earnest young man, very intelligent, who, however, lacks a practical sense of things. If he lives and studies society better, he will become an influential man in the destiny of his country: at the moment he demonstrates the power of conception but the inability to act: he lacks, as do many of his friends,

the essential element for a fruitful activity, the faith in experienced and reasonable principles, a faith which he will perhaps acquire with time. When that happens, he will have modified his ideas radically." See La Democrazia, Apr. 8-9, 1876.

[12]See the cited report from the police inspector of Forlì to the prefect of Forlì, Oct. 27, 1879.

[13]Subprefect of Cesena to the prefect of Forlì, Jan. 30, 1880, A.S.F., Gab. Pref., vol. 94, fasc. 262.

[14]A list of "the most feared and influential of the Internationalists" in Rimini, signed Jan. 11, 1879, contained the names of eleven persons, all ex-republicans (A.S.F., Gab. Pref., vol. 84, fasc. 11).

[15]Subprefect of Rimini to the prefect of Forlì, May 26, 1880, A.S.F., Gab. Pref., vol. 95, fasc. 296.

[16]Subprefect of Rimini to the prefect of Forlì, Dec. 25, 1879, A.S.F., Gab. Pref., vol. 95, fasc. 262.

[17]Subprefect of Rimini to the prefect of Forlì, Feb. 28, 1880, A.S.F., Gab. Pref., vol. 94, fasc. 247/b.

[18]Report to the prefect of Forlì, A.S.F., Gab. Pref., vol. 84, fasc. 13.

[19]On Oct. 13 of that year the prefect of Bologna wrote the prefect of Forlì declaring that the two parties were coming together in his province, but that this process was occurring not so much in the city of Bologna as in near-by Imola (A.S.F., Gab. Pref., vol. 83, fasc. 1).

[20]For a biographical sketch of Sassi (1853-1902), see Romeo Galli, "Luigi Sassi," Il Resto del carlino, Aug. 23, 1941.

[21]Memorie, p. 29.

[22]Cita /Giuseppe/ Mazzini, Imola d'una volta, I (Milan: Gastaldi, 1942), 166. Gigino is an affectionate form of Luigi, and significantly it was by that name that Sassi was known among the Imolesi.

[23]Lotti, I repubblicani in Romagna, p. 38.

[24]Codronchi's judgement of Sassi in 1874: "He is by

231

nature a troublemaker: it is because of him that many
inexperienced youngsters were recruited into the subversive party." See report to the pretore of Imola, Aug.
14, 1874, Procedimento Costa, vol. 1.

[25]Marabini, Prime lotte socialiste, p. 55.

[26]Letter to the prefect of Forlì, Feb. 22, 1880,
A.S.F., Gab. Pref., vol. 94, fasc. 247/b. In the same
month (n.d.) the Minister of Interior also cautioned
against a possible insurrection in the Romagna by both
parties working in concert. See letter to the prefect
of Forlì, A.S.F., Gab. Pref., vol. 95, fasc. 279.

[27]On Mar. 21, 1880, the subprefect of Rimini informed
the prefect of Forlì that Alfonso Leonesi had arrived in
the seaside city from Pesaro two days before. "In his
conversations," the subprefect stated, "he supposedly
lamented the failure, except in Rimini, of the attempts
made to bring about the fusion with the republicans"
(A.S.F., Gab. Pref., vol. 94, fasc. 247/b).

[28]La Plebe, Dec. 12, 1880.

[29]Diario Guarini, Jan. 2, 1881, quoted in Aurelio
Lolli, Cronologia repubblicana forlivese, I (Rocca San
Casciano: Cappelli, 1962), 63.

[30]Subprefect of Rimini to the prefect of Forlì, Jan.
22, 1881, A.S.F., Gab. Pref., vol. 96, fasc. 322. The
events in Forlì and Cesena were isolated incidents.
Writing a few days after the tumults, Federico Comandini
noted that in general great progress had been made in im-
proving the relations between the two parties during the
last few years. See Adige, Jan. 14, 1881.

[31]The initial attempt to bring peace in Cesena was
made by Valzania, who proposed that the two parties sign
a manifesto openly declaring conciliation. Led by Galli,
though, the Internationalists of the city met on Jan. 12
and rejected Valzania's idea 270-78. Thereafter antagonism became so intense in Cesena that the party heads never
left their homes unless accompanied by their comrades.
See report from the Forlì carabinieri to the prefect of
Forlì, Jan. 18, 1881, A.S.F., Gab. Pref., vol. 97, fasc.
346.

[32]On June 26, 1881, the carabinieri in Forlì informed
the local prefect that it was difficult to make a true

distinction between the socialists and the republicans in the province because "they are completely united" (A. S.F., Gab. Pref., vol. 96, fasc. 325).

[33]La Plebe, Dec. 21, 1880, quoted in Manacorda, Il movimento operaio italiano, pp. 158-59. Costa made his position known the day before his speech in an article which appeared in the first number of Il Moto, Oct. 30-31, 1880. At the Comizio dei comizi--the greatest demonstration for universal suffrage during this period--held in Rome in February, 1881, these views were again presented in a letter (dated Feb. 8 and published in Il Moto, Feb. 12-13, 1881) which Costa addressed to the organizing committee of the Comizio. The Romagnol repeated these opinions the following month in an article in La Vita nuova (Rimini), May 15, 1881.

[34]Costa's view of universal suffrage is very similar to that of Fratti. "Universal suffrage," Fratti wrote in La Democrazia of Apr. 8-9, 1876, "can serve us as a means of gaining a certain civil education...but surely it does not make the people sovereign, as certain political mesmerizers would want to make it believe....Even were universal suffrage to be granted, there would still be the indisputable Statuto, and above all there would still be a supreme Authority which can always free itself of the people's representatives, if these became troublesome, at its pleasure."

[35]Della Peruta, "Il socialismo italiano...," p. 333, suggests that Costa had arrived at this conclusion by mid-1880.

[36]As it was there developed much opposition to the resolutions accepted at Bologna. According to information received by the Minister of Interior, the various socialist meetings taking place in the Romagna between March and September, 1880, tended to repudiate these deliberations (Minister of Interior to the prefect of Forlì, Sept. 15, 1880, A.S.F., Gab. Pref., vol. 97, fasc. 339).

[37]See the P.S.R.R. program, in Manacorda, Il movimento operaio italiano, pp. 362-71.

[38]Even this position, though, was too much for the most intransigent of the anarchist die-hards, who rejected the very idea of candidacies. See, for example, the letter by Vittorino Valbonesi in Catalina, May 1, 1881.

[39]Catalina, July 10, 1881. In order to evade the strict surveillance to which he was subject in the province of Bologna, Costa ceased publication of Avanti! in May and later moved to Cesena, in the province of Forlì, where he took over Catalina, a socialist organ formerly published by Carlo Rotondi. The Imolese put out four numbers of the paper under the old title--this issue is the first--before resurrecting the name Avanti! on Aug. 21, 1881.

[40]Supplement to Avanti!, Sept. 6, 1881.

[41]Costa again championed negative candidacies in his letter Ai miei amici ed ai miei avversari (Sept. 15, 1881) and in Avanti!, Feb. 5, 1882.

[42]Avanti!, Oct. 30, 1881.

[43]Ibid., Dec. 26, 1881.

[44]"It is easy to surmise," wrote Palomba, the subprefect of Imola, "that the city of Imola has been selected, among the other cities in the Romagna, as the best place to hold such a meeting primarily because it has a more numerous and active group of socialists and also because it is the residence of Andrea Costa, who is the incarnation of the sect and is unable to leave the city on account of his ammonizione." See report to the prefect of Bologna, Feb. 16, 1882, A.S.B., Gab. Pref., cat. VII, 1882. In her chronology of Costa's life (p. 191), Lipparini makes note of an electoral meeting held in Imola on Feb. 26, 1881. This is a mistake: apparently she was thinking of the gathering which took place exactly one year later.

[45]Subprefect of Imola to the prefect of Bologna, Apr. 4, 1882, A.S.B., Gab. Pref., cat. VII, 1882. The other outsiders, according to the subprefect: Giovanni Robertini and Ettore Tondini of Cesena, Giusto Goldini of Rimini, Corradini (probably Ugo) from Ravenna, Pietro Plata from Medicina, and the Buscaroli brothers and a certain Corazza from Bologna. Quite possibly Secondo Cappellini might have been there also (prefect of Bologna to the Minister of Interior, Mar. 3, 1882, A.S.B., Gab. Pref., cat. VII, 1882). Ettore Serpierri of Savignano and Antonio Bartoli of Gambettola are other possibilities (subprefect of Imola to the prefect of Bologna, Feb. 27,

1882, A.S.B., Gab. Pref., cat. VII, 1882).

[46]For a description of the proceedings at the Imola meeting, see Avanti!, Mar. 5, 1882. Manacorda relies heavily on this account in Il movimento operaio italiano, pp. 173-76.

[47]Judging from the poor attendance at the meeting, the subprefect of Imola stated on Feb. 27, "it would seem...that the Romagna has not responded in the way that the socialists of Imola, and their leader Costa, expected. See report to the prefect of Bologna, A.S.B., Gab. Pref., cat. VII, 1882.

[48]The subprefect of Rimini had noted on Feb. 23 that few socialists from his city would go to Imola, as their course of action had already been decided (report to the prefect of Forlì, A.S.F., Gab. Pref., vol. 103, fasc.78).

[49]Dall'internazionalismo di Andrea Costa al cortegianismo di Leonida Bissolati (Imola: Galeati, 1914), pp. 25-26.

[50]The Don Chisciotte appeared on May 1, 1881. At this time, Costa stated, "It has a program which is not completely our own, but to which we could in part subscribe." See Avanti!, Apr. 30, 1881. In fact, the authorities labeled it "republican with socialist tendencies." See questore's report of 1882 /n.d./, A.S.B., Gab. Pref., cat. VII, 1882. The Bologna paper's chief editor was Barbanti-Brodano and its editorial staff included Pradelli and Carducci.

[51]Letter of Mar. 20, 1882, Avanti!, Mar. 26, 1882.

[52]Telegram from the prefect of Ravenna to the prefect of Bologna, Mar. 21, 1882, A.S.B., Gab. Pref., cat. VII, 1882. Informed of this possibility, the subprefect of Imola replied that in his city, "where conspiracy is permanent and where the subversive parties always demonstrate public activity," the socialists and republicans were concerned with the coming elections rather than with plans for insurrection. He warned, however, that after the elections anything was possible. See report to the prefect of Bologna, Mar. 23, 1882, A.S.B., Gab. Pref., cat. VII, 1882.

[53]Anonymous note from Bologna to the Minister of Interior, Mar. 27, 1882, A.S.B., Gab. Pref., cat. VII, 1882.

[54]According to word received by the Minister of Interior, at their meeting of Feb. 26 the socialists decided to propose a list of candidates to include Costa, Fratti, Valzania, and Amilcare Cipriani. See Minister of Interior to the prefect of Bologna, Mar. 13, 1882, A.S.B., Gab. Pref., cat. VII, 1882. This information is probably incorrect; Costa maintained that candidates were not even discussed at the gathering. See Avanti!, Mar. 5, 1882.

[55]Subprefect of Imola to the prefect of Bologna, Apr. 1, 1882, A.S.B., Gab. Pref., cat. VII, 1883. The subprefect does not include the exact date of the association's creation, but its program, according to him, consisted of three main goals: popular sovereignty to be carried out by means of universal suffrage, the emancipation of the working classes, and the abolition of all privilege.

[56]A.S.B., Gab. Pref., cat. VII, 1882. Some idea of Costa's influence on the republicans--and also on the anarchists--at this time can be gained from a subprefect's report dated Mar. 28. Adamo Mancini and Luigi Sassi had spoken at the Circolo Imolese on the 18th. According to the official, these speeches "are conceived by...Costa because neither Sassi nor Mancini are capable of expressing themselves with those ideas and that form which is so characteristic of Costa." See note to the prefect of Bologna, A.S.B., Gab. Pref., cat. VII, 1882.

[57]Report to the prefect of Bologna, Aug. 23, 1882, A.S.B., Gab. Pref., cat. VII, 1882.

[58]Writing about Fortis during his electoral campaign in 1880, Fratti declared, "I feel sympathy and affection for him, but even if he were my beloved brother I would not vote for him, I would not say anything in his favor; I would fight him as I will always fight false promises, ambiguous positions, betrayals." Quoted by Casali, "Il movimento mazziniano in Romagna...," p. 46.

[59]Issue of Jan. 8, 1882.

[60]Ibid.

[61]Speech of Mar. 10, quoted in Il Moto, Mar. 12, 1882.

[62]"The fusion of the republicans and socialists continues to progress," the prefect of Ravenna informed the

Minister of Interior on June 30, 1882. See Archivio
Centrale di Stato, Rome (hereafter A.C.S.R.), Ministero
Interno Gabinetto--Rapporti dei prefetti (1882-90),
busta 13.

[63]Avanti!, June 29, 1882.

[64]According to a carabiniere report, the comizio at
Imola was attended by the socialists Costa, Friscia, and
Covelli, and by the republicans Sassi, Saffi, Ferrari,
Saladini, Fortis, Bovio, and Ceneri (report to the pre-
fect of Bologna, June 27, 1882, A.S.B., Gab. Pref., cat.
VII, 1882).

[65]Report to the prefect of Bologna, July 24, 1882,
A.S.B., Gab. Pref., cat. VII, 1882.

[66]Costa's name had been put on the electoral list
early in April but had promptly been removed by the authorities on account of his status as an ammonito (prefect of Bologna to the questore, Apr. 11, 1882, A.S.B.,
Gab. Pref., cat. VII, 1882). On June 30, through his
lawyer Aristide Venturini, Costa had taken his case to
the Bologna Court of Appeals (Avanti!, July 9, 1882),
and shortly afterward his name was ordered back on the
list.

[67]Avanti!, Aug. 20, 1882.

[68]Ibid. For the program established at the meeting,
see Il Moto, Sept. 3, 1882.

[69]Avanti!, Sept. 2-3, 1882. Among those in attendance
were Venturini, Barbanti-Brodano, Mattioli, Lodovico Nabruzzi, Gaetano Zirardini, Rito Balducci, and the Corradini brothers, Tullo and Ugo (subprefect of Imola to the
prefect of Bologna, Aug. 27, 1882, A.S.B., Gab. Pref.,
cat. VII, 1882). For an account of the meeting, see Il
Sole dell'avvenire (Ravenna), Sept. 3, 1882.

[70]Letter, n.d., in Il Sole, Sept. 16, 1882. Casali,
"Il movimento mazziniano in Romagna...," gives Saffi much
credit for intuiting that his party had to enter into the
political life of the country (see p. 46); however, the
A.R.U. chieftain never did actively encourage republican
entry into the Chamber of Deputies.

[71]See the supplement to Il Moto, Oct. 7-8, 1882. Earlier in 1882 Il Dovere, the authoritative republican news-

paper, had ceased publication when Alberto Mario, its editor, died. The defunct paper was succeeded by La Lega della democrazia (also based in Rome), which now became the leading organ of the republican party in Italy.

[72]The electoral alliance--which was directed by the Comitato Elettorale Democratico in this college--did not include all the democratic factions in Imola; it was composed mainly of republicans and socialists. The Associazione Democratica Imolese represented a third democratic element in the city. The Associazione, however, fearing identification with the socialists, refused to join the alliance (see Avanti!, Oct. 5-6, 1882) and thereby caused a schism within its own ranks--a minority of its members seceded and supported the Costa list.

[73]Issue of Oct. 1, 1882. This number also described the candidates. In regard to Costa it had this to say: "Andrea Costa is too well-known to all of us...to all of Italy, to have to speak of him here...he is not only a socialist, but the most authoritative representative of the socialist party in Italy."

[74]Codronchi was a staunch law and order man. He had served as the prefect of Palermo in 1874 and would later become the prefect of Naples (1888-90) and of Milan (1900-03). Even his political adversaries, however, held him in high regard. Romeo Galli, one of Costa's socialist comrades in Imola, later described the Count in these terms: "Giovanni Codronchi, though being...a man devoted to his ideas of order, of firm civil and political discipline, was a man of magnanimous manners and a heart which was genuinely Romagnol." See Il Diario (Imola), May 7, 1932.

[75]Quoted in Avanti!, Oct. 28-29, 1882.

[76]Under the old law Imola had had only 575 eligible voters (Avanti!, Mar. 18, 1882); under the new list, of the 11,112 voters in the college, Imola had 2534 (Il Moto, Oct. 15, 1882).

[77]The results in Imola: Filopanti, 1,025; Costa, 1,009; Venturini, 931; Codronchi, 861; Inviti, 749; and Berti, 668. See Il Moto, Nov. 5, 1882.

[78]Ibid.

[79]Ibid., Oct. 28-29, 1882.

[80] Ibid., Nov. 5, 1882.

[81] "Imola elected three radicals as its deputies," commented Il Moto on Nov. 5, "and if the rurali /country people/ from Castel Maggiore gave the victory to the moderates, that in no way affects our local interests."

[82] Bertani would later opt for Milan and his seat would be contested by Venturini, for the radicals, and Count Pier Desiderio Pasolini, the eventual winner, for the moderates.

[83] Zirardini attended the Imola comizio on June 25 as a representative for the Circolo Istruttivo Educativo Razionalista of Florence and also for the Federazione Fiorentina dell'Associazione Internazionale dei Lavoratori. See report from the Bologna carabinieri to the prefect of Bologna, June 27, 1882, A.S.B., Gab. Pref., cat. VII, 1882.

[84] Zirardini was the secretary of the committee which prepared the comizio. See L'Alfabeto, Aug. 27, 1882. Prior to the young art student's return to Ravenna the city's socialist party lacked a strong personality. Writing on June 30, 1882, the prefect of Ravenna remarked: "There is no one of any worth at the head of the local International, of the hoodlums /who compose it/. Their pontiff is Costa, who sends encouragement.../and/ ordains priests and deacons from Imola." See report to the Minister of Interior, A.C.S.R., Min. Int. Gab.--Rapporti dei prefetti, busta 13.

[85] Il Sole dell'avvenire became the third major socialist newspaper in the Romagna at this time. The others were Costa's Avanti! and Pellegrino Bagli's Alfabeto in Rimini. The latter was first published in August, 1882.

[86] Il Sole, Oct. 28-29, 1882.

[87] Avanti!, Sept. 2-3, 1882.

[88] Il Sole, Sept. 3, 1882.

[89] Avanti!, Sept. 2-3, 1882.

[90] Il Sole, Sept. 30, 1882.

[91] Ibid. Generally speaking, republicanism in the

province of Ravenna was more "closed and sectarian" than that in the province of Forlì, according to Caseli, "Il movimento mazziniano in Romagna...," p. 48.

[92]Supplement to Il Sole, Oct. 21-22, 1882.

[93]Quoted in Il Sole, Oct. 28-29, 1882.

[94]Il Ravennate is described as a "government newspaper" by Antonio Mambelli, Il giornalismo in Romagna: Rassegna di tutta la stampa quotidiana e periodica dalle origini ad oggi (Forlì: Camera di Commercio, Industria, e Agricoltura, 1966), p. 251.

[95]Avanti!, Oct. 28-29, 1882.

[96]Il Sole, Nov. 4-5, 1882.

[97]Ibid. Despite the results of the election Il Sole was not completely satisfied. The abstentionists, Zirardini felt, had robbed the democrats of a clear-cut victory: "If some of our friends had understood the situation and gone to the polls, our victory, the victory of Democracy, would have been complete and definitive...."

[98]Letter of Oct. 30, 1882, B.C.I., no. 216.

[99]See La Plebe, Sept., 1881, for the Milanese attitude toward socialist candidacies. La Favilla, according to Avanti!, Mar. 26, 1882, had accepted the complete program adopted at Imola on Feb. 26 except for "the imperative mandate regarding the giuramento."

[100]L'Alfabeto, Nov. 19, 1882.

[101]Report to the prefect of Bologna, Nov. 16, 1882, A.S.B., Gab. Pref., cat. VII, 1882.

[102]An account of the meeting is found in Don Chisciotte, Nov. 22, 1882. The questore of Bologna reported that on Nov. 3 Costa had met with the socialists of Bologna and it appeared that he had been instructed to take the oath (note to the Bologna prefect, Nov. 4, 1882, A.S.B., Gab. Pref., cat. VII, 1883). This seems unlikely, however, as the Bolognesi had no jurisdiction in this affair.

[103]Issue of Sept. 30, 1882. The article went on to say: "The possibility of useful and serious reforms does not exist for us socialists except in the sphere of mu-

nicipal administration. Once those legal reforms which
are immediately possible are obtained, this sphere should
not stop but should ardently proceed along the road which
has been traced for it by the necessities of human nature,
the inspirations of the popular masses, and by the latest
results of science."

[104]It is significant that in the letter of Oct. 30,
Zirardini had asked Costa what he planned to do; the Ravennati, it seems, would abide by their leader's decision.

[105]Questore of Bologna to the prefect of Bologna, n.d.,
A.S.B., Gab. Pref., cat. VII, 1883. Among those Costa
talked to, apparently, were Lodovico Nabruzzi and Gaetano
Zirardini. Both attended the Nov. 17 meeting and sup-
ported the resolutions passed there. See Don Chisciotte,
Nov. 22, 1882.

[106]Il Sole, Nov. 25-26, 1882.

[107]Paradoxically, in Imola, where he was supported by
Sassi and the republicans, Costa failed to win election,
but in Ravenna, where he won, he did so largely in spite
of the republicans rather than because of them.

[108]His decision came as a surprise even to those who
knew Costa best. On Nov. 28, for example, Kuliscioff
wrote him and declared: "I was extremely surprised that
you swore to it /the oath/, especially since I do not
know what reasons, outside of the mandate, induced you
to do it" (B.C.I., no. 229).

CHAPTER SEVEN

COSTA AND THE ANARCHISTS, 1879-1883

The Anarchists and the Svolta

Even more intransigent than the republicans in their attitude toward parliamentary institutions were the anarchists.[1] Understandably, then, Costa's success in the elections and his subsequent acceptance of the giuramento created a furor among his old comrades. Costa's decision to enter Parliament came as a shock. The anarchists--which is to say, those socialists who still adhered to the program of the old International--had been able to reconcile themselves to the election, but Costa's acquiescence with respect to the giuramento was unforgivable, for it signified reconciliation with the state and its institutions. Thus only now, in 1882, did Costa's break with his anarchist past become irreparable.

The Italian Internationalists' reaction to Costa's letter to his friends in the Romagna had been surprisingly mild in comparison with their attitude toward his latest move. The famous letter of 1879 had dire implications as far as the old Internationalist program was concerned. How then can we account for the relatively weak response which it evoked? Several explanations may be suggested. First of all, at that time the International all over Italy was being subjected to intense government persecution. Hence the time was hardly propitious for self-criticism. Struggling to survive, the party was in no position to engage in polemics which would only divide its adherents. Then, too, the leading apostles of the International--those most able to discern the Costian heresy and to counter it effectively--had been forced into exile; such, for example, was the fate of both Cafiero and Malatesta. Consequently, the Romagnol had the field pretty much to himself in 1879-80. Finally, and perhaps most importantly, the Internationalists were slow to perceive the full implication of the new approach being proposed--a failure attributable, at least in part, to the vagueness with which Costa presented his ideas. All these considerations suffice to explain the

243

anarchists' inability to respond forcefully to Costa's initial revision of his old position.

The only effective opposition which Costa encountered in 1879 took the form of a circular, dated September 27, issued by the Italian Commission of Correspondence, now residing in Naples.[2] "We...do not want to deny anyone the right to make peaceful propaganda," the circular stated. "In fact even we ourselves want to do it, insofar as it is possible, but at the same time we want to reorganize the party around a plan of action to be accomplished more or less in the immediate future. Without this plan of action propaganda is useless and fruitless. Propaganda divorced from conspiracy /lavoro secreto/ makes us soft, it accustoms us to feed people sentences and words, to lull ourselves with hopes; propaganda divides us: conspiracy unites us."

Quite possibly the publication may have been the work of Francesco Saverio Merlino (1856-1930), who lived in Naples during this period.[3] Certainly by the following year it was Merlino who led the anarchist opposition to Costa. On April 14, 1880, he wrote to the Romagnol from Naples. Conciliatory but firm, Merlino stated: "Perhaps I am mistaken, but I was under the impression that an evolutionary approach could very well be put into practice in such a way as not to hinder the other approach /that of revolution/, which is the principal one. You want to make us look like exclusivists, like absolutists; but you know that I too cooperate willingly in the work of propaganda, and even in the evolutionary approach."[4]

By this time, too, Malatesta had become concerned over the course Costa was intent upon pursuing. Writing from Paris on April 15, he informed the Romagnol that he considered "the direction which you would give to the socialist movement in Italy to be dangerous." He assured Costa, however, that he could not succeed. "Still," he continued, "it makes me sad to see you waste an activity and compromise a position which would have rendered our cause many other, and more effective, services." He declined to elaborate on his view, having no wish "to engage in a polemic with you because it would not serve any purpose unless it were brought before the public."[5]

Up to now the Internationalists in Italy and abroad had maintained cordial relations with the Romagnol. In

his letter of April 15, for instance, Malatesta concluded by saying, "Be very careful to avoid arrest: you
know that they would keep you in prison for at least two
years, and that would profit only our enemies." Such
camaraderie became more difficult with the publication
of the Rivista internazionale del socialismo in May, 1880.
After reading Costa's program there could be no doubt
that he had embarked on a course antithetical to that of
the old International, and anarchist criticism inevitably
became less temperate.[6]

The full force of the anarchist reaction against
Costa was vented at the Congress of Chiasso which took
place on December 5-6, 1880, in a small Swiss town near
the Italian border. The meeting, attended by nineteen
representatives, was convened in order to lay the basis
for a solid socialist organization which would embrace
both legalitari and anti-legalitari.[7] Among the principal defenders of Internationalist orthodoxy present
were Matteucci, Grassi, and Egisto Marzoli. But the
ranking figure there was Carlo Cafiero, who presided.

Up to now Cafiero had refrained from open involvement in the polemic against Costa. This is not to suggest that his attitude toward the svolta was a neutral
one; on the contrary, he was vigorously opposed to the
Imolese's new orientation.[8] By late 1880, as a consequence, Cafiero and Costa were no longer on speaking
terms, and despite efforts made by Kuliscioff, who like
the Pugliese was in Swiss exile at Lugano during this
time, conciliation between the two men proved to be impossible. Still, open confrontation was avoided. At
Chiasso, however, all of this changed: Cafiero directed the attack on the Costian program.

Costa himself was unable to attend the meeting, for
he had been arrested on November 1 and was serving his
term at Perugia. His position was more or less represented at Chiasso by the Legalitarians, who were led by
Bignami, Gnocchi-Viani, and Giuseppe De Franceschi.

The meeting had been called by the Milanesi for purposes of unification; the result was quite different.[9]
At Chiasso the breach between the two camps widened.
For the anarchists the meeting was a resounding victory.
The reformists' program was rejected. Socialist candidacies, in both political and administrative elections,
were voted down.

Understandably, Costa was upset by the resolutions passed at the Swiss conference.[10] Kuliscioff disagreed with him, and Costa sensed it. Strangely puzzled, he asked her: "What do you think of what I have told you? Do you feel as I do? I don't know why, _Nina mia_, but I'm afraid that you are not generally in agreement with me; that the resolutions of the Congress of Chiasso seem acceptable to you. I fear that you have not assumed a sufficiently strong stand /against the resolutions/.... If I am mistaken, set me straight."[11] The fact is, Kuliscioff did accept the resolutions--that is, if we are to believe Carlo Monticelli, who talked with her shortly after the gathering.[12] Evidently at this time Costa had ventured further than she along the road from anarchism to socialism.

By the beginning of 1881 the anarchists, fortified by their recent victory at Chiasso, stepped up their attack on Costa. The crest of intense government persecution against them had passed, and now they were able to deal with Costa more effectively. Spearheading the opposition was Merlino, who in February began publishing _Il Grido del popolo_ in Naples. Yet the criticism of Costa which appeared in the Neapolitan paper was noticeably restrained, with Merlino concentrating on Costa's principles, not the man himself.

The anarchists abroad were not so charitable as Merlino. Embittered by years of exile, these men reacted with a passion. Among the most vociferous were Matteucci in Cannes and Covelli in Switzerland. The latter was the more effective critic, for he could air his views in _I Malfattori_, a magazine he had founded in Geneva in May.[13]

The wave of anarchist attack originating at Chiasso peaked in mid-1881. By August even Merlino, temperate as he had been in criticizing Costa, had lost his scruples.[14] The impetus for this new offensive was the Congress of Rimini held on July 24--an event of considerable moment to Costa's former comrades, for there he had established the _P.S.R.R._ on the basis of his antirevolutionary program. The words of Carmelo Palladino, now one of his bitterest critics, epitomize the anarchists' evaluation of Costa at this time:

Now that Andrea Costa's desertion is a _fait accompli_ and has provoked a new schism in the heart of the Italian International, silence is no longer permis-

sible: I consider...it to be every true socialist's
duty to lift his voice so that this new phylloxera
be confined to the few places it has infected and
so that those that have been deluded return to the
straight and narrow road....It is not hatred nor
spite which has impelled me to write. I have always loved and esteemed Costa more than a brother;
but now that he abandons the cause of the Revolution, I do not hesitate an instant to call him the
principal enemy of the workers.15

But the most unrestrained attack came from Cafiero.
Three days before Rimini, on July 21, 1881, Il Grido del
popolo published a letter to Vittorino Valbonesi and
Ruggero Moravalli (originally from Perugia but now living in Forlì) in which the Pugliese, referring to Costa,
declared: "My duty is to reveal the treachery; yours
to judge and to shoot the traitor....But act, for god's
sake; do something; do not remain inert in front of this
spectacle....Friends, if you do not want the people to
curse the revolution as a new false god and a deception,
do justice to the wicked charlatan, or cruelly shoot me
as a slandering rogue."16 Costa, writing in Catalina,
took issue with Cafiero's diatribe. He attacked Valbonesi, Moravalli, and the Neapolitan paper, defended his
position, then concluded: "We continue on our way confident and serene; hurt because we can no longer shake
the hands which, at one time, were fraternally extended
to us, but convinced that we have neither provoked nor
merited the base treatment to which we and our ideas
are subjected."17

In response to these anarchist attacks which had
proliferated after the Congress of Rimini,18 and with
Cafiero's words still very much on his mind, Costa published an open letter, dated September 15, bearing the
salutation, "To my Friends and to my Enemies." In it
he first dealt with Cafiero's recent assault: "It is
not in this way that we can pretend to reshape the world!
Before converting others, it is necessary that we aim at
converting ourselves; we cannot effectively reproach the
bourgeoisie for its vices, its defects, its intolerance,
its egoism, when, put to the test, we are no better than
it." The rest of the Costa letter was a defense of the
program he had been advocating for the past two years.
Reform, he insisted, was only "a means of agitation";
revolution was still the ultimate end. He unequivocally
denounced conspiratorial methods, though, and concluded
by reviewing his achievements: "Because of our efforts,

socialism has publicly asserted itself in Bologna, Mantua, Leghorn, Forlì...." This, then, was the Imolese's answer to the anarchist opposition.

Cafiero's letter and its sinister implications stirred up the Romagna, and its effects were to prove beneficial to Costa. The anarchist chieftain had in fact done for his new adversary what Costa had been unable to accomplish for himself over the past few months: Cafiero had discredited the cause of his followers and, certainly without intention, had united the Romagnols behind Costa's banner. To understand how this turn of events came about an examination of the happenings in the Romagna over the previous two or three years is essential.

Costa and the Romagnols

Costa's open letter, "To my Friends of the Romagna," as we have seen, had encountered little resistance among the Internationalists of that region; indeed, it had met with some unexpected enthusiasm. Certainly by the following year, 1880, Costa could count on the support of most of his old comrades there. Opponents of his new program--the anti-costiani, as they came to be known--were not very much in evidence. These anarchists were so weak, in fact, that early in 1880 government authorities were still unable to detect significant cleavages within the ranks of the local International.[19] Nor were discrete groupings apparent even at the socialist gathering in Bologna of March 14, 1880.

As the year wore on, however, opposition to Costa gradually manifested itself. By May the International had split into two clearly defined factions, one of which followed Costa while the other supported Cafiero and Malatesta.[20] An indication of the growing strength of the anarchists at the time was their reversion to conspiratorial organization. At least one anarchist association of this type had been established by mid-1880.[21]

Also during the course of the year the various International meetings held in the Romagna tended to be dominated by the anarchist element: the resolutions that were passed opted for revolution and rejected the Costian program formulated at Bologna in March.[22] Reportedly, by the end of 1880 the anarchists had grown so strong that even though Costa's program of political struggle had been accepted in Bologna and Emilia, in Tuscany and the Romagna

Merlino's call for armed struggle was predominant.[23]
While this report may have been exaggerated, the anarch-
ists had unquestionably made considerable progress in the
Romagnol provinces.

How can we account for this development? Undoubtedly
the burgeoning anarchism in the Romagna reflected its increasing popularity beyond the region. It was not until
May that Merlino and the other leading anarchists moved
against Costa in an effective way. This thrust must have
had telling repercussions in the Romagna. Certainly Merlino's influence there was weighty, for he had numerous
contacts within the region.[24]

The force of Merlino's arguments, however, cannot
wholly account for the situation. Equally important was
the fact that during most of 1880 Costa was in prison,
hence unable to offer much resistance to the mounting
criticism. Significantly, only after Costa's arrest were
the anarchists able to make any headway in the region.[25]
Costa was released in early 1881, and as soon as he returned to the Romagna the tide turned in his favor.[26]
The Imolese's efforts now were so fruitful that Carlo
Rotondi, one of his followers from Cesena, must have been
correct when he declared in March of that year that in
the Romagna only a minority followed the "bloody theories
of the Russian socialists and the French Communards...."[27]

But, as already noted, after the Congress of Chiasso
Merlino and the anarchists in exile launched a new offensive against Costa. This campaign, directed by Il Grido
del popolo after February, was carried into the Romagna
where it had many violent manifestations, especially with
the Congress of Rimini approaching.

Costa's opposition in the region came mainly from
the province of Forlì. There the two most active centers
of anarchism were Rimini and Forlimpopoli. The anarchist
element in Rimini had been rather weak at the beginning
of 1881,[28] but experienced a revival within the next few
months. On March 30 the local subprefect reported the
appearance of new anarchist associations in Rimini and
the surrounding territory. Each secret organization was
said to be governed by a triumvirate and to have Cafiero
and Malatesta as its honorary presidents.[29]

The majority of the Riminesi, however, continued to
adhere to Costa's program.[30] By 1881 the local party was
headed by Pellegrino Bagli, who had now replaced Francolini

as <u>capo-partito</u>. Francolini had been tried the year before for publication of subversive literature, and since
that time he had gradually withdrawn from political life
and subsequently lost much of his influence.[31] Bagli,
as the columns of <u>L'Alfabeto</u>, his newspaper, confirm,
continued to be one of Costa's staunchest supporters.

In Forlimpopoli, a town located between Forlì and
Cesena, anarchist sentiment was even more pervasive than
in Rimini. In contrast to the situation there, the anarchists in Forlimpopoli were able to rely on a dynamic
personality, Valbonesi, soon to establish himself as the
ranking <u>anti-costiano</u> in the Romagna.[32] In 1879, at the
age of twenty-two, Valbonesi was already recognized as
the outstanding local Internationalist.[33] During 1880 he
had made an all-out effort to heal the split within his
party between <u>costiani</u> and <u>anti-costiani</u>.[34] But by this
time he was definitely aligned with the latter, and at
the Congress of Rimini young Valbonesi was the most vocal
of Costa's opponents.[35]

In Forlimpopoli, as in Rimini, anarchists constituted
a minority. According to a police report on the condition
of the International's local section during the first tri-
mester of 1881, the association, known as <u>Sofia Perovoskaya</u>
and headed by Valbonesi, had eighty members who supported
Cafiero and a hundred who supported Costa.[36]

In Cesena, Ravenna, and the other major Romagnol cities, anarchist presence was even weaker than in Forlimpopoli and Rimini. At Imola opposition to Costa was practically nil. At this time Bennati, Castellari, and Mancini, the most militant of the local Internationalists,
were still on good terms with their old comrade in arms.[37]
Mancini aided Costa with the publication of <u>Avanti!</u>, which
appeared in late April, and Bennati, who helped finance
the publication,[38] was described as "very friendly" with
the socialist chieftain even as late as February, 1882.[39]

Nevertheless, as the Congress of Rimini approached
anarchist opposition to Costa mounted in the Romagna.
Seemingly, he was going to have a hard time convincing
the delegates to adopt his program.[40] This was the moment
just three days before the Congress, when <u>Il Grido del
popolo</u> published Cafiero's letter. The result was not at
all what the Internationalist champion had foreseen. The
suggestion that Costa was a traitor and should be dealt
with accordingly provoked almost universal condemnation
of Cafiero throughout the Romagna. Valbonesi and his

friends were completely inundated by the ire their standard-bearer had stirred up.

The reaction against Cafiero and the anarchists was most evident at the Congress of Rimini. Now that they had been discredited, the anti-costiani were not able to make much of an impression at the meeting. Their ineffectuality at Rimini was not due solely, however, to the Cafiero missive. The Romagnol correspondent for Il Grido del popolo (probably Valbonesi himself) insisted that the anarchists ought to have made a better showing there, but, he lamented:

> It is...necessary to admit that Andrea exerts a kind of fascination on the minds of certain dull-witted people, since one such person from Ravenna publicly stated at the congress that the anarchist group which he represented opposed Costa's political program and wanted to support the program of 1872, but that he, although under mandate to conduct himself accordingly, nevertheless was fully convinced by Costa's words, would vote with him, and was in agreement with him.
> But what surprised me more than anything else was to see that the representative from Bologna was Costa's paladin and his firmest supporter, while previously he had said that he was an anarchist of the first order, and had never accepted any program which did not represent rebellion against everything that now exists.[41]

The furor created by Cafiero did not die with the Rimini Congress. A series of local meetings was held throughout the Romagna during the following weeks in defense of Costa. The carabinieri reported one such gathering in Savignano on August 16. The Imolese was present to defend himself against a representative who had been dispatched by Cafiero. The reaction against the latter was overwhelming: the socialists of Savignano, led by Francesco Squadrani, signed a firm declaration in which Cafiero was roundly censured for the personal nature of his attack, and Valbonesi and Moravalli were condemned for their indiscretion in publishing the letter.[42]

The Romagnol anarchists were dealt a crippling blow during this period, and they recovered from it very gradually. In other sections of the country, however, opposition to Costa's position was considerably stronger. Here the offensive against the Imolese and his P.S.R.R.

program formulated at Rimini continued to be directed by Merlino. Increasingly, though, Tuscany began to rival Naples as the center of anarchist disaffection in Italy. Already in July La Riscossa, the Florentine organ of the Tuscan Internationalists, had vigorously opposed Costa's views on universal suffrage. Its editors, Fortunato Serantoni and Pezzi, argued that universal suffrage was not something about which true anarchists could get unduly excited. What was needed, after all, was revolution, not reform.[43]

For the next few weeks Costa was kept busy defending his position on reform. In August he wrote in Avanti! "Let us understand each other: we do not support the agitation that aims at reforms for the reforms themselves.... We support the agitation...not for that which it can or will give; but because if we know where it begins, we do not know where it will end."[44]

The Tuscan Internationalists were still unconvinced, and after the Congress of Rimini they took a firmer stand. Late in August they published a manifesto reaffirming their faith in revolution and denouncing the Romagnol program established at Rimini. Costa, in a rather transparent argument, insisted that there was no essential difference between his program and the Tuscans': "If we are legalitarians, so too are the Tuscan Internationalists; our program and conduct do not differ from theirs."[45]

Needless to say, the Florentines, who controlled the International in Tuscany, saw the matter from a different perspective. Yet before long they too had been lured by the prospects which the coming election held out, and began to participate in the agitation for reform.[46]

The Tuscans emulated the Romagnols in more than their support for reform. By November they announced their plan to organize themselves into a regional party. Costa congratulated them and assured them they were on the right path.[47] The name they adopted for their party, however, the Federazione Toscana dell'Internazionale, indicated that they were not ready to abandon their old program. Still, they continued to move toward Costa's position. By the beginning of 1882 they had decided not only to participate in the elections, but at a meeting at Poggibonsi on March 16 voted to propose candidates as well. These candidacies were to serve as means of protest: should their man be elected he was to refuse the giuramento. Professor Masini sees Costa's influence as having been

responsible for the decision,[48] which could well have
been the case, for certainly by this time both the Tuscans and the Romagnols were of the same mind regarding
candidacies.

Yet one doubts whether Costa's authority could have
been this decisive. The polemics which took place in the
preceding year clearly suggest that the Tuscans were not
easily moved by the Romagnol. Why, then, would they now
come to accept protest candidacies? Perhaps the answer
can be found in the Cipriani affair. Amilcare Cipriani
(1845-1918) represents one of the most interesting personalities of the Italian socialist movement.[49] A man of
action more than a man of thought, Cipriani, like Malatesta, was viewed by his contemporaries as the incarnation of revolution, a quite natural identification since
Cipriani had devoted all his life to revolt both at home
and abroad. He began his career as a Garibaldian during
the _Risorgimento_. Once Italian unification had been completed, he fought in Greece and later in France. It was
among the French that the soldier of fortune established
his reputation, for he became a Communard (rising to the
rank of colonel) and as a result spent a number of years
as a political prisoner in New Caledonia. By the time
he returned to Italy in 1881 his deeds had become legendary.

For these reasons a great cry of protest arose when
Cipriani was arrested upon his return to his homeland in
late January, 1881. Although he came home ostensibly to
visit his father, who was very ill, his motives were probably mixed; Cipriani, an Internationalist, had spent
the first part of the month in Switzerland among his old
comrades and had assured them of his intention to foment
revolution in Italy.[50] The protests that arose in 1881,
however, were nothing compared to those of the year following. Cipriani was tried in Ancona in February, 1882,
for murdering three men in Alexandria, Egypt, fifteen
years earlier. Though the evidence was weak, the verdict
was guilty, and Cipriani was condemned to twenty-five years
in prison. The clamor which ensued spread throughout
the peninsula and was by no means confined to anarchists
and socialists; all the liberal parties demanded Cipriani's
release.

The agitation at this time was not entirely negative.
Soon after the outrageous verdict, Cipriani's candidacy
for Parliament in the coming elections was seriously considered, with his most enthusiastic supporters being the

AMILCARE CIPRIANI
Archivio di Stato, Forlì

anarchists. They saw the possibilities which the elections opened up for their imprisoned hero and this realization was no doubt a weighty consideration in their decision to accept protest candidates in 1882.

The Cipriani affair was not the sole factor working in favor of electoral participation. In the course of the year the Tuscans' decision to involve themselves in the coming elections was reinforced by the conversion of Carlo Cafiero to legalitarianism. The Tuscans had always held the Pugliese in the highest regard. In Florence he was the most popular of the anarchist leaders. Consequently Cafiero's conversion was bound to have powerful repercussions in Tuscany.

Cafiero announced his conversion in April: "Today the party has resolutely set out on this new /legalitarian/ path....So it seems to me that the question has been posed in precise and decisive terms: to submit or to resign....To resign from the defense of the people's rights has never appealed to me; consequently, I have submitted to the party, frankly accepting its new line of conduct."[51] Costa was happy to see his old friend take this new position. But Cafiero had gone too far for the Romagnol, who now warned, "Throwing himself today in the opposite path of legality, he jumps in all the way, going beyond the point that we ourselves have gone: it is true that we intend to profit from legality, but we want, at the same time, to keep our powder dry."[52] Costa insisted that his program must remain revolutionary.

By this time Cafiero had begun to show symptoms of the psychosis which would plague him the rest of his life.[53] To what extent his conversion was attributable to illness is a matter of conjecture. One can be sure, though, that Cafiero's ideological change could hardly have failed to impress those Internationalists who had been so close to him in the 1870's. Such was certainly the case in Tuscany, where the anarchists came more and more to accept participation in the coming elections. An indication of the Tuscans' more positive attitude toward Costa and his ideas was to be found in Pezzi's friendly letter of congratulation to Il Sole dell'avvenire--whose program was clearly of Costian inspiration--after the appearance of its first number, in September.[54] Also indicative of the prevailing accord between Romagnols and Tuscans was the fact that in the last few months before the elections Avanti! no longer engaged in polemics with the Florentines concerning the electoral question.

Nor was Merlino posing much of a problem now. While
he continued to speak out against the legalitarian line,
his effectiveness seemed to be waning even in his native
city. This decline is alluded to in a letter Costa received from the Neapolitan, Giuseppe Sarno, in July. According to Sarno, Costa had overestimated Merlino, who
was without influence in Naples, where everyone was in
agreement with the Romagnol.[55] Moreover, even Merlino,
though insisting that he was "poles apart from the Romagnols," had come to endorse electoral agitation, on the
eve of the election, as a means of propagating socialist
ideas.[56]

The exiled anarchists remained the most unyielding,
but here too signs of fatigue began to appear.[57] Even
Errico Malatesta, now one of the most zealous of Costa's
critics abroad, began to withdraw from personal confrontation with the Romagnol. After the Congress of London
in July, 1881--which brought together all the leading
European anarchists in an effort to re-establish the old
International[58]--Malatesta, who had been a delegate there,
concerned himself more and more with developments outside
Italy. Also, his London exile took him too far away to
have much effect any longer on the political situation
within his homeland.

The Tito Vezio Meeting

Anarchist strength in the Romagna, like that outside
the region, had declined between the Congress of Rimini
and Costa's election the next year. Late in 1881, just
after the Congress, the anarchists were holding their own
and in some places had even been growing in number. In
October, 1881, for instance, the subprefect of Rimini reported that the split between costiani and anti-costiani
had become more marked over the last few months and that
while "the great majority of the Internationalists of the
district is still following Costa....the propaganda of
Cafiero's apostles becomes more active every day."[59] By
the following year the situation had changed. In October,
on the eve of the elections, L'Alfabeto, the organ of Rimini's Internationalists, was urging the election of Cipriani, Costa, and Gnocchi-Viani.[60] The slate was accepted
by all the Riminesi: a few days later the local police
reported that the Internationalists in the city would
vote as a unit.[61] The division within the local party
had apparently been healed.

The same thing was happening elsewhere in the Romagna.
On the eve of the elections the two socialist factions were
working together all over the region, and mainly for two
reasons: the preceding February the anarchists had been
assured that the P.S.R.R. would limit itself to protest
candidacies, and both sides had agreed that Cipriani should
be one of these protest candidates.

Nowhere in Italy was Cipriani more popular than in
the Romagna. Cipriani, after all, was a Romagnol; although he had been born in Anzio he was raised in Rimini.
Among the anarchists in the region, especially the Riminesi, he found enthusiastic support: not only was he a
Romagnol, but he was an ardent anarchist as well. The
Cipriani affair had therefore led many anarchists to agree
in principle to protest candidacies. Thus by the time of
the elections the P.S.R.R. had achieved some semblance
of unity.

All this came to an end with Cipriani's electoral
defeat as a candidate in Forlì. But even more contribu-
tive was Costa's acceptance of the giuramento. The reaction of the anarchists was so violent that even in
Imola, where they had always cooperated with Costa, the
P.S.R.R. became bitterly divided.[62] In November, at a
socialist reunion in Imola, Costa was asked to justify
his conduct. His explanations were not altogether satis-
factory, and the local anarchists, led by Mancini, passed
to the opposition.[63] After this incident the cleavage
between socialists and anarchists in Imola became permanent.

In the rest of the Romagna Costa's popularity likewise deteriorated. In Forlimpopoli during the early part
of 1883 the local party was sharply divided between Costa's
supporters and those of Cipriani (who now replaced Cafiero
as the paragon of orthodoxy). Reportedly, though, Costa's
following was dwindling.[64]

In Rimini, where Cipriani had considerable support,
the polarization was even more pronounced. One sign of
anarchist growth there was the development by the end of
1882 of the Circolo Amilcare Cipriani, founded earlier
that year, into the most powerful socialist organization
in the area.[65] The antagonism between the rival factions
there became more heated early in 1883. At this time
Costa addressed a political gathering in Rimini at which
the local party members revealed the disfavor into which
he had fallen: scheduled to speak on the function of the

socialist deputy, Costa was confronted by the Riminesi
who, hoping to embarass him, demanded that he make a
speech on the Cipriani affair. In spite of severe criticism the Imolese insisted on addressing the original
theme and evidently did so.[66]

Finally, in Savignano the reaction to Costa's political behavior had even more serious repercussions. According to a police report, sometime in late 1882 the
local association had "completely changed direction, and
through the efforts of the socialist group headed by the
Squadrani brothers and Briani and Cattoli, it assumed
an anarchist character."[67]

During this period--following the elections and his
entrance into Parliament--Costa was under tremendous
pressure from the anarchists outside as well as within
the boundaries of the Romagna.[68] On December 4, 1882,
for example, a banquet in Rome honoring the new socialist deputy was disrupted by local anarchist militants
who were outraged by Costa's "treachery."[69] An event
of even greater moment occurred soon after. Early in
the following year the Internationalists of the Marches,
who had heretofore generally sympathized with the Costian position, met at Ancona and turned against the Roma-
gnol--the beginning of an anarchist resurgence in this
region which would last for many years.[70]

The reaction against Costa gathered momentum throughout the country until the middle of February, 1883, when
the crisis culminated in the Tito Vezio meeting in Milan.[71]
The offensive on the socialist deputy was now led by Carlo
Monticelli and the anarchists of the Lombard capital.[72]
By February Monticelli had determined that the Milanesi
should come together to discuss the Costa affair,[73] and
a conference--sponsored by his paper, Tito Vezio--was
held on the 18th of that month.

According to La Plebe, the main question on the
agenda was of two parts: "whether the agitation that a
socialist deputy can make in Parliament is useful, and
what should his conduct be."[74] In truth the purpose of
the gathering, as Costa's friends knew, was to disavow
the new deputy.[75] Consequently, when the meeting opened,
Monticelli's objections notwithstanding, Costa was there
to defend himself. Aside from the deputy the gathering
was attended only by Milanesi, both costiani and anti-
costiani,[76] with the Legalitarian Bignami presiding.
Leading the opposition alongside Monticelli was Paolo Val-

258

era.

First, Monticelli made the following forthright statement of the anarchist position on parliamentary participation:

We anarchists are against socialist participation in parliamentary life because the parliamentary atmosphere was from experience recognized to be a corrupter and ruiner of men, and because whenever the electoral struggle and legal means are advocated, the people are deluded and are distracted from their true objective, which is that economic emancipation which cannot be obtained by legal means. The propaganda which a socialist can make in the hostile atmosphere of Montecitorio is much less fruitful than that which he can make in the bosom of the people....

In response, Costa asserted that a man could be corrupted outside of Parliament as well as inside; it depended, he said, on the individual. As for misleading the people, Costa agreed that a deputy would be doing just that if he promised them he could bring about their emancipation through Parliament. But, he added, when a deputy made it clear, as he had done, that Parliament was to be exploited simply as a platform for propaganda, then he was making his function unmistakably plain. "To send deputies of the people to Parliament to affirm its claims," Costa concluded, "is a declaration of war, not... a surrender: how can it be said that the declaration of war is in contradiction to the war of which it is the necessary antecedent?"

Costa's argument was convincing: Monticelli's resolution, which declared parliamentary activity to be useless, was rejected, and Giuseppe De Franceschi's declaring that the party should utilize all methods of struggle was approved.77

Costa's personal conduct during the first few months after his election was the next item on the agenda. Costa admitted that he had been working with bourgeois democrats in Parliament. He added, however, that this was the only way anything positive could be accomplished at Montecitorio. He further justified his posture by insisting that "it is necessary...to extend the propaganda to all democrats in order to draw them to our ideas, something much more fruitful certainly than to predicate solely among

259

those who are already convinced."

Following Costa's declaration, the assembly--"in great majority," according to La Plebe--approved the following resolution: ...the Milanese socialists, deploring the way in which the personal question was raised in regard to the parliamentary conduct of comrade Costa, reconfirm all their confidence in him."

The Tito Vezio encounter thus proved to be a personal as well as political triumph for Costa.[78] The anarchists had hoped to discredit him, but they had failed. If anything, it was Monticelli who had been humbled. Even Valera, his closest ally, turned against him. As Valera wrote to Costa on March 1: "You are certainly right. Monticelli is a great impostor. Let us not give another thought to him, nor to his acolytes, nor to his newspaper. His personalismo has completely nauseated me. After all, he is too cowardly, too vile, too deceitful for me to lend myself to his tricks."[79] Costa had hoped to convert the anarchists in Milan to his point of view,[80] and apparently he had succeeded.

In fact, the Romagnol's prestige soared to unprecedented heights throughout the Italian peninsula. His old adversary Merlino, on the other hand, seemed to be losing ground, especially in his own city of Naples. Early in March, after a recent trip there, Costa was reported to have said that all the Neapolitan anarchists were behind him and that "Merlino is followed by only eight or ten imbeciles...who help him today and combat him tomorrow."[81]

The story was the same, of course, in the Romagna, where Costa had fortified his position vis-à-vis the anarchists. In March the questore in Bologna reported that there were almost no anarchist socialists left in the province (which is to say, in Bologna and Imola).[82] In Ravenna Costa encountered even less opposition.[83] By March, 1883, he had seemingly stifled all anarchist opposition.

Conclusion

To understand the difficulties Costa faced when trying to restore vitality to the socialist movement by creating a new foundation for it, we must have some insight into the environment in which he was operating. The Romagna

posed formidable problems for Costa. We have seen that
the republicans, far more numerous there than the socialists, had always opposed the development of a viable socialist organization in the region. Rivalry between the republicans and the Internationalists went back to the
1870's, and that tradition was still alive at the beginning of the following decade. Indeed, Costa had to utilize all the political acumen he possessed to overcome
republican resistance to his reorganization of the socialist movement through the P.S.R.R.

Even more opposed to Costa's program during these
years were the anarchists, who cherished the old Internationalist program and vigorously combatted Costa's efforts to direct them along new paths.

Although Costa's svolta of 1879 surprised the old
Internationalists, in the Romagna it hardly caused deep
indignation. Where this reorientation would lead was
not yet clear--perhaps not even to Costa himself. But
antagonism soon appeared and continued to grow over the
next three years with each step in Costa's venture away
from the program of the old International, markedly with
the publication of the Rivista internazionale del socialismo in 1880, then the Congress of Rimini in 1881, and
finally Costa's election and acceptance of the giuramento
in 1882.

Anarchist denunciation within the Romagna was profoundly influenced by the same kind of condemnation beyond the region. This campaign against the socialist
leader was spearheaded by Merlino in Naples, and to a
lesser extent by the old Internationalists in Tuscany.
Still more violent was the reaction from abroad, especially from the exiled Cafiero and Malatesta who were
the most authoritative of the anarchist leaders at the
time.

Yet Costa was able to ride out each wave of criticism. The salient factor in his favor was the fact that
the environment in which he found himself operating demanded a fresh approach. And not only was the moment
ripe--Costa seemed to be the man to seize it. Time and
again we see him appear on the scene to revitalize what
otherwise promised to be a hopeless situation. His personal intervention was crucial, for even more persuasive
than his arguments were Costa's eloquence and the charismatic force of his personality when presenting his ideas.

Despite the remarkable effectiveness of his efforts

in developing cohesion, however, the Internationalists polarized into two camps. All over Italy, though particularly in the Romagna, the cleavage manifested itself in terms of costiani and anti-costiani. Prior to 1882 both factions could be found within the same associations in the Romagna, but after that time each camp would establish its own separate organizations. Thus only in the wake of Costa's election did the break become definitive, and not until then could a clear-cut distinction be made between socialists and anarchists.

Does all of this mean, as some anarchist critics have suggested, that Costa was responsible for the destruction of the International in Italy? Obviously, in retrospect, Costa was a contributing factor, but he can hardly be viewed as the main cause of this process. By the time Costa came forward with his new program the International was already dying. The repressive blows directed at it by the Italian government in the late seventies had proved fatal, though at the time that fact was not evident. After 1880 the International was finished as an effective force. The coup de grâce was administered in 1882 with the extension of the suffrage, which opened up the possibility of working within the parliamentary system rather than destroying it. At the most, therefore, Andrea Costa should be seen as a catalyst in the International's demise.

NOTES

[1]This chapter is based heavily on Masini, _Storia degli anarchici italiani_.

[2]The circular is reproduced in Romano, _Storia_, III, 575-78.

[3]Though Professor Romano attributes the authorship of the document to Cafiero. See _Storia_, II, 672. Merlino's initial reaction to the _svolta_ was very mild, revealing that he had not yet grasped the full potential of Costa's position. See Merlino's letter, dated Aug. 6, published in _La Plebe_, Aug. 17, 1879.

[4]Quoted in Pier Carlo Masini, "Lettere inedite di anarchici e socialisti a Andrea Costa (1880)," _Movimento operaio e socialista_, 13 (1967), 58-59.

[5]Ibid., pp. 59-60. Perhaps the letters by Merlino and Malatesta in April were written in response to a correspondence by Costa, dated Mar. 23, which was published in _La Stella d'Italia_, Mar. 29-30, 1880. In this article the Romagnol presented his ideas in a somewhat clearer fashion than he had the previous year. Bonfiglioli insists that ideologically this document "is certainly more significant and explicit than the famous open letter _Ai miei amici di Romagna_." See _Su compagni, in fitta schiera: Il socialismo in Emilia-Romagna dal 1864 al 1915_, ed. Luigi Arbizzani, Pietro Bonfiglioli, and Renzo Renzi (Bologna: Cappelli, 1966), p. 27.

[6]Even now, though, his ex-comrades were reluctant to repudiate Costa altogether. Writing on Dec. 24, 1880, Malatesta admitted that despite political differences "my personal sentiments for him remain the same...I love and esteem Costa from the bottom of my heart." See letter to Amilcare Cipriani, reproduced in Della Peruta, _Democrazia e socialismo_, p. 430.

[7]See Kuliscioff's letter to Costa, Dec. 6, 1880, B.C.I., no. 110.

[8]Kuliscioff to Costa, Oct. 20, 1880, B.C.I., no. 82.

[9]An account of the meeting is given in La Plebe, Dec. 12, 1880.

[10]He had been informed of the proceedings by Kulisciof in a letter dated Dec. 7, 1880, B.C.I., no. 112. This correspondence is quoted by Lipparini, Andrea Costa, pp. 169-70.

[11]Letter of Dec. 12, 1880, B.C.I., no. 116. Quoted in Lipparini, Andrea Costa, p. 164, and Romano, Storia, II, 682.

[12]Avanti della domenica (Florence), Jan. 1-4, 1903.

[13]"It is unnecessary to add," Costa wrote in regard to I Malfattori, "that we strongly recommend the new magazine to...our comrades, because we desire that socialist though be diffused in all of its breadth and be discussed even in its subtlest nuances." See Avanti!, May 7, 1881. Costa, it is evident, took great pains during this period to preserve the unity of the party.

[14]Masini, Storia degli anarchici italiani, p. 183.

[15]Letter of Sept. 7, 1881, published in Il Grido del popolo, Sept. 18, 1881. Many coreligionists would agree with Palladino in seeing the Rimini Congress as the great turning point in the Romagnol's career; Camillo Berneri would later write that "from 1881 to his death, Costa was a nonentity." See Volontà, 2 (Apr. 15, 1948), 66. In general the anarchists have tended to give Costa very little credit. The same goes for historians who sympathize with the anarchist movement. Professor Masini, for example, in one of his earlier writings--one which in all probability he would like to forget--declared that "on the basis of the most recent research, we have to advance the thesis of a Costa who was not an anarchist, never an anarchist, we have to...deny Costa's supposed anarchism, his pseudo-Bakuninism, that anarchic communism that he recklessly professed for a certain period." See "Il Caso Costa: psicologia dell'opportunismo," Volontà, 2 (Apr. 15, 1948), 61. Cf. with Masini's more recent view: "Andrea Costa will never deny, not even when he will be vice-president of the Chamber of Deputies, that exultant and fiery youthful adventure /anarchism/; in fact, he will often stress its educative, propagandistic, and experimental value. But it was to be he--he, who had lived it in a more intense way than others had, even more than Cafiero and Malatesta...--who would set in motion that process

that would lead socialism in a legal and pacifistic direction." See Storia degli anarchici italiani, p. 172.

[16]The original copy of this letter, signed June 8, 1881, is contained in A.S.F., Tribunale Civile e Correzionale, Procedimento contro Valbonesi Vittorino ed altri (1882) (hereafter this set of documents will be designated Procedimento Valbonesi), fasc. 15. Apparently the contents of Cafiero's letter were not entirely unknown in the Romagna before the publication of the correspondence. See report of the prefect of Bologna to the prefect of Forlì, July 4, 1881, A.S.F., Gab. Pref., vol. 95, fasc. 300.

[17]July 31, 1881.

[18]For the anarchist reaction to Rimini, see the Romagnol correspondence, probably written by Valbonesi, in Il Grido del popolo, Aug. 19, 1881.

[19]Minister of Interior to the prefect of Forlì, Jan. 8, 1880, A.S.F., Gab. Pref., vol. 94, fasc. 262.

[20]Minister of Interior to the prefect of Forlì, May 26, 1880, A.S.F., Gab. Pref., vol. 97, fasc. 339.

[21]On July 9 the local carabinieri informed the prefect of Forlì that they had captured a manifesto calling for insurrection and signed by a Comitato Segreto Rivoluzionario Propaganda Anarchica Socialista in Cesena (A.S.F., Gab. Pref., vol. 96, fasc. 310).

[22]Minister of Interior to the prefect of Forlì, Sept. 15, 1880, A.S.F., Gab. Pref., vol. 97, fasc. 339.

[23]Minister of Interior to the prefect of Forlì, Dec. 4, 1880, A.S.F., Gab. Pref., vol. 97, fasc. 339. The subprefect of Cesena referred to these programs as lavoro morale and mezzi violenti (report to the prefect of Forlì, Dec. 10, 1880, A.S.F., Gab. Pref., vol. 97, fasc. 339).

[24]Already in November, 1879, Merlino was in correspondence with Francolini, Carpesani, and Zavoli in Rimini, and Brunelli and the Battistini brothers in Cesena (Minister of Interior to the prefect of Forlì, Nov. 14, 1879, A.S.F., Gab. Pref., vol. 83, fasc. 1).

[25]Minister of Interior to the prefect of Forlì, May 26, 1880, A.S.F., Gab. Pref., vol. 97, fasc. 339.

[26]Even before Costa's release, however, the two op-

posing factions were beginning to come together once more. This, at least, was the case in Rimini (subprefect of Rimini to the prefect of Forlì, Jan. 6, 1881, A.S.F., Gab. Pref., vol. 84, fasc. 11).

[27]Subprefect of Cesena to the prefect of Forlì, Mar. 28, 1881, A.S.F., Gab. Pref., vol. 96, fasc. 322.

[28]On Jan. 22, 1881, the subprefect of Rimini reported that all the Internationalists in the city agreed on universal suffrage (report to the prefect of Forlì, A.S.F., Gab. Pref., vol. 96, fasc. 322). This would seem to indicate that the anarchists, who had no faith in reform of this kind, were a negligible element within the city.

[29]Report to the prefect of Forlì, A.S.F., Gab. Pref., vol. 96, fasc. 331.

[30]Subprefect of Rimini to the prefect of Forlì, June 4, 1881, A.S.F., Gab. Pref., vol. 96, fasc. 306.

[31]Subprefect of Rimini to the prefect of Forlì, Feb. 25 1881, A.S.F., Gab. Pref., vol. 96, fasc. 306. The reasons for his withdrawal, according to the subprefect, were pressure from his relatives, all of them conservative-minded; "his nature which is basically timid and lacking of all energy and which led to a decline in his prestige among his coreligionists, a prestige which was originally conferred upon him by social position and a more than discreet education; and...the ambition and preponderant activity of Pellegrino Bagli who had aspired to local supremacy for a long time."

[32]Police report to the prefect of Forlì, July 6, 1881, A.S.F., Gab. Pref., vol. 95, fasc. 300.

[33]See the "List of Internationalist associations in Forlimpopoli," Jan. 1, 1879, A.S.F., Gab. Pref., vol. 83, fasc. 3. The association, the only one in the city, was quite small at this time; there were only eleven affiliates among its membership.

[34]Police report to the prefect of Forlì, Apr. 5, 1880, A.S.F., Gab. Pref., vol. 95, fasc. 300.

[35]See Valbonesi's cited letter to Malatesta of Aug. 14, 1881.

[36]"Statistics of the Association of Forlimpopoli,"

n.d., A.S.F., Gab. Pref., vol. 101, fasc. 30.

[37]All three men, according to the local prefect, "belong to the class of Internationalist which is the most dangerous and capable of any excess." See report to the prefect of Bologna, A.S.B., Gab. Pref., cat. VII, 1882.

[38]Mancini, Gazzetta dell'Emilia, Jan. 21-22, 1910.

[39]Subprefect of Imola to the prefect of Bologna, Feb. 2, 1882, A.S.B., Gab. Pref., cat. VII, 1882.

[40]On July 6, 1881, Valbonesi wrote to an anonymous correspondent--perhaps it was Vito Solieri, now in London--informing him that the anarchists in the Romagna had held a meeting on June 26 to prepare for the coming Rimini Congress and unanimously decided "not to move one millimeter from the program of 1871." See Procedimento Valbonesi, fasc. 21.

[41]Il Grido del popolo, Aug. 19, 1881. The fascination which Costa exerted on the Romagnols was the subject of a letter Valbonesi wrote to Malatesta on Aug. 14: "The majority of the socialists in Romagna--stupid or deluded--do not permit anyone to attack their supreme duce for whom they are more fanatical than the Indians are for their Buddha....Let he who touches the holy, the infallible Andrea beware!" See Procedimento Valbonesi, fasc. 13.

[42]Report to the prefect of Forlì, Aug. 18, 1881, A.S.F., Gab. Pref., vol. 96, fasc. 323. A similar declaration, dated July 30, 1881, was also issued by the Cesenati. Among the signers were all of the city's leading socialists, including the Battistini brothers and Valducci. A copy of this document is found in Procedimento Valbonesi, fasc. 27.

[43]See Catalina, July 17, 1881.

[44]Issue of Aug. 21, 1881.

[45]Letter, signed Aug. 29, published in La Favilla, Aug. 31, 1881, and again in Avanti!, Sept. 11, 1881.

[46]Avanti!, Sept. 25, 1881. Now, paradoxically, it was Costa who counseled caution by warning Serantoni and Pezzi not to identify themselves too closely with non-socialist democrats.

[47]Avanti!, Nov. 13, 1881.

[48]"Il Caso Costa...," Volontà, 3 (Sept. 15, 1948), 161.

[49]For biographical information see the chapter on "Amilcare Cipriani: il guerriero permanente della rivoluzione sociale," in Emiliani, Gli anarchici, pp. 113-44.

[50]Perhaps this revolution was to be focused in the Romagna (subprefect of Rimini to the prefect of Forlì, Feb. 20, 1881, A.S.F., Gab. Pref., vol. 96, fasc. 306). Late in the previous year Cipriani had written a manifesto--signed by Zarandelli and Lodovico Nabruzzi, among others--urging revolution in Italy. A copy of this document, addressed "Agli oppressi d'Italia," is found in A.S.F., Gab. Pref., vol. 96, fasc. 331.

[51]La Favilla, Apr. 9-10, 1882; Avanti!, May 13-14, 1882.

[52]Avanti!, May 13-14, 1882.

[53]For this last period of his life, see Gianni Bosio, "Carlo Cafiero nei manicomi di Firenze e di Imola, attraverso le carte personali inerenti e le cartelle cliniche," Movimento operaio, 2 (1950), 368-84; 3 (1951), 437-49.

[54]The letter was published by Gaetano Zirardini in the first issue of his paper, on Sept. 3, 1882.

[55]Letter of July 21, 1882, B.C.I., no. 174.

[56]See Merlino's letter to Antonio Murgo, Mar. 6, 1882, reproduced in Della Peruta, Democrazia e socialismo, p. 446. Valbonesi, another of Costa's old antagonists, was prepared to go even beyond this point. Writing from a Forlì prison on Sept. 16, 1882--he had been arrested in October of the previous year--Valbonesi sent Costa a friendly letter in which he agreed that socialist propaganda in Parliament would indeed be useful. Published in L'Alfabeto, Sept. 24, 1882.

[57]Emilio Covelli, for example, probably the most extreme of the intransigents (see his letter to Murgo, Aug. 26, 1882, in Della Peruta, Democrazia e socialismo, pp. 424-25), had come to accept protest candidacies on principle. See Covelli's letter to Costa, Aug. 31, 1882,

B.C.I., no. 183.

[58]Costa's attitude toward the gathering: "We are a long way, certainly, from accepting all the resolutions of the Congress of London: some of them seem in contradiction with the modern socialist movement; others...appear superfluous; generally, we think that the Congress of London has produced much less than some had hoped; nevertheless, the spirit that animated the delegates at London was the spirit of revolution; and when the revolution passes, we cry: Viva!" See _Catilina_, Aug. 7, 1881. The Romagnol himself, however, refused to attend the meeting, for, as the anarchists correctly surmised, he was afraid that he would be forced to clarify his reformist position there. See _La Révolution Sociale_ (Saint-Cloud), July 3, 1881.

[59]Report to the prefect of Forlì, Oct. 8, 1881, A.S. F., _Gab. Pref._, vol. 83, fasc. 3.

[60]Issue of Oct. 22, 1882.

[61]Report to the prefect of Forlì, Oct. 25, 1882, A.S.F., _Gab. Pref._, vol. 103, fasc. 78.

[62]Marabini, _Prime lotte socialiste_, p. 71.

[63]According to Mancini, Costa "presents himself among his old comrades at the Albergo della Campana, answers evasively, and says that he would have liked to imitate the republican Falleroni /who was elected to Parliament, too, then refused to accept the _giuramento_/ but that he had sacrificed himself...for his electors in Ravenna." See _Gazzetta dell'Emilia_, Jan. 21-22, 1910. This explanation is indeed weak, since, as we have seen, the decision was made by Costa himself rather than by his electors.

[64]Anonymous report to the prefect of Forlì, Jan. 14, 1883, A.S.F., _Gab. Pref._, vol. 101, fasc. 30.

[65]Anonymous report to the prefect of Forlì, n.d., A.S.F., _Gab. Pref._, vol. 101, fasc. 30. The association was led by Carpesani and Alceste Cipriani, Amilcare's brother.

[66]Subprefect of Rimini to the prefect of Forlì, Feb. 17, 1883, A.S.F., _Gab. Pref._, vol. 106, fasc. 151.

[67]Report to the prefect of Forlì, July 3, 1884, A.S. F., Gab. Pref., vol. 101, fasc. 30.

[68]Early in 1883 the new deputy's life was threatened in the Romagna, according to Mancini, Gazzetta dell'Emilia, Jan. 21-22, 1910.

[69]Masini, Storia degli anarchici italiani, p. 185.

[70]Enzo Santarelli, "Democrazia e socialismo nelle Marche dal 1882 al 1889," Movimento socialista e operaio, 8 (1962), 163. The Ancona meeting took place on Feb. 4, 1883.

[71]By this time the anarchist attacks were getting worse every day, according to Kuliscioff (letter to Costa, Feb. 15, 1883, B.C.I., no. 246).

[72]For Monticelli's position on the question of socialist participation, see his letter of May 31 published in I Malfattori, June 4, 1881.

[73]This decision was bitterly resented by La Favilla, Feb. 16, 1883, which insisted that the Milanesi had no right whatsoever to judge the socialist leader.

[74]Issue of January, 1883.

[75]See the letter from Agostini, a Milanese, to Costa, Feb. 11, 1883, B.C.I., no. 245.

[76]The following account of the meeting, including the quotes, was taken from La Plebe, February, 1883. Other accounts of the conclave can be found in La Favilla, Feb. 22 and 25, 1883, and Tito Vezio, Mar. 5, 1883.

[77]There were 24 votes cast for the proposal and only 6 against it (Tito Vezio, Mar. 5, 1883).

[78]Commenting on the Imolese's performance at Milan, Covelli lamented, though not without a certain amount of admiration: "Costa was shrewder than Depretis /Italian Prime Minister, nicknamed the "Wizard of Stradella"/; he already deserves to be a minister of the Kingdom of Italy." See letter to Murgo, Mar. 3, 1881, in Della Peruta, Democrazia e socialismo, pp. 426-27.

[79]B.C.I., no. 248.

[80]See _questore_'s report to the prefect of Bologna, Feb. 18, 1883, A.S.B., _Gab. Pref._, cat. VII, 1883.

[81]_Questore_ to the prefect of Bologna, Mar. 12, 1883, A.S.B., _Gab. Pref._, cat. VII, 1883.

[82]Report to the prefect of Bologna, Mar. 17, 1883, A.S.B., _Gab. Pref._, cat. VII, 1883.

[83]Subprefect of Imola to the prefect of Bologna, Mar. 3, 1883, A.S.B., _Gab. Pref._, cat. VII, 1883.

CHAPTER EIGHT

THE RISE AND FALL OF ROMAGNOL SOCIALISM, 1883-1886

Malatesta and the Riminesi

During the period 1879-1882 Costa gradually abandoned the intransigent program characteristic of the First
International and came to espouse parliamentary institutions, an attitude resembling that of the Milanesi. Conditioned by his past and his environment, he had been
rather slow to adopt this position. But by 1882, the
year of his first election to Parliament, his evolution
was complete: Costa had, in effect, made the transition
from anarchism to socialism.

His political metamorphosis was reflected in the
Romagna, now one of the strongholds of the socialist movement in Italy. Indeed, it is not an overstatement to say
that socialism took its most progressive strides in this
region from 1883 to 1886. Evidence of this advance was
to be found in the development of the P.S.R.R. After
1882 Costa not only persevered in consolidating the party,
but also attempted to extend its authority and organization beyond the borders of the Romagna. In effect, he
tried to construct a national socialist party. Though in
the end the attempt proved to be abortive, it was not
without significance. Through this effort, Costa and his
Romagnols were to exert their greatest influence on the
Italian socialist movement. The years 1883-86 witnessed
one of the most seminal periods in the history of Romagnol
socialism.

Preoccupied after the election of 1882 with parliamentary affairs, Costa was slow to resume his work of organizing the socialist movement.[1] But by the beginning
of 1883, Il Sole--now merged with Avanti!, and the official organ of the P.S.R.R.--began to call for reorganization once again.[2] The Romagnols hoped to convoke a
national congress in which all Italian socialists would
be able to create an Italian socialist party. Immediately, however, organization was to take place at the regional level. Only when the party had firm foundations in
the various regions could there be a national gathering.

Consequently, the Romagnols set out to organize a regional congress and urged their comrades throughout the country to follow their example.3

Unfortunately, a long-standing obstacle was still in their way at both the local and national levels: the anarchists. While Costa was able to defend his position convincingly at the _Tito_ _Vezio_ meeting in February, that victory over his adversaries was short-lived. Soon the anarchist attack was more aggressive than ever. The leader of this new offensive, which was to last for more than a year, was Errico Malatesta, who had returned to Italy at the end of 1882.4 Fresh from exile Malatesta initiated his attack in a letter published in _L'Ilota_ on April 1, 1883, in which he violently criticized Costa and "the about-face which has...euphemistically been called the evolution of Costa." Regarding Costa's efforts at reorganization Malatesta had this to say: "Let us organize ourselves through our own efforts. Let us gather together all the forces of our party, yes, but let us remember that as far as we are concerned...the _parlamentaristi_ do not belong to our party....Our party should be _our_ party, our organization should be _our_ organization. And this organization should be the International Workingmen's Association, whose program...continues to be: Communism, Anarchy, Revolution."5

Malatesta did not stop at attacking Costa's ideas; he insisted that his old comrade had abandoned the International and was therefore a traitor to the cause. The letter was written in so personal a vein that even the Florentines, who had been intensely opposed to the legalitarian program, now turned to Costa's defense. In a letter dated April 5, Natta and Pezzi, Florence's top-ranking anarchists, stated their position on the matter. Malatesta's communication, they declared, was "largely erroneous in its affirmations."6 Moreover, they said, Malatesta had not attacked Costa's ideas but rather the man himself. They censured Malatesta for this personal attack and concluded: "It seems incredible! For some time we socialists have preoccupied ourselves more with Costa than with the people's misery, their suffering, their toils, with the revolution."

But Malatesta had no intention of stopping here. On April 22 _L'Ilota_ published a second letter from him in which he continued his campaign: "Costa's conduct has become too clearly opposed to that of a socialist, too clearly dangerous for me to shirk my duty of denouncing him as a traitor."

Natta and Pezzi again insisted that Malatesta was
being unfair. According to them, Costa was no traitor;
he had always acted on good faith. Furthermore, the difference between their program and the Romagnol's was not
so wide as it seemed, for disagreement had arisen not
over principles but methodology. Malatesta had accused
the Romagnols of being duped by their chief. But the
Florentines refused to condemn their friends to the north.
Socialists in every region, they stated, had the right
to choose their own means of realizing the common goal--
the state of anarchy.[7]

Costa himself remained quiet during this period, a
silence caused by his having been stricken with typhus
on March 30.[8] The illness was so serious that for a
time it was expected to be fatal. Costa recuperated
very slowly. For three months he was virtually immobil-
ized in Imola, where he was under Kuliscioff's care.[9]

In addition to the Florentines Costa found an able
defender in Gaetano Zirardini. The young Ravennate felt
compelled to protect the honor of his fellow Romagnols
and their champion. In an article in Il Sole entitled
"The Bigots of Socialism and of the Republic," Zirardini--
writing under the pseudomym Noto--defended Costa against
the inveighing of the intransigent republicans on the
one hand and of Malatesta on the other.[10] He was particularly critical of Malatesta and the anarchists, whom
he described as "revolutionary hydrophobes when it comes
to talking." Both factions, though, were condemned for
belonging to the "school of absolutism and doctrinairism."
Zirardini concluded: "Today...we can no longer remain
silent, especially when a socialist /Malatesta/ has recklessly joined a republican /G. Ippolito Pederzoli/ to an-
athematize the Revolutionary Socialist Party not just of
the Romagna, but of Italy, since whenever socialism af-.
firms itself...it follows the path that we in the Romagna
follow."

Malatesta was no doubt infuriated by having been
placed in the same category with republicans, of whatever
hue. But he was unable to reply to Zirardini's article
because in May he and Merlino were arrested for having
distributed subversive literature on March 18, during
the celebration of the Paris Commune.[11]

In April the Romagnols rallied to Costa's banner.

On April 29 the Ravenna federation of the P.S.R.R. (all
the major cities in the Romagna had their own federations)
met and voted overwhelmingly to back Costa in this crisis.[12] The position adopted by Zirardini and the Ravennati must have reflected the prevailing sentiment in the
region. Still, not all Romagnols were in agreement. As
already observed, at a very early date there was a strong
anti-Costian current in Rimini. The Riminesi looked to
Cipriani, the anarchist, rather than to Costa, the socialist. Not surprisingly, then, when the polemic between
Costa's defenders and Malatesta got under way, the Southerner found considerable sympathy in Rimini and the surrounding area. Furthermore, his arrest in May did nothing to stem Rimini's flourishing anarchist sentiment.

Meanwhile, efforts to organize the Romagnol Congress
went forward. On February 26 the socialists of the province of Ravenna met at that city and proposed that a
regional congress be convoked as soon as possible.[13]
Other provincial meetings were also held in Bologna, Pisa,
and Ancona more or less simultaneously, and all had the
same objective: the convocation of regional congresses.[14]
During February and March the Romagna prepared for its
assembly.[15] The date of the meeting, however, was not
announced. Even by June, no date had been set. "We have
to procrastinate," Zirardini lamented, "because of im-
pelling circumstances beyond our control."[16]

Perhaps Zirardini was referring here to Costa's illness; not until July 14 at a comizio in Imola calling for
the reform of the communal and provincial laws was Costa
able to make a public appearance.[17] Or perhaps Zirardini
had in mind the editors of Il Sole then being tried for
the publication of seditious material.[18] But quite possibly the complications were due to the schism which was
beginning to split the party in the Romagna.

Throughout Italy the more intransigent anarchists
were intent upon frustrating the movement to reorganize
the old International along Costian lines. They were
naturally opposed to the Romagnol Congress, for, they
contended, it could result only in Costa's manipulation
of the socialist movement in the Romagna with its subsequent loss to the cause of anarchy. By July this point
of view had been adopted by the Riminesi. Though this
split in the P.S.R.R. had not been aired in the columns
of Il Sole, it is amply documented in the police records
of the state archives.

On July 15 a meeting was held in Rimini in which
P.S.R.R. representatives from all over the Romagna tried
to persuade the local federation, now dominated by the
anarchists, to participate in the coming Congress. Thirty
persons joined in the discussion held at the home of Bruto
Zavoli.19 Among the outsiders was Costa, flanked by Gaetano Zirardini, Pradelli, Cappellini, and Valducci.20
What occurred at the gathering is not too clear, but apparently the disagreement between the costiani and the
Riminesi was heated, and the meeting almost ended in
violence (Costa's adversaries were said to have ripped
his deputy's medal off his chest, but the authorities
later discounted this rumor).21

One thing is certain: the conclave did not accomplish its purpose. A few days later, on July 22, a second one was held, this time in Forli. Again an attempt
was made to reconcile the Riminesi, represented by Bagli,
Francolini, and Goldini. Acting as delegates for the
P.S.R.R. were Costa, Cappellini, Fortuzzi, Rito Balducci,
and Gaetano Zirardini, along with other Romagnols. Altogether, forty persons were present.22 Again the discussion was fiery and the results few, with most of the
representatives firmly committed to Costa's program but
the Riminesi unrelenting in their intransigence.23

By now Pellegrino Bagli's pre-eminence in Rimini
was a thing of the past. Bagli, as we know, had been a
strong supporter of Costa at the time of his election in
1882, and he was still espousing Costa's political philosophy. On July 31, writing in L'Alfabeto, Bagli pleaded
for union between intransigents and legalitarians and urged participation in the coming Romagnol Congress.24 But
Bagli was hardly the spokesman for the prevailing sentiment in Rimini. Much more influential were the leaders
of the anarchist Circolo Amilcare Cipriani, Luigi Carpesani and Alceste Cipriani.

Neither of these men was present, however, at the
July 22 meeting. There the anarchists' point of view
was represented by Francolini who, having made a political comeback, had managed by 1883 to supersede Bagli as
the capo-partito in Rimini. All his efforts had the whole-
hearted backing of Carpesani and Alceste Cipriani, even
though Francolini himself did not belong to their association.

The Riminesi stuck to their intransigent guns, for
when the Second P.S.R.R. Congress convened at Ravenna on

August 5 only Bagli was present.25 According to <u>Il</u> <u>Sole</u>,
the delegates were to determine the party's program and
its line of conduct.26 Of the more than eighty representatives almost all were from the Romagna, though Florence,
Pisa, Parma, Venice, Rome, and Naples did send delegates.27
Presiding over the Congress was a commission composed of
Costa, Traversi, Baldini, Pradelli, Alfredo Mazzotti, and
Gaetano Zirardini,28 who, according to Professor Manacorda, was the "animator" of the gathering.29 Unfortunately, the authorities had known about the Congress long before it convened; as soon as it assembled the police appeared and ordered the representatives to disperse.30 A
melee followed, and the meeting was finally broken up,
though not before Bagli, Pradelli, and Giovanni Zirardini
--Gaetano's brother--had been arrested.

Unwilling to give in so easily, seventy of the Congress' delegates reassembled early the next morning.
This time they were able to carry on their business without interruption. A resolution was passed condemning
the government for violating freedom of assembly. It was
also decided to hold another session of this Congress at
Forlì in November.31 Finally, a commission of nine members was elected and charged with organizing an Italian
congress as soon as possible.

No sooner had the Ravenna session of the Second
<u>P.S.R.R.</u> Congress ended than the anarchists resumed their
vituperative repudiation of Costa and his program. This
time it was not Malatesta (who was still in prison) nor
the Riminesi, but the anarchist exiles who led the attack
Early in August <u>Le</u> <u>Réveil</u> <u>des</u> <u>Travailleurs</u>, a socialist-
republican newspaper in Nice, published a letter from
Ariodante Facchini, an old Internationalist from Bologna
then in French exile, in which he launched a vicious personal assault on Costa.32 The aggrieved Romagnol responded with a letter--dated August 17--to <u>Le</u> <u>Réveil</u> in
which he challenged Facchini and proposed that each of
them appoint three persons to a jury to investigate the
charges and announce a verdict.33 Costa himself named
as his seconds Gnocchi-Viani, Gaetano Zirardini, and
Serafino Mazzotti, but Facchini ignored the invitation
and continued to assail Costa, and <u>Il</u> <u>Sole</u> for having
defended him.34

Despite the fact that Facchini was never able to
furnish evidence in support of his allegations,35 anarchists both in Italy and in exile latched onto the Bolognese's anti-Costa crusade. In Italy the most rabid criti-

278

cism of Costa came from Proximus Tuus in Turin,[36] L'Op-presso in Pergola (the Marches), and Il Popolo--directed by Grassi, Marzoli, and Icilio Ugo Parrini--in Florence. Facchini also received particularly zealous support from his fellow exiles in France.[37]

The anarchists aroused great indignation in the Romagna, where Zirardini and Il Sole once more took up Costa's defense.[38] The Ravennate and his paper, in turn, were attacked by Il Popolo and Proximus Tuus.[39] Soon all the Romagnols were embroiled in the conflict. On October 7, socialists from all over the region met at Forlì to counter the abuse being heaped on Costa and Zirardini. Among the most important Romagnol chieftains in attendance were Baldi, Cappellini, Pradelli, Baldini, Buggini, Lanzoni, and Cesare Lombardi of Dovia.[40] The gathering accomplished its purpose and as a result a formal protest against the anarchists, signed by socialists from all over the Romagna, was published in Il Sole on October 20, 1883.[41]

There were no Riminesi, though, among the signers. According to the authorities, moreover, the Riminesi had not attended the October 7 meeting. Instead, they had sent a message declaring they had found nothing offensive in the articles in Le Réveil.[42] At a meeting on October 11 the socialists of Rimini decided not to adhere to the protest made at Forlì.[43]

Costa's troubles at this time were not confined to attacks from the anarchists: the government now renewed its suppression of the socialist movement. On September 9, at a comizio in Cesena for the unveiling of a bust of Garibaldi, the authorities prevented Costa from speaking and a riot ensued. A similar occurrence took place at a second comizio held in Faenza later that day.[44] The authorities were determined to move against the socialists. As a result of the first incident Valducci was arrested for assaulting a police official with a knife and Costa was charged with complicity.

These setbacks notwithstanding, Costa was determined to hold the second session of the Second P.S.R.R. Congress. Accordingly, on November 18, 1883, the party convened at Oreste Randi's villa near Forlì,[45] presided over by a commission composed of Costa, Cappellini, Baldini, Gaetano Zirardini, and Gaspare Bagli.[46] Over sixty cities were represented, all Romagnol. The chief accomplishment of the gathering was the approval of the party program which

279

had been formulated at the Congress of Rimini in 1881.
The representatives also nominated a Commission of Correspondence to be located at Ravenna and composed of
three representatives from that city and one each from
Cesena, Forlì, Imola, and Bologna. It was also decided
to hold an International Workers' Congress at Turin during the Universal Exposition scheduled for 1885. The
meeting closed with a vote of solidarity with Cipriani,
with Valducci, now being held for the Cesena incident in
September, and with Malatesta, who had been released from
prison late in October.

Although the Riminesi had made a token appearance
at the first sitting of the 1883 Congress in the person
of Bagli, none of them attended the Forlì session. Instead, they sent a letter to the Congress explaining
their absence:

> Considering that the meetings which have been
> called over and over again for the formulation of
> programs...have resulted up to now in completely
> negative results for the true propaganda:
> Considering that the proposals and approvals are
> not part of his own sentiments because the worker is
> still incapable of understanding formulas which are
> purely rhetorical; and that the vote of a few per-
> sons, a vote inspired by one man, forms the great
> majority on which the many results realized up to
> now are based:
> Considering that other much more effective and
> energetic means are available for the eradication
> of the bad seed which is the work of one man and
> which has taken root in the camp of the true Revolu-
> tionary Socialist party:
> It has been decided not to adhere to the invita-
> tion to...the Congress but...to apply ourselves to
> projects which are much more useful to the unravel-
> ling of that single problem /the "bad seed" mention-
> ed above?/ which was and continues to be the only ob-
> stacle to the realization of the great Ideal.[47]

The resistance of the Riminesi to Costa's program
was now strengthened by the fact that upon Malatesta's
release from prison he resumed his battle against Costa.
To implement his objective he founded a Florentine newspaper, La Questione sociale, in December, one month after
the Congress at Forlì.[48] He waged his campaign into 1884
appealing in January directly to the Romagnols in an article entitled "To our Friends of the Socialist Party of

Romagna," in which he condemned the program the Romagnols had adopted and suggested that they had been deceived by Costa. The P.S.R.R., Malatesta added, "has ceased to be socialist and revolutionary in fact and has become an appendix to the democratic bourgeois parties: a stupendous base of operation for those renegades from our party who need to be accepted by the bourgeoisie and appreciated by the government."[49]

What Malatesta had in mind here, as others had before him,[50] was the P.S.R.R.'s participation in the Fascio della Democrazia. From the time of his election Costa had cooperated with the radicals and the republicans--the parties of the Estrema Sinistra (Extreme Left)--in Parliament. An attempt to extend this parliamentary alliance to the country at large resulted in the creation of an organization called the Fascio della Democrazia at the Congress of Bologna on May 5, 1883, where socialists, radicals, and republicans all agreed to cooperate in their opposition to the government.[51]

But Costa--who was unable to attend the Bologna Congress because of his illness--and the socialists were not wholly in accord with their allies. The socialists could not in good conscience accept the Fascio program, which was of radical inspiration. Consequently, at the second Congress of the Fascio, again in Bologna, on August 8-9, 1883, the socialists presented a declaration of their dissatisfaction with the program, yet agreed to remain in the Fascio for the time being.[52] That the socialists were willing to participate actively in the Fascio became apparent when Costa accepted his nomination to its Central Committee (which also included Felice Cavallotti, a radical, and Giovanni Bovio, a radical with strong republican sympathies).

Costa responded to Malatesta's charges by addressing the Romagnols himself. He acknowledged that the P.S.R.R. had been working with bourgeois parties, but defended this tactic by insisting that "just propagating our ideas and just organizing ourselves no longer sufficed."[53] He concluded by dismissing as ridiculous Malatesta's insinuation "that all that which has occurred...from 1879 to the present was thought up, foreseen, and desired by me, and that you have been nothing more than the unconscious instrument of that which I desired."

By now Malatesta had had enough of this "mystification." Late in January, 1884, he and Pezzi, who now waxed

281

equally intransigent, went to Ravenna for a direct confrontation with Costa and his supporters.[54] The P.S.R.R. leader, flanked by the Ravennati, met with Malatesta on January 20 and again the following day.[55] Malatesta, according to his own testimony, demanded that Costa, "resign from the Fascio and denounce this organization as bourgeois and anti-revolutionary, make an interpellation in Parliament on Cipriani's behalf with a speech which would strongly...affirm the socialist program, even at the cost of provoking laughter, howls, and hisses, and ...hand in his resignation as deputy and invite his electors to vote for Amilcare Cipriani."[56] But Costa rejected his demands and was able to counter Malatesta's charges effectively. The Ravennati continued to give him their support.[57] The meeting was finally adjourned with the two adversaries farther apart than ever.

Once again Malatesta had raised the question of Cipriani's candidacy. Soon his followers seized on this issue as a means of embarrassing Costa. On March 5--four days after Costa had made a speech at Brescia in favor of Cipriani's election there--the anarchist circle at Forlimpopoli demanded that Costa dismiss himself from Parliament and call for the election of Cipriani in his place. The suggestion, published in La Questione sociale, received an enthusiastic response. The adherents of the proposal, according to Professor Masini, gave a clear indication of the strength of the anarchist movement at the time: endorsements came from anarchist sections in Bologna, Cesena, Faenza, Ravenna, Rimini, Milan, Rome, Genoa, Palermo, Ancona, Pesaro, Camerino, Osimo, Recanati, Sassoferrato, Terni, Florence, Galluzzo, Pisa, Prato, Pistoia, S. Giovanni Valdarno, S. Croce sull'Arno, Cascina, Aulla, Gello, Leghorn, Padua, Legnano, Adria, Badia Polesine, Este, Monselice, Turin, Alessandria, Reggio Calabria, Rocca Imperiale, Naples, Sorrento, Foggia, Aquila, and Antrodoco.[58]

At the end of January Malatesta and Merlino were brought to trial again and charged with a variety of offenses, the most serious of which was sedition. Both were found guilty on February 1. Malatesta was sentenced to three years in prison and Merlino to four, but pending a new trial before a Court of Appeals both were given their freedom. Malatesta, as the petition in favor of Cipriani demonstrates, continued to inveigh against Costa. By now, though, he was heading in a more positive direction: the reorganization of the anarchist movement throughout Italy.

The Forlì Congress of 1884

With the anarchists, particularly Malatesta, preoccupied with the reorganization of the Italian International, Costa was again able to concentrate on parliamentary affairs in Rome and on the organization of the P.S.R.R. in the Romagna. He also resumed publication of Avanti!, now published in Rome, with the first number of the new series appearing on April 6, 1884.[59] The paper was no longer an organ of the P.S.R.R.; in fact, in it there was hardly any mention of the party. Instead, Costa concentrated on strengthening his alliance with the republicans both in and out of Parliament.[60]

Still, Costa was determined to hold the Third Congress of the Romagnol party. Consequently he ceased publication of Avanti! on June 24, and when the parliamentary session ended the following month he returned to the Romagna to prepare his followers for the gathering.

Although Il Comune--which succeeded the defunct Sole as Ravenna's socialist organ in late 1883 and was published by Claudio Zirardini--gave no sign that a major congress was imminent, this became clear on July 7 when the Federal Commission of the P.S.R.R. had the party program published. About two weeks later, on July 20, the Third Congress of the P.S.R.R. opened in Forlì.[61] Presiding was Gaspare Mariotti, with Baldi, Cappellini, and Baldini serving as secretaries. Present were representatives from throughout the Romagna.[62] Although it was intended only Costians would be allowed at the Congress, three anarchists were there when the meeting opened: Antonio Fantini from Forlimpopoli, Pietro Toni from Faenza, and Romeo Mingozzi from Ravenna. After some deliberation the anarchists were permitted to remain and participate in the discussions, but not to vote.

Three problems confronted the delegates: the democratic alliance, the Cipriani affair, and the need for party organization. The socialist position at the coming Congress of the Fascio della Democrazia at Turin was first considered. The discussion was dominated by Costa, who began by giving a brief history of the Fascio. He admitted that Fascio efforts had been productive in only a few areas, notably Lombardy and Piedmont,[63] and blamed the republicans for hindering rather than aiding its development.[64] But despite the alliance's limited accomplishments, the Imolese emphasized its potential. P.S.R.R. participation in the Congress of Turin was therefore de-

cided upon, though with the reservation that the socialists would not accept the _Fascio_'s radical program.

The discussion then moved to Cipriani. As already
mentioned, the anarchists had proposed that Costa resign
as deputy for the province of Ravenna so that Cipriani
could replace him there. Of course, the anarchists were
not primarily concerned with Cipriani but rather with embarrassing Costa, and the conferees were well aware of
this fact before the discussion of the anarchist proposal
opened. Costa's friends (Costa dismissed himself from
the discussion) led the opposition to the Cipriani candidacy at Ravenna. Antonio Lanzoni and the Ravennati--
especially Baldini and the Zirardini brothers, Claudio
and Giovanni--claimed that Cipriani could not win in that
province,[65] and Cappellini assured the delegates that Cipriani's chances were more promising in Forlì, since this
electoral college included Rimini, the Romagnol city where
the anarchist champion aroused the most enthusiasm. The
Congress voted overwhelmingly to propose Cipriani at Forlì rather than Ravenna, thereby confirming its confidence
in the party's leadership.

The last major question before the Congress was organization. After a long discussion in which Cappellini,
Costa, and Luigi Musini all took part, it was determined
that the _P.S.R.R._ should henceforth be known as the _Par-
tito_ _Socialista_ _Rivoluzionario_ _di_ _Italia_ (_P.S.R.I._) and
to set it in motion throughout the peninsula a national
congress should be held in Rome in the near future. Apparently Costa was now convinced that his party had the
strength to project itself beyond the Romagna.[66]

In late August the _P.S.R.I._'s Federal Commission published the program established at Forlì as the basis for
the national congress.[67] Several developments toward the
end of the year, however, prevented the Romagnols from
carrying through with the assembly.

First, the party continued to be plagued by government persecution. In October Fortuzzi, Cappellini, Enrico
Zani, Giacinto Donati, and Alfredo Turci were brought to
trial for publishing the _P.S.R.R._ program in July, on the
eve of the Forlì Congress.[68] The loss of these activists
weakened the party in the Romagna. Costa also found himself involved in court proceedings. Late in August, 1884,
both he and Valducci were finally brought to trial for
the Cesena affair of the preceding year, and were found
guilty on September 3 and sentenced to one year in prison.

Valducci had already put in his time behind bars while awaiting trial, so he was immediately released. By virtue of his immunity as a deputy, Costa had spent no time in jail, but in the following months the government made a sustained drive to have Parliament authorize his imprisonment. Even though these executive pressures were to no avail in the end, with this possibility hanging over his head Costa's efforts to convoke the national congress were moderated to say the least.

As usual, another factor working against the effective organization of the P.S.R.I. was the opposition of the anarchists. Certainly Costa had been too optimistic in believing that their criticism to his program had ebbed sufficiently to permit the expansion of the party. On the contrary, anarchist strength had recently been on the upswing. For example, in a visit in mid-1884 to Pisa, one of the few Tuscan cities where his svolta had been judged positively in the past, Costa was informed that only one hundred of the local 800 socialist workers were behind him.[69]

This trend was equally evident closer to home. The Riminesi, who earlier in 1884 had organized themselves into a loose federation of local sections,[70] had been conspicuous at the July Congress by their absence. Still opposed to the Costians after the Forlì Congress, the Riminesi decided to form a regional organization of their own to combat their opponents more effectively. On August 24 they convoked an anarchist convention at Ronco, near Forlì, and there the Federazione Romagnola dell'Internazionale was created.[71]

For the first time the anarchists in the region were able to combat Costa's party with a united opposition, and they lost no time making their attitude known. On September 17 the Federazione drew up a declaration accusing the P.S.R.I. of causing a schism within the socialist movement in the Romagna. They attacked the very foundation on which the rival party had been built: "the creation of the so-called revolutionary socialist party...is a fact which is contrary to reality, because not all the revolutionary socialists of the Romagna, much less of Italy, are in agreement with the program and method which that party has adopted."[72] In the next few months the Federazione Romagnola, using these arguments, was able to make some progress at the expense of Costa's supporters.[73]

The Decline of the Socialist Movement

Unlike the Riminesi, Malatesta had interpreted the P.S.R.I. Congress of Forlì as affording hope for the anarchist cause. To him the Congress proved that the Costians were losing ground, because its attendance, from a legalitarian point of view, had been disappointing. He predicted: "If we continue to be active, Costianism will soon be dead and all or almost all the socialists in Ital will advance toward the Revolution together."[74]

Malatesta's autopsy on the legalitarian movement was premature, however, Within a few months, it would be the anarchist party in Florence that would be in crisis. After his trial in February, as already noted, Malatesta directed his energies to reorganizing the Italian International.[75] The center of this activity was to be in Tuscany, more specifically Florence. By the end of 1884, though, the anarchist movement in that city had fallen on bad times.

After Malatesta's February trial fifty-eight of his friends in Florence signed a declaration emphatically protesting his unjust sentence. Ironically, this declaration was used as grounds for a new trial: in September the fifty-eight Florentines who had signed the protest were found guilty of showing disrespect for the fundamental laws of the realm. Understandably, the International in Florence went into crisis. The local questore described the effect of the trial in this way: "These sentences...though foreseen by the defendants, have nevertheless produced the greatest depression among them, and among all those affiliated with the sect. Although Natta Grassi, and Pezzi /among those sentenced/ attempt to keep the spirit of sacrifice...alive among their comrades, no one fails to recognize the mortal blow which socialism has received in Florence."[76]

The immediate result was a mass exodus of anarchists from the Tuscan city. Most of those convicted managed to escape before their sentences were imposed. Among these were Malatesta, Natta, Pezzi, and the latter's wife, Luigia Mingozzi, all of whom were living in Argentina by the beginning of 1885.[77] By this time the anarchist party in Florence was indeed dead,[78] and several years would elapse before the Florentines would again exert any influence on Italy's socialist movement.[79]

Yet the will to reorganize the old International did

286

not die with the departure of the Florentine anarchists. Instead, the initiative passed to the Romagna. There the main instigators for the formation of this party were not the Riminesi, as one might expect, but rather Romeo Mingozzi, a Ravennate living in Forlì at this time. Mingozzi wanted to hold a national anarchist congress in the Romagna. A gathering of the region's anarchists met at Forlimpopoli in December, 1884, and endorsed the idea: a national assembly was to be held in the Romagna as soon as possible.[80]

Immediately following the Forlimpopoli meeting the anarchists in the Romagnol provinces came alive. Mingozzi observed: "Propaganda makes headway in the Romagna. I have been making the rounds for about ten days, and I have observed a great awakening. They begin to understand. Meldola, Castel Bolognese, Granarolo, and Lugo have already initiated, and effectively, Internationalist propaganda."[81]

Several postponements notwithstanding, the Congress finally took place in Forlì on March 15, 1885.[82] Its chief accomplishment was the establishment of a national anarchist organization, the Branca Italiana dell'Associazione Internazionale dei Lavoratori. Though some disagreement surrounds the actual purpose of this organization, more than likely the Branca was formed as a weapon against the Costians.[83] Mingozzi himself suggested as much a few months earlier. In a letter to Emilio Castellani dated December 12, 1884, he concerned himself with "the present antagonism between the Italian Socialist Party and the International," and noted that both parties were competing for followers. He concluded: "It is therefore necessary to expand the International actively among the people."[84] As a matter of fact, one of the resolutions passed at the Forlì Congress called for the Branca "to combat the so-called revolutionary socialist party as it would any other bourgeois party."[85] In light of these facts one is inclined to agree with Enzo Santarelli's conclusion that anarchist efforts at association during this period occurred in reaction to the formation of Costa's own party.[86]

The Branca was to have a short life, however; indeed, its organization disintegrated almost before it began. The main reason for its failure can be traced to the internal conflicts splitting the anarchists in Italy at this time:[87] the anarchici-collettivisti wanted to institute a socialist society in which members received ben-

efits according to what they produced; the anarchici-comun
isti, following Kropotkin, called for a society whose members received according to their need. In practice, the
communists in Italy tended toward intransigent positions
and individual action; the collectivists placed larger
emphasis on propaganda and adhered to ideas which resembled those of the P.S.R.I.[88] Actually, there was considerable cooperation between the anarchici-collettivisti
and Costa's party.[89]

But the majority of the anarchists in Italy were communists; hence they were reluctant to accept the resolutions of the Forlì Congress, which more or less reflected
a collectivist position. At Forlì, for example, the anarchists were urged to organize workers' federations.
The intransigent communists saw such action as compromising their revolutionary stand. What was needed, they insisted, was revolution, not organizations which would inevitably lull the workers into an acceptance of the status quo. Consequently, there were few adherences to the
Branca in the first few weeks after its creation. As Mingozzi wrote: "It is a glacial and distressing silence."[90]
By May the situation had not improved, and Mingozzi was
thinking of publishing a newspaper in Forlì so that "the
Internationalist party will be able to organize itself
and do something serious and positive"[91]--evidence, no
doubt, of the Branca's meager accomplishment.

By late 1885 the effort had fallen apart. Nowhere
was the anarchists' failure to organize themselves more
obvious than in their old stronghold of Rimini, where in
November the local subprefect noted that the Circolo Cipriani's efforts to create an anarchist federation in that
city had not been productive. A local federation, he insisted, was nothing more than a wish.[92]

Yet if the anarchist movement waned in 1885, the
same was also true of Costa's party. A sure sign was its
inability to convoke a national congress in that year.
Nor was the P.S.R.I. able to establish a newspaper outside the confines of the Romagna. The attempt to construct a national party had apparently come to a halt.
More and more Costa understood that before the party could
be created socialist ideas had to be implanted in Italy's
soil. Toward the end of 1884 he turned his attention to
propagandizing his ideas throughout the peninsula, especia
ly in the northern part of the country.[93] By the following year propaganda had definitely superseded organization
as the main socialist thrust.

Even in the Romagna, the only region where the P.S.
R.I. did have some foundation, party organization began
to crumble. Costa's long absences were to have a detri-
mental effect on the movement there. The process had
manifested itself in the latter part of 1884. In November Gaetano Zirardini wrote to Costa from Paris: "I know
that in certain towns in Romagna, and especially in Ravenna, the party's organization has broken up. This is bad,
very bad."94

Zirardini's concern over the disintegration of the
party in his home town of Ravenna was well founded, for
there the P.S.R.I. had its widest support, and that following had to be preserved at all costs. Yet by early
1885 the situation there had not improved. On January
6 Costa was in Ravenna to confer with the P.S.R.I.'s
local federation. Mingozzi explained the reason for this
visit: "Costa had to make himself visible once more, in
order to impede the separation of many socialists from
his program and their espousal of that of the International."95

The decline of the P.S.R.I. in the city of Ravenna
reflected the situation in the entire province. According to prefect reports, the "public spirit" (i.e., the
attitude of the populace toward the government and its
institutions) had been getting worse there every year
from 1879 to 1883.96 Concurrently the subversive parties,
especially the socialists, had been growing stronger and
stronger. In July, 1884, the prefect of Ravenna informed
the Minister of Interior that the public spirit during
the first half of the year was about the same as that of
the one before--bad.97 He noted, though, that the P.S.R.
I. was beginning to experience some difficulties in the
province: many party members were refusing to pay their
dues or were dropping out of the organization altogether.
Part of the cause of this disaffection was the expulsion
of Armando Armuzzi, the president and founder of Ravenna's
Associazione Generale degli Operai Braccianti, from the
socialist party.98

Armuzzi's expulsion stemmed from a seemingly harm-
less controversy over the fate of the extensive pine forest (pineta) which then existed in the eastern part of
Ravenna province.99 Armuzzi's cooperative was calling
for reclamation of some of this land, an operation which
would provide sorely-needed work for its members, but the
leaders of the local P.S.R.I. federation were very much
against the destruction of the forest, for ecological rea-

289

sons. Unwilling to follow the dictates of the party,
Armuzzi was thrown out, a decision which alienated many
members of the braccianti's cooperative, the backbone of
the P.S.R.I. in Ravenna.

But there was also a second cause for the trouble
within the ranks of the party, the local prefect added,
one which would provide a more serious threat to the P.S.
R.I.'s existence than would the question of the pineta:
anarchist dissatisfaction with Costa's failure to resign
from Parliament and to call for the election of Cipriani
in his place.[100] During the second half of 1884 this dis-
sent increased, and the anarchists, led by Lodovico Nabruz
zi, mounted a relentless campaign against Costa and his
lieutenants in the province.[101] The beginning of the
P.S.R.I.'s demise in Ravenna dates from this period.[102]

In the rest of the Romagna the story was much the
same. The condition of the P.S.R.I. in the province of
Forlì was not quite as bad as in Ravenna, but there too
the situation was less than rosy. Such was the case, certainly, in the city of Forlì, where on February 28, 1885,
a socialist circle was founded on the initiative of Amedeo Ghetti. Although the new association had no connection with the local anarchist group, it maintained its
independence vis-à-vis the Costians.[103] Thus even in
Forlì, where the P.S.R.I.'s Commission of Correspondence
was in residence, the party was losing its preponderance.
But perhaps the most telling sign of the P.S.R.I.'s plight
in the Romagna was the fact that in August its official
organ, Il Comune, ceased publication.[104] The apparent
cause of its failure was financial difficulties, by no
means the least of the party's problems.[105]

Costa and the Partito Operaio Italiano

As the P.S.R.I. began to decline, however, other developments were taking place to augur for the socialist
movement in Italy a brighter future. One such occurrence
was the creation of the Partito Operaio Italiano (P.O.
I.).[106] While the P.O.I. had its inception in 1882, not
until the Congress of Milan in 1885 (the first session of
which was held on April 12 and the second on May 3) did
the party formally come into existence.[107]

Created in Milan, Italy's industrial capital, by
Costantino Lazzari, Giuseppe Croce, Augusto Dante, and
other workers of that city, the P.O.I. had earlier been

influenced and its growth aided by Gnocchi-Viani and the Milanese socialists. But a significant difference persisted between the programs of the two groups: principally, the fact that unlike the socialists the <u>operaisti</u> restricted their membership to the proletariat. Thus the Marxian concept of class warfare was projected to its logical extreme.

The anti-bourgeois bias of the <u>operaisti</u> was also evident in the fact that there was always a strong current within the party which repudiated political action; hence the <u>operaisti</u> were especially opposed to participation in political elections. Here they displayed a certain similarity with the anarchists, since both viewed Parliament as a corrupt bourgeois institution. In this respect, too, the <u>operaisti</u> differed from the socialists, who were primarily concerned with gaining control of those institutions which the <u>P.O.I.</u> was intent upon destroying. Instead of political goals, the <u>P.O.I.</u> leaders sought economic gains. The worker, they insisted, had to better his material condition as soon as possible. Only when this was done could he turn to political action. He must improve his economic status, however, not through social legislation, which the <u>P.O.I.</u> claimed was philanthrophy, but rather through direct action, specifically the strike.

Costa had looked favorably on the <u>P.O.I.</u> since its inception in 1882,[108] believing the <u>operaisti</u> to be a valuable arm of that national socialist party which he hoped to create.[109] But the idea of fusion of the two parties, or even cooperation between them, had always met with powerful resistance from the Milanesi. Their strict class orientation and intransigence with respect to political involvement were insurmountable obstacles to unification of the Romagnol and Lombard movements. Moreover, to the <u>P.O.I.</u> heads Costa was the personification of the fate of socialism when it begins to work within the system, for it seemed to them the Romagnol was sacrificing his ideals as he cultivated closer contacts with the bourgeois parties in Parliament. His entrance in 1884 into the Masonic movement, the bourgeois institution par excellence, did nothing to enhance his popularity in Milan.[110] At times, in fact, outright hostility erupted between Costa and the <u>operaisti</u>.[111]

Discouraged by the <u>P.S.R.I.</u>'s inability to hold its congress in 1885, Costa saw the possibility of a national party being formed in the immediate future rapidly diminishing. At the same time, however, he could see a pro-

mising potential developing in Milan: by 1885 the P.O.I.
was gaining momentum. On December 6-7 the operaisti held
their Second Congress, this time in Mantua.[112] This assembly was perhaps even more important than the founding
Congress earlier that year, for it was at Mantua that the
Confederazione Operaia Lombarda was incorporated into the
workers' party. This development was a sizable one, for
the Confederazione, which had formerly been under the control of the Milan radicals, was now the largest workers'
organization in the province of Lombardy. At Mantua,
therefore, the P.O.I. had vastly expanded its power. The
Romagnols were rapidly losing their ascendancy over the
Italian socialist movement.

If ever there had been any doubt in Costa's mind that
the best way of creating a national socialist party was
through the merger of the P.O.I. and P.S.R.I., it vanished in late 1885. He was now determined to effect this
fusion.[113] This was his prime objective at the Second
Congress of the P.S.R.I., finally held in 1886.

Although the P.S.R.I. had not held a national congress during the previous year, hope of doing so was
never abandoned. On April 26, 1885, a meeting had been
held in Forlì for the purpose of preparing the congress,
but nothing had been accomplished.[114] In the following
months, though, Costa continued to work toward this end,[115]
and in December, on the eve of the P.O.I. Congress, he
finally issued a call for his own party's Congress, to be
held on April 25-26, 1886, in Mantua.[116]

Costa, like the operaisti, had a special reason for
selecting that site. Mantua was located in the Lombardy
and was therefore very close to Milan, where Costa was
banking on making the biggest impression. But an even
more weighty consideration was the fact that by the mid-
1880's Mantua had become the center of Italy's peasant
movement--a reputation Mantua had built up by virtue of
a series of agricultural strikes which broke out in the
surrounding area (the mantovano) in 1884-85.[117]

The Italian countryside witnessed a series of agricultural strikes in the 1880's, especially in the Po Valley. The impetus for this agitation was the economic crisis tormenting the country during this period.[118] The
outstanding effect of this depression in the Po Valley
was the creation of an agricultural proletariat, the braccianti. As economic conditions worsened in the 1880's
the mezzadri were driven off their lands and were replac-

ed by the braccianti,[119] who formed the backbone of the militant movement responsible for the wave of strikes that began in the Polesine, "the Romagna of Venetia,"[120] around 1882, gradually spread all over the Po Valley, and culminated in the famous Mantua strikes of 1884-85. Organized by Eugenio Sartori and Francesco Siliprandi, and inspired by La Favilla, the peasant associations of the mantovano practically revolutionized the countryside in these years. The immediate outcome was the trial in Venice from February 16 to March 27, 1886, of the strike organizers, including Sartori, Siliprandi, and Alessandro D'Atri, the editor of La Favilla. But bearing a long-range impact was the thorough radicalization of the peasantry in the mantovano. The countryside had finally become fertile ground for the planting of socialist ideas --which was the reason both the operaisti and Costa selected Mantua as the site of their party congresses.

Costa's prime objective at Mantua was to reach an understanding with the Milanesi. He was also concerned, however, with spreading socialist propaganda into the countryside. Unlike some Italian socialist leaders, Costa was keenly aware of the problems of the peasants as well as of the contribution they could make to the socialist movement.[121] He was always careful, therefore, to address himself not only to workers in the city, but also to the peasants--both braccianti and mezzadri--in the countryside (see, for example, his letter, "To my Friends of the Romagna"). Costa's concern for the peasant found expression in a number of other ways: in the many speeches he gave in the small villages and hamlets in the Romagna and throughout Italy; in his efforts in Parliament to help the braccianti's cooperative of Ravenna; in his defense of the agricultural strikes in Mantua and the rest of the lower Po Valley;[122] and even in his antimilitary campaign of the 1880's and 1890's, which he used to attract the peasant to the cause of socialism.[123] All these manifestations of concern for the agricultural worker were undoubtedly rooted in Costa's anarchist past, for the Internationalists had always seen the peasant as innately revolutionary and had therefore stressed the radicalization of the countryside.

The Second Congress of the P.S.R.I. opened in Mantua on April 23, 1886. Presiding was Siliprandi; the Directing Commission was composed of Costa, Musini, D'Atri, and Dante.[124] Dante's presence on the Commission was significant since he was a high-ranking P.O.I. member.

Yet the stated purpose of the Congress was not the
fusion of the Romagnol and Lombard movements per se, but
rather the creation of a truly national socialist party.
Immediately, however, it became manifest that this scope
had not been accomplished. Although there were delegates
from Piedmont, Liguria, Venetia, Emilia, Tuscany, Lazio,
and the Marches, the overwhelming majority of the representatives came from two areas--the mantovano and the
Romagna.[125]

After opening remarks by Domenico Ratti, a Piemontese
on the pressing need for reforms, D'Atri (like Ratti a
close friend of Costa) set forth the most urgent issues
to be discussed by the Congress: the utility of participation in political and administrative elections; the
necessity for the socialist coalition with democratic
parties; and closer relations with the operaista party.

The last was the question of most import. Dante
realized this, and thanked the Congress for the consideration it had given his organization. But, he added, he
felt compelled to clarify one point: though both parties
had a common end, inasmuch as both were essentially socialist, they did differ markedly on the question of means
The P.O.I., he reaffirmed, had little faith in the state,
and in fact sought its abolition. Dependence on this
bourgeois institution would lead only to inertia; the liberation of the proletariat must originate not with the
state but with the proletariat itself. Plainly the P.O.I.
was unwilling to compromise on this point.

Thus the distinction between the two parties was
still a crucial one. If the P.O.I. maintained its intransigence, no union would ever be possible. Costa had
to address himself to this problem. As the last speaker
before the Congress, he exhorted its delegates to unite
within the ranks of the socialist movement. Although he
was concerned with the anarchists, who incidentally had
been excluded from the sessions again,[126] Costa was interested primarily in the operaisti. Both the P.O.I. and
the P.S.R.I., he declared, had common origins in the old
International, as well as a common end. The question,
he conceded, was indeed one of means. Turning to Dante's
objection, Costa assured the P.O.I. representative that
the P.S.R.I., too, had little faith in the state. But,
he counseled:

The state exists; and as long as it exists we
should deal with it. The state, Dante has said, is

the organization of the bourgeoisie. All right.
But why? Because the state is in the hands of the
bourgeoisie. Once we take it over, it comes into
the hands of the workers; and, instead of being the
enemy, as it is today, it will become the powerful
lever by which the social revolution will be completed.

The knife which, in the hands of the bourgeoisie,
is pointed against our chest today--if we take this
knife by the handle we can turn it against the bourgeoisie. It is just for that reason that I believe
our activity should aim, politically, at gaining
control of the state; it is just for that reason
that we frankly state in our Statute that the revolution is first of all the temporary dictatorship
of the working classes: that is, the accumulation
of all social power (economic, political, military)
in the hands of the workers.

Costa then dealt with Dante's argument that the acceptance of the state would inevitably result in general
inertia. He insisted that under the present circumstances,
political and economic victories could be obtained only
through legislation--a product not of inertia but of "the
activity and pressure of the masses." In attempting to
enact these reforms, therefore, the socialists were demanding action, not passivity. Anarchists, socialists,
and operaisti, Costa concluded, were members of one all-
encompassing socialist party. That all its factions
should agree on means was not necessary; what was imperative was that they cooperate without trying to impose
their ideas on each other, since a polemical battle would
dissipate their vitality and benefit only their common
enemy: the bourgeoisie.

The Congress closed with a series of resolutions.
The party approved the need for economic reform, collectivization of the land, workers' cooperatives, electoral
participation and democratic coalitions, and close cooperation between the various schools of socialism. Finally,
it recommended "that our own Federal Commission come to
an agreement with the Central Committee of the Partito
Operaio in order to bring about the objectives which
both parties have in common."

This last proposal was the most meaningful, for it
provided a concrete plan of action which would lead to
larger cooperation between the two parties and, it was
hoped, to their eventual fusion. But in Milan the pro-

gram established at the Mantua Congress of the P.S.R.I.
met with apathy.[127] Seemingly, Costa's argument had little effect on the intransigent position of the operaisti.

A few months after the Congress, however, the operaisti would be more receptive to the idea of cooperation
with the Costians. In fact, for a time there would be a
real possibility of fusion. What caused the P.O.I. to
take this new position?

The situation began to change with the political e-
lections of May, 1886. Despite their reluctance to participate in political life, the operaisti decided to propose
candidates in these elections. The inevitable result of
this P.O.I. decision was the antagonizing of the radicals
of Milan (with whom relations had always been strained),
who saw that any gains which the P.O.I. might make in
Lombardy would be made at the expense of their party.

Though the operaista candidacies were unsuccessful,
tension between the two parties intensified after the
elections. Late in May, Cavallotti created a bombshell
when he charged that the P.O.I. had been financed by the
authorities. In effect, he said, the operaisti were nothing but a gang of government spies. Lazzari and his
friends, though often unforbearing themselves, were shocke
by the accusation. Before long a full-scale war broke out
in Milan, with the "battles" fought in the columns of Il
Fascio operaio and Il Secolo.[128]

On June 23 the polemic was suddenly terminated when
the government moved against the P.O.I., arresting its
leaders--including Lazzari, Croce, and Dante--and suppress
ing its newspaper. Since, as we have said, the operaisti
had grown unusually strong by this time, Agostino Depretis
then Prime Minister, had good cause to fear them. Now,
with the democratic Left so divided, the moment seemed
ripe to him for crippling the Milanesi. His reasoning
was excellent, for the operaisti were indeed isolated by
this time, an isolation as much a product of their own
intolerance as of Cavallotti's accusations. Beset by
these circumstances, the operaisti were forced to turn
to Costa for assistance.

Even before the 1886 elections, Costa had sided with
the P.O.I. in its conflict with the radicals.[129] Pressing as he was for the union of socialist forces, Costa's
choice was a logical one. The decision was made easier,
moreover, by the fact that his faith in an alliance with

296

the republicans and the radicals--a position he had defended from 1882--had been severely shaken by the inability of these parties to cooperate in the Fascio. By 1885 the Fascio had ceased to exist. Costa had every reason, then, to come to the aid of the operaisti.

Costa made an impassioned defense of the operaisti in the Chamber of Deputies on July 2, 1886.[130] His activities in and out of Parliament made plain that he had for some time been one of the staunchest defenders of the suppressed party, and thus demonstrated that the solidarity of the two socialist parties was not simply a fiction he had conjured up at the Mantua Congress. His efforts won him much sympathy from the operaisti; in fact, they now began to consider that party union which they had earlier rejected.[131] Apparently Depretis had done what Costa had been unable to do at Mantua.

But in the next few months this union was not consummated. Whether or not the operaisti were acting in good faith in suggesting cooperation is unclear. What is certain is that the possibility of fusion between the P.O.I. and P.S.R.I. which existed in mid-1886 soon disappeared.

Without the alliance, the P.S.R.I. faded rapidly. Already the Mantua Congress in April had revealed the weakness of the party outside the Romagna. One final effort was made at that time, however, to broaden the party's power base by transferring the Commission of Correspondence from the Romagna to Parma.

But in the Emilian city the new Commission, composed of Musini, Attilio Orland, Cino Cordero, Giuseppe Tommasini, and Augusto Ruffini, was unable to accomplish anything. In June the Central Committee of the P.O.I. wrote Costa from Milan: "Give us news of the Commission of the Socialist Party which is based in Parma. It seems to be a little indolent. Arouse it!"[132]

Although this is precisely what Costa tried to do, the response from Parma was not very encouraging. On August 5, 1886, Musini wrote Costa:

We have set up a meeting for today between myself, Tommasini, Orland and Cordero and something will be done. But there is so much apathy here, and most of all demoralization, that...the strongest will is necessarily weakened before the obstacles, which derive not so much from our enemies...but from our very friends. You should not judge the conditions of our party around Parma by those in Romagna. There is no unity of principles and of conviction here, there is no discipline of any kind: if to this /state of affairs/ you add the continual defeats, the influences and the overbearing action of the government, of the bourgeoisie...you will easily understand our situation.[133]

On August 26 the Commission issued a circular, apparently drawn up at the August 5 meeting referred to by Musini, in which it admitted its impotence. The Commission had been ineffectual for many reasons, "most important of these, the lack of cooperation from those who should have and could have helped us, apathy, general indifference....."[134]

The demoralization at Parma more than anything else shows the degree to which the P.S.R.I., its title notwithstanding, remained a Romagnol party. Outside the Romagna, even in Parma where Musini was extremely popular, the party was ineffective in projecting its organization. Disintegration was inevitable. The Commission made one feeble effort to save face: it proposed that a new congress be held on September 26-27, 1886. The congress never convened, for by that time the P.S.R.I. was all but finished.

Conclusion

The creation of the Partito Socialista Rivoluzionario di Romagna in 1881 established the Romagnol provinces as the leading stronghold of the budding Italian socialist movement. This reputation was enhanced during the next few years by the initiative taken by Costa to make the P.S.R.R. the basis for a national socialist party--the first such attempt made on the peninsula. This period of Romagnol pre-eminence did not last very long, however; the hegemony won by Costa and his followers was soon threatened from Lombardy, where the Partito Operaio Italiano was making steady progress in the eighties. In the Romagna itself, moreover, the socialist party began to lose its momentum after the middle of 1884. The resistance which their program encountered in the region proved to be insurmountable, and the Costians grew increasingly lethargic. Trying to avert this spiraling decline, Costa stepped up his efforts to found an Italian socialist party.

But by 1886 the attempt had come to naught. In re-

trospect, it is clear that the most promising possibility
for the creation of an Italian socialist party under the
leadership of the Romagnols rested in the Mantua Congress
of that year.[135] Thereafter Costa's prime objective elud-
ed him, and the Romagna suffered a crushing defeat. What
accounted for this failure? The answer is also elusive.

To say that the P.S.R.R. declined because of its inability to project party organization beyond the confines
of the Romagna is stating the obvious. The real question,
then, is why the P.S.R.R. remained almost exclusively a
Romagnol party. Certainly one reason is to be found in
the reluctance of the P.O.I.--the only other effective
socialist organization in the eighties--to combine its
forces with those of the Romagnols. Had the two groups
fused or even cooperated effectively after 1886, a national socialist party might have come into being.[136] But
the Milanesi refused to abandon their conception of a
pure proletarian party concerned exclusively with economic questions. Thus on principle the two parties were
incompatible.

But the impasse did not arise out of principles alone.
Another consideration was regionalism. As noted earlier,
this tendency in Italy remained a significant characteristic even into the twentieth century, and in the nineteenth century it had a vital bearing on political life.
Insofar as the socialist movement was concerned, the effect of regionalism was largely negative--each section of
the country tried to maintain its autonomy vis-à-vis other
sections,[137] and undoubtedly this was one of the reasons
the operaisti of Milan hesitated to cooperate with the
Romagnols. The Milanesi were unwilling to subordinate
themselves to a movement controlled by outsiders, especially by Romagnols, a people they must have had considerable difficulty in understanding, so vast were the differences in their environments.

Another factor contributing to the P.S.R.R.'s inability to expand was the weakness of the party's organization
even in the Romagna itself. Had the P.S.R.R. been stronger
there, perhaps the operaisti could have been induced to
enter into an alliance. Throughout the period 1881-86
the party was repeatedly holding congresses, deliberating,
and reorganizing, but the objectives of all this repeti-
tious activity never seemed to be realized. There was
always a striking discrepancy between Costa's feverish
efforts in the Romagna and his few accomplishments there
in the way of organization. With these circumstances pre-

vailing in the Romagna, the party's prospects of prolifer-
ating into sections beyond that region, even under the
best of circumstances, could never have been bright.

Yet just why was the party weak in the Romagna?
Guglielmo Ferrero, writing in 1893, suggested an explanation that is still widely accepted. The formation of
the party, Ferrero contended, was illogical "at a time
and in a region in which economic conditions were not
those that are the necessary prerequisite of a socialist
party."[138] Ferrero was of course referring to the non-
existence of an industrial proletariat in the Romagna
during the 1880's. Without such a base, he reasoned, the
party was inevitably weak.

While Ferrero's explanation has much truth in it,
his view is not wholly accurate. His assumption that a
socialist party can be based only on an industrial proletariat is debatable. If the history of the Italian
Socialist Party, created in 1892, is any guide, one can
deduce that the countryside rather than the city constituted the popular base of the Italian socialist movement.[1]
In fact, in 1892 a significant proletariat existed only
in Milan;[140] the country was still overwhelmingly agricultural. That the Romagna had no industrial proletariat
was hardly a crucial factor.

Still, Ferrero is absolutely right when he says that
the P.S.R.R. did not have a popular base. Here lies its
main source of weakness. Conceivably the party might have
cultivated this indispensable popular base in the agricultural proletariat, a class that was burgeoning, particularly in the Romagnol provinces, throughout the 1880's. But
in fact this was not possible. The P.S.R.R. did not creat
a mass party partly because it did not want to.[141] But
even had the P.S.R.R. been so inclined, success would
hardly have followed since the countryside was not ready
to be organized. The peasants were numerous, but in the
1880's they were not aware of their own class interests.[14]
Development of class consciousness would therefore have
been a prerequisite to effective party organization. What
was needed was propaganda, and though the P.S.R.R. did
propagandize the countryside, socialist ideas took time
to penetrate.

Economic factors also have a weighty bearing on whether or not an environment is ready for socialist ideas.
The economic crisis of the eighties would coerce Italy's
peasants into accepting more radical solutions and thus

make them susceptible to socialist propaganda. In the
early 1880's, however, the full impact of this crisis
was yet to be felt. For this reason, too, a mass party
based on the peasantry was still out of the question, at
least in the Romagna.

Consequently, instead of relying on the peasantry,
the P.S.R.R. was forced to rely on the artisan classes
in the small towns, a source which necessarily restricted
party membership. In examining police files, one is
struck by the fact that the same names come up again and
again. Incidental to so small a membership was the party's
vulnerability to financial problems; witness, for instance,
the sporadic publication of many socialist newspapers.
Not relieving this intraparty problem, of course, was the
economic crisis which Italy suffered in those years.

Besides the lack of a popular base and financial resources, one must remember that the P.S.R.R.'s program
in the Romagna was always hampered by both the republicans
and anarchists.[143] Possibly it was the competition from
these groups, more than any other single factor, which
was at the core of the party's impotence in the region.
Republican antagonism was no mean obstacle to Costa's ambitions, given the numerical superiority and prestigious
leadership of the Consociazione Romagnola. And yet the
anarchist element proved to be the Imolese's more formidable opponent. While anarchism had begun to die out in
Italy after 1880, in the Romagna its adherents held on
to a semblance of their old power throughout the following decade. As a party, perhaps, the anarchists constituted no inordinate threat to the P.S.R.R., but anarchist
sentiment pervaded the whole region and was strong even
among Costa's most loyal supporters. With few exceptions,
the socialist party's functionaries had been Internationalists in the seventies. For many of these men, as for
Costa himself, anarchist ideology died hard.[144] These
former ties were a more or less constant source of dis-
unity within the P.S.R.R. during this period. In fact,
police authorities often had trouble distinguishing between socialists and anarchists.

Conditions inherent in the Romagnol environment,
then, played a major role in undermining the P.S.R.R. and
preventing it from projecting its organization elsewhere
in Italy. This failure had become obvious to everyone
by the end of 1886, signaling that the primacy of Romagnol
socialism was no more.

NOTES

[1] After the elections, according to a <u>carabiniere</u> report dated Nov. 27, 1882, Costa "appears for the moment to have abandoned every effort to bring about the congress" (note to the prefect of Bologna, A.S.B., <u>Gab</u>. <u>Pref</u>., cat. VII, 1882).

[2] See <u>Il Sole</u>, Jan. 6-7, 1883.

[3] This appeal met with a favorable response in several regions throughout the peninsula, especially in Tuscany, where <u>L'Ilota</u>, an anarchist newspaper in Pistoia, echoed <u>Il Sole</u> in its plea for reorganization. See <u>L'Ilota</u>, Feb. 25, 1883.

[4] Conti, <u>Le origini del socialismo</u>, p. 279.

[5] Quoted in part by Masini, <u>Storia degli anarchici italiani</u>, p. 209.

[6] <u>L'Ilota</u>, Apr. 8, 1883, and later in <u>Il Sole</u>, Apr. 14, 1883.

[7] <u>L'Ilota</u>, Apr. 29, May 6, 1883; <u>Il Sole</u>, May 22, 1883.

[8] <u>Il Moto</u>, Apr. 14, 1883.

[9] <u>L'Alfabeto</u>, Apr. 22, 1883. Kuliscioff had been living in Switzerland during this period. By now the relationship between the two had cooled off considerably, and when Costa recovered, Anna returned to Switzerland with their daughter, Andreina (born in late 1881), nevermore to be reunited with the Imolese.

[10] <u>Il Sole</u>, Apr. 22, 1883. Professor G. Ippolito Pederzoli, writing in the republican newspaper, <u>L'Intransigente</u> of Jesi, had attacked Costa's conduct in Parliament: by allying with the deputies of the Left, Pederzoli charged, Costa had turned his party into a legalitarian one. This criticism was also made by Malatesta.

[11] Ibid., May 12, 1883.

[12] Ibid., May 6, 1883. Zirardini had been shot on Apr.

22 (see Il Sole, Apr. 23), apparently by intransigent republicans who took issue with the young socialist for his
article aimed at the republicans of the Marches. The reunion of Apr. 29 was originally called on account of the
shooting.

[13]Ibid., Mar. 3-4, 1883.

[14]Ibid., Mar. 10-11, 1883. The gathering at Ancona--
held on Feb. 4--like that of Pisa, was dominated by the
anarchists. According to Il Risveglio (Ancona), Mar. 18,
1883, the Ancona Congress completely rejected "legal
means." This article is reproduced in Enzo Santarelli,
Bakuninisti e socialisti nel Piceno (Urbano: Argalìa,
1969), pp. 52-53.

[15]"News of the reorganization of our party reaches us
from every part of the Romagna," Il Sole announced on Mar.
10-11, 1883.

[16]Ibid., June 10, 1883. The Congress had earlier been
announced --Il Sole, Apr. 29--for the end of May.

[17]Il Sole commented on the comizio on July 14, 1883.

[18]The entire staff was eventually convicted, and all
the members given short prison terms (ibid.).

[19]Subprefect of Rimini to the prefect of Forlì, Aug.
22, 1883, A.S.F., Gab. Pref., vol. 107, fasc. 235.

[20]Subprefect of Rimini to the prefect of Forlì, July
16, 1883, A.S.F., Gab. Pref., vol. 107, fasc. 235.

[21]Subprefect of Rimini to the prefect of Forlì, Aug.
22, 1883, A.S.F., Gab. Pref., vol. 107, fasc. 235.

[22]Report of the carabinieri to the prefect of Forlì,
July 23, 1883, A.S.F., Gab. Pref., vol. 107, fasc. 235.

[23]According to the prefect of Forlì, at the end of the
meeting Costa received enthusiastic applause. See report
to the Minister of Interior, July 24, 1883, A.S.F., Gab.
Pref., vol. 107, fasc. 235.

[24]The carabinieri reported on Aug. 11, 1883, that Costa and Bagli had been seen together in Rimini only a few
days after the stormy meeting of July 15. Apparently,
they concluded, the two socialist leaders were still on

friendly terms. See report to the prefect of Forlì, A.S.
F., <u>Gab</u>. <u>Pref</u>., vol. 107, fasc. 235. It should be noted,
however, that Bagli had serious reservations about Costa's attempts to encourage closer ties with the radicals
and republicans. See <u>L'Alfabeto</u>, June 5, 1883.

[25]The date of the Congress had been determined at a
meeting held on July 14 at Ravenna. See <u>Il</u> <u>Sole</u>, July
28, 1883.

[26]Ibid.

[27]The delegates from Florence and Pisa came despite
a circular issued by the Florentine anarchists, dated
July 20, asking all Tuscans to boycott the Congress. The
circular is contained in an undated letter from Egisto
Marzoli to his "friends" (?), B.C.I., no. 327.

[28]<u>Il</u> <u>Sole</u>, Aug. 19, 1883. The chronicle of the Congress is to be found in this number, on which this account
is based unless otherwise indicated.

[29]<u>Il</u> <u>movimento</u> <u>operaio</u> <u>italiano</u>, p. 194. Manacorda's
account of the meeting is also based on <u>Il</u> <u>Sole</u>.

[30]See note from the Minister of Interior to the prefect of Forlì, July 12, 1883, A.S.F., <u>Gab</u>. <u>Pref</u>., vol.
107, fasc. 235.

[31]The <u>carabinieri</u> mistakenly reported that the site
of this session was to be Rimini (report to the prefect
of Forlì, Aug. 11, 1883, A.S.F., <u>Gab</u>. <u>Pref</u>., vol. 107,
fasc. 235.

[32]According to Alcibiade Moneta, ex-director of <u>La</u> <u>Fa-</u>
<u>villa</u> in Mantua and--like Facchini--an exile in France
during this period, Facchini had been encouraged to write
his letter by Florido Matteucci. See letter from Moneta
to Costa, Sept. 10, 1883, B.C.I., no. 291.

[33]Both Facchini's and Costa's letters were later published in <u>Proximus</u> <u>Tuus</u>, an anarchist newspaper in Turin,
on Sept. 8, 1883. This was the paper's first number; its
last was that of Mar. 18, 1885.

[34]<u>Il</u> <u>Popolo</u> (Florence), Sept. 21, 1883. Facchini's
letter was addressed from Menton, in France, and dated
Sept. 12, 1883.

[35]According to Gnocchi-Viani, Mazzotti, and Zirardini,

Il Comune (Ravenna), Dec. 8-9, 1883.

[36]See issue of Oct. 22, 1883.

[37]See the letter from the anarchists in Nice, published in Proximus Tuus, Sept. 8, 1883.

[38]Il Sole, Sept. 2, 1883.

[39]On Sept. 21 and 22 respectively.

[40]Report of the carabinieri to the prefect of Forlì, Nov. 20, 1883, A.S.F., Gab. Pref., vol. 107, fasc. 235.

[41]The protest was also published by the republican newspaper La Democrazia of Forlì, Oct. 14, 1883. The protest: "The undersigned delegates of the Partito Socialista Rivoluzionario della Romagna convened at Forlì on the 7th day of this month...energetically disapprove and condemn the conduct which was and still is maintained by a self-styled revolutionary socialist press...and affirm their complete political and personal confidence in comrade Andrea Costa...."

[42]Minister of Interior to the prefect of Forlì, Oct. 11, 1883, A.S.F., Gab. Pref., vol. 107, fasc. 245.

[43]Subprefect of Rimini to the prefect of Forlì, Oct. 24, 1883, A.S.F., Gab. Pref., vol. 107, fasc. 245. The subprefect was not entirely aware of what the situation was in his city: he concluded that the evolutionists were led by Carpesani and the intransigents by Bagli (sic).

[44]See Il Sole, Sept. 16, 1883, for the events of Sept. 9.

[45]The date of the congressional session was determined at a preliminary meeting of the organizing committee--which included Costa--in Forlì on Oct. 11 (Minister of Interior to the prefect of Forlì, Oct. 20, 1883, A.S.F., Gab. Pref., vol. 107, fasc. 245).

[46]Unlike the Congress at Ravenna, this meeting was kept secret. The delegates gathered at Forlì on the pretense of holding a comizio. This ploy apparently worked well, for on Nov. 20 the carabinieri reported that a meeting, presided over by Costa, Zirardini, and Ugo Corradini, had been held in that city on the 18th, but that prior to the meeting--which numbered 200 persons--these leaders and

a few other followers had taken a trip to villa Bondi (sic). See report to the prefect of Forlì, A.S.F., <u>Gab. Pref.</u>, vol. 107, fasc. 245. The Congress was described in <u>La Favilla</u>, Nov. 29, and in <u>Il Sole</u>, Dec. 1, 1883. Unless otherwise indicated, it is the latter account-- which also contained a list of all the representatives present--which has been used here.

[47]Letter "To the President of the Romagnol Socialist Congress," Nov. 17, 1883, B.C.I., no. 311. Of the major socialist leaders in Rimini, only Luigi Carpesani signed this declaration.

[48]The first issue appeared on Dec. 3, 1883, the last on Aug. 3, 1884.

[49]<u>La Questione sociale</u>, Jan. 5, 1884. Parts of this letter are quoted in Manacorda, <u>Il movimento operaio italiano</u>, p. 197.

[50]See, for example, <u>Il Popolo</u>, Sept. 2, 1883.

[51]For the birth of the <u>Fascio</u>, see Alessandro Galante Garrone, <u>I radicali in Italia (1849-1925)</u> (Milan: Garzanti, 1973), pp. 214-16. Giampiero Carocci, <u>Agostino Depretis e la politica interna italiana dal 1876 al 1887</u> (Turin: Einaudi, 1956), p. 539, says that Costa was responsible for the founding of the <u>Fascio</u>, a theory effectively countered by Galante Garrone (p. 214), who credits the radicals with the initiative.

[52]According to <u>Il Sole</u>, Aug. 19, 1883, the Congress was attended by thirty socialists, including Costa and Gaetano Zirardini.

[53]Letter, dated Jan. 18, published in <u>Il Comune</u>, Jan. 23-24, 1884.

[54]This after Leonesi, Pradelli, and others had made futile efforts earlier in the month to reconcile Costa and Malatesta. See <u>questore</u> of Bologna to the prefect of Bologna, Feb. 29, 1884, A.S.B., <u>Gab. Pref.</u>, cat. VII, 1884.

[55]Unfortunately, Gaetano Zirardini was no longer in a position to be of any assistance. Early in January he had left Italy and had gone into exile in France. The cause of his departure was government persecution. As editor of <u>Il Sole</u>, he was convicted of publishing subversive literature on June 27, 1883 (<u>Il Sole</u>, July 8, 1883) and

early in January, 1884, another court decision was made against him (see Il Comune, Jan. 23-24, 1884). Though Costa tried to persuade him not to leave--see Zirardini's letter to Costa, Jan. 31, 1884, B.C.I., no. 349--the Imolese had been of great help to his friend by putting him in contact with some of the leading figures of the French socialist movement, including Paul Brousse. In Paris, where he settled down, Zirardini made his living by writing for socialist newspapers. He was Italian correspondent, for example, for Emile Massard's Cri du Peuple, published in the French capital. See Zirardini's letter to Barbanti-Brodano, July 9, 1886, Carte Barbanti-Brodano, MS. 303.

[56] La Questione sociale, Feb. 10, 1884. Quoted in Enzo Santarelli, Il socialismo anarchico in Italia, 2nd ed. (Milan: Feltrinelli, 1973), pp. 64-65.

[57] Il Comune, Jan. 23-24, 1884, reported that everyone at the meeting had supported Costa, but Baldini (who had just gotten out of prison after being found guilty, like Zirardini and the other members of the editorial staff of Il Sole, of publishing subversive material) wrote Costa on Jan. 26 to inform him that not all the Ravennati had been in agreement: "A comrade," he reported, "informs me that some socialists from Ravenna have backed Malatesta and because he tells me their names and because I know them well, I will tell you the kind of socialists they are and the kind of regard they should be held in when you come to Ravenna" (B.C.I., no. 343). Baldini made his own position very clear: "I am certainly not surprised at Malatesta whose lack of good manners I am already familiar with; but it is quite another matter with Pezzi who without a doubt can now be called a great beguiler." He went on to attack the ex-Ravennate Pezzi, "his jesuitism and his cowardice."

[58] Storia degli anarchici italiani, pp. 213-14. But this list is somewhat misleading; in the Romagna, for example, only Rimini and Forlimpopoli could be said to have anarchist majorities.

[59] According to Avanti!, Apr. 13, 1884, Costa's collaborators and correspondents included Malon, Brousse, Gaetano Zirardini, and Alcibiade Moneta, in France; in Italy, Barbanti-Brodano, Gnocchi-Viani, Giuseppe Dante, Filippo Turati, Luigi Musini--who in January became the second socialist to sit in Parliament--and Ettore Socci. Not included in this list was Camillo Prampolini, who collab-

orated on <u>Avanti!</u> but did not want to do so publicly, as his father was opposed to his political activity. See Prampolini's letter to Costa, Apr. 1, 1884, B.C.I., no. 393.

[60]See Costa's articles on "The Republicans and Ourselves" in <u>Avanti!</u>, Apr. 13, Apr. 20, May 4, May 18, and June 24, 1884.

[61]Described in <u>Il Comune</u>, July 26-27, 1884.

[62]In addition to Costa the most prominent of the Romagnols in attendance were Pradelli, Fortuzzi, Mussolini, Lanzoni, Claudio and Giovanni Zirardini, the brothers Amadeo and Pellegrino Ghetti from Forlì, and Antonio Mancini, a young Imolese. Also present was Musini from Parma. Altogether there were about 70 representatives at Forlì. See prefect of Forlì to the Minister of Interior, July 21, 1884, A.S.F., <u>Gab</u>. <u>Pref</u>., vol. 107, fasc. 245.

[63]Even in Piedmont, however, the <u>Fascio</u> was very weak See the letter from Canuto Borelli of Asti to Costa, Jan. 15, 1884, B.C.I., no. 337.

[64]The republicans had been afraid to be identified too closely with the <u>Fascio</u> because of its connection with Parliament; in the republican party the Mazzinians, who maintained their political intransigence, still dominated policy. This reluctance on the part of the republicans was already clear at the Bologna Congress of August, 1883 when Saffi and Ceneri, both republicans, were elected to serve on the Central Committee of the <u>Fascio</u> together with Cavallotti but declined the nomination. See Luigi Musini <u>Da Garibaldi al socialismo: Memorie e cronache per gli anni dal 1858 al 1890</u>, ed. Gianni Bosio (Milan: Avanti!, 1961), p. 212.

[65]Not all the Ravennati agreed, though: on Aug. 4 the <u>Circolo Operaio Socialista</u> of Ravenna voted for the Cipriani candidacy. This shows the extent to which the Cipriani question was dividing the socialists even in Ravenna, Costa's major source of strength in the Romagna. The resolution voted on Aug. 4 was issued as a circular, signed by Romeo Destefini and Aristide Trerè, which is contained in a letter from Mingozzi to Emilio Castellani, Dec. 24, 1884. The letter is reproduced in Letterio Briguglio, <u>Il partito operaio italiano e gli anarchici</u> (Rome: Storia e Letteratura, 1969), p. 243.

[66]This confidence was also expressed by Il Comune, July 26-27, 1884, "The Partito Socialista Rivoluzionario Romagnolo, strong from its numerous sections and federations, which extend even to the humblest hamlets and to the most distant countryside, now has a solid and unshakable base."

[67]The federal commission, which was elected after the Forlì Congress by the federations of Imola, Lugo, Ravenna, Cesena, and Forlì, was composed of Fortuzzi, Cappellini, Valducci, Baldini, Rito Balducci, Ido Germinani, and Enrico Zani (Il Comune, Oct. 4-5, 1884). The program, which was signed by Cappellini, Balducci, and Fortuzzi, appeared in Il Comune, Aug. 30-31, 1884.

[68]Il Comune, Oct. 18-19, 1884.

[69]Nicola Badaloni, "Le prime vicende del socialismo a Pisa (1873-1883)," Movimento operaio, 7 (1955), 881.

[70]See Il Comune, Feb. 9-10, 1884. In addition to the Circolo Amilcare Cipriani there were five other sections in the federation.

[71]According to Il Comune, Sept. 27-28, 1884, the P.S. R.I. had four times as many members as the Federazione Romagnola. For the Ronco Congress, see Il Pane (Padua), Aug. 30, 1884.

[72]The declaration was graciously published by Il Comune, Sept. 27-28, 1884. Among the Riminesi who signed the document were Alceste Cipriani, Carpesani, Goldini, Francolini, and Pellegrino Bagli--who apparently was now firmly in the anti-Costian camp.

[73]"From the Romagna we have great news. The Romagnol Federation of the International is doing extremely well." See letter from Malatesta to Argante Vecchi, Oct. 31, 1884, reproduced in Briguglio, Il partito operaio italiano, p. 230.

[74]Letter to Castellani, Aug. 20, 1884. Also reproduced in Briguglio, Il partito operaio italiano, p. 228.

[75]"What," Malatesta asked, "should we do today? Above all, we have to firmly organize the anarchist party under the flag of the International" (ibid.).

[76]Sept. 20, 1884. Quoted in Conti, Le origini del

socialismo, p. 239.

[77]See Merlino's letter to Castellani, Jan. 24, 1885, reproduced in Briguglio, Il partito operaio italiano, p. 234. The departure of Malatesta and his friends created much discord in the ranks of these anarchists who remained in Florence, as they felt abandoned by their leaders. See Arturo Mazzanti's letter to an anonymous correspondent, Nov. 22, 1884, B.C.I., no. 499.

[78]While Florence had always been the headquarters of the Tuscan International, by the end of 1884 it was Pisa which came to hold this position: "After the departure of Malatesta and the other influential leaders, it /Pisa/ became in fact the true organizing center of the entire region," writes Briguglio, Il partito operaio italiano, p. 19.

[79]Even by the end of 1886 there was no socialist association whatsoever in Florence. See the letter from C. Vinattieri and O. Santemi to Costa, dated Florence, Sept. 2, 1886 (B.C.I., no. 710).

[80]Present at the meeting were representatives of "the most important cities of the Romagna, the Republic of S. Marino, and 30 other small localities, especially around Rimini and Cesena." See Mingozzi letter to Castellani, Dec. 24, 1884, in Briguglio, Il partito operaio italiano, p. 242.

[81]Ibid. Undoubtedly the anarchist revival was aided by the increased interest which the Cipriani candidacy aroused at this time. "The Cipriani question absorbs everyone in Romagna," Mingozzi wrote to Castellani on Feb. 3, 1885. See Briguglio, Il partito operaio italiano p. 255.

[82]Part of the reason for the delay, according to Mingozzi, was "the inertia of our comrades from Rimini." See letter to Castellani, Feb. 18, 1885, reproduced in Briguglio, Il partito operaio italiano, p. 257. The anarchists in Rimini did indeed seem to be in decline relative to those in the rest of the Romagna: in 1885 L' Intransigente of Venice—the most prestigious anarchist newspaper in the area—had 34 subscribers in Forlì, but in Rimini only 5. See Briguglio, pp. 214-15. Among the major Romagnol cities represented at the Congress were Ravenna, Forlì, Cesena, Rimini, Imola, Faenza, and Forlimpopoli, according to Il Paria (Ancona), Apr. 26, 1885.

For an account of the proceedings at the Congress, see
this issue of Il Paria. See also the letter from Mingozzi, Mar. 16, 1885, to the socialists of Rome informing
them of these proceedings (this letter was sent to the
prefect of Forlì by the Minister of Interior on Mar. 26,
1885, A.S.F., Gab. Pref., vol. 110, fasc. 23).

[83] Briguglio, Il partito operaio italiano, suggests
that the Branca was formed partly to combat the influence
of the P.O.I. (p. 46), but primarily to heal divisions
within the anarchist ranks (p. 47).

[84] This letter is reproduced in Briguglio, Il partito
operaio italiano, p. 238.

[85] Il Paria, Apr. 26, 1885.

[86] Il socialismo anarchico in Italia, p. 72.

[87] "As far as the first effort to form an anarchist
'party' goes, we would have to say that at Forlì, in '85,
the division between collectivist and communist anarchists was so decisive that it impeded the rise of any unifying party organization," writes Briguglio, Il partito
operaio italiano, p. 42.

[88] Santarelli, Il socialismo anarchico in Italia, p.
73.

[89] Mingozzi, who belonged to the collectivist school,
was able to get along well with Costa, even during this
period. See Mingozzi's letter to Castellani, Apr. 3,
1885, in Briguglio, Il partito operaio italiano, p. 263.
The Costians, however, held Mingozzi in scant regard.
See Cappellini's letter to Barbanti-Brodano, July 8, 1886,
Carte Barbanti-Brodano, MS. 723. In the late 1880's Mingozzi increasingly drew nearer to the socialists in Ravenna and by the mid-1890's he had become a member of the
Italian Socialist Party.

[90] Letter to Castellani, Apr. 3, 1885, in Briguglio,
Il partito operaio italiano, p. 261.

[91] Castellani letter to Arturo Callegari, May 6, 1885,
in Briguglio, Il partito operaio italiano, p. 138.

[92] Report to the prefect of Forlì, Nov. 13, 1885, A.S.
F., Gab. Pref., vol. 110, fasc. 23.

[93]Costa's efforts were not altogether successful. A-
mong the towns the touring deputy visited at this time
were Ferrara and Argenta, where he was received with a
"great indifference," a reception which forced him to cut
short his trip in that area. See prefect of Ferrara to
the Minister of Interior, Feb. 20, 1885, A.C.S.R., Min.
Int. Gab.--Rapporti dei prefetti, busta 6.

[94]Letter of Nov. 5, 1884, B.C.I., no. 489.

[95]Mingozzi letter to Castellani, Jan. 12, 1885, in
Briguglio, Il partito operaio italiano, p. 246.

[96]Memo by the Minister of Interior, Mar. 13, 1884, A.
C.S.R., Min. Int. Gab.--Rapporti dei prefetti, busta 13.

[97]A.C.S.R., Min. Int. Gab.--Rapporti dei prefetti,
busta 13.

[98]Ibid.

[99]For the pineta controversy and its effect on the
socialists of Ravenna, see Alfeo Bertondini, "La vita politica e sociale a Ravenna e in Romagna dal 1870 al 1910,"
in Nullo Baldini nella storia della cooperazione, pp. 277-
96.

[100]See the July, 1884, report previously cited. Another related cause of dissension in Ravenna at this time was
the anarchist opposition to the local socialist alliance
with the republicans. See letter from Giorgio Giorgi to
Costa, Nov. 11, 1884, B.C.I., no. 495.

[101]Prefect of Ravenna report on the public spirit in
his province during the second half of 1884 to the Minister of Interior, Jan. 28, 1885, A.C.S.R., Min. Int. Gab.--
Rapporti dei prefetti, busta 13. The socialist party, the
prefect noted, had lost much influence in the province
during the last months, especially in and around the city
of Ravenna.

[102]Semiannual reports by the prefect of Ravenna to the
Minister of Interior indicate the public spirit in his
province steadily improved from 1884 to 1890 (A.C.S.R.,
Min. Int. Gab.--Rapporti dei prefetti, busta 13).

[103]Prefect of Forlì to the Minister of Interior, May 1,
1885, A.S.F., Gab. Pref., vol. 110, fasc. 5. The local
anarchist section was the Circolo Michele Bakunin, founded

in January, 1884, by Moravalli, Bazzocchi, Ravaioli, Zola, and Fabbri. Early in 1885, according to the carabinieri, the circle had 30 members but "no importance" (report to the prefect of Forlì, Jan. 9, 1885, A.S.F., Gab. Pref., vol. 110, fasc. 5).

[104]The last number was that of Aug. 22-23, 1885.

[105]An appeal for money was made by the Federal Commission to the party members in Il Comune, May 14-15, and Aug. 1-2, 1885. Costa resigned himself to the loss of the party organ; his only advice to Claudio Zirardini: "If, in fact, you are forced to suspend once again the publication of the Comune, please do not announce it. Let the affair drop without regrets, without laments, without anything. It would be more honorable for all of us that way." See letter of Aug. 21, 1885, reproduced in "Carteggio C. Zirardini--A. Costa," Movimento operaio, ed. Gianni Bosio, 3 (1951), 637.

[106]We will not spend as much time on the relations between Costa and the P.O.I. in the 1880's as they merit; this subject will be treated very thoroughly in the next volume--as yet unpublished--of Hostetter's history of the Italian socialist movement.

[107]For the early history of the party, see Gnocchi-Viani, Il partito operaio italiano, 1882-1885 (Milan: Stefani e Pizzi, 1885).

[108]The P.O.I. program had been published in Avanti! on Aug. 13, 1882.

[109]As Costa visualized it, his Romagnol followers would form the center of this great party and the anarchists and operaisti the two extremes. See Liliano Faenza, Marxisti e "riministi." La Conferenza di Rimini e l'Internazionale italiana: vent'anni di storia del movimento operaio (1872-1892) (Rimini: Guaraldi, 1972), p. 71.

[110]All the democratic parties in Italy established close ties with the Masonic movement, and the socialists were no exception (nor the anarchists: even Bakunin and Malatesta had been Masons). Given the nature of the subject, very little is known about this connection between the democrats and Freemasonry--a subject which would form the basis of an interesting and rewarding study.

[111]See, for example, the letter from Lazzari and other

313

operaisti to Costa, Dec. 10, 1884, which is reproduced in Manacorda, Il movimento operaio italiano, pp. 380-83.

[112]The Congress is described in Il Fascio operaio (the organ of the P.O.I., located in Milan), Dec. 12-13, 1885.

[113]This idea was already apparent in April when Il Comune--Apr. 12-13, 1885--extended its salutations to the representatives of the Milan Congress: "The Federal Commission of the Partito Socialista Rivoluzionario Italiano rendering itself the interpreter of all the socialists of Italy, salutes the Representatives...gathered in Milan, hoping that in the near future the Partito Operaio and the Partito Socialista Rivoluzionario will become one single organization, the objective for which they fight being a single one: the emancipation of labor."

[114]Il Comune, May 14-15, 1885.

[115]Il Paria, Oct. 6, 1885, reported that Costa had expressed his intention to convoke this meeting before a group of anarchists in Turin earlier that same month. Il Paria opposed the idea of the gathering, as did the majority of anarchists.

[116]In La Questione sociale (Turin), Nov. 29, 1885 (Proximus Tuus had been renamed La Questione sociale--not to be confused with Malatesta's old paper--on Apr. 5), and La Favilla, Dec. 3, 1885. The article calling for the general assembly is unsigned, but Manacorda, Il movimento operaio italiano, p. 240, identifies Costa as its author.

[117]The best interpretation of these developments is to be found in Richard Hostetter, "Lotta di classe nelle campagne: il movimento contadino di resistenza nella Val Padana, 1884-1885," Movimento operaio e socialista, 16 (1970), 45-72.

[118]The causes of this crisis are given in Hostetter, "Lotta di classe...," 47.

[119]This process is described very well in Emilio Sereni Il capitalismo nelle campagne, 1860-1900, 2nd ed. (Turin: Einaudi, 1968). See also Luigi Preti, Le lotte agrarie nella valle padana (Turin: Einaudi, 1955). This transformation was especially notable in the Romagna, where 30% of the mezzadri became braccianti in the years between 1880 and 1890. See Casali, "Il movimento mazziniano

in Romagna...," p. 52.

[120]Giuseppe Zangarini to Costa, Apr. 20, 1884, B.C.I., no. 412.

[121]This is one of the important differences between Costa, on the one hand, and Turati and the Milanesi, on the other, according to Renato Zangheri, "Andrea Costa e le lotte contadine del suo tempo," Movimento operaio, 7 (1955), 11.

[122]See, for example, his article on Giuseppe Barbiani, a young peasant leader from Cremona, in Il Messaggero (Rome), Feb. 22, 1886.

[123]Zangheri, "Andrea Costa e le lotte contadine del suo tempo," p. 19.

[124]An account of the Mantua Congress is to be found in La Rivista italiana del socialismo, 1 (1886), 23-28.

[125]Among the chief Romagnol leaders at the Mantua Congress were Cappellini, Piselli, Valducci, and Rito Balducci, according to Musini, Da Garibaldi al socialismo, p. 278.

[126]See Cappellini letter to Costa, Apr. 6, 1886, B.C.I., no. 631.

[127]Manacorda, Il movimento operaio italiano, p. 246.

[128]For this episode, see Galante Garrone, I radicali in Italia, pp. 235-46.

[129]See the letter of E. Moneta, director of Il Secolo (Milan), to Costa, Mar. 14, 1886, B.C.I., no. 626.

[130]See Discorsi parlamentari di Andrea Costa (Rome: Stab. Tip. Carlo Colombo, 1972), pp. 96-105.

[131]See the letter from the Central Committee of the P.O.I. (Croce, Casati, and Dante) to Costa, June 4, 1886, reproduced in Manacorda, Il movimento operaio italiano, p. 384. "Our comrades (at least a large part of them) are very much afraid to frankly call themselves socialists," the letter read; "and while we would view a union with the Socialist Party with immense satisfaction (as you can imagine!), we are forced to be very cautious so that they do not resign from the association."

[132]The letter, signed by Dante and Casati, is dated June 20, 1886, and is reproduced in Manacorda, Il movimento operaio italiano, p. 387.

[133]Reproduced in "Carteggio Musini--Costa," Movimento operaio, ed. Gianni Bosio, 2 (1950), 74.

[134]The circular is reproduced in Musini, Da Garibaldi al socialismo, p. 275. This explanation failed to satisfy the Romagnols. "You...should not suppose," Musini wrote Costa early in the following year, "that the faith in those common ideals that motivate and guide us has ebbed in me, but for now, believe me, nothing can be done here among us. In fact, I have written about this very subject to our Lanzoni of Lugo, who sent Tommasini an almost peremptory letter, reproaching us severely for our inertia in regard to the party...of whose direction we were put in charge, despite ourselves, at Mantua." See letter of Mar. 16, 1887, reproduced in "Carteggio Musini--Costa," p. 75.

[135]Gastone Manacorda, "Il centenario della nascita di Andrea Costa," Rinascita, 8 (1951), 589.

[136]I do not mean to suggest that this party would have been "national" in the sense of having strong influence throughout the peninsula. This did not happen even in 1892 when the Italian Socialist Party was in fact born.

[137]"The chief obstacle to a social revolution," Costa remarked in an interview in Paris in 1889, "is not found in governmental institutions; it is rather in the diversity of the regions which make up Italy." Quoted in Il Secolo, July 24-25, 1889. During this interview before the French, incidentally, Costa also described the condition of his country's socialist movement in these terms: "Italian socialism does not really exist except in Lombardy and the Romagna. And still some qualification is necessary. In Lombardy the workers' movement is economic, that is, the worker seeks simply to better his condition without having the notion of a complete and radical transformation of the social system. In the Romagna, on the other hand, the workers' party is clearly socialist /and/ revolutionary, and the great majority of its members belong to the agricultural class: they are braccianti, who work in the countryside from one day to the next."

[138]Il mondo criminale italiano, p. 301. Ferrero himself provides a good example of the strength of regional

feeling in this period. Ferrero, a Milanese, found it
very difficult--as is apparent from reading his articles
--to understand the Romagnol environment. His description of the Romagna is full of exaggerations; see especially Part V of his work where he concerns himself with "the
two /only two?/ faces of the Romagna, the violent Romagna
and fraudulent Romagna."

[139]Gastone Manacorda, "Formazione e primo sviluppo del
Partito socialista in Italia. Il problema storico e i
più recenti orientamenti storiografici," Il movimento operaio e socialista. Bilancio storiografico e problemi storici (Milan: Gallo, 1965), p. 154; Giuliana Ricci-Garotti
and Alberto Cossarini, La cooperazione: Storia e prospet-
tive (Bologna: A.P.E., /1974/), p. 109.

[140]This proletariat in Italy would become numerous only
after the turn of the century. By 1901 only about 15% of
the work force (and this figure includes artisans) was employed in industry, writes Giuliano Procacci, La lotta di
classe in Italia agli inizi del secolo XX (Rome: Riuniti,
1970), p. 4.

[141]Ferrero (p. 296) recalled talking to a socialist
leader in Russi, in the Romagna, and inquiring why the
local socialist section was so small. The old socialist
responded, "Among us the entire association is responsible
for the actions of the member;...it is necessary to move
slowly in admitting new members, otherwise the rowdiness
of one individual brings everything to ruin. Even if a
member engages in a knife attack the others, at least
morally and often even materially, are answerable for it."
This clannish attitude on the part of Romagnol associations, Ferrero concluded, was responsible for the fact
that "every association has an intimate and unconscious
fear of extending itself too much, of becoming too numerous."

[142]See Atti della Giunta per la Inchiestra agraria e
sulle condizioni della classe agricola, II (Rome: Forzani,
1881), 229. Even in the nineties the Romagna was still
distinguished, generally, by this absence of class consciousness. According to Ferrero, p. 280, "The circles
of the Romagna are characterized by the almost total lack
of this spirit and consciousness of class: the classes
there are confused; the small proprietor, the larger proprietor, the industrialist, the nouveau-riche contractor
and the worker all gather there as good friends, they
drink and they play together, they all feel themselves to

be...men of the same class."

[143]As was also true in the Marches. See Enzo Santarelli, _Aspetti del movimento operaio nelle Marche_ (Milan: Feltrinelli, 1956), p. 26.

[144]The federative structure of the P.S.R.R. is only one example of lingering anarchist influence, but an especially important one because it contributed to the weakness of the party by discouraging strong party discipline. It must be admitted, however, that the structure of the party was not so much a cause of weakness as it was an indication of an existing state of affairs.

CHAPTER NINE

A TIME OF TROUBLES, 1887-1890

The Anarchist Resurgence

The years from 1887 to 1890 witnessed a further deterioration in the fortunes of the P.S.R.I., a decline which worsened as the years passed. Bearing some responsibility for this state of affairs was Costa himself. After the Mantua Congress of 1886 Costa began to lose interest in the party and its reorganization, as he became more and more preoccupied with parliamentary affairs. In this period his orientation shifted from the Romagna to Rome, where he was primarily concerned with Italian foreign policy.

By the mid-1880's Italy had become deeply involved in colonial expansion.[1] This interest was, of course, a reflection of developments affecting all the major European powers in the last quarter of the nineteenth century. Agostino Depretis, the nation's Prime Minister for most of the decade, was not an ardent believer in the acquisition of empire. Nevertheless, the urge for expansion became so powerful that some concessions had to be made. In 1882, the year Costa entered Parliament, Italian sovereignty was declared over Assab, an African port on the Red Sea. Three years later the process was repeated at Massawa, located just north of Assab.

The attempt to extend Italian influence into the interior of the African continent came to an abrupt halt on January 26, 1887, however, when the Italians suffered a serious defeat in Dogali at the hands of the Ethiopians. Although the Italian people had never been enthusiastic about expansion into Africa, the defeat momentarily altered the situation. The Italians now rushed to the defense of the nation. This wave of patriotism had telling repercussions in Parliament, which immediately after Dogali voted to increase military appropriations to five million lire; the army had to be strengthened, the defeat avenged. So pervasive was patriotic sentiment at this time that even Cavallotti and the Extreme Left approved the appropriations bill. Only five deputies resisted the tide and voted against the measure, and one of them was Costa.

As a good socialist, Costa opposed imperialism on
principle. Humanitarianism permeated his political philosophy. Socialism to him meant not only material but moral progress as well. During his anarchist period, in
fact, the moral implications of socialist ideology were
the ones Costa emphasized. In January, 1874, for example,
he proclaimed that what he and his comrades in the International wanted was "that the worker stop being a machine
and become a man; that as such he have the right to life,
instruction, and education." In a word, he said, they
wanted "to be a society of men, not of beasts."[2] As a
socialist, Costa never lost sight of the humanitarian and
moral aims of socialism as he understood it. "Our rebellion," he wrote in 1886, "is a rebellion for the conquest of all that is good, beautiful, true, just: it is
the fight for work, for liberty, for science."[3] The humanitarianism inherent in these words was implemented on
many occasions. When cholera epidemics swept through
Naples in 1884 and Palermo in 1885, Costa was among the
first volunteers to reach the cities and bring aid to the
sick.[4] This same concern for humanity guided him in his
active opposition to the African venture.

Apart from the principle of humanitarianism, Costa
was concerned with the more tangible consequences of colo-
nialism. The government, he correctly reasoned, was following a suicidal policy in developing an Italian Empire.
There were grave problems at home, and they would not be
resolved in Africa. The most pressing of these domestic
problems was the social question. These considerations
led the Romagnol deputy to oppose the annexation of Massawa in 1885.[5] In fact, throughout the 1880's it was
Costa who spearheaded the anticolonial opposition in Parliament.[6]

In 1887 the colonial question consumed Costa's attention almost exclusively. On February 3 he gave his most
famous speech in Parliament, declaring that he and his
friends in the Chamber of Deputies would vote "not one
man, nor one cent" for the African campaign.[7] In May and
June he again condemned colonial expansion before the
Chamber.[8] He also agitated outside Parliament: On April
17 he gave a speech on "Colonial Policy and the Socialists" in Siena, and on October 30 he presided over a comizio in Ravenna growing out of Italy's expansion in Africa.[9] Certainly in 1887, then, Costa's attention was focused on affairs outside of the Romagna.

320

Also in the same year the P.S.R.I. was encountering problems at home. The Cipriani affair was still suffi- ciently alive to create serious divisions within the so- cialist movement. Moreover, the cause célèbre was strength- ening the anarchists at the expense of Costa's party.

Yet perhaps it was in the previous year of 1886 that the Cipriani affair had had the most profound impact, a- long with its most brilliant successes. In May Cipriani had won the protest elections in the provinces of Ravenna and Forlì, but Parliament had nullified his victories. In July and in December Cipriani was again proposed in both provinces and was re-elected. Since these elections were also annulled, by 1887 the Romagnols had begun to doubt the wisdom of protest elections. By May of that year even the Riminesi had become discouraged.[10] The ex- tent of this flagging interest in Cipriani's candidacy manifested itself on April 3 and June 26, 1887, when Cip- riani failed to win election in either Forlì or Ravenna. The reason for these defeats lay in the disagreement be- tween socialists and republicans.[11]

The Consociazione Romagnola had never developed much enthusiasm for Cipriani, a natural reaction considering the republicans' bias against electoral participation of any kind. When the agitation began, however, the Romagnol republicans championed the cause, viewing the agitation not so much pro-Cipriani as antigovernment; through Cip- riani they hoped to discredit the institutions of the mon- archical state. Moreover, at that time they could see no alternative, for they feared that witholding support would alienate the party's rank and file. In that event both the anarchists and socialists--who did support Cipriani-- would gain new members at the republicans' expense.

But by the mid-1880's the situation was changing. The Romagnols were weary of the whole matter, a circum- stance which had the effect of encouraging the republi- cans to return to their intransigence as regards politi- cal involvement. Saffi himself made it plain in May, 1887, that he would not support another campaign for Cipriani's re-election.[12] By this time the republicans were convin- ced that the Cipriani agitation was benefiting only the anarchists.

The socialists were equally convinced that protest was futile, and for the same reason. This attitude was especially pronounced in Ravenna, where Costa's follow- ers decided against the Cipriani candidacy as early as

321

the first months of 1886.[13] This stance, though, was over
come by the anarchists, who pushed the candidacy hard and
eventually gained the reluctant support of both the republicans and the socialists.[14] The anarchists achieved only
a partial victory: Cipriani did indeed win at the polls
on May 23, but his election, as we have seen, was invali-
dated. The same thing occurred following Cipriani's election on July 18. The anarchists were determined to try
again. By this time, though, socialist opposition had
mounted and was no longer confined exclusively to Ravenna.
On October 3, consequently, the Romagnols called a meeting
at Forlì to settle the matter. The discussion was a fiery
one,[16] but the _ciprianisti_ apparently maintained the upper
hand, since their champion was proposed in both Ravenna
and Forlì at the end of the year and again won.

Costa himself shared the republicans' lukewarm feeling on the Cipriani question, and like them, too, he could
not afford to alienate his followers. In public, therefore, he did everything possible to further the cause of
the "prisoner of Ponte Longone," as Cipriani had come to
be known. Not only did Costa campaign for his fellow Romagnol whenever requested, but he also took the initiative
in bringing the Cipriani question before Parliament on
several occasions.[17] He displayed no real conviction in
these efforts, however. Perhaps Costa's attitude toward
this cause is best expressed in his letter of February
16, 1887, to the chief editor of the _Rivista_ in Ferrara:
"I would have been against a fourth election of Cipriani,
and I would have said it frankly to my friends, if, after
an extensive discussion in the Chamber, the question, in
one way or another, would have been resolved; but, in the
present situation, when no discussion whatsoever has tak-
en place, I persist...in the attitude that I have always
taken: let my friends and the voters do as they please.[18]

Costa's coolness toward the Cipriani affair was not
an expression of personal antagonism, for the two men respected each other.[19] Costa opposed the pro-Cipriani agitation because he knew it antagonized the republicans.
He was anxious to maintain good relations with the republican chieftains, and the Cipriani affair put these relations in jeopardy. Perhaps even more pertinent was
Costa's awareness that the anarchists were championing
Cipriani's fight not in defense of justice alone, but as
an offensive tactic against Costa himself. Certainly
their will to discredit him was evident when the anarchists of Forlimpopoli demanded that he resign his parliamentary seat and propose Cipriani in his place. Costa

saw Cipriani as a tool of the anarchists; hence his restraint in aiding the cause.

By 1887 the P.S.R.I., what was left of it, was no longer cwatrianista. Yet by this time, unfortunately, the Cipriani question had had an adverse effect on the party's development. Not only had the affair created serious divisions within the P.S.R.I., but it had also succeeded in fortifying the anarchist camp at the expense of the Costians. The anarchists were now very active in Rimini, Ravenna, and Forlì,[20] and in each city their resurgence was closely related to the Cipriani question. Led by Alceste Cipriani and Carpesani, the anarchists in Rimini had been in the forefront of the battle since 1882. Pro-Cipriani sentiment was in fact so dominant in that city that at the height of the agitation even members of the local republican association, including Cajo Renzetti, the ranking republican in Rimini, enlisted in the cause. In Ravenna, on the other hand, the anarchists had been much weaker than the socialists. By 1885-86, though, the anarchists, uniting under the banner of Cipriani, had gained in number sufficiently to dissociate themselves from the local socialist federation. Thus in Ravenna the Cipriani affair was definitely responsible for the cleavage between the two camps. By the mid-1880's, however, the main Romagnol citadel of anarchism had shifted from its traditional strongholds of Ravenna and Rimini to Forlì. Forlì had not witnessed a conflict between costiani and anti-costiani in the early eighties, but after 1886 this changed. The anarchists of that city were then able to strengthen their party and before long were to predominate over the socialist element.

This resurgence of the anarchist movement in Forlì was associated with the name of Germanico Piselli, the old Internationalist. Unlike Mingozzi, who had been Forlì's foremost anarchist in the early eighties, Piselli was a communist rather than a collectivist. Yet there were also meaningful similarities between the two men, the most significant of which was that both wanted to create a unified anarchist movement in the Romagna that would take the initiative in reorganizing the old Italian International along anarchist lines.[21]

Still Piselli's understanding of how this goal ought to be implemented was a little different from Mingozzi's: Mingozzi thought to organize only the anarchists, whereas Piselli aimed for an organization including both socialists and anarchists (to be controlled by the latter, of course).[22] With his sights fixed on this objective, Piselli began publishing La Rivendicazione in Forlì on November 16, 1886.

Piselli, a sincere ciprianista, recognized the Cipriani question as a useful instrument to bring together Romagna's many socialist factions. In the first months of its existence, therefore, La Rivendicazione was largely devoted to this affair. By the next year, however, when the Cipriani candidacy had begun to lose its appeal, Piselli turned his attention to Costa. He would try to build the party on an anti-Costian foundation.[23]

Early in 1887 Costa began to encounter intense opposition from Piselli.[24] At first the criticism was indirect. On May 21, 1887, for example, La Rivendicazione attacked the sectarianism of the Masonic movement. "Well, after all that," Piselli concluded, "is it not surprising that some socialists should belong to this sect? But we will never be masons, because all that is declared to be beautiful and good by masonry, we believe instead to be ugly and bad." Since Costa was the most eminent socialist belonging to the order, Piselli's target was self-evident. By July, though, Piselli was more explicit: "The excessive tenderness which Costa displays toward opposing parties and vice versa both irritates and shocks us. Costa may remain at his post, but he should not become too much of a deputy and an opportunist."[25]

Here, of course, Piselli was referring to the republican alliance. Like all anarchists, he was adamantly opposed to socialist coalitions with democratic parties, especially with the republicans. In Forlì even Costa's followers distrusted the republicans and were most reluctant to deal with them.

The republican alliance which Costa had cultivated in the Romagna early in the decade had never been popular in Forlì, where the republican preponderance obviated the need to attend to pleas for cooperation from the small socialist minority. Almost all Forlì's republicans, like their chief Saffi, were strict Mazzinians and therefore against participation in national elections as well as electoral coalitions of the kind Costa was proposing. Yet in administrative elections the republicans were glad to work temporarily with their adversaries. In the municipal elections of 1884, for instance, the republicans in collaboration with the socialists, now led by Sesto Fortuzzi, captured control of the city council. When cooperation was not to their advantage, however--which was usually the case--the republicans shunned alliances, an attitude that generated much friction between the two groups.

Moreover, the republicans' stand on the pro-Cipriani agitation did nothing to improve relations. As their opposition to Cipriani became more evident, the republicans met with increasing hostility from the socialists. Among the most intransigent opponents was Piselli, who after 1886 never missed a chance to assail them in his newspaper.

Friction between the two parties grew more pronounced, and on several occasions during 1887 almost erupted in violence.[26] This heightened tension was reflected in the columns of La Rivendicazione. "Between us and them," Piselli wrote on July 23, in reference to his adversaries, "there is always an abyss and it will not be filled until the republican worker comes to recognize that socialism wants his complete emancipation." As for Piselli's attitude toward the republican leaders: "We may perhaps be able to remain good personal friends, but let us not entertain illusions that one day they will come to adhere to our economic theories." On August 6 he declared: "Socialists have nothing in common with republicans, if by socialists we are not referring to /Domenico/ Berti, Bismarck, and Leo XIII."[27] By the beginning of 1888, Piselli was even more incisive: "Why hide it? The republicans are our enemies."[28]

Piselli's two-pronged attack, against Costa and the republicans, began to produce tangible results. Gradually the anarchists gained the upper hand over the socialists in Forlì. A clear indication of the trend was Piselli's displacement of Fortuzzi as Forlì's leading socialist (using the term in its wider sense). Prior to 1887 Fortuzzi had been recognized as the head of the party in Forlì, but Piselli's attacks on Costa early that year had put Fortuzzi between two fires. For a while he tried the role of peacemaker;[29] by mid-1887, though, he definitely had been superseded by Piselli.[30] Fortuzzi resigned from the local P.S.R.I. federation in September, apparently because of the opposition he was encountering from his more aggressive rival.[31]

Secondo Cappellini, Costa's old friend and another party chieftain in Forlì, likewise crossed swords with Piselli and met the same fate. Unable to work effectively with Piselli owing to marked personal and political

325

differences, Cappellini was coerced into semi-retirement.
In March, 1887, he explained the situation to Costa:
"Piselli wants to be a dictator and...so he is, and as
such he does as he pleases both with his newspaper and
in everything; I personally have retired as a simple
soldier, without interfering any more, but with the right
as a socialist to make my observations as I do with you,
and as I did today with some friends in regard to the
language which La Rivendicazione uses against you...."[32]
In August, 1888, Cappellini left for Marseilles,[33] and
later that year emigrated to South America, eventually
settling in Buenos Aires.[34] The reason for his exile
was apparently as much financial as political.[35]

By mid-1887 Piselli had established himself as the
unchallenged head of the socialist movement in Forlì. By
this time, too, the local federation of the P.S.R.I.,
weakened by the loss of Fortuzzi and Cappellini, almost
ceased to exist.[36] Similar developments were taking place
throughout the Romagna at this time. Everywhere the anarchists still dominated as they had from the beginning
of the decade, only more so. And in Ravenna the situation
was only slightly better, with the absence of Gaetano Zirardini, still in Paris, undoubtedly contributing to the
condition there. By 1887 the only real socialist paper
in the Romagna was La Rivendicazione; clearly the anarchists had been able to make progress at the expense of
the costiani. Indeed, at this time the resurgence of the
anarchist movement was readily discernible all over Italy.

The moment seemed propitious for the reorganization
envisaged by Piselli. In August, 1887, he created the
Federazione Internazionalista Forlivese, to be his first
step in a general reorganization of the party throughout
the Romagna.[38] This initiative, though, was almost fruitless. The Federazione was never able to extend its organization beyond Forlì,[39] and even there the party was still
divided.[40] The anarchists had made some gains in the Roma
gna, but apparently unification had not gone very far.
The socialists, especially in Imola and even in Ravenna,
continued to adhere to the Costian program.[41] The anarchists themselves were plagued by dissension, with many of
them opposing Piselli because he was confusing their program with that of the socialists. By this time, too, the
Cipriani question was just about a dead issue.[42] All thes
things worked against Piselli's efforts to forge a Romagnol organization based on anarchist principles.

The Twilight of the Socialist Movement in the Romagna

Meanwhile, Costa occupied himself with affairs outside the Romagna. His seat in the Chamber of Deputies took up a good deal of his time.[43] But along with his parliamentary activity, he continued to work for a P.O.I.-P.S.R.I. alliance, which he believed still had a chance of being effected in 1887. Not only had he received encouragement from some of the P.O.I. leaders, but circumstances also seemed conducive to unification. The P.O.I. had been dealt a crippling blow by the government in 1886-87, and it was slow in recovering. This situation, according to Costa, was favorable for the reception of his ideas by the Milanesi. Moreover, Costa's position on the African question had generated much sympathy among them.[44]

Costa's hopes were kindled at the Third Congress of the P.O.I., held at Pavia (Lombardy) on September 18-19, 1887.[45] Although the party had never allowed bourgeois representatives at its congresses, at Pavia Costa and two anarchists, Luigi Galleani and Luigi Molinari, were permitted to attend the sessions and participate in the deliberations.

But the possibility that the strict class orientation of the P.O.I. might be altered quickly disappeared. A proposal submitted by Costa that nonworkers be allowed to join the party--a prerequisite for the fusion of his movement with that of the operaisti--was overwhelmingly defeated. The delegates also remained intransigent with respect to political involvement, for a resolution which would have established the principle of party participation was likewise rejected. Instead, the P.O.I. adhered to its old formula: each individual party section was free to determine whether or not to propose candidates in these elections.

If Costa had been hopeful prior to the Pavia Congress, the deliberations had done nothing to justify his expectations.[46] Fusion was still opposed by all but one of the P.O.I. leaders. Only Giuseppe Croce seemed to support the idea of close cooperation. In a speech before the workers of Imola on November 1, 1887, introduced by Costa, Croce declared that the socialists and the P.O.I. ought to unite.[47]

None of the other ranking operaisti, however, shared Croce's opinion. Lazzari, the most inflexible among them, was notoriously hostile to Costa and his ideas.[48] Dante sympathized more with Costa's opponents, the anarchists, than he did with the Imolese.[49] Casati got along well with Costa; yet he, too, had some reservations regarding unification. On July 21 both he and Costa spoke before the Società Operaia of Bologna.[50] The local questore reported that Casati's speech did not arouse much enthusiasm.[51] Probably the moderate response was due to Casati's attitude toward union.

During this period, then, the possibility of close cooperation was feeble indeed. This reality made itself plain at the Fourth Congress of the P.O.I., held in Bologna on September 8, 9, and 10, 1888. The choice of Bologna, on the edge of the Romagna, as a site for the meeting was indicative not, as one might suppose, of any wish to give a symbolic gesture of union between the P.S.R.I. and the operaisti, but rather of an attempt to extend the party's authority as far as possible. Bologna was on the perimeter of the P.O.I.'s sphere of influence; in the Romagna, despite the presence of an operaista section in Imola,[52] the Milan-based party was almost nonexistent, and certainly not influential.[53]

In fact, fusion was not even an issue at the Bologna Congress; instead, discussion was limited largely to matters of party organization.[54] The only controversial questions considered were participation in administrative, though not political, elections, a proposal which was approved by one vote,[55] and the suggestion that only workingmen represent workers' associations at party congresses. On this matter of delegate eligibility a divergence of views within the party's Central Committee manifested itself: Croce--who presided over the gathering--argued strenuously against the proposal; Lazzari argued just as vehemently for it.[56] In the end Lazzari's opinion was upheld by the delegates.

At the time of the Bologna Congress the idea of union was no longer feasible. Perhaps Costa was well aware of this fact, inasmuch as he limited himself in his speech before the assembly to expressing his solidarity with the operaisti.[57] The P.O.I. Congress had done nothing to alter its party program to accommodate an alliance. Moreover, apart from Croce, none of the leading operaisti seemed to be interested in the possibility. But probably the overriding reason why fusion was no longer tenable was that neither the P.O.I. nor the P.S.R.I. had sufficient energy to make such an alliance effective. Costa's party, as already noted, was badly disorganized;[58] the P.O.I.'s condition was not much better. Very little was heard from the operaisti. A speech given by Costa near Milan in early 1888 and sponsored by the P.O.I. was that party's most important public demonstration in two years, according to the Sozialdemokrat, the authoritative organ of the German Social Democrats.[59] The Congress of Bologna a few months later further demonstrated the advanced state of the party's decline. Beyond the inordinate amount of time the assembly spent on organizational matters, the weakness of the party was evident in its decision to hold national congresses only on the initiative of two-thirds of the party's sections; the P.O.I. could no longer afford annual meetings. Furthermore, only forty or fifty representatives had been able to attend[60]--an indication that the P.O.I., its title notwithstanding, was a regional organization which possessed little strength in central Italy, let alone in the rest of the country. Obviously, the repression of 1886-87 had accomplished its purpose.

With the prospects of fusion at an end and his own party all but totally disintegrated, Costa retreated more and more into Imola, an environment he could control. Local politics became one of his major interests in the next two years. This development was already apparent in late 1888 when he began consolidating his authority in his native city, certainly a far more modest, albeit realistic goal than forging an alliance between the P.O.I. and P.S.R.I., or even of reorganizing the latter. Yet neither Costa's decline nor that of his party was to end here.

On December 20, 1888, a comizio was held in Rome to commemorate Guglielmo Oberdan, an Italian patriot.[61] When the authorities tried to disperse the demonstrators, an altercation ensued. Among those involved was Costa, one of the principal speakers. The events of December 20 were to have far-reaching repercussions on the Romagnol's career over the next few years.

Early in 1889 the government moved against Costa for his part in the Oberdan riot. Charged with fomenting rebellion, the socialist deputy was brought to trial on April 3, found guilty two days later, and sentenced to three years in prison with a fine of one hundred lire.[62] A new wave of repression was gathering momentum.[63] Francesco Crispi, who had succeeded Depretis as Prime Minister on August 6, 1887--a few days after the latter's death--was restoring internal order to Italy before concentrating on foreign policy, his prime interest.[64]

Nevertheless, the following year the Romagna was to witness a slight revival of the socialist movement. In early 1889 the **P.S.R.I.** was languishing, as it had been since 1886. Apathy was deepest in the province of Forlì, where the two major cities, Rimini and Forlì, were now under the sway of the anarchists. In fact, just about all the socialists in the province, according to the prefect of Forlì, belonged to the anarchist party.[65] Nor was the **P.S.R.I.** in much better shape in Ravenna. In March, Cesare Golfarelli wrote to Costa and informed him that in Ravenna only a single Circolo Socialista adhered to the **P.S.R.I.** program.[66] There too, according to Golfarelli, the anarchists--then organized into a Federazione Ravennate dell'Internazionale--were able to provide an effective opposition to the socialists. Of the major Romagnol cities, only in Imola had the socialist party maintained a dominant position vis-à-vis the local anarchist circle.[67]

By mid-1889, however, the **P.S.R.I.** had begun to show signs of life. Taking the initiative in this reorganization was not Costa, but Gaetano Zirardini, who had returned in late 1888 from French exile. One sign of the revival was Zirardini's resumption of Il Sole. Its first number, on June 29, 1889, called for the reorganization of th **P.S.R.I.** in the Romagna. The next day, June 30, the party held a gathering at Forlì, the first general reunion of the **P.S.R.I.** since 1886.

The meeting included not merely costiani, but also the anarchists, who found their champion in Piselli. In fact, Piselli was the instigator of the gathering, according to Ravenna's prefect.[68] Like Zirardini, Piselli was still interested in the unification of Romagnol anarchists and socialists into one party. Unlike Zirardini, though, Piselli wanted unification along anarchist lines and under an anarchist program. Both currents therefore met at Forlì intent upon dominating each other.

Besides Costa, the chief advocates of the legalitarian program in attendance were Baldini, Gaetano Zirardini, Alessandro Balducci, and Umberto Brunelli.[69] The anarchist element was represented primarily by Piselli and Nicola Sandri, both of La Rivendicazione. Most of the other representatives--among them Valducci, the Battistini broth ers, Mussolini, G.B. Lolli, and the Squadrani brothers-- took an intermediate position.[70]

330

The specific purpose of the Forlì reunion was to determine exactly what the P.S.R.I.'s attitude should be toward the two international socialist congresses scheduled for late July in Paris. While the socialist movement had declined somewhat in Italy during the late eighties, in other parts of Europe, notably Germany and France, the movement had made steady progress. By 1889 the socialists in Western Europe were ready to organize the movement on an international scale. Unfortunately, though, by this time schism had divided the movement into two schools--hence the two congresses.

Both assemblies, the Marxists' and the "possibilists'," extended invitations to the socialists of the Romagna. At Forlì a decision had to be made whether to accept these invitations. The principal speakers at the meeting were Costa and Piselli. Apparently there was little disagreement between the two as to what was to be done, for the delegates unanimously approved a proposal, offered by Baldini, that the Romagnols not only participate at both congresses, but also do their utmost to effect a merger between the Marxists and the "possibilists." Elected as the P.S.R.I.'s representatives to Paris were Costa, Piselli, Cipriani, Brunelli, and Alessandro Balducci.

The delegation--Brunelli was replaced by Valducci at the last moment--arrived in Paris just before the Marxist Congress opened on July 14, 1889. After an unproductive effort there to achieve union between the two schools, it was decided, in keeping with the Forlì resolution, that representatives should attend both congresses; accordingly, Costa and Balducci chose to attend the "possibilists'," and Piselli, Cipriani, and Valducci, that of the Marxists.[71] Of the two meetings, the Marxists' proved to be the more significant. It was there that the Second International was born.

Costa, who was well acquainted with many of the French socialist leaders, particularly Malon and Brousse, was recognized by the French as heading Italy's representation at the two assemblies.[72] Piselli, obviously getting along better with his rival at the time,[73] reported that Costa, "when he arrived...in Paris, was met by 14 or 15 deputies and municipal councilmen, all of whom recognized the young representative of the Italian nation, who possesses beautiful and honest qualities, and wanted to approach him personally to give him a hearty welcome."[74]

Once the assemblies were over, Costa learned that he could not return to Italy right away. With his immunity as a deputy, the sentence imposed on him in April could not be enforced as long as the Chamber of Deputies was in session, but by July the parliamentary session had adjourned. To avoid imprisonment, therefore, Costa was compelled to stay in France until Parliament convened again at the end of the year.75

Costa was extremely upset by this turn of events. Contributing to his frustration was the financial burden of living in France, but, more heavily, he had been banking on the P.S.R.I.'s ability to take over the municipal administration of some of the Romagnol cities in the administrative elections to be held in Italy in October and November. Control of municipal government was one of the party's prime goals. In 1881 the P.S.R.R. had made this one of the main planks of its program. Since that time the battle cry of socialists both in and out of the Romagna had been: "Let us gain control of the commune." Gaetano Zirardini in Il Sole had stressed this objective; in fact, when his newspaper expired at the end of 1883 it had been replaced, appropriately enough, by Il Comune, under the editorship of his brother, Claudio.

The title of this newspaper referred, of course, to the Paris Commune. In Italy, as Ernesto Ragionieri points out, the major significance of the Commune had been as a revolt against centralism; as such it was the anarchist aspect of the Commune that the Italians emphasized.76 Ragionieri, though, is only partially correct when he attributes to the party's anarchist origins the emphasis which the P.S.R.R., and later the P.S.R.I., placed on city government. Actually, this phenomenon had deeper roots, namely in Italy's own long-lived communal tradition. From the Renaissance and even earlier, the commune had been a source of special pride. By the nineteenth century loyalty to one's city was more meaningful than even pride in one's region, and regionalism, as we have seen, was by no means weak. Such amor patrio was particularly evident in the Romagna. Alessandro Fortis expressed this opinion in one of his parliamentary speeches in 1884: "We...are proud of...our communal traditions, which we will never renounce. And when I say we, I am not referring just to the democrats: not even the conservatives in the Romagna will ever renounce these traditions of which I speak: since we do not consider the commune to be a purely administrative body. Our tradition is different: and we will conserve it such as it is."77

The same civic pride characterized a Romagnol who
was quite unlike the Honorable Fortis. As Armando Borghi,
the noted anarchist from Castelbolognese, put it: "The
world is very big, and...I have traveled over it far and
wide, and everywhere I met people whom I loved and those
whom I hated. But it was only within the walls of Castel
Bolognese that I never hated anyone."78

The socialists in the Romagna had been advocating
the conquest of city governments for almost a decade;
yet their participation in administrative elections had
always been sporadic, since the chances of success had
never been bright. But all of this changed in 1889. The
electorate eligible to vote in municipal and provincial
elections was now enlarged along much the same lines as
the political franchise had been expanded in 1882. There
was now a good chance of success. Moreover, at the Congress of Naples on June 20-24 of that year the A.R.U. had
finally abandoned its intransigence regarding elections.
Working in concert with the republicans, the socialists
stood to make real inroads in the Romagna.

By mid-1889 Costa had decided that at the next administrative elections the P.S.R.I. would participate
wholeheartedly. Consequently, at the Forlì reunion, a
few days after the republican Congress of Naples, the
socialists not only deliberated on the Paris Congresses,
but they also adjourned their reunion with the proposal
to meet soon at Bologna "to discuss a common program for
the struggle in the administrative elections."79

Exiled in France, Costa was determined that the P.
S.R.I. should still engage in the administrative election.
He therefore encouraged the party to establish a minimum
program, which would serve as an electoral platform, in
accordance with the decision reached at Forlì.

A meeting took place on August 22 in Castelbologn-
ese.80 Alessandro Balducci opened the session by relating what had happened in Paris. A proposal presented by
Gaetano Zirardini approving the Romagnol delegation's
conduct there was accepted unanimously. The gathering
then approved participation in the forthcoming administrative election, and a commission of five men--Zirardini,
Baldini, Brunelli, Piselli, and Balducci--was elected to
draw up a minimum program. This was done on August 26,
and on September 14 both Il Sole and La Rivendicazione

published the document. The program opened with the following general statement of principles: "The emancipation of the working classes should be obtained by these classes themselves: the economic emancipation of the proletariat is the great end to which every political impulse should be subordinated as a means: social misery and political dependence are products of the economic slavery of the workers imposed by the owners of the means of production (land and capital): economic emancipation should spring from the solidarity of all the workers." Eighteen specific proposals followed, the most important of which stated that the commune should abolish all indirect taxes, provide a lay education based on socialist principles, help the worker to better his living conditions, and support the establishment of workers' organizations.

On the basis of this program the socialists of the Romagna participated in the elections of October and November. Working with the republicans, they made significant gains throughout the area. Only in Rimini did the moderates consolidate their position. The reason for the democrats' defeat there was that the local anarchists (who in Rimini outnumbered its socialists) abstained from voting.[81]

In Forlì the republicans regained their control of the municipal government, and Alessandro Balducci was elected to the city council. In Cesena the democrats were also victorious; in fact, the socialists fared even better there than at Forlì.[82] In Ravenna the Comitato Popolare Elettorale Amministrative, representing eighty socialist and republican associations,[83] made a remarkable showing. In the elections held in Ravenna on November 10, the democrats won forty-eight of sixty seats on the city council; in the race for the provincial council seven of the eleven candidates elected were democrats and of these, four were socialists--Baldini, Zirardini, Armuzzi, and Gregorio Pozzi.[84] The democrats also triumphed in Cervia, Cesenatico, Castrocaro, and several of the smaller Romagnol cities.[85]

The most resounding democratic victory, however, occurred in Imola: on November 27 the socialists, aided by the republicans, took over the city council. The four candidates whom the democrats proposed for the provincial council--Costa, Franco Paglieroni, Giuseppe Gottardi, and Girolmo Baldrati--also won. The campaign had been directed by Costa from abroad, but the real architects of the

victory were Negri and Sassi. Together they had been
able to win three crucial victories during the year: on
February 3, Quirico Filopanti, a republican, had been
elected deputy for the electoral college of Imola; on
May 28, Musini was elected as the second deputy; and now
came the victory in the administrative elections--the
most meaningful one, since the election of November 27
marked the first time that the socialists had gained control of a city council in Italy.[86]

The administrative elections of 1889 had produced
a great democratic victory throughout the Romagna. Yet
prospects were not altogether reassuring. An ominous
sign was the friction between the socialists and the republicans in the course of the campaign. On the eve of
the elections Gaetano Zirardini had commented, "The electoral struggle has resurrected old conflicts and has created new ones between socialists and republicans."[87] The
animosity broke out in all the major Romagnol cities save
Imola, but it was most serious in Lugo.[88] In Forlì, interparty strife soon forced Balducci to resign his seat
on the city council, an event which did nothing to en-
dear Piselli--already reluctant to work with his old ad-
versaries--to Saffi and the Mazzinians of that city.[89]

The situation worsened later in 1889 when the relations between the two parties degenerated almost to the
level of the 1870's. What had caused this state of affairs? The answer is to be found in the fact that, as
in the 1870's, the socialists were sapping the republicans' strength. Now, however, the plight of the republicans was far more critical. It was at this time,
in the late eighties, that the Consociazione Repubblicana
began to lose its clear advantage over the socialists in
the Romagna.[90]

The trouble began in Imola in 1887 when Sassi started
to abandon his republican faith.[91] Although he still adhered to Mazzini's political teachings, Sassi began to
question the master's economic ones. The conflict between
classes, according to Mazzini, could be resolved only by
organizations in which the worker and the employer would
come together to discuss their problems. Through association, he believed, social conflict could be eliminated.
Such a view was no longer acceptable to Sassi. Heavily
influenced by Costa and his socialist ideas, Sassi now
believed that through collectivization, not association,
the social problem would be solved.[92]

335

In the late eighties this socialist ideology began attracting new adherents among the republicans in Italy, especially in the Romagna. By 1889 a socialist-republican (or collectivist-republican) current had manifested itself within the Consociazione Romagnola. Besides Sassi, the most notable representatives of the school were Ernesto Monti and Giuseppe Nardi of Ravenna, Antonio Bianchedi and Quinto Gaudenzi of Forlì, and Cajo Renzetti of Rimini.

In anticipation of the republican national congress in Naples in June, 1889, a preparatory meeting of the republican workers' associations in the Romagna was held at Rimini on May 18-19 of that year.[93] Here the socialist-republicans scored their first victory. Led by Renzetti, Sassi, and Decio Fantini, another Imolese, the collectivists managed to get the assembly to adopt a resolution which established collectivization rather than association as the basic economic tenet of the Romagnol republicans. This triumph in the Romagna, the Mazzinians' traditional stronghold, came as a total surprise.[94]

On their arrival at the Congress of Naples on June 20-24, the Mazzinians were prepared to crush the heresy.[95] The collectivists, represented by a dynamic contingent of Romagnols along with numerous Southerners, were led by Enrico DeMarinis, a Neapolitan, who presented the assembly with a resolution similar to that of Rimini. The Mazzinians, however, under Fratti's guidance, defeated the socialist proposal by a vote of 411 to 108. Obviously the collectivist current could count on only a few adherents beyond the Romagna.

The Romagnols refused to accept defeat. At the end of 1889 they concentrated their efforts on increasing their forces. In November they began to organize on a local scale. In that month a Federazione Operaia Repubblicana Ravennate adhering to the collectivist program was founded in Ravenna.[96] The Federazione, however, was still to be a part of the Consociazione Repubblicana Romagnola.

By the time of the administrative elections of 1889, socialist ideas were making a deep impression among the republicans. The fear of this subversive influence quickly spread among the old republican chiefs in Italy, especially among the Mazzinians in the Romagna, where the threat was the most alarming. Under these circumstances, the alliance between socialists and republicans was bound to suffer.

As ideological differences continued to split the Romagnol republicans--and after the death of Saffi in April, 1890, the schism widened--they reacted more vigorously against Costa's party. Relations between the republicans and the socialists did not improve during the early 1890's. This state of affairs was a reflection of the degree to which the republican program was then being threatened by that of the socialist-republicans.

On June 8, 1890, the _Consociazione Romagnola_ held a meeting at Forlì.[97] Thirty-three collectivists, led by Sassi and Renzetti, tried to impose their socialist program at the gathering. Opposed by about sixty Mazzinians, though, the collectivists abandoned the meeting. On October 15, again in Forlì, the collectivists had a gathering of their own at which they proceeded to organize themselves into a _Confederazione Repubblicana Collettivista Romagnola_, a body that was given a solid foundation on March 22 of the following year.[98] On May 26-29, 1892, at the Palermo Congress, which was the national assembly of republican factions, the collectivists dominated, despite the absence of the Romagnols.[99] The collectivists continued to gain strength until the following year, when they reached the height of their power, then rapidly disintegrated. In 1893 some members of the _Confederazione_ returned to the republican party, but the majority joined the socialists. Among the latter group were Gaudenzi, Nardi, and, most important of all, Sassi, who together with his followers in Imola had by this time totally embraced the socialist program. By the mid-1890's the collectivist movement within the republican party had ceased to exist. What had been its effect on that party? Luigi Lotti gives this answer: "Internal quarrels, and consequently an inertia which had lasted for years, an increase in the number of socialists, the loss of the entire _imolese_, these were the consequences of the collectivist movement in the Romagna for the republican party."[100]

The End of the P.S.R.I.: The Ravenna Congress of 1890

Parliament reconvened in November, 1889, and Costa was able to return to Italy. He went first to Imola,[101] then proceeded to Rome, where he resumed his parliamentary seat at the end of December. The situation had apparently returned to normal, but in reality 1890 was to

337

be another bad year for Costa. Early in February he was struck by a grave illness, which seriously hampered his activities into the following month.[102] No sooner had he recovered from this malady than new difficulties presented themselves: on March 20 Parliament authorized the government to execute the sentence of April, 1889. Late in March, Costa was once more forced into exile in France.

Crispi's persecution of Costa now made an even more profound impression than that of the preceding year. The reaction was quick to come. On March 25 Musini resigned his seat in Parliament in protest over the action by the Chamber of Deputies, a gesture wholeheartedly supported by the Imolesi. The Romagna demonstrated its support for Costa by electing him deputy of Ravenna--a post he had resigned on March 27--on April 20.[104] A protest election also took place in Imola, where Costa was elected to fill Musini's vacancy on May 18.[105]

These electoral successes, together with the victories which had been obtained at the polls during the preceding year, encouraged Costa, still in exile in France to continue to work for the election of democratic candidates in the Romagna. Accordingly, in the first days of August he sent the following letter to Gaetano Zirardini and the Ravennati:

My dear friends,
The general political elections (which will perhap take place in October) are just around the corner.
Perhaps we should begin to prepare for them?
Up to now our party has been able to do very littl in Parliament.
Whether our party will be able to accomplish more both in and out of Parliament depends on us.
Let us learn a lesson from the German socialists.
Let us prepare, then!
The next elections, even if they would perform no other function, will permit us to effectively propagandize our ideas.
But, so that our labors might have their maximum effect, it is necessary that we come to some understanding.
For that reason a congress is necessary.
Do you want to take the initiative?
It has been such a long time since we have gotten together that surely this meeting will be of use to
Everyone will be able to contribute his opinions.
If the congress cannot be held in Italy, let us

have it abroad, at the end of August, or at the be-
ginning of September at the latest!
Let us invite all those members of the socialist
party and of the workers' party who accept the prin-
ciple of electoral participation....
What do you think?
Publish this letter and make an appeal to our
friends throughout Italy.
Do you like the idea?
Then let us do something.[106]

Costa's proposal was enthusiastically accepted by
the socialists in the Romagna. Zirardini and the Ravennati were in complete agreement[107]--likewise the Imolesi.
According to La Lega democratica, Costa's letter "inter-
prets a thought, a common desire: that of discussing and
agreeing upon the conduct of the workers' and socialist
parties on the eve of the general political struggle."[108]
This was also the opinion of Il Martello, another democratic newspaper in Imola.[109]

The anarchists were opposed to the congress, however,
for, being against electoral participation on principle,
they were to be excluded from the meeting. Consequently,
Piselli declared that he could not adhere to the proposed
assembly.[110] Instead of concerning itself with electoral
questions, the anarchists protested, a national congress
should be held which would attempt to organize all schools
of the socialist movement, from the anarchists to the P.O.
I., into one strong socialist party.[111] In August and
September, the anarchists began preparations for a national congress of their own--to take place in Switzerland
--which would concern itself with this organization.[112]

Outside the Romagna the idea of an assembly which
would deal with the coming elections met with a mixed reception among the socialists. In August Zirardini reported: "Numerous letters of adherence have been sent to us,
and we can affirm that in all of Italy the idea of the
congress has found enthusiastic acceptance."[113] There were
those, though, who saw little value in such a meeting.
One of these critics was Gnocchi-Viani, who, like the anarchists, thought the question of reorganization should
be resolved as soon as possible.[114] Even before Costa had
called for his congress, Gnocchi-Viani had sent a letter
to the Circolo di Studi Sociali in Bologna urging it to
take the initiative in this reorganization. The P.O.I.
had already reorganized itself, Gnocchi-Viani declared;
now the socialists--or "collectivists," as he preferred

to call them--should do likewise. This reorganization,
he added, would exclude the anarchists, "socialists not
capable of being organized." Gnocchi-Viani concluded his
letter with an appeal to action: "Therefore, forward finally! Collectivists! Have the civil courage to proclaim
yourselves a socialist school with your own historic, scientific, social reasons for existence. Let the name of
the collectivist school be proclaimed on high; a name which
up to now has been kept semi-hidden as if it were a ridiculous and shameful thing. Let us have a strong initiative! A congress, even a local one, of collectivists!"[115]

Like Gnocchi-Viani, the **P.O.I.** also lamented the disorganization in the ranks of the socialist party. In August, **Il Fascio operaio** declared that the participation
of the **P.O.I.** in Costa's proposed congress would be nothing but a waste of time, in view of the state of confusion
which existed among the socialists.[116] Undoubtedly, too,
the operaisti were concerned about the fact that the gathering would deal with electoral participation. Their intransigence on this question had still not completely disappeared.

Despite these misgivings, in August the Ravennati
took the initiative in preparing the congress. In that
month the **Lega Socialista**, an organization of the various
socialist associations in Ravenna, met and approved the
project.[117] The meeting, it was decided, would take place
in that city on October 19. The conferees also nominated
a commission which would organize it, consisting of Piazza
Baldini, and Gaetano Zirardini.

Before the congress could be held it became necessary
to consult Costa on his view of the coming elections. Since
the Imolese was still unable to return to Italy, this meeting had to be held in France. On October 8 Gaetano Zirardini, Alessandro Balducci, Baldini, and other friends of
Costa, about thirty socialists in all, met with him at
Modane, a French city near the Italian border.[118] It was
here that the exact scope of the Congress of Ravenna was
determined.

Once more it was decided that the proposed congress
should concern itself primarily with the electoral question, and that the anarchists should be excluded. But by
now Costa was forced to make some concessions to the anarchists and those in his own party who were primarily
concerned with the problem of organization. While the
work of reorganization could not take place at Ravenna,

it was decided that after the assembly there the socialists would take the initiative in convening a second congress sometime within the immediate future to reorganize
the socialist party. This body would include all schools
of the socialist movement: socialist, anarchist, and operaista.[119]

The Third Congress of the P.S.R.I. convened on Sunday,
October 19, in Ravenna.[120] The meeting was presided over
by Gaetano Zirardini and was attended by 130 to 140 dele-
gates--all of them Costians.[121] Zirardini opened the
session with a speech in which he echoed Costa's ideas
at Modane: the immediate concern of the assembly would
be the next political elections; the general scope would
be the reorganization of the party. He also announced
the agenda of the gathering, which had been determined
at a preliminary meeting the previous day:[122] first, a
salute to the workers of the world; second, a discussion
on the projected Italian congress, which would concern
itself with reorganization; and third, a discussion on
the party's attitude toward the coming political elections.

After affirming the necessity of celebrating May 1
throughout Italy--in accordance with the deliberations
which had taken place at the Marxist Congress in Paris
in 1889--the delegates turned to the question of reorganization. Since the anarchists were not present at
the meeting there was little disagreement on this subject.
The assembly approved, with only three votes against, the
following resolution:

> The Congress, inspired by the sentiments and needs
> of the Italian Socialist Party, and also by the ideas
> prevailing in the deliberations of the circles and
> associations adhering to it, affirms the utility of
> a socialist congress in Italy, the scope of which is
> to be the coordination of all the forces of the Party
> ...for the attainment of common goals, and it dele-
> gates the Lega Socialista di Ravenna to get in contact
> with all factions /the reference is to the anarchists/,
> in order to prepare the said congress and to deter-
> mine the subjects to be discussed.[123]

The third question, that of the elections, was the
real reason the meeting had been called, and it was on
this subject, appropriately enough, that the delegates
spent the most time. The subject was introduced by Danielli and Barbanti-Brodano, who described the general program
which should inspire the participation of the party in the

341

elections. Since 1882, they declared, individual socialists had presented themselves as candidates during political elections, but at no time had the socialists participated in the elections as a party. It was now time
for them to affirm their existence by participating in
the coming elections as a party and with a definite program of their own. What should be the principles which
should determine this program? According to Danielli and
Barbanti-Brodano, "Class struggle, the defense of labor,
the complete separation from all bourgeois programs and
parties: this is the cry with which we will go into battle." These ideas were presented as a resolution and met
with the overwhelming approval of the delegates--there
was only one dissenting vote.

Likewise, there was little disagreement on the cri-
teria the party should establish in selecting its candidates. The discussion on this question was brief. It
was agreed that the party could present only candidates
who would affirm that they were socialists publicly, and
who would wholeheartedly embrace the socialist program.

But what about alliances? Should the socialists
make electoral alliances with other democratic parties?
On this question, the official report stated, "the discussion is very lively." Finally, however, it was decided that in areas where the socialists controlled a
majority of the votes they should present their own exclusive slate of candidates; in those areas where there was
no socialist majority "coalition becomes a duty, in order
that the candidates of the reactionary bourgeoisie not
profit from the discord between the popular parties and
succeed at the polls."

Even without the presence of the anarchists the ques
tion of alliances aroused much disagreement (the official
report significantly fails to give the vote on this issue
and Zirardini himself stepped down from the presidency to
moderate the discussion. The reason for the difference
of opinion here was that this proposal seemed to contra-
dict the previous one which had suggested that the party
represent itself before the electorate with a program
based entirely on socialist principles. Alliance, to
many of the socialists, meant compromise. Moreover, this
form of cooperation was being elevated to a general principle, since nowhere did the party actually have sufficient strength to allow it to enter the elections by itself.

But despite these differences on the matter of inter-party cooperation the proposal was approved, and the meeting ended with the delegates in general agreement.[124] While no minimum program had been formulated at Ravenna, the socialists there had succeeded in establishing the principles which would govern their participation in the coming elections.

In a more general sense, however, the Third Congress of the P.S.R.I. had been a failure. The P.O.I. had failed to send any delegates to the meeting, claiming that the conditions of the socialist party in Italy "prevented its doing so."[125] Turati, too, excused his absence by saying that he had been tied up by professional responsibilities.[126] Prampolini, who was very much against the Ravenna Congress, declared that he had been impeded from attending it because of his health.[127] The Ravenna Congress did not, in fact, seem to stir up much enthusiasm.[128]

Indifference was perhaps justified; what the socialists needed in 1890 was organization, and in this problem the Congress of Ravenna had had only a peripheral interest. Despite its concern for a future gathering which would resolve the problem of organization, it was obvious that the Congress of Ravenna had not really been keen on the question. Costa by this time seems to have given up on the reorganization of the party. What concerned him now was the question of the elections. One might possibly arrive at the conclusion, as Professor Manacorda does, that the October gathering had been proposed by Costa only in order to insure his re-election in the Romagna, a re-election which would permit him to return to Italy.[129]

But if the scope of the meeting was rather limited, it was also realistic, as Costa's triumph and return to Italy would soon prove. Allied with the republicans, the socialists in the Romagna campaigned vigorously for Costa's candidacy in the November elections. In Imola (the II electoral college of Bologna) Costa was part of the democratic slate which included Venturini, a republican, and Giovanni Visani-Scozzi, a socialist-republican.[130] In Ravenna, where the democrats had some difficulty in agreeing upon a common slate,[131] he was entered in a list that included a radical and two republicans. On November 23 Costa was elected at both Ravenna and Imola--he opted for the latter. At the end of the month a general amnesty was granted to the Italian exiles abroad. After spending most of the year in France, Costa returned to Imola on December 5, amidst the cheers of his friends throughout the Romagna.[132]

Conclusion

     The second half of the 1880's witnessed a general
decline of the workers' and socialist movement in Italy.
The **P.S.R.I.**, the **P.O.I.**, the peasant movement, and even
the anarchists--despite a deceptive resurgence--were all
part of this general trend. Nothing illustrated the decay more clearly than the scant success of socialist newspapers during the period. Il Fascio operaio (the **P.O.I.**
organ), for example, had a very irregular existence. Undoubtedly the most important cause of this deterioration
was the persecution which the government had initiated
in the mid-1880's and which was to continue under Crispi
into the following decade.

     Of the various "schools" of socialism which declined
in this period, none experienced the debacle of the Romagnols. The **P.S.R.I.** had never been a strong party, but
when it gave up on its efforts to reorganize itself it
practically disappeared. Increasingly in the late eighties, Costa, who controlled the destiny of the party, turned away from organization. In part this reflected his
failing health, in part the persecution which he exper-
ienced--in 1889-90 he spent fourteen months in exile.
But the main reason for his neglect of this problem was
the difficulties inherent in organizing the party, especially in the Romagna.

     Increasingly in this period Costa turned from organ-
ization to more immediate and attainable goals. Local
politics and parliamentary affairs became his main concerns. This new orientation became especially clear at
the Ravenna Congress of the **P.S.R.I.** in 1890, which dealt
not with organization, which had consumed Costa's efforts
in the preceding years and which had now become the most
pressing problem facing the movement, but rather with the
electoral question. The Imolese, it had become obvious,
was no longer interested in the reorganization of his
party. Having lost its vitality, it was not long before
the party would disappear altogether; the proposed national congress which had been discussed at Ravenna never
took place.

     By 1890, then, the workers' and socialist movement
was in decay throughout Italy. In concluding, though,
it should be made clear that this general deterioration

involved only socialism at an organizational level. Socialism as an ideology was not affected adversely at all. In fact, the persecution of the eighties was to strengthen socialist sentiment rather than sap it. This was to become evident during the following decade.

NOTES

[1]For Italian foreign policy in the last decades of the nineteenth century, see Chabod, *Storia della politica estera italiana*.

[2]See the first revolutionary circular issued by the *Comitato Italiano*. This same moral tone is apparent in the second circular of the *Comitato*, which was dated March, 1874, and was also written by Costa. In this circular Costa insisted that, "This sensitivity toward humanity which is within us will render us invincible."

[3]*I diritti dell'operaio e la necessità dell'associazione* (Borgo S. Donnino: Tip. Donati, 1886). The emphasis which Costa placed on morality was clearly seen in the *P.S.R.R.* program. As has been observed, the rebellion which this program called for "concerns a revolt which is essentially ethical....The socialists want a world in which one can feel himself to be a human being living among other human beings...." See Pier Paolo Rampazzi, "Sogni e programmi politici di Andrea Costa," *Storia e politica*, 6 (1967), 503-04.

[4]According to Ernesto Nathan, the Grand Master of the Italian Masonic movement ca. 1900, the mission which Masonry sought to fulfill was primarily a moral one. See *La massoneria: Sua azione--suoi fini* (Rome: Stab. Tip. Civelli, 1901), p. 16. This emphasis on morality may be what attracted Costa to a movement which his comrades, at least a majority of them, so violently attacked as a bourgeois institution. When Costa went to Naples during the epidemic, incidentally, he went as part of a relief brigade sponsored by the Masons.

[5]See his speech before the Chamber of Deputies of May 7, 1885, in *Discorsi parlamentari*, pp. 66-68.

[6]Manacorda, *Il movimento operaio italiano*, p. 293.

[7]*Discorsi parlamentari*, pp. 113-19.

[8]Speeches of May 26-27 and June 30, 1887, ibid., pp. 142-43.

[9]See Musini's account of the *comizio* in *Da Garibaldi al socialismo*, p. 284.

[10]Letter from Cappellini to Costa, May 3, 1887, B.C.
I., no. 771. According to Cappellini, by this time the
Riminesi had decided to suspend the agitation in Cipri-
ani's favor.

[11]Carocci, Agostino Depretis e la politica interna
italiana, p. 580. The division between republicans and
anarchists was especially wide. See prefect of Ravenna
to the Minister of Interior, July 1, 1887, A.C.S.R., Min.
Int. Gab.--Rapporti dei prefetti, busta 13.

[12]Il Lupo (Ravenna), May 7-8, 1887.

[13]Prefect of Ravenna to the prefect of Forlì, Aug. 19,
1886, A.S.F., Gab. Pref., vol. 127, fasc. 77.

[14]Sectarian ties, the fear of reprisal, and the menace of a monarchist victory all played a part in encouraging this support, according to the prefect of Ravenna
(report to the Minister of Interior, Aug. 23, 1886, A.C.
S.R., Min. Int. Gab.--Rapporti dei prefetti, busta 13).

[15]Even Francolini and the Riminesi had second thoughts
about renominating Cipriani in mid-1886. See the letter
from Achille Sendi, a Forlivese, to Francolini, June 25,
1886, Biblioteca Civica Gambalunga, Rimini, Fondo Francolini-Lettimi.

[16]Telegram from the prefect of Forlì to the Minister
of Interior, Oct. 5, 1886, A.S.F., Gab. Pref., vol. 127,
fasc. 77. The gathering was attended by 114 anarchists
and socialists from throughout the Romagna. Among the
conferees were Carpesani, Cappellini, Fortuzzi, Francolini, Mingozzi, Nabruzzi, Valbonesi, Valducci, Ugo Corradini, Cajo Renzetti, and Francesco Squadrani. Costa
was not at the meeting. See prefect of Forlì to the Minister of Interior, Oct. 4, 1886, A.S.F., Gab. Pref., vol.
127, fasc. 77.

[17]He defended Cipriani before the Chamber of Deputies
on June 16 and Nov. 26, 1886, and on Mar. 11 and Apr. 23,
1887. See Discorsi parlamentari, pp. 86-93, 122-26.

[18]B.C.I., no. 746.

[19]Unlike the ciprianisti, Cipriani himself remained
on good terms with Costa. Some indication of the esteem
Cipriani had for the Imolese is evident in a letter he
wrote him on Dec. 27, 1890. Addressed to "My very dear

347

Andrea," Cipriani's letter continued, "Believe me, my dear friend, the insults which have been hurled at you hurt me very much. I do not understand so much hate, I do not understand why belonging to one party one should have to coarsely insult those that belong to another." See Masini, Storia degli anarchici italiani, p. 341.

[20]Even in Imola the anarchists had had a minor resurgence. By the following year the carabinieri report that a Comitato Elettorale Socialista Anarchico Operaio had been formed in Imola. Its scope: "to oppose the socialist party led by the honorable Costa, Andrea, and to create propaganda on its own behalf in order that it may... intervene in municipal administration." See report to the prefect of Bologna, Dec. 1, 1888, A.S.B., Gab. Pref., cat. VII, 1888.

[21]Piselli, like Mingozzi, was interested in the organization of the peasantry, and, in fact, in February, 1887, he reorganized Mingozzi's old cooperative of braccianti in the forlivese. See Briguglio, Il partito operaio italiano, p. 71. Piselli served as secretary, and other officers of the association included the socialists Fortuzzi, Randi, and Arturo Zambianchi.

[22]See La Rivendicazione (Forlì), July 23, 1887.

[23]During 1886 Piselli had not been especially critical of Costa. Sometimes, in fact, the latter was treated sympathetically in Piselli's newspaper. See, for example, Cappellini's article in La Rivendicazione, Nov. 24, 1886, on Costa's trip to Piedmont.

[24]Letter from Lanzoni to Costa, Feb. 5, 1887, B.C.I., no. 743.

[25]La Rivendicazione, July 23, 1887.

[26]See letter from Cappellini to Costa, Sept. 8, 1887, B.C.I., no. 805. According to Cappellini, "The other evening in the suburb of Mazzini /in Forlì/an armed party of socialists and an armed party of republicans were about to come to blows and a slaughter would have taken place if peacemakers had not arrived, thus the fratricidal battle was momentarily postponed." The day before, Cappellini continued, Amedeo Ghetti, one of the younger members of the party, had fired on a republican but fortunately had missed.

[27]Berti, a moderate, had sponsored a project in 1882

which proposed to initiate a limited program of social reform in Italy.

[28]La Rivendicazione, Jan. 7, 1888.

[29]See letter from Fortuzzi to Costa, Apr. 2, 1887, B.C.I., no. 765.

[30]Prefect of Forlì to the Minister of Interior, Aug. 14, 1887, A.S.F., Gab. Pref., vol. 121, fasc. 48.

[31]Cappellini letter to Costa, Sept. 8, 1887. According to Cappellini, "Fortuzzi has already dismissed himself from the Federation, accompanying his dismissal by a very long letter in which he described the motives for his resolution at length, motives of political conduct and of men whose aims are confusing...."

[32]Letter of Mar. 28, 1887, B.C.I., no. 759.

[33]Prefect of Forlì to the Minister of Interior, Aug. 18, 1888, A.S.F., Gab. Pref., vol. 128, fasc. 80. According to the prefect, Cappellini, who had been the local correspondent for Il Secolo (the Milanese newspaper), a position Costa had obviously procured for him, left this position to Alessandro Balducci.

[34]See Cappellini's letter to Costa from Buenos Aires, n.d. /but November, 1889/, B.C.I., no. 4189.

[35]Letter from Rito Balducci to Costa, Oct. 18, 1888, B.C.I., no. 841.

[36]See the cited letter from Cappellini to Costa, Mar. 28, 1887.

[37]Santarelli, Il socialismo anarchico in Italia, p. 76.

[38]Carabiniere report to the prefect of Forlì, Oct. 26, 1887, A.S.F., Gab. Pref., vol. 121, fasc. 48.

[39]On Sept. 12, 1887, the prefect of Forlì observed that Piselli's plan to organize the movement in the Romagna had not succeeded; his program had received so few adherences that he had been forced to confine the Federazione to Forlì (report to the Minister of Interior, Sept. 12, 1887, A.S.F., Gab. Pref., vol. 121, fasc. 48).

[40]On Aug. 9 the local anarchist circles Amilcare Ci-

priani and <u>Carlo</u> <u>Pisacane</u> had met and merged to form the
<u>Federazione</u>. They had been unsuccessful, however, in per-
suading the <u>Circolo degli Studi Sociali</u>, which still adhered to the program of the <u>P.S.R.I.</u>, to join their organization. See prefect of Forlì to the Minister of Interior, Aug. 14, 1887, A.S.F., <u>Gab. Pref.</u>, vol. 121, fasc.
48.

[41]The socialist opposition to Piselli in the Romagna
at this time was apparently led by Nullo Baldini. See
Baldini's letter to Costa, Aug. 15, 1887, B.C.I., no. 803

[42]On Apr. 1, 1888, the prefect of Forlì reported that
despite Piselli's efforts the socialists in his province
would refuse to repropose Cipriani's candidacy. They
wanted, instead, to vote for Vendemini, a republican. See
report to the Minister of Interior, A.S.F., <u>Gab. Pref.</u>,
vol. 127, fasc. 77.

[43]During the period 1886-88 Costa also took a "very
active part" in a campaign to help the unemployed in the
Italian capital. See "Andrea Costa a Roma," <u>Avanti!</u>, Jan
21, 1910.

[44]This can be seen from the report, written mainly by
Lazzari, which the <u>operaisti</u> sent to the American socialists meeting at the Congress of Buffalo on Sept. 16, 1887
This document--reproduced in <u>La Rivista italiana del so-
cialismo</u>, 2 (1887), 281-86--related the history of the so
cialist and workers' movement in Italy up to 1887. According to the report: "...fortunately a favorable occasion for the <u>Italian Socialist Party</u> to demonstrate to th
public its sincerity and loyalty in the practice of the
principles of human regeneration has recently presented
itself. After the Italian government had declared war a-
gainst Abyssinia (Africa) in order to take over part of
its territory, the Italian socialists pronounced themselv
resolutely and boldly against the principles of violence
and militarism which sustain this war, a war in which mil
lions of dollars and thousands of soldiers are sacrificed
The good sense, the courage, the force of this anti-bel-
ligerent campaign by the socialists won for them a great
deal of sympathy and interest."

[45]For the Pavia Congress, see Manacorda, <u>Il movimento
operaio italiano</u>, pp. 266-72.

[46]The report submitted to the Congress of Buffalo gav
this judgement of Costa's party: "The <u>Italian Socialist</u>

Party...has not really created a current of ideas in public opinion which could clearly mark out a distinct path
to socialist aspirations in all the various phases of political and popular life, and up to now it has dedicated
itself instead to undertakings in which the effect and
success have counted for more than principles; but this
proves that it has still not been able to create an environment...in which to develop the struggle of its principles against those of bourgeois privilege." See La Rivista italiana del socialismo, 2 (1887), 284. Costa, at
the Pavia Congress, took exception to this and other crit-
icisms contained in Lazzari's report. See La Rivista i-
taliana del socialismo, 2 (1887), 286-87.

[47]Subprefect of Imola to the prefect of Bologna, Nov.
1, 1887, A.S.B., Gab. Pref., cat. VI, 1887. Croce and
Costa had just returned from Ravenna, where they spoke at
a P.O.I.-sponsored comizio on Oct. 30, according to Maragi, Storia della Società Operaia di Bologna, p. 299.

[48]An antagonism which was implicit in the report to
the Buffalo Congress.

[49]La Rivendicazione, Sept. 24, 1887, carries a letter
from Dante in which he declares that he is in complete a-
greement with the political ideas that Piselli expounds
in his newspaper. A second letter from Dante appears in
La Rivendicazione on Oct. 15, 1887.

[50]Through Enrico Forlai, its president, the circle was
greatly influenced by Costa. See the report from the questore to the prefect of Bologna, Aug. 10, 1885, A.S.B., Gab.
Pref., cat. VI, 1887.

[51]Report to the prefect of Bologna, July 22, 1888,
A.S.B., Gab. Pref., cat. VI, 1888.

[52]This section, entitled Lega dei Lavoratori, was apparently created sometime in 1887, perhaps through Costa's
initiative. See subprefect of Imola to the prefect of Bologna, July 1, 1888, A.S.B., Gab. Pref., cat. VII, 1888.

[53]Two days before the beginning of the Bologna Congress the local questore reported that of the 19 associations which adhered to the meeting up to then, only two
were from the Romagna: the Società Operaia of Bagnacaval-
lo and the Società Operaia of S. Pietro in Casale (report
to the prefect of Bologna, Sept. 6, 1888, A.S.B., Gab.
Pref., cat. VII, 1888). Hostetter makes it clear that the

P.O.I. never really extended its organization beyond the borders of Lombardy. In fact, he insists that "the Lombard peasant associations never established substantial organizational ties with the P.O.I." See "Lotta di classe...," p. 71.

[54]Manacorda gives an account of the meeting--based on the report of Il Fascio operaio, Sept. 22-23, 1888--in Il movimento operaio italiano, pp. 272-75.

[55]Report from the questore to the prefect of Bologna, Sept. 11, 1888, A.S.B., Gab. Pref., cat. VII, 1888.

[56]Ibid.

[57]Report of the questore to the prefect of Bologna, Sept. 8, 1888, A.S.B., Gab. Pref., cat. VII, 1888.

[58]In addition to the "noted" division between socialists and anarchists, the prefect of Ravenna observed on Mar. 9, 1889, the party was also hampered by personal rivalries within the ranks of both factions. Costa, the prefect continued, had attempted to unite the party in Ravenna, "but it must be added that for him too the best days...have passed." See report to the Minister of Interior on the public spirit in Ravenna during the second half of 1888, Mar. 9, 1889, A.C.S.R., Min. Int. Gab.-- Rapporti dei prefetti, busta 13.

[59]See the Milan correspondence in the issue of Jan. 22, 1888.

[60]Report from the questore to the prefect of Bologna, Sept. 11, 1888, A.S.B., Gab. Pref., cat. VII, 1888.

[61]Oberdan, a republican from Trieste, had attempted to assassinate the Austrian emperor Franz Joseph in 1882 in the name of Italia irredenta (that part of Italy still under Austrian control). The attempt failed and Oberdan was executed in that same year. In Italy the event made a deep impression. Italian nationalism had found a martyr in Oberdan. He was especially revered by the republicans, who were fervent irredentisti. Costa, on the other hand, was not concerned at all with the question of Italia irredenta; this was generally the case with the socialists, who preferred to concentrate on the social question. See Il Sole, Aug. 3, 1889.

[62]The real reason for Costa's arrest: "The govern-

ment is afraid of socialism and aping Bismarck it hunts down the socialists. It sees socialist ideas advance with giant strides, and in order to destroy them it attacks the men who propagate them so vigorously. There is no one, beginning with Crispi, who does not recognize in Costa the head of the socialist party. And it is at the leader that they /the authorities/ aim." See La Lega democratica (Imola), June 15, 1889. After the demise of Il Moto--the first series--on July 8, 1886, the democratic party in Imola had been without a newspaper. But on Jan. 13, 1889, Sassi, Negri, Baldi, and the other members of the old newspaper staff began publication of La Lega democratica. The program of both papers was exactly the same.

[63]In May the government would also move against the P.O.I., thereby adding to the party's already deteriorating state of disorganization.

[64]It was said, nevertheless, that Crispi held Costa in "great personal esteem." See Carlo Monticelli, "Dalle memorie di un internazionalista," Andrea Costa: episodi e ricordi, p. 54.

[65]Report to the Minister of Interior, Apr. 26, 1889, A.S.F., Gab. Pref., vol. 140, fasc. 68. According to the prefect, there were about 2,000 anarchists in his province: 350 in Forlì, 100 in Forlimpopoli, 40 in Predappio, 80 in Meldola, 300 in Cesena, 215 in Rimini, 45 in Sant' Arcangelo, 40 in San Giovanni Magnano, and 792 in the smaller cities. Though the anarchists were stronger than the socialists, they too were considered a weak party. According to the prefect, the anarchists were "not dangerous" because they lacked organization, good leaders, and, most of all, money.

[66]Letter of Mar. 1, 1889, B.C.I., no. 854. Among the members of the Circolo Socialista, according to the correspondence, were Baldini, Golfarelli, Piazza, Santandrea, Traversi, and Zirardini.

[67]On Mar. 2, 1889, the questore of Bologna reported to the local prefect, informing him that no formal organization of anarchists existed in the province--which included Imola (A.S.B., Gab. Pref., cat. VII, 1889). An anarchist section--which contained fewer than 40 members-- was only established in Imola during the following year (subprefect of Imola to the prefect of Bologna, Aug. 29, 1890, A.S.B., Gab. Pref., cat. VII, 1890).

[68]Note to the prefect of Forlì, June 27, 1889, A.S.F, Gab. Pref., vol 135, fasc. 86.

[69]Hereafter Brunelli becomes one of the main protagonists in the history of the socialist movement in the Romagna. For his life, see Mario Santandrea, Umberto Brunelli (Bologna: Tip. Accorsi, 1961).

[70]In all there were 60 representatives present. See prefect of Forlì to the Minister of Interior, July 3, 1889, A.S.F., Gab. Pref., vol. 135, fasc. 86. Most of these delegates and the associations they represented are listed in La Rivendicazione, July 6, 1889, and in Il Sole, July 6, 1889.

[71]See Piselli's correspondence in La Rivendicazione, July 27, 1889. Aside from the Romagnols there were several other Italians at Paris. Of these, according to Piselli, a certain Negri (?) from Turin, and Ezio Foraboschi and Francesco Cini, both of Leghorn, joined Costa at the "possibilist" Congress; Piselli, in turn, was joined by F.S. Merlino--who had been in exile in London--and by Achille Vittorio Pini. Balducci, in his correspondence to Il Sole, July 20, 1889, also makes mention of some anarchist exiles: Molinari, Bertoia, Pichi, and Giannetto Zirardini. In addition, Croce represented the operaisti.

[72]His correspondence concerning the Paris Congresses is reported in Il Sole, Aug. 3, 1889.

[73]The two had worked together shortly before in promoting the Lega Latina, a loose association of French and Italian democrats which aimed at preserving the peace between the two Latin peoples. The more intransigent anarchists were violently opposed to the Lega, for its membership was largely bourgeois. See the letter from Virginio Condulmari, an anarchist from Recanati, to Francolini (who was sympathetic toward the Lega), Nov. 6, 1888, Fondo Francolini-Lettimi.

[74]La Rivendicazione, July 27, 1889.

[75]While in Paris, Costa was able to make his living as a correspondent for Italian newspapers, notably the liberal Roman paper Il Messaggero. During Costa's visits to the French capital he generally resided in Montmartre. See Talamini, "Parigi socialista e l'agonia di A. Costa." Avanti!, Jan. 21, 1910.

[76]"la formazione del programma amministrativo socialista in Italia," Politica e amministrazione nella storia
dell'Italia unita (Bari: Laterza, 1967), p. 197.

[77]Atti parlamentari, June 21, 1884, quoted in Questa
Romagna, ed. Andrea Emiliani, 2nd ed. (Bologna: ALFA,
1963), II, 499.

[78]Vivere da anarchici, ed. Vittorio Emiliani (Bologna:
ALFA, 1967), pp. 40-41. More than anything else, perhaps,
the quotation shows the degree to which class conflict
was absent in the cities of the Romagna during the last
century.

[79]La Rivendicazione, July 6, 1889.

[80]It is described by Gaetano Zirardini in Il Sole,
Aug. 25, 1889. This issue also included a list of all
the representatives present.

[81]Il Sole, Oct. 26, 1889. In general, however, the
anarchists in the Romagna had agreed to participate in
the elections. At the meeting of Forlì, in fact, only
the anarchists of Rimini--who by now wanted to have nothing to do with the P.S.R.I.--had been absent. Piselli,
the major anarchist leader in the region, had not only
attended, but had also helped to write up the minimum
program, and had published it in his newspaper, albeit
with some reservations. See Il Sole, Sept. 14, 1889.

[82]At Cesena the local federation of the P.S.R.I. presented as its candidates Epaminonda and Pio Battistini,
Emilio Giorgi, Giuseppe Gozzi, Giacomo Lucchi, Turci, and
Valducci. See Ragionieri, "La formazione del programma
amministrativo...," p. 242.

[83]Il Sole, Oct. 5, 1889.

[84]Il Sole, Nov. 27, 1889. The three republicans on
the provincial council were Luigi Cilla, Epaminonda Farini, and Tullo Ginnasi Corradini.

[85]Il Sole, Oct. 26, 1889.

[86]For important documents relating to the campaign,
see the Appendix in Giorgio Amendola, Anselmo Marabini e
Imola Rossa (Imola: Galeati, 1969).

[87]Il Sole, Oct. 19, 1889.

[88] _Il Sole_, Nov. 9, 1889.

[89] Balducci, _Alessandro Balducci_, p. 40.

[90] Luigi Lotti, "Il movimento operaio in Romagna nei primi decenni dell'Unità," _L'azione dei mazziniani in Romagna_, p. 64.

[91] Lotti, _I repubblicani in Romagna_, p. 10.

[92] Ibid.

[93] This regional gathering was sponsored by the republican society _Istruzione-Libertà-Benessere_ of Imola and the _Consociazione Romagnola_. See _La Lega democratica_, May 11, 1889.

[94] Manacorda, _Il movimento operaio italiano_, p. 284.

[95] Ibid., pp. 276-94.

[96] Lotti, _I repubblicani in Romagna_, p. 11.

[97] See _La Lega democratica_, June 14, 1890.

[98] At this time the party's Commission of Correspondence was entrusted to Sassi, Fantini, and Antonio Emiliani, the latter from Castelbolognese (prefect of Bologna to the prefect of Forlì, Apr. 15, 1891, A.S.F., _Gab. Pref_. vol. 145, fasc. 72). In this same month the police inspector of Forlì reported that "the collectivist Federation, which has its major associations in Rimini and Imola, has recruited, to this moment at least, only about twenty adherents in Forlì" (report to the prefect of Forlì, Apr. 4, 1891, A.S.F., _Gab. Pref_., vol. 145, fasc. 72.

[99] Manacorda, _Il movimento operaio italiano_, p. 335.

[100] _I repubblicani in Romagna_, p. 18.

[101] Costa's visit to Imola was probably aimed at settling a difference of opinion which had arisen within the ranks of the local democratic party during the course of the recent administrative elections. The dispute (which stemmed from the composition of the democratic slate submitted during the elections) involved Sassi and Negri on the one hand and Baldi and Elviro Lunati on the other. Thanks to Costa's intervention the two factions were reconciled. See _La Lega democratica_, Dec. 8, 1889.

[102]See the letters from Giovanni Floretto to Costa, Feb. 5, 1890, and from Maria Giuffrida to Costa, Mar. 2, 1890, B.C.I., nos. 959 and 972.

[103]Before he left, Costa had a word of advice for those deputies who had authorized his arrest: "In political life, a little heart is not a bad thing /non fa male/. Humanity tempers the fierceness and harshness of disagreement. Victors today, O gentlemen, you may be losers tomorrow; remember that." Quoted in Lipparini, _Andrea Costa_, p. 335.

[104]Costa found great support among the Ravennati at this time. "You and we are one single entity," Gaetano Zirardini and Baldini wrote him on Mar. 26, 1890, B.C.I., no. 987.

[105]So strong was the sympathy in Costa's favor that in Imola even some of his enemies abstained from voting against him. See letter from Ercole Mondini to Costa, June 19, 1890, B.C.I., no. 1027. Costa's election in Imola was nullified by virtue of the fact that he had already been elected at Ravenna. In the new election which took place in Imola on July 13 the conservative candidate, Francesco Isolani, triumphed; the democratic party in Imola abstained. See _La Lega democratica_, July 12, 1890. But this abstention was due not so much to a desire to express solidarity with Costa as it was to the fact that his chances in a new election were slight. Costa himself was against abstention (see his letter to Negri, July 10, 1890, B.C.I., no. 1036). His friends in Bologna, the radicals of _Il Resto del carlino_, wanted the Imolesi to propose Venturini, a republican, and Costa was in agreement (Costa to Negri, June 17, 1890, B.C.I., no. 1026). This created problems in Imola, however; Sassi and Negri apparently wanted to repropose Musini, who had made a good impression on them earlier in the year and who, moreover, was a socialist rather than a republican. The disagreement led Sassi and Negri to propose abstention even despite Costa's opposition. See Costa's letter to Negri, June 30, 1890, B.C.I., no. 1033, and to Sassi, July 2, 1890, B.C.I., no. 1034.

[106]The letter, dated July 30, appeared in _Il Sole_, Aug. 10, 1890, and _La Lega democratica_, Aug. 16, 1890.

[107]_Il Sole_, Aug. 10, 1890. Zirardini had resumed publication of _Il Sole_ on July 6, 1890, after a suspension of several months. The old series stopped on Nov. 27,

1889. The paper had apparently made many enemies, for as the prefect of Ravenna commented early in 1890: "When the loathsome periodical ceased /publication/ for lack of financial support, no one regretted it--perhaps not even its inspirators, who after having exhausted the complete dictionary of the most trivial and provocative epithets ..., found themselves isolated and in an atmosphere of glacial indifference." See report to the Minister of Interior, Apr. 14, 1890, A.C.S.R., Min. Int. Gab.--Rapporti dei prefetti, busta 13. Perhaps the paper's most vindictive detractors were the anarchists, who insisted that its scope was purely electoral. See letter from Condulmari to Francolini, Mar. 4, 1890, Fondo Francolini-Lettimi.

[108] Issue of Aug. 16, 1890.

[109] Issue of Aug. 17, 1890. It seems that the trouble between Baldi and the other members of the democratic party in Imola had resurfaced. On July 20 Baldi began publication of his own weekly, Il Martello. This paper, if it was more clearly socialist in orientation, had a program very similar to that of La Lega democratica. Il Martello was not popular, however; on Aug. 29, 1890, the subprefect of Imola commented on the "near indifference with which it is received by the public which continues to consider the old newspaper, La Lega democratica, as the organ of the great democratic party." See report to the prefect of Bologna, A.S.B., Gab. Pref., cat. VII, 1890. The subprefect also declared that in addition to Baldi the paper's staff included Lunati, and the publication was backed by Paolo and Romeo Renzi.

[110] La Rivendicazione, Oct. 4, 1890.

[111] This point of view is best expressed in a letter which Guglielmo Schiralli, an anarchist from Apulia, sent to Zirardini and which was published in Il Sole, Sept. 27, 1890.

[112] Manacorda, Il movimento operaio italiano, pp. 298-99

[113] Il Sole, Aug. 24, 1890.

[114] Another was Prampolini, who on Aug. 14, 1890, wrote Costa declaring that he had no faith in congresses and that he did not understand what good Costa's proposed assembly would do (B.C.I., no. 1041).

[115] Il Martello, July 27, 1890. Baldi published this

letter because, "We believe it is time that the parties differentiate themselves completely one from the other." In recognizing that the socialists should separate themselves from the anarchists, Baldi had arrived at a clearer conception of a modern socialist party than had Costa and Zirardini, both of whom continued to insist that the anarchists should be included in the party.

[116]Il Martello, Aug. 31, 1890, disagreed: like Costa, the editors felt that the P.O.I. should attend the gathering. Baldi was especially concerned with the criticism of disorganization which had been made against his party. This lack of unity, he suggested, was more apparent than real, for if there were serious differences between regions and between associations, within the individual associations there was a great deal of cohesiveness.

[117]Il Sole, Sept. 27, 1890. The newspaper had failed to appear during the previous month. One reason was that Zirardini had been occupied with the work of organizing the congress at this time. Another was that during this month Zirardini had been involved in a dispute with Il Ravennate, Ravenna's conservative organ, a dispute which culminated with a duel--Zirardini's seconds were Baldini and Baroncelli--against Tullo Poletti, one of the editors of Il Ravennate, on Aug. 20. For the details of this affair, see Zirardini's letter to Costa, Aug. 18, 1890, B.C.I., no. 1042.

[118]Il Secolo, Oct. 10, 1890.

[119]These decisions were announced in Il Sole, Oct. 15, 1890.

[120]The official report of the Ravenna Congress--drawn up by Gaetano Zirardini, Barbanti-Brodano, and Baldi--appears in Il Sole, Oct. 25, 1890, and in Il Martello, Oct. 28, 1890.

[121]Musini, Da Garibaldi al socialismo, p. 328.

[122]From the official report it appears that those in attendance at the Saturday meeting included (in addition to the Ravennati) Baldi, Musini, Barbanti-Brodano, Alessandro Balducci, Jacopo Danielli of Florence, Edoardo Alfieri of Parma, Vincenzo Girotto of Rovigo, Francesco Salmaso of Adria, Bruto Fiorentini of Polesine, and Vincenzo Griggi of Alessandria.

[123]Among those voting against this proposal was Anselmo Marabini, who agreed on the need for the proposed congress but wanted it to be held abroad. Marabini describes the Congress of Ravenna--the first national assembly he had ever attended--in Prime lotte socialiste, p. 123.

[124]"The Congress has left an excellent impression--few speeches, no rhetoric, calm and serene discussion." See letter from Panfilo Marchesini to Costa, Oct. 20, 1890, B.C.I., no. 1059.

[125]Letter to the Congress in Il Sole, Oct. 25, 1890.

[126]Also in Il Sole, Oct. 25, 1890.

[127]Letter to Costa, Oct. 27, 1890, B.C.I., no. 1064. Prampolini did, however, accept the resolutions made at Ravenna. See Costa letter to Barbanti-Brodano, Oct. 28, 1890, Carte Barbanti-Brodano, MS. 165. Quoted in Barbanti-Brodano, Un uomo, un tempo, p. 294.

[128]In his diary Musini relates that upon returning to Borgo San Donnino on Oct. 20, "I find several friends whom I tell about the Congress; I become aware, however, that they have little interest in it" (Da Garibaldi al socialismo, p. 330).

[129]Il movimento operaio italiano, p. 298.

[130]The failure of the Imolesi to include Musini on the democratic slate left the latter embittered toward them and toward Costa. See Da Garibaldi al socialismo, p. 331. It was, in fact, probably Costa who had Musini excluded from the list, for he had never been enthusiastic about Musini's nomination in Imola in 1889 (Da Garibaldi al socialismo, p. 288). Costa's hostility to Musini in this period appears to have stemmed from the latter's lax efforts on behalf of the party; busy with his duties as a doctor, Musini was unable to fulfill his commitments as a socialist.

[131]The socialists in Ravenna wanted to include both Costa and Zirardini on the democratic list. The republicans opposed the idea: they would allow the socialists only one representative. They were especially opposed to Zirardini, a stance which was due, it seems, to the personal antipathy which Tullo Corradini, the leader of the republicans in Ravenna, felt toward him (Baldini's letter to Costa, n.d., B.C.I., no. 4107). Together with Baldini,

Costa persuaded Zirardini to withdraw his candidacy for
the sake of the alliance (letter from Ratti to Costa,
Dec. 2, 1890, B.C.I., no. 1089), a compromise which lost
them the support of many of their followers throughout
the province (Baldini to Costa, n.d., B.C.I., no. 4108).
In the province of Forlì, the situation was worse: there
no alliance was possible. The republicans, in fact, abstained. Il Secolo, Nov. 24-25, 1890, reported that "in
general, apathy and abstention prevailed" in Forlì.

[132]Ragionieri, "La formazione del programma amministrativo...," p. 245, correcting Marabini, writes Nov. 5 (sic).

CHAPTER TEN

THE CREATION OF THE ITALIAN SOCIALIST PARTY,
1891-1892

The Romagna on the Eve of the Milan Congress

The Ravenna Congress of 1890 had called for the convocation of a national congress which would create an
Italian socialist party. Preparations for this gathering
began after Costa's return to Italy. On January 18, 1891,
as Costa was recuperating from another in a series of illnesses which plagued him in these years, the Romagnols
met at Ravenna once more and began to plan for the national assembly. The most important result of this Ravenna
meeting was the creation of a commission to take charge
of organizing the proposed congress. In addition to Costa, this commission included the new deputies Giacomo
Maffei, Pietro Casilli, and Camillo Prampolini, and also
Giuseppe Veraldi.[1] The latter, in his capacity as secretary of the commission, was given the responsibility of
informing the various socialist associations throughout
the peninsula of the coming congress, to be held on March
10 in Bologna, and of soliciting adherences to it.

A circular announcing the assembly was published in
late January.[2] Though it was distributed throughout the
peninsula, however, it met with a disappointing response.
There were but a handful of adherences.[3] Even among the
Bolognesi themselves the idea of the congress was received with little enthusiasm.[4] Consequently it was decided
that the meeting should be postponed to the first days of
April, when it would take place in Rome.[5] But general
apathy continued and instead of the national congress, a
regional gathering of the socialists of Emilia-Romagna
met at Bologna on April 26.[6]

Little was accomplished at this meeting. Rather than
taking a strong initiative, the gathering limited itself
to the appointment of a second commission to aid the one
elected at Ravenna in January in creating the long-awaited national congress. The new commission, which was headed by Costa and included Barbanti-Brodano and Alessandro
Balducci, met on June 24 and, according to Il Moto, "held

the most urgent deliberations concerning the convocation
of the coming Italian Socialist Congress."7

Exactly what concrete proposals were made at this
meeting are not known. It is apparent, though, that by
this time the Romagnols could only talk of the general
assembly rather than convoke it. Early in the following
year Costa's friends continued to speak of "that famous
Congress, which is never held,"8 but by now any possibility of the constitution of an organized socialist party
under the leadership of the Romagnols had completely disappeared.

By the early nineties the socialists in Italy were
tired of preparatory meetings, and these, it seemed, were
all the Romagnols were capable of. Perpetual congresses,
but little in the way of concrete results: these appeared
to be the only fruits of Costa's efforts during the past
decade. By this time, consequently, the Romagnols found
themselves isolated. Unable to exert any significant influence on the socialist movement outside their own boundaries, the Romagnols had lost the initiative in creating
the Italian socialist party. Costa himself seemed to
sense this, a realization which helps to explain his feeble efforts to convoke the proposed congress in 1891. By
this time his interests lay elsewhere.

After his return to Italy in December, 1890, Costa
withdrew more and more within the friendly confines of
his native Imola. Municipal government now became his
chief concern. Early in 1891 he was elected president
of the local Congregazione di Carità, the municipality's
leading welfare organization, and in February he was e-
lected mayor of the city. Despite the efforts of friends
to encourage his participation in the affairs of the socialist party outside of Imola,9 Costa continued to occupy himself almost exclusively with local problems. While
this activity at the municipal level brought some good results, outside the Romagna these efforts were judged in
less positive terms. Antonio Labriola, for example, was
extremely critical of Costa's new orientation. Since Costa had been amnestied during the preceding year, Labriola
complained to Friedrich Engels, "he has enclosed himself
in his Imola, and says that 'his office of mayor and president of the Congregazione di Carità oblige him to demonstrate that the socialists are mature enough for the government of the State' (sic)."10

Labriola was also critical of another of Costa's con-

364

cerns during this period: his preoccupation with the cooperative movement.[11] This current had begun to prosper
in Italy during the eighties, especially among the braccianti of the Po Valley.[12] The socialists' view of the
movement was ambivalent. They opposed this form of economic association in theory because they feared that once
the worker became involved in the cooperative, he would
embrace the status quo and thus be lost to the cause of
revolution.[13] But in fact most of the socialists came
to accept the cooperative, and even to promote it. They
did this in order to attract the worker, who saw the cooperative in a favorable light, to their movement, and
also because in the cooperative they saw a way of ameli-
orating the terrible economic condition of the working
class.

    This ambivalent attitude was reflected in Costa, who
recognized the limitations of the cooperative movement
but supported it for both humanitarian and practical reasons.[14] This encouragement is apparent throughout the
eighties in the many efforts he made to help the Associazione Generale degli Operai Braccianti of Ravenna both
in and out of Parliament.[15] By the early nineties, as
Labriola notes, Costa was very much involved with the cooperative movement. In 1891, when Labriola commented on
his activity, Costa was the president of Imola's bracciante cooperative.[16] During that year he was also one of
the principal movers in the creation of the Società Con-
sorziale dei Braccianti di Romagna, an organization which
was to coordinate the efforts of the various bracciante
cooperatives in the region.[17]

    Concerned with municipal government in Imola and
with the cooperative movement in the Romagna, Costa withdrew more and more from the socialist movement. The sligh
possibility that the initiative taken by the Romagnols at
the Congress of Ravenna in 1890 would succeed soon vanished altogether as Costa lost interest in promoting the national congress.

    Somewhat more successful in bringing unity to their
movement were the anarchists. Excluded from the Ravenna
Congress of 1890, the anarchists took the initiative in
calling for a congress of their own. The main instigators
of this gathering were the Romagnols, led by Piselli and
Lodovico Nabruzzi, and the anarchist exiles of Lugano in
Switzerland.[18] After a preparatory meeting at Faenza on
October 13,[19] the anarchist congress was held at Capolago,
in Switzerland, on January 4-6, 1891.[20] The object of the

meeting was to reorganize the socialist party in Italy under the flag of the old International. All factions of the party were therefore encouraged to be present.[21]

In one sense the Capolago Congress failed miserably, for the socialists, including Costa, generally stayed away. As a matter of fact, only two Legalitarians, Danielli and De Franceschi, were in attendance. On the other hand, some unity was given to the splintered anarchist movement, which at Capolago was divided into three groups: those represented by Piselli, Malatesta, and Paolo Schicchi.[22]

Piselli and the Romagnols were on the extreme right of the anarchist movement.[23] While they professed anarchist goals, the Romagnols were sometimes willing to work within the system. On the question of political elections, for example, they at times failed to follow a strict anarchist line, and participated not only in municipal elections but occasionally in political elections as well. In 1890, in fact, Piselli had worked hard for the re-election to Parliament of Fortis, a fellow Forlivese but a staunch supporter of the status quo.[24] In practice, it is clear, Piselli and his followers had much in common with the costiani.

Schicchi and his followers were on the extreme left wing of the anarchist movement in Italy. This group of activists carried the concept of anarchy to its logical extreme: the "individualists," as they were called, were against any form of organization, even that of an anarchist party, which they said was a contradiction in terms. The individual, not the group, they argued, should be the backbone of the anarchist movement. They naturally opposed the creation of workers' associations, and were very hostile to Piselli and his group, which generally encouraged such organizations. As far as political participation was concerned, Schicchi and his followers were completely intransigent, as they were in their attitude toward social legislation. During the nineties these "individualists" were to lean more and more toward the use of terroristic methods. In general, however, the "individualists" were exiles, and their methods never won wide acceptance in Italy.[25]

Malatesta represented the large majority of anarchists in Italy. Together with Amilcare Cipriani, who had been given his freedom in June, 1888, he dominated the Capolago gathering. Unlike Schicchi, Malatesta saw that power could

come only through organization; thus he was determined
to create a unified anarchist movement. On the other
hand, he was opposed to the formation of an anarchist
party along the lines which Piselli envisaged. For Malatesta and the orthodox anarchists, Piselli's "socialist-
anarchist" approach was too similar to that advocated by
Costa. Malatesta was determined to make no concessions
either to the right or to the left.

It was Malatesta's tendency which triumphed at Capolago. The gathering reaffirmed its intransigence toward
political elections, and condemned electoral alliances
of any kind. But its most important accomplishment was
the formation of an anarchist party, the Federazione
Italiana del Partito Socialista-Anarchico-Rivoluzionario,
which was created despite the objections of the "individualists."

Some concessions where made to the latter. The Federation, for example, was given a very loose organization:
there would be no central organ to direct the activities
of the various regional commissions of correspondence.
Despite these concessions, Schicchi and his group never
reconciled themselves to the party. Piselli's followers,
on the other hand, readily accepted the program of the
Congress of Capolago, and immediately set out to implement its decisions.

Late in January Cipriani arrived in the Romagna to
initiate the work of reorganization in accordance with
the program which had been voted at Capolago. Cipriani
was no longer as influential among the Romagnols as he had
once been,[26] but together with Piselli he was able to make
a good deal of progress. His efforts were rewarded on
February 2 when a Romagnol federation of the anarchist
party was created at a meeting held in Ronco near Forlì.[27]
The Ronco Congress approved an anarchist program,[28] and
elected a Commission of Correspondence which was to have
its seat in Forlì and which was composed of Temistocle
Bondi, Ugo Facchi, Luigi Gottarelli, Lodovico Nabruzzi,
Piselli, and Valducci.[29]

The Congress at Ronco was only partially successful.
The carabinieri reported that Cipriani was disappointed
with the results.[30] Apparently the chief source of Cipriani's dissatisfaction was his failure to entice the socialists of the Romagna into the new organization. Unlike Malatesta, Cipriani wanted to create a party which
would not be confined exclusively to those socialists who

accepted anarchist principles. He also wanted Costa's supporters to enroll in the anarchist federation.[31]

On January 19, before the Ronco Congress, Cipriani held a meeting in Forlì with some of the major leaders of both the anarchist and socialist factions in the Romagna. The anarchists were represented by Piselli, Valbonesi, Bondi, and Nabruzzi; the socialists by Gaetano Zirardini and Alessandro Balducci.[32] "The principal scope of the meeting," according to the prefect of Forlì, "was to initiate attempts to bring about an agreement between legalitarian socialists and anarchists, thus the presence at the meeting of Zirardini and Balducci, the leaders of the legalitarian socialists in Ravenna and Forlì respectively."[33] Nothing was resolved at this gathering. The socialists were unwilling to commit themselves to an alliance with the anarchists. At the Ronco Congress, consequently, Costa's followers failed to appear.

But the refusal of the socialists to adhere to the anarchist federation was not Cipriani's only worry. Complete agreement at Ronco had been impossible even among the anarchists themselves.[34] A few days after the meeting it was reported that Cipriani's efforts to unite the anarchists had not been successful thus far.[35] These divisions within the ranks of the anarchist movement in the Romagna, it seems, did not take place over questions of ideology, but resulted rather from personal antagonisms between the various chieftains of the party. In Cesena the old rivalry between Valducci and the Battistini brothers continued;[36] in Forlì personal differences separated Piselli and Francesco Bazzocchi;[37] and in Rimini the most serious rivalry took place between Amilcare Cipriani and Cajo Zavoli, "on account of old grudges...which had never been settled."[38]

Despite these difficulties, the meeting at Ronco did produce some positive results: a measure of unity was brought to the anarchist movement in the Romagna. The same thing was occurring everywhere in Italy. Soon after the Ronco Congress other regional congresses took place throughout the peninsula.[39] These gatherings laid the basis for the creation of an effective anarchist party with a nation-wide organization. What the socialists had failed to accomplish, the anarchists appeared on the verge of doing during the first half of 1891.

But this progress came to a sudden halt in May. The cause of the new collapse of the anarchist movement after this date was the repression which followed the May 1 celebrations throughout Italy.[40] At the Congress of Capolago the anarchists had decided that they would observe the May 1 celebration, which had first been proposed at the Marxist Congress at Paris in 1889. Annually on this date the workers of the world were to hold celebrations which would demonstrate the solidarity of the working class across national borders.

Though the majority of anarchists were in agreement that the May 1 observance should limit itself to peaceful demonstrations, there were others who wanted to use the celebration for revolutionary purposes. Accordingly, on May 1 some anarchists in Rome attempted to incite the workers to rebel. The police reacted quickly and indiscriminately; among those arrested at Rome was Cipriani, who had attempted to calm the crowd rather than incite it. Official repression of the anarchist movement ensued during the next few months and culminated in the following year when Cipriani was condemned to four years in prison.

The repression was also felt in the Romagna. In Imola, Mancini, Castellari, and Francesco Cremonini, the heads of the local anarchist party, were all arrested in March.[41] One result of the repression was the mass emigration of anarchists from the Romagna after May, 1891. Many of them departed for the Americas.[42] Government persecution kept those who remained in the region in line.[43] By the following year the anarchists there were in a sad state of disorganization,[44] and the same was true throughout the country. The repression of 1891-92 had destroyed the anarchist federation almost as soon as it had been born. The anarchist party never recovered from this blow.

The Milan Congress of 1891

By the middle of 1891 both Costa and the anarchists had failed in their attempts to create a national socialist party. But it was precisely at this time that a new effort was begun. The center of the initiative was no longer the Romagna but rather Lombardy. It was at the Congresso Operaio Italiano held at Milan on August 2-3, 1891, that the work began which led to the creation of the Italian Socialist Party.

The initiative in calling the Milan Congress was taken by Filippo Turati (1857-1932).[45] Turati, the man

369

who was to be primarily responsible for the creation of the Italian Socialist Party, had become a socialist rather late in his life. Starting out as a conservative, Turati had embraced radical-republican ideas by the time he left the University of Bologna. In Milan, however, he became increasingly interested in socialism and began to associate himself with the leaders of the operaista party. In 1886, when the bitter polemic took place between Cavallotti and the P.O.I., Turati chose to defend the latter. It is from this date that his socialist period really begins.[46]

As a student, Turati had come into contact with the positivist ideas which were current among the intellectuals of that period. These ideas were reinforced in Milan, where the intellectual environment was strongly permeated by the positivist philosophy. In view of his early development, therefore, it is hardly surprising that when Turati turned to socialism, he became interested not in the anarcho-socialist ideas which had been popular in Italy up to that time, but rather in the concepts which were associated with "scientific" socialism--that is to say, with Marxism.[47] Perhaps the determining influence leading the young Lombard in this direction was that exerted by Anna Kuliscioff,[48] whom he met in 1884 in Naples, where she lived. By this time Kuliscioff's romantic involvement with Costa was a thing of the past,[49] and shortly thereafter she transferred to Milan, where she and Turati initiated a close personal and political association which would last until Anna's death in 1925.

Turati's transition from positivism to Marxism, however, was never complete. For him, as for the other intellectuals in Milan, Marxism remained tinged with positivist elements. There was a conscious effort among these intellectuals, in fact, to wed both philosophies, first in Arcangelo Ghisleri's influential journal, Critica e cuore (1886-90), in which Turati was an assiduous collaborator, and after January 15, 1891, in Turati's own Critica sociale.

Through Critica sociale, Kuliscioff and Turati hoped to popularize Marxism among the Italian intelligentsia.[50] By the late eighties Turati had come to see the need for an Italian socialist party, and he realized that these intellectuals would provide the party's leadership. But he was also aware of the importance of providing a popular base for this party. In Milan this could be accomplished only through an alliance between the intellectuals

DOTT. FILIPPO TURATI.
Deputato al Parlamento.

FILIPPO TURATI
Biblioteca Comunale di Imola

ANNA KULISCIOFF
Biblioteca Comunale di Imola

and the members of the workers' party. The first practical steps toward this end were taken in 1889 when, under Turati's leadership, the Lega Socialista Milanese was founded in the Lombard capital. Among the members of this socialist association were some of the operaisti, including Costantino Lazzari, one of the directors of the party. The operaista intransigence on the question of middle-class alliances was apparently coming to an end. Undoubtedly the repression which the P.O.I. had suffered in the late eighties had done much to persuade the party's leaders to modify their stance on this question.[51]

Over two years passed before Turati had sufficiently cemented the alliance to the point where he felt that a socialist party based on the old P.O.I. was possible. By the middle of 1891, after it became clear that the Romagnols would fail in their efforts to convoke a national congress, Turati decided that he and his friends must take the initiative in organizing the party. A start in this direction was made at the Milan Congress in August.[52]

The Milan Congress was little more than a regional meeting of representatives of the workingmen's associations in Lombardy.[53] Yet its significance should not be underestimated, for it was to be an integral part of the process which would culminate in the formation of the Socialist Party in Italy during the following year. The gathering was dominated by Turati, who, with the assistance of Lazzari and Croce, was able to win over the majority of the operaisti to his point of view. Despite the opposition of the intransigent P.O.I. members, led by Angiolo Cabrini, and of their anarchist allies, Turati was able to get the delegates to accept social legislation on principle. In effect, this meant that the operaisti had at long last abandoned their opposition to political action.

Turati dealt next with the traditional prejudice the operaisti had displayed against working with middle-class elements. Backed by Lazzari, who had long since overcome his prejudice, Turati was able to present his arguments effectively. Though Cabrini and his followers refused to give in completely on this point, Turati was able to convince most of the delegates to accept his position in substance if not in form.

Once the majority of operaisti had been persuaded to abandon their intransigent position on the question of political action and their insistence on a pure work-

373

ers' association, it became a relatively easy matter to get them to agree to the constitution of a socialist workers' party on principle. Because of the lack of time, however, it was decided that the formation of the party would take place at a congress to be held in Genoa during the following year. In the meantime, a commission composed of Antonio Maffi, Enrico Bertini, Silvio Cattaneo, Carlo Cremonesi, Anna Maria Mozzoni, and Lazzari was entrusted with the task of formulating the party's program and statutes, both of which would be submitted at Genoa for approval.

After the Milan Congress, it became clear that the initiative in creating a national socialist party had passed from the Romagnols to the Lombards. During the last months of 1891, moreover, the socialist party in the Romagna underwent a steady decline.[54] This decay reflected Costa's inactivity during this period. Despite invitations from the Milanesi, Costa refused to attend the Milan Congress, just as Turati had failed to appear at the Congress of Ravenna the previous year.[55] He continued to isolate himself in Imola.

In September Costa was suddenly aroused, though only temporarily, from his apathy. Trouble between the republicans and the socialists of Cesena had been brewing all during the year.[56] This antagonism peaked on September 7 when Pio Battistini, Costa's old friend and one of his chief aides, was murdered by a group of republicans. The cause of the assassination, reminiscent of that of Piccinini at Lugo in 1872, was the defection of some of the younger members of the republican movement into the ranks of Battistini's party. Immediately after the assassination it appeared that the incident would provoke bloody battles between the two factions throughout the region. As he had in 1872, though, Costa, together with the ranking republican leaders, was able to restore order.[57]

After this crisis had been resolved, Costa returned to his secluded life in Imola. He now preoccupied himself exclusively with local affairs; in effect, he had gone into semi-retirement. This withdrawal from active life also seems to have been accompanied by a serious personal degeneration. An allusion to this breakdown was made by the anarchists of Imola early in 1892. Speaking of Costa, the anarchists "declared him to be a man who was morally wasted, adding that in Imola, where he is almost always found, he abandons himself to a thoughtless life and to continual drinking which earn him the disrespect of every-

374

one."[58]

While the testimony of the anarchists, Costa's enemies, may be suspect,[59] the same cannot be said of comments made by Antonio Graziadei in this regard. Graziadei, who after Costa's death in 1910 was to succeed him
as Imola's deputy in Parliament, later recalled his first
contacts with the aging recluse, contacts which, judging
from the exchange of correspondence between the two, began in 1891.[60] Graziadei wrote of Costa: "I must confes
with regret that I met him when his decadence had already
begun. For some time he had taken up the fatal habit of
stimulating his declining energies with artificial stimu-
lants. He seemed to me to be a man who had lost the habi
of study, and who, under new political conditions, no lon
er found a function comparable to that of the past."[61]

As Costa declined, he seems to have become something
of a misanthrope. Increasingly he withdrew into his own
private world and displayed a marked unwillingness to get
along even with old friends.[62] During the course of 1892
he had a serious falling out with Franco Baldi.[63] In Sep
tember of the same year he was obliged to fight a duel
with Elviro Lunati, another of his old comrades (though
a member of the republican party), the cause of which was
Costa's insult of Lunati's wife.[64]

Some historians have been puzzled by Costa's inertia
during the period of the Genoa Congress of 1892.[65] It
seems probable, however, that this apathy, and the moral
collapse which became evident at the same time, derived
in part, as is suggested by Graziadei's comments, from
Costa's failing health. Never very strong physically,
the Imolese, especially after 1890, seems to have been
continually plagued by a variety of illnesses, something
made abundantly clear in his correspondence.[66] Not the
least of the causes of Costa's maladies at this time, and
this holds true for a number of his companions, were the
many years which he had spent in prison during his youth.
Beset by illness, Costa grew melancholy and tended to
isolate himself more and more from the activities which
had taken up so much of his time before.

The Genoa Congress of 1892

Costa's isolation was very evident early in 1892.
But by this time, preparations had commenced for the Geno
Congress, which was to be held in August, and Costa's

friends now began to fear that he might excuse himself
from this crucial gathering just as he had from the Milan
Congress of the previous year. Among those who were most
concerned with Costa's apathy was Carlo Monticelli. "Look,
Andrea," he wrote in May, "it is a mistake...to remain...
in the shell of your Imola, while the Italian working-class
and socialist movement is in such need of organization. I
understand that you wanted to rest a little; but it is
time that you get going again."[67]

Also urging Costa to make an appearance at Genoa
were Kuliscioff and Prampolini, both of whom anticipated
trouble with the intransigent operaisti and the anarchists
and wanted Costa's aid in defeating these foes.[68] On the
eve of the Genoa Congress, Costa was still reluctant to
leave Imola,[69] but in the end the significance of the
event did not escape him, and when the meeting opened on
August 14 Costa was among the most illustrious of the representatives present.

In contrast to the gathering of the preceding year,
the Congress at Genoa was truly a national one.[70] Though
there was a preponderance of delegates from Lombardy and
Emilia, all regions were represented. There were over
two hundred delegates in attendance when the meeting was
convened.

No sooner had the first session started than it became evident, as had been feared, that the intransigent
operaisti, led by Cabrini, and their anarchist allies,
headed by Pietro Gori, would pose serious problems. On
the first question on the agenda, that of nominating the
presiding commission, the operaisti made their position
clear by insisting that this commission should be composed exclusively of workingmen. They thus brought up an
issue which had apparently been resolved during the previous year: the question of the class composition of the
party. The operaisti had no intention of permitting the
creation of a socialist party based on Turati's program;
in fact, they had no intention of permitting the construction of any party at all. Throughout the course of the
session the operaisti and the anarchists resorted to obstructionist tactics. The socialists stood their ground,
and the atmosphere soon grew very tense. By the end of
the session, tempers on both sides were practically at
a boiling point.[71]

As a result of the obstructionist campaign, absolutely nothing was accomplished at the first session. The

Congress threatened to end in complete fiasco. The socialists were uncertain as to what to do. Following the session, therefore, they held a private gathering, dominated by Turati, Kuliscioff, and Prampolini,[72] in which it was decided that the socialist majority should abandon the original Congress and convoke a second gathering to be restricted to representatives who accepted the use of elections to conquer political power. In effect, this formula would exclude both intransigent operaisti and anarchists.

The following morning the two allied factions found themselves alone at the Sala Sivori, the original site of the Congress. The socialists met at a new location, the Sala dei Carabinieri Genovesi. Unfortunately, not all the socialists had been informed of the change in plans, and many of these found out what had happened only when they arrived at the Sala Sivori. Among those who had not been informed were Costa and the Romagnols.[73]

Costa was understandably upset when he arrived at the boycotted meeting and was informed of the schism. He proceeded to express his view on the matter. According to one report: "Although convinced, after what had happened yesterday, that it had to come to a separation, he /Costa/ deplores the method by which this separation has come about; he believes that the /executive/ committee and the presidency should have returned to their post at the Sala Sivori and provoked an explicit vote on a concrete proposal and regulated their conduct accordingly, instead of making such an important decision behind closed doors, as was done."[74] Costa and the Romagnol delegation then marched to the socialist gathering where, instead of taking part in the deliberations, they again expressed their displeasure at the way the schism had been brought about and requested that the socialists return to the Sala Sivori. But Turati and his followers would not hear of it; they were in no mood to spend the little remaining time they had in fruitless discussions.

Unable to bring about the union of the two gatherings Costa refused to have anything to do with either of them. He and his Romagnols left Genoa that same day,[75] followed by Monticelli and the Venetians and by numerous other individuals, including the Genovese Pietro Chiesa. Ironically, then, Costa was to be absent at the founding of the Socialist Party which he had worked for so long to bring about. The creation of the party was to take place at the famous second session of the Genoa Congress, where

CAMILLO PRAMPOLINI
Biblioteca Comunale di Imola

the party's program and statutes were formally approved.

The preparation of this program and statutes had been entrusted to the commission nominated at Milan. Both, however, were presented in a very unsatisfactory form. Dominated by Maffi, a radical deputy from Milan, the commission had adopted and only slightly modified the old program and statutes of the P.O.I., with the result that many objectionable operaista elements were retained. During the course of the second session Turati was able to iron out some of the difficulties. Although the statutes were not altered significantly, Turati convinced the assembly to amend the program, which was much more important than the statutes, in a decidedly socialist direction. He was thus able to insure that the party, christened the Partito dei Lavoratori Italiani would be a socialist rather than merely a workers' party.

A few days after the Genoa Congress, Costa made it clear that he accepted the socialist rather than the anarchist program.[76] He refused, though, to adhere to the newly-created party. Why was Costa unwilling to endorse the very party which he had labored for so many years to create?[77]

It has been suggested that what upset Costa was the omission of the anarchists from the party.[78] To be sure, Costa felt a natural sympathy for his old comrades, and as late as the preceding year he and his friends had made it clear that they thought there should not be a separation between their organization and that of the anarchists.[79] It is unlikely, though, that it was the exclusion of the anarchists which caused Costa's estrangement from the socialist party. At Genoa, after all, had he not declared that he thought the schism to be inevitable?[80] Then, too, Il Moto, whose views were identical with those of Costa, asserted after the gathering that the disorder which had resulted there could have been avoided had the Genoa Congress included only socialists who thought along the same lines. "Having permitted, instead, everyone to attend, that which would inevitably happen happened."[81] The implication here is that the meeting should have been restricted exclusively to socialists in the first place. And, in fact, this is the line which Costa had followed for years in practice if not in theory; the gatherings of the P.S.R.I. had generally excluded the anarchists. Their exclusion from the Genoa Congress, then, did not explain Costa's apparent antagonism toward the party.

There is little reason to doubt Costa's sincerity
when he insisted that he had been upset not by the separation itself, but rather by the way it was brought a-
bout. Certainly this statement goes a long way in explaining his behavior. One characteristic which could
be observed consistently throughout the course of Costa's
life, from his early anarchist days to his death in 1910,
was his rejection of authoritarian methods. Though we
may disagree in view of the way the anarchists conducted
themselves at the Sala Sivori, Costa believed that Turati
and his followers had made their decision at Genoa in an
arbitrary fashion. He was understandably upset. Yet in
refusing to adhere to the new party, Costa seems to have
overreacted. Behind the method of separation there was
a far more important motive for Costa's discontent and
subsequent behavior.

The Congress of Genoa represented a triumph for the
Milanesi and a defeat for the Romagnols; the source of
Costa's dissatisfaction was to be found in this fact.[82]
The party which Costa and his followers had done so much
to create during the preceding decade had finally come
into being in 1892. The real architects of the party at
this time, however, had not been the Romagnols, but rather
the socialists in the Lombard capital. What the Romagnols
had sown, Turati and his friends had reaped. The Congress
of Genoa clearly demonstrated that the hegemony of the
socialist movement in Italy had passed to the latter.
This process had been evident from the mid-eighties on,
and Costa himself had not been ignorant of its development. But this did not make it any easier for him to
accept the results of the Genoa Congress.

The party which had been formed through the initiative of the Milanesi, moreover, represented the triumph
of ideas which Costa did not fully comprehend. His socialism, and that of the Romagnols, was idealistic and
humanitarian; it had little in common with that of the
Milanese intellectuals of the Critica sociale. The difference between Milan and the Romagna, in fact, was the
difference between two environments in sharp contrast,
the one urban and industrial, the other rural and agricultural. Unable to understand Milan and its brand of socialism, the Romagnols were naturally very reluctant to
accept a party which bore its imprint so distinctly.

Costa's attitude toward Milanese socialism is reflected in his relationship with Turati, its foremost exponent. During the early eighties this relationship was

cordial.[83]   But as Turati consolidated his position as
the leader of the socialist group in Milan, Costa grew
increasingly cool in his attitude toward him.[84]   On the
eve of the Genoa Congress, when it became obvious that
Turati had become Costa's heir,[85] Costa was no longer on
friendly terms with the young Milanese--a state of affairs
which was not helped any by Turati's intimate association
with Kuliscioff, Costa's ex-love.[86]   Turati's handling
of the anarchist question at Genoa certainly did nothing
to abate Costa's resentment.   His failure to consult
Costa on the advisability of the socialist withdrawal
from the Sala Sivori, or to inform him of the decision
once it had been made, must have been construed by the
latter, by now perhaps overly sensitive to "insults" of
this kind, as a personal affront.[87]

The Aftermath of the Genoa Congress

Increasingly after the Genoa Congress the futility
of Costa's gesture became recognized.   It was not long
before the Socialist Party was able to win wide endorsement throughout Italy.   Costa's position on the question
of adherence did not gain much support.[88]   The Socialist
Party began to make some progress even in the Romagna.
Not all of Costa's old friends there were willing to accept his position regarding the decisions made at Genoa;
a few of them, notably Alessandro Balducci and Umberto
Brunelli, were enthusiastic supporters of the newly-formed party from the very beginning.[89]   However, the initiative for a general acceptance of the Socialist Party in
the Romagna was taken by some of the younger socialists
of the region.

Late in August the socialist circle of Russi, a small
town in the province of Ravenna, called for the convocation of a regional assembly of socialists to be held at
Russi.[90]   The object of the meeting was to be the organization of the socialists of that province and their adherence to the Partito dei Lavoratori Italiani.[91] The
Russi Congress was held on October 9.   Despite the heated
opposition of Gaetano Zirardini and some of Costa's old
comrades, the majority of the delegates there, led by
Brunelli and Ilo Gherardini of Russi, voted to adhere to
the party.   The decision at this meeting seriously weakened Costa's position.

The decision seems to have upset Costa's friends
more than Costa himself, however.[92]   After his initial

negative reaction, Costa's opposition to the Socialist
Party appears to have slackened. In fact, he seems to
have forgotten about the party almost entirely. Once
more he sank into the lethargy which he had displayed in
the previous few years. Not heeding the pleas of his
friends, he refused to appear at the Russi Congress. Later in the year he also excused himself from Monticelli's
Venetian Congress (which condemned the decisions made at
Genoa), though he was in nominal agreement with the position endorsed there.93

This apathy on Costa's part did much to erode his
authority. A measure of the degree to which Costa's supremacy had been undermined in the Romagna was to be seen
in the way the Imolesi reacted to the Genoa Congress.
The young socialists in Imola, led by Anselmo Marabini,
a personal friend and a disciple of Costa, found themselves in disagreement with their old champion after the
gathering; they were of the opinion that an immediate adherence should be made to the party. Though there is
some question as to exactly what happened, it appears
that these young dissidents broke away from the local
socialist circle (which completely accepted Costa's position), formed an organization of their own, the Circolo
di Studi Sociali, and voted to adhere to the Partito dei
Lavoratori Italiani.94 This adherence was given in October, 1892.95 Even in Imola, then, Costa's traditional
power began to be threatened.96

As if to underline the irreparable decline which he
had suffered by 1892, in November of that year Costa failed in his effort to win re-election as Imola's deputy to
Parliament--this was to be the only period after 1882 in
which he would be absent from Montecitorio.97 This defeat,
more than anything else, illustrated the degree to which
Costa's prestige had ebbed during these years.

Conclusion

The Italian Socialist Party, or the Partito dei Lavoratori Italiani as it was originally called, was founded at the Genoa Congress of 1892. The gathering itself
was the product of two years of preparation. The party,
though, had been in the process of formation all through
the preceding decade. During the 1880's many personalities contributed to its development. The most important
of these was Costa, who in his efforts to make the P.S.R.R.
the nucleus of a national party had been the first to at-

tempt to give the idea of an Italian socialist party a
concrete form. But Costa was too advanced for his times:
in the 1880's existing conditions in Italy precluded the
possibility of a party of the type he envisaged. Propitious conditions did not come about until the 1890's.

By this time the Italian economy had finally advanced
to a point where a proletariat, both industrial and agricultural, which would serve as the foundation of a mass
party, had developed. Perhaps more important was the
fact that by this time socialist ideas had begun to penetrate into the consciousness of the intellectuals, and
in some places, notably Milan and the Po Valley, into
that of the masses. The formation of the Italian Socialist Party in 1892 can be understood only in the light of
these processes.

If Costa had played a leading role in the early development of the party, he had little to do with its actual formation at the Congress of Genoa. The real architect of the party there was Turati. Aided by existing
conditions, but also displaying unusual talents which
permitted him to take full advantage of the situation,
Turati was able to forge the party despite still formidable obstacles.

During 1891-92, Costa retained a good deal of prestige;[98] never, however, was he to have as little influence
on the course of events as in these crucial years. Beset by illness, tired and depressed, Costa displayed little interest in the affairs of his party. Content to occupy himself almost exclusively with local questions in
Imola, he remained there in self-imposed isolation. Despite the efforts of his friends to rouse him from his
apathy, he refused to have anything to do with the momentous work being accomplished. At the Congress of Genoa,
consequently, his impact was minimal.

Not only did Costa refuse to help in the preparation
of the meeting, but he also refused to accept its decisions. It is not hard to explain Costa's negative attitude toward the Genoa gathering and the party which it
had created. The hegemony of the Romagnols over the socialist movement, brought about by virtue of their efforts
to create a national socialist party, had effectively disappeared by the late eighties. But Costa, despite his
awareness of his own personal slump, had never accepted
the fact that the Romagnol initiative had come to an end.
At the Congress of Genoa it was no longer possible to hide

the fact. The Milanesi, it was clear, were the victors at Genoa, the Romagnols the vanquished. The party formed at Genoa symbolized his defeat; Costa's immediate reaction, therefore, was to reject this party.

In refusing to adhere to it, Costa acted illogically. This, after all, was the very party which he had worked to create for over a decade. The contradiction in Costa's behavior was apparent even to the Romagnols, many of whom now followed Balducci in his opposition to Costa. Perhaps this contradiction did not escape Costa himself, whose resistance to the initiative of the Milanesi was generally of a passive nature.

NOTES

[1] A sign of the importance the socialist movement in Italy was beginning to assume at this time was the success the socialists encountered in the political election of 1890. In addition to Prampolini and Maffei, both from Reggio Emilia, other socialists elected to Parliament in this year included Gregorio Agnini, Nicola Badaloni, and Giuseppe De Felice Giuffrida. The latter, a deputy from Sicily, is especially significant because he demonstrates the extent to which the socialist program penetrated even the backward South. Casilli, from Naples, though not a socialist, sympathized with socialist ideas and was a good friend of Costa.

[2] A copy of the circular, published in Rome on Jan. 29, is found at the Biblioteca Comunale in Imola.

[3] See the letter from Veraldi to Costa, Feb. 21, 1891, B.C.I., no. 1149. Quoted, in part, in Manacorda, Il movimento operaio italiano, p. 315.

[4] The socialist circle, F. Lassalle of Bologna, while it adhered to the gathering, suggested that it be held in some other city. See letter from Barbanti-Brodano, the circle's secretary, to the organizing commission, Mar. 11, 1891, B.C.I., no. 1158.

[5] Prefect of Forlì to the Minister of Interior, Mar. 11, 1891, A.S.F., Gab. Pref., vol. 145, fasc. 72.

[6] La Lotta (Forlì), Apr. 29, 1891.

[7] Issue of June 28, 1891.

[8] Letter from Barbanti-Brodano to Costa, Feb. 12, 1892 B.C.I., no. 1181.

[9] See Angiolo Cabrini's letter to Costa, May 20, 1891, B.C.I., no. 1189.

[10] Letter of July 31, 1891, reproduced in La corrispondenza di Marx e Engels con italiani, p. 397. Kuliscioff, too, was worried about the implications of Costa's preoc-

cupation with local affairs. See her letter to Costa, Apr. 29, 1891, B.C.I., no. 1181.

[11]Labriola, who was against the cooperative movement because of its anti-revolutionary character, wrote Engels: "This business of the cooperatives is especially flourishing in Romagna and Emilia, where many people make their living from it, as middle-men, string-pullers, book-keepers, and secretaries. It is to this business that Costa has now given himself, running continually to prefects and ministers, and without this industry he would never be... re-elected as deputy for Imola...." See letter of Aug. 14, 1891, La corrispondenza di Marx e Engels con italiani, pp. 401-02.

[12]For a recent study on this movement, see "La cooperazione in Italia," in Ricci-Garotti and Cossarini, La cooperazione. Of more local interest are Sergio Nardi, "Il movimento cooperativo ravennate dalle origini al fascismo," in Nullo Baldini nella storia della cooperazione, pp. 389-566, and Nazario Galassi, La cooperazione imolese dalle origini ai nostri giorni (1859-1967) (Imola: Galeati, 1968).

[13]This is one of the reasons the republicans enthusiastically supported the cooperatives. For a comparison of the socialist and republican views of the cooperative, see Costa's article on the braccianti in Avanti!, July 6, 1884.

[14]Though he was convinced that cooperation would not solve the social question, Costa insisted that it would serve as a means of educating the worker. See his article on the braccianti of Ravenna in Avanti!, Apr. 27, 1884.

[15]Zangheri, "Andrea Costa e le lotte contadine del suo tempo," p. 17.

[16]He was elected president in 1889, according to Galassi, p. 69.

[17]Il Moto, May 24, 1891.

[18]Manacorda, Il movimento operaio italiano, p. 299.

[19]Compte-rendu in I Malfattori (Imola), Oct. 18, 1890 (the only issue of this paper, published by Adamo Mancini). See also a Rimini correspondence, dated Oct. 15, in La

Campana (Ancona-Macerata), Oct. 19, 1890. According to
the latter article, all the delegates (who represented every major city in the Romagna), with the exception of thos
from Cesena and Savignano, "strongly affirmed their revolutionary anarchist faith." Castellari, Francolini, Mancini, Mazzotti, and Nabruzzi were among the conferees.

[20]The Capolago Congress is described in La Gazzetta
ticinese (Lugano), Jan. 4, 8, and 9, 1891, and in La Riven
dicazione, Jan. 10, 1891. Its deliberations were publishe
in Piselli's paper on Jan. 18.

[21]The anarchists made it clear that this gathering was
not to be confined exclusively to members of their own fac
tion, but rather it was intended to unite both anarchists
and socialists into one strong party. See Gaetano Benzi's
letter, dated Dec. 10, published in La Rivendicazione, Dec
27, 1890. It is clear, however, as Manacorda points out,
that the anarchists had no intention of compromising their
program; in reality, they wanted to force the socialists
to abandon their legalitarian principles (Il movimento
operaio italiano, p. 310).

[22]Manacorda, Il movimento operaio italiano, p. 309.

[23]The Romagnols at Capolago included Piselli, Sandri,
Bondi, Valbonesi, Giovanni Merendi, Luigi Gottarelli, Giu-
lio Marchese, and Cajo Zavoli (questore to the prefect of
Bologna, Jan. 23, 1891, A.S.F., Gab. Pref., vol. 146, fasc
79).

[24]Labriola described him as "the great elector of Fortis." See letter to Engels, May 21, 1892, La corrispondenza di Marx e Engels con italiani, p. 433.

[25]Outside Italy, on the other hand, the "individualists" were very active. It was an Italian anarchist, Dante Jeronimo Caserio, who assassinated Sadi Carnot, President of the French Republic, on May 24, 1894. Michele An-
giolillo, another Italian anarchist, assassinated Antonio
Cánovas, the Spanish Prime Minister, on Aug. 8, 1897. And
another Italian, Luigi Luccheni, assassinated Elizabeth of
Bavaria, Empress of Austria, on Sept. 10, 1898. Significantly, it was an exile, Gaetano Bresci, recently returned
from the United States, who killed King Umberto I on July
29, 1900.

[26]Subprefect of Rimini to the prefect of Forlì, Jan.
26, 1891, A.S.F., Gab. Pref., vol. 146, fasc. 79.

387

[27]An account of the Ronco Congress is given in La Rivendicazione, Feb. 7, 1891.

[28]A copy of this program is contained in a communication from the Minister of Interior to the prefect of Forlì, Feb. 16, 1891, A.S.F., Gab. Pref., vol. 146, fasc. 79.

[29]Prefect of Forlì to the Minister of Interior, Feb. 13, 1891, A.S.F., Gab. Pref., vol. 146, fasc. 79. According to the police, the following were chosen as section leaders at Ronco: Valducci, Alfredo Turci, and Giuseppe Gozzi at Cesena; Serafino Mazzotti at Faenza; Gottarelli at Lugo; Nabruzzi and Cajo Gherardini at Ravenna; and Cajo Zavoli at Rimini (report to the prefect of Forlì, Feb. 11, 1891, A.S.F., Gab. Pref., vol. 146, fasc. 79).

[30]Note to the prefect of Forlì, Feb. 17, 1891, A.S.F., Gab. Pref., vol. 146, fasc. 79.

[31]There is also some evidence that Cipriani was trying to persuade the collectivist republicans to accept the party program. On Jan. 25 he promoted a reunion of anarchists in the city of Rimini. The scope of this meeting, according to the local subprefect, was to bring about an agreement between the anarchists, on the one hand, and the socialists and collectivist republicans, on the other. Both socialists and collectivists, though, refused to adhere to the meeting, and Renzetti, the head of the local collectivist republican group, refused to attend. See report to the prefect of Forlì, Jan. 26, 1891, A.S.F., Gab. Pref. vol. 146, fasc. 79.

[32]Prefect of Forlì to the Minister of Interior, Jan. 20, 1891, A.S.F., Gab. Pref., vol. 146, fasc. 79.

[33]Ibid. Significantly, Costa was absent from the meeting. He had probably been invited but had refused to go to Forlì, just as he had done earlier in the month when he declined an invitation to attend a Forlì meeting which was held to discuss the Capolago program. See report from the prefect of Forlì to the Minister of Interior, Jan. 9, 1891, A.S.F., Gab. Pref., vol. 146, fasc. 79. Costa, it seems, was losing his interest in the activity of the party even in his own region.

[34]The meeting at Ronco was supposed to unite the anarchist party in the provinces of Forlì, Ravenna, Bologna, and Ferrara. According to the prefect of Forlì, however, Bologna sent only two representatives to the meeting (one

of them was Castellari from Imola) and Ferrara did not send any at all. See report to the Minister of Interior, Feb. 13, 1891, A.S.F., Gab. Pref., vol. 146, fasc. 79.

[35]Report of the subprefect of Rimini to the prefect of Forlì, Feb. 6, 1891, A.S.F., Gab. Pref., vol. 146, fasc. 79.

[36]Prefect of Forlì to the subprefect of Cesena, Mar. 21, 1891, A.S.F., Gab. Pref., vol. 145, fasc. 77. On Feb. 1, Valducci founded a new Fascio Operaio Socialista in competition with the older socialist circle in Cesena which was headed by the Battistini brothers. The carabinieri reported that Valducci's organization was "almost anarchist." See report to the prefect of Forlì, Mar. 19, 1891, A.S.F., Gab. Pref., vol. 145, fasc. 77. The ideological difference between the circle headed by Valducci and that headed by the Battistini brothers, however, must not have been too great, since it is reported that Valducci's association was represented by La Lotta, Balducci's legalitarian newspaper at Forlì. See the list of new associations in Cesena signed Mar. 18, 1891, A.S.F., Gab. Pref., vol. 145, fasc. 77.

[37]Report of the police inspector to the prefect of Forlì, Apr. 2, 1891, A.S.F., Gab. Pref., vol. 145, fasc. 79. Bazzocchi, a local anarchist, had helped Romeo Mingozzi organize the anarchist movement in Forlì during the mid-1880's.

[38]Subprefect of Rimini to the prefect of Forlì, Jan. 25, 1891, A.S.F., Gab. Pref., vol. 146, fasc. 79. Later in the year, the subprefect of Rimini noted that though Zavoli was the most dangerous anarchist in this city, he had little influence among the other members of his party, for in the last election he had backed a monarchist candidate, and therefore he was considered a traitor even by his friends. See report to the prefect of Forlì, June 12, 1891, A.S.F., Gab. Pref., vol. 149, fasc. 74.

[39]Manacorda, Il movimento operaio italiano, p. 314.

[40]Santarelli, Il socialismo anarchico in Italia, p. 84.

[41]Subprefect of Imola to the prefect of Bologna, Mar. 21, 1891, A.S.B., Gab. Pref., cat. VI, 1891.

[42]Subprefect of Rimini to the prefect of Forlì, Sept.

30, 1891, A.S.F., Gab. Pref., vol. 149, fasc. 73. Emigration was not limited to the Romagnols. Among those who
fled to the New World in this year was Malatesta, who remained absent from Italy for many years.

[43]Subprefect of Rimini to the prefect of Forlì, Dec.
15, 1891, A.S.F., Gab. Pref., vol. 149, fasc. 73.

[44]On Apr. 6, 1892, the prefect of Bologna informed
the Minister of Interior that while there were many socialists in his province, the anarchists were few in number, disorganized, and in need of funds (A.S.B., Gab.
Pref., cat. VI, 1892).

[45]Useful biographies: Alessandro Schiavi, Filippo
Turati (Rome: Opere Nuove, 1955); Franco Catalano, Filippo Turati (Milan: Avanti!, 1957).

[46]For Turati's early development see Turati giovane:
Scapigliatura, positivismo, marxismo, ed. Luigi Cortesi
(Milan: Avanti!, 1962).

[47]"As far as socialism is concerned, essentially, I
believe that there is only one, the Marxist form, unless
you want to consider the various forms which are characteristic of thought which varies from person to person and
nation to nation, but which varies in form rather than
substance, if it wants to be a scientific and positive
socialism." See letter from Turati to Costa, Sept. 30,
1890. Quoted in Manacorda, Il movimento operaio italiano,
p. 403.

[48]Giuseppe Mammarella, Riformisti e rivoluzionari nel
partito socialista italiano, 1900-1912 (Padua: Marsilio,
1968), p. 14.

[49]Though Lipparini suggests that it was only in 1885
that the romance ended definitively. See Andrea Costa,
p. 240.

[50]See Lazzari's "Memorie," Movimento operaio, ed.
Alessandro Schiavi, 5 (1952), 789.

[51]An account is to be found in Critica sociale, Aug.
20, 1891, and in Il Moto, Aug. 9, 1891. The latter expressed a very favorable opinion on the proceedings at
Milan.

[53]Manacorda, Il movimento operaio italiano, p. 326.
The Romagnols displayed little interest in the meeting

(<u>questore</u> to the prefect of Bologna, June 3, 1891, A.S.B., <u>Gab</u>. <u>Pref</u>., cat. VI, 1891). In fact, it does not appear that any of the leading Romagnols attended the sessions; certainly this is true of the socialists in the province of Forlì (<u>carabinieri</u> to the prefect of Forlì, June 23, 1891, A.S.F., <u>Gab</u>. <u>Pref</u>., vol. 145, fasc. 72).

[54]Subprefect of Rimini to the prefect of Forlì, Sept. 30, 1891, A.S.F., <u>Gab</u>. <u>Pref</u>., vol. 149, fasc. 73.

[55]On July 21, Croce had written him: "A great many invitations to the Congress of Milan...were sent to Romagna, but up to now zero adherences! I therefore turn to you for news, certain that you will want to concern yourself with the matter in these last few days before the Congress, which will be well-attended and important for the working-class and socialist movement. Will you come?" Quoted in Manacorda, <u>Il</u> <u>movimento</u> <u>operaio</u> <u>italiano</u>, p. 391

[56]In February, Antonio Fratti wrote to Costa informing him of the friction which existed between the two parties in Cesena during that period (letter of Feb. 13, 1891, B.C.I., no. 1144).

[57]On Sept. 20, <u>Il</u> <u>Moto</u> carried a letter from the leaders of the republican and socialist parties in the Romagna asking the Cesenati of both parties to remain calm. Apparently Costa had already written a personal letter to this effect to Battistini's followers. See the letter from the socialist federation of Cesena to Costa, Sept. 16, 1891, B.C.I., no. 1230. The Cesenati were irritated by Costa's request but reluctantly complied.

[58]Minister of Interior to the prefect of Bologna, Apr. 23, 1892, A.S.B., <u>Gab</u>. <u>Pref</u>., cat. VII, 1892. Costa's personal deterioration may have been responsible for the fact that while the anarchists of the Romagna generally grew weaker in 1892, in Imola a large number of socialists entered into the ranks of the local anarchist party. See subprefect of Imola to the prefect of Bologna, May 16, 1892, A.S.B., <u>Gab</u>. <u>Pref</u>., cat. VII, 1892.

[59]Anarchist attacks on Costa had not stopped even during this period. See Luigi Cortesi, <u>La</u> <u>costituzione</u> <u>del</u> <u>partito</u> <u>socialista</u> <u>italiano</u> (Milan: Avanti!, 1962), p. 103.

[60]The first letter from Graziadei to Costa, who obviously was not acquainted with the young man at this time

seems to be that of Jan. 13, 1891, B.C.I., no. 1133.

[61] *Memorie*, p. 28.

[62] See Kuliscioff's letter to Costa, July 15, 1892, B.C.I., no. 1343. In this letter, Kuliscioff expressed surprise that Costa had been so short with her. The exact nature of his criticism, however, is not made clear.

[63] So serious was the misunderstanding that Costa tried to have Baldi fired as Imola's correspondent to *Il Secolo* and to have Marabini replace him. Moneta, the publisher of *Il Secolo*, refused to accede to Costa's wishes, however. See Moneta's letter to Costa, June 26, 1892, B.C.I., no. 1339. Not satisfied with Moneta's refusal, Costa answered the letter of June 26 "rudely," according to Moneta. See letter to Costa, July 9, 1892, B.C.I., no. 1342. The trouble between Baldi and Costa seems to have been due mainly to the latter, for as Moneta informed Costa (letter of July 9): "Baldi never said anything against you ...." The nature of the disagreement between Baldi and Costa is not known; in fact, it escaped even their mutual friends. See Barbanti-Brodano's letter to Costa, Apr. 10, 1892, B.C.I., no. 1302.

[64] Costa felt that Signora Lunati, who owned a small business in Imola, had taken unfair advantage of two of her young apprentices. For the documents related to the duel see Elviro Lunati, *Vertenza Costa-Lunati* (Imola: Tip. Sociale, 1893). Sassi and Gaetano Zirardini, incidentally, acted as Costa's seconds in this duel.

[65] Cortesi, *La costitutione del partito socialista italiano*, p. 23.

[66] See, for example, the letters to Costa from Giovanni Florito, Feb. 5, 1890, B.C.I., no. 959; Francesco Cini, Jan. 28, 1891, B.C.I., no. 1140; and Kuliscioff, July 26, 1892, B.C.I., no. 1351.

[67] Letter of May 16, 1892, B.C.I., no. 1326. Quoted, in part, in Cortesi, *La costituzione del partito socialista italiano*, p. 99.

[68] Letters from Kuliscioff to Costa, July 26, 1892, cited above, and Prampolini to Costa, Aug. 7, 1892, B.C.I., no. 1356. Monticelli, however, thought that at the assembly Costa should serve a different function: "At the Congress of Genoa it will be necessary...to carry the good

word and try to tone down disagreements, to conciliate tempers, to unite the various forces, and no one can fulfill these functions better than you." See letter to Costa, Aug. 5, 1892, B.C.I., no. 1355.

[69]See Monticelli's letter of Aug. 5, 1892, cited above.

[70]The most important descriptions of the gathering are to be found in Lotta di classe (Milan), Aug. 20-21, and in Il Moto, Aug. 21, 1892. Both accounts are included in the Appendix to Cortesi, La costituzione del partito socialista italiano.

[71]"A fist fight was avoided by a hair," according to L'Ordine, Aug. 20, 1892, an anarchist newspaper based in Turin.

[72]After Turati and Costa, Prampolini is probably the most influential figure in the history of the Italian socialist movement of the nineteenth century. Biographies of the Emilian leader include: Giovanni Zibordi, Saggio sulla storia del movimento operaio in Italia: Camillo Prampolini e i lavoratori reggiani, 2nd ed. (Bari: Laterza, 1930); Renato Marmiroli, Camillo Prampolini (Florence: Barbèra, 1948); and Luigi Arbizzani, Camillo Prampolini (Milan: Il Calendario del Popolo, 1967).

[73]Felice Anzi, one of the participants at the meeting, recalled that all through the first session Costa had appeared discouraged and sad. Costa's decline was evident even in his appearance. See "Tenersi alla corda," Genova, 1892: Nascita del partito socialista in Italia (Milan: Avanti!, 1952), p. 24.

[74]Il Moto, Aug. 21, 1892.

[75]Not all the Romagnols, though, followed Costa: Alessandro Balducci stayed on and took a very active part in the deliberations at the Sala dei Carabinieri. Costa was so upset with Balducci that he refused to talk to his old friend before leaving Genoa. See Balducci, Alessandro Balducci, p. 56.

[76]Il Moto, Aug. 21, 1892.

[77]Even Marabini, in that period very close to Costa, was unable to explain why Costa took this contradictory stand. See Prime lotte socialiste, p. 145.

[78]Cortesi, _La costituzione del partito socialista italiano_, p. 108.

[79]The Imolesi had protested when in 1891 the anarchists were expelled from the international Congress of Brussels. See _Il Moto_, Sept. 6, 1891.

[80]_Il Moto_, Aug. 21, 1892.

[81]Ibid.

[82]Manacorda, _Il movimento operaio italiano_, p. 350.

[83]See Turati's letter to Costa, Apr. 5, 1884, reproduced in Manacorda, _Il movimento operaio italiano_, p. 392.

[84]Despite Turati's repeated invitations, Costa refused to collaborate on _Critica sociale_. See Turati's letter to Costa, May 20, 1892, reproduced in Manacorda, _Il movimento operaio italiano_, pp. 408-09.

[85]In his letter of May 16, 1892 (see above), Monticelli had tried to persuade Costa to attend the Genoa meeting because, as he said, "I would be very happy to see you resume the leadership of our movement, to that position to which Turati, who does not have your glorious past of struggle and suffering, aspires under the stimulus of Anna Kuliscioff." He went on to inform Costa that, "I have not been the first to see things this way: I repeat this after having heard it from the lips of Maffei and Prampolini, and I repeat it without ulterior motives and without the comments which the others...make."

[86]Despite their lengthy separation, Costa appears to have retained something of his romantic affection for Kuliscioff (see Kuliscioff's letter of July 15, 1892, cited above; also Kuliscioff to Costa, July 7, 1903, B.C,I., no. 3195, quoted in Pala, _Anna Kuliscioff_, pp. 114-15), and a certain amount of jealousy toward Turati would not have been unnatural. In the voluminous correspondence which Kuliscioff exchanged with Costa after 1884, when she met the Milanese, there is, discreetly, hardly ever any mention of Turati.

[87]On his part, Turati always seems to have maintained a great deal of respect for Costa, whom he admired for his role as a pioneer in the socialist movement. See _Critica sociale_, June 1, 1892. In the crucial period 1891-92, Turati rather than neglecting the apathetic Costa

tried to solicit his cooperation. He sought Costa's collaboration in the publication of both Critica sociale and
Lotta di classe. See letter from Turati to Costa, July
17, 1892, reproduced in Manacorda, Il movimento operaio
italiano, pp. 410-11. He also attempted to get Costa to
take an active part in preparing the Genoa Congress. See
his letter to Costa, June 17, 1892, reproduced in Manacorda, Il movimento operaio italiano, p. 410.

[88]Monticelli, who shared Costa's views, tried to convoke a regional congress at Venice in order to initiate
the formation of a second socialist party. The gathering
of October 16, however, drew little support and proved
to be a complete failure. See Cortesi, La costituzione
del partito socialista italiano, p. 133.

[89]Balducci, through his newspaper La Lotta, which in
1891 had been transferred from Forlì to Bologna, soon became the leading advocate of Romagnol adherence to the
Socialist Party. See La Lotta, Aug. 20, 1892.

[90]This circle, together with the bracciante cooperative of Castelbolognese, had been represented at Genoa
by Turati, according to Cortesi, La costituzione del partito socialista italiano, p. 300. This shows the extent
to which Costa's influence was being superseded in the
Romagna by that of the Milanesi.

[91]The circular announcing the meeting was published
in Lotta di classe, Aug. 27-18, 1892. The Milanese paper
later carried a short account of the assembly. See issue
of Oct. 15-16, 1892.

[92]"This provincial socialist meeting at Russi," Claudi
Zirardini wrote to Costa on Sept. 24, 1892, "...carries
the promise of an important discussion and decision; and
that does not set well with everyone on first sight. Must
we really forget...the tradition of the old Romagnol socialist party which has its history and content ourselves
by wearing the new shirt of class struggle? If only it
were another red shirt! ...we cannot accept, only in part
never completely, the blandishments of the new program...
in the Romagna we should conserve our own form of revolutionary socialism, of which you were and still are the
recognized leader" (B.C.I., no. 1379, reproduced in "Carteggio C. Zirardini--A. Costa," pp. 639-40).

[93]Letter from Costa to Monticelli, Oct. 1, 1892, published in Socialismo popolare, Monticelli's newspaper in

Venice, Oct. 16, 1892.

[94]Cortesi, La costituzione del partito socialista italiano, p. 200. Cortesi bases his account on that of Graziadei (Memorie, p. 32), one of the young dissidents. Marabini, however, insisted that there had been no schism; the young socialists, he claimed, had persuaded the others to accept their point of view, and all the Imolesi, therefore, had adhered to the new party in 1892. See Prime lotte socialiste, pp. 145-46.

[95]Lotta di classe, Oct. 15-16, 1892.

[96]According to Marabini, p. 146, Costa's defeat was not total, for when informed by his young followers of the course they planned to follow, he said he was in agreement with them and even presided over the meeting in which they made a formal adherence to the Socialist Party. Cortesi, while he disagrees with Marabini on other points, says that this was entirely possible. See La costituzione del partito socialista italiano, p. 222. Costa, it seems, had accepted the formation of the Partito dei Lavoratori Italiani on principle; only pride prevented his formal adherence to it.

[97]The main reason for Costa's defeat seems to have been the scant interest which he took in the election. He very reluctantly accepted the candidacy. See Il Moto, Oct. 21, 1892. In fact, there was serious doubt that he would accept the nomination even if elected. See Amilcare Zamorani's letter to Costa, Oct. 14, 1892, B.C.I., no. 1398. Apparently, too, the conservatives had won by cheating at the polls. But despite the efforts which the Masons in Rome made on his behalf--see the letters from M. Bacci to Decio Fantini, Dec. 13 and 20, 1892, B.C.I., nos. 1409 and 1412--the government refused to annul the election of Costa's opponent.

[98]"Come...because among these workers you are more beloved than God once was." See letter to Costa from Pietro Munari of Schio (in Venetia), July 24, 1891, B.C.I., no. 1211. In the South, too, Costa continued to be widely admired at this time. Gaetano Salvemini, then a young socialist, wrote to Turati in 1892 and asked him if Costa might be persuaded to make a speech in Molfetta (in Apulia). "...having carefully studied the situation," Salvemini wrote, "it seems to me that it is now time for some socialist deputy to come here; and this deputy should be Costa, who has an extremely popular reputation among the

workers and in the last elections received 398 votes in our city against the 1,000 given to the radical; and it was his first attempt." See letter of Aug. 12, 1892, B.C.I., no. 1359.

CHAPTER ELEVEN

CONCLUSION

The minor role which Costa played at Genoa and his
general decline during those years tend to obscure his
historical importance. But it should not be forgotten
that Costa was one of the patriarchs of Italian socialism.[1] In the decade which preceded the Genoa Congress
it was Costa, more than any other individual, who provided the leadership for the socialist movement in his
country. During that period he made several important
contributions to the movement.

Without a doubt Costa was the decisive figure in the
transition from anarchism to socialism in Italy.[2] This
is not to say that the Romagnol leader was the first major Internationalist to make this conversion; others,
notably the Milanesi, did it before Costa. But their defection from the I.W.A. did not weaken it to any great
extent. Costa's svolta, on the other hand, had far more
serious implications: his letter to his friends in the
Romagna in 1879 caused a mass exodus from the old International. (Because Costa "was the man most loved in the
cities where the Internationalists were most numerous,"
Malatesta later admitted, "he cast schism and confusion
among us and was among the principal causes of the death
of the Association").[3] It was only after his initiative
that socialism became a significant force in Italian life.
The part he played in bringing about this process is certainly the most noteworthy of Costa's achievements.

In order to give practical effect to the ideas he
came to embrace after 1879, Costa set out to create a socialist organization--this was another major contribution
which he made to the socialist movement. Costa's efforts
to create a national socialist party extended all through
the 1880's. As we have seen, this attempt met with scant
success. Outside of the Romagna--and a few isolated areas
--the P.S.R.R. never really had much vitality. It seemed
that Costa's efforts had been in vain. But his failure
was more apparent than real, for if the party had all but
disappeared by the end of the decade, Costa left an important legacy: he had put forth the very important idea

of the organization of a socialist workers' party. This was the party which was created at the Congress of Genoa in 1892. Consequently, while Costa played only a minor role at that time, it is clear that his pioneering efforts at organization did much to prepare the socialists for the events which took place in the Ligurian city.

Another form of organization which Costa encouraged was that of the cooperative movement. As an anarchist, he had vehemently opposed it. Associations of this kind, he insisted, tended to lull the worker into an acceptance of the status quo.[4] As he made the transition to socialism, however, he gradually changed his attitude toward the movement. While he always remained conscious of its drawbacks and insisted that the workers should not put too much faith in it, during the 1880's he came to accept the cooperative on principle.[5]

He was especially sympathetic toward the bracciante cooperatives, and did much to encourage their growth.[6] Costa believed that they could be used as a means of radicalizing the countryside. He was probably correct. In 1891 a contemporary student of the agrarian problem in Italy--a conservative--noted that the braccianti of the South, though more miserable economically than those of any other part of Italy, did not rebel while the Romagnols did. The Southerners were passive, she concluded, "because they are not organized: in the Romagna they are, and therefore...they are prepared to fight against the proprietors and the authorities in order to extort through violence that which they desire."[7] Costa's efforts on behalf of the cooperative movement, as is clear from this account, had far-reaching consequences, and it is for this reason that they constitute one of his major achievements.

Unfortunately, Costa's role as an educator and teacher has generally not been recognized.[8] In popularizing socialist ideas, nevertheless, Costa proved to be much more successful than he was in making the transition from anarchism to socialism and in creating effective socialist organizations. His propaganda had an impact throughout Italy. Its most powerful effect, though, was felt in the Romagna and the surrounding area. By the beginning of the twentieth century the Partito Socialista Italiano drew its greatest support from the region of Emilia-Romagna.[9] Today this same region forms the backbone of the Communist Party, the heir to the socialist tradition in Italy. Undoubtedly Costa's propaganda has much to do with the radicalism which has characterized this area in our century.

Certainly this is true in Imola, where the vast majority of citizens were already staunch socialists by the eve of World War I.[10] The city's socialist composition, in fact, soon became legendary. In the late twenties, in one of his best novels, Ernest Hemingway had occasion to allude to it when he described a conversation between his protagonist and a group of Italians:

"Are you really anarchists?" I asked.
"No, Tenente. We're socialists. We come from Imola."
"Haven't you ever been there?"
"No."
"By Christ it's a fine place, Tenente. You come there after the war and we'll show you something."
"Are you all socialists?"
"Everybody."
"Is it a fine town?"
"Wonderful. You never saw a town like that."
"How did you get to be socialists?"
"We're all socialists. Everybody is a socialist. We've always been socialists."
"You come, Tenente. We'll make you a socialist too."[11]

As a propagandist Costa had few equals. A trememdous orator, he dominated the various meetings at which he spoke. "The speaker who aroused the most sympathy," a contemporary recalled, "who attracted, electrified, fanaticized, was always Andrea Costa."[12] Years later, Giovanni Merloni, a socialist from Cesena, recalled the strong impression Costa's speeches had first made on him:

The first time that I heard Andrea Costa speak, that I saw and heard him, I might have been ten or eleven years old. The impression of that day has remained strong in my mind....I do not remember what he said. More than the words, I felt the wave of his powerful and brilliant voice, and I was moved by the impetus of the warlike song which he seemed to raise high over the flags and the people gathered there. It was music, harmonious and strong, which excited /us/ like the sound of a reveille, like a blasting trumpet before the attack.[13]

Even during the period of his decline Costa's speeches continued to stir his audiences. Describing a speech

401

ANDREA COSTA
Biblioteca Comunale di Imola

which the Imolese had made at Rovigo in December, 1892, Carlo Monticelli wrote: "The learned, lofty, and inspired word which aroused the assembly to enthusiasm has moved, as if we were neophytes, even us--even us, who after seven years of propaganda consider ourselves to be old veterans."[14]

Students of the Italian workers' movement are familiar with Costa's propaganda among the workers and artisans of the cities. Yet few of these scholars realize the extent to which he was able to popularize socialist ideas in the Italian countryside. Costa took a special interest in the peasantry.[15] His agitation played a large part in making Emilia-Romagna the center of the Italian peasant movement after 1890.[16] The impact of Costa's ideas among the peasantry has been underestimated largely because it was indirect. While he often spoke before the peasants who lived in and around the smaller villages, particularly in his own region, Costa generally concentrated on spreading his ideas in the larger cities, where he had wider audiences. Many of the peasant leaders, however, came under his spell, and it was through them that socialist ideas found their way into the countryside.[17] One of the first of these men was Leonida Bissolati, who propagandized the district around Cremona. As a young student at the University of Bologna, Bissolati had witnessed Costa's trial at that city in 1876. Afterwards, he wrote Costa: "I...have felt a repugnance when confronted by the enormous injustices of this society and have dreamed of devoting myself to combatting it from the time that I was a child, and when I saw so many convinced and active /followers/ with you, I felt it resurge powerfully within me and incite me to the fight."[18] Another of Costa's disciples was Prampolini, the greatest of the socialist agitators in the countryside. Ideologically, there were many ideas which the two men had in common: they agreed on the need to establish socialist alliances with other democratic parties; both believed that the primary function of the socialist deputy was propaganda outside of Parliament; both stressed the moral content of socialist ideas. These similarities were not altogether casual, for, as has been pointed out, Prampolini was "an intellectual son of Costa."[19]

In 1908 Michels commented that one of the essential differences between socialism in Germany and in Italy was that in the latter country its moral purpose seemed to be much more pronounced.[20] The emphasis placed on morality was indeed one of the outstanding aspects of the movement in Italy. It was a characteristic which Costa helped to give it--yet another of his major contributions to the socialist tradition in his country.

Costa was aware that in order to improve society, its economic foundations had to be altered. But he also knew that the socialists needed to do more than change the material environment. "Let us remember that, above all else," he once said, "ours is also a great task of human education...."[21] On another occasion he insisted, "Socialism is not just a struggle for material existence, but is the highest expression of human sentiment...."[22]

In popularizing his ideas Costa chose to emphasize the ethical scope of socialism. So did most of the other leaders of the Italian movement. Undoubtedly the emphasis on morality was a legacy which had been transmitted by the old International. Recalling the International and his participation in it, in 1898 Costa noted this very aspect of the organization: "Our problem was human. We considered it thus. It was man. The humanization of man." The Internationalists were motivated, he recalled, not by economic conditions, but "by the idea of natural equality, of dignity, of human liberty...."[23] Their rebellion was therefore a moral one.[24]

Concerned primarily with the ethical ends of socialism, the Italians tended to de-emphasize its impersonal elements. One result was that Marxism, a mechanistic and scientific philosophy, was accepted only hesitantly in Italy, and it was never completely understood.[25] This was true throughout the peninsula, but particularly in the Romagna, where the character of the people rebelled against an ideology of this kind;[26] hence the persistence of anarchist elements there long after they had exhausted their currency in other regions.

Costa himself embraced Marxism but found it difficult to accept many of its basic tenets. The humanitarian ideas of his anarchist past never completely gave way to the more scientific ones which were to be found in Marxist thought. Costa did not see socialism as a system, he wrote in 1882, "but as the widest expression of the perfectibility of man...."[27] The Marxian concept of class struggle, in particular, always remained foreign to his way of thinking.[28] As Pier Paolo Rampazzi points out, Costa's ideas were largely pre-Marxist: they found their source of inspiration in the French Enlightenment and the utopian socialism which sprang from it both in France and in Italy.29

The role played by French thought in shaping Costa's ideas was intensely felt. While Turati and the Milanesi patterned their program after that of German Marxism, Costa's socialism had much in common with that of Benoît Malon and the French Integralists. Malon opposed class struggle on principle; he insisted that all means, both revolutionary and reformist, should be used to create a perfect society; and in order to achieve this end he even encouraged the formation of democratic alliances.30 This humanitarian and eclectic socialism was also characteristic of Costa. Ideologically, it seems, the Romagnol had gained much from his personal contact with his old adversary. And yet while it is important to understand the intellectual roots of Costa's thought, they should not be overestimated. Costa's philosophy, after all, was not primarily intellectual. His socialism, like that of Garibaldi--and even Turati--was above all a socialism of the heart rather than of the head.31

The transition from anarchism to socialism, the organization of socialist associations, the popularization of socialist ideas, and the shaping of these ideas in a more humanitarian direction--Costa played a major role in all these processes. Perhaps his greatest contribution to the movement, though, came during his darkest hour, during the period immediately following the Congress of Genoa.

By 1893 Costa had still not adhered to the Socialist Party, nor had the majority of the Romagnols. The Second National Congress of the Partito dei Lavoratori Italiani was to be held at Reggio Emilia in September of that year. As the date of the meeting approached, it became necessary for the Romagnols to make a decision. On August 27 they held a regional gathering at Imola and, after a brief discussion, unanimously adopted Gaetano Zirardini's proposal that the Romagnols join the party.32 They also formed a regional organization of the party, the Federazione Socialista Romagnola. One of the officers of the federation was Costa.33

Costa was also chosen to serve as president at the Reggio Emilia Congress. Though he had not formally committed himself to the Partito dei Lavoratori Italiani, Costa had in fact joined it. His official adherence came in December, at a regional congress which was held in Faenza.34 It was here that Costa was nominated to the

405

party's National Council. He now took his rightful place
among the party's leading representatives. Unwilling to
divide the new organization, Costa had submitted to its
dictates. "This," as Turati noted many years later, "...
was the main service which he rendered; the truest kind
of heroism."35

NOTES

[1]Renato Marmiroli, Socialisti, e non, controluce
(Parma: La Nazionale, 1966), p. 44.

[2]Lelio Basso, "Ritratti critici di contemporanei:
Andrea Costa," Belfagor, 7 (1952), 55.

[3]Quoted in Masini, Storia degli anarchici italiani,
p. 212.

[4]See Costa's letter to Il Nettuno, Oct. 1, 1877,
quoted in Zangheri, "Il Nettuno...e il suo direttore Domenico Francolini," pp. 255-56.

[5]Another champion of the cooperative movement was
Camillo Prampolini. His attitude toward the cooperatives,
though, was much more positive than Costa's. See his letter to Costa, n.d., B.C.I., no. 4471. Abetted by Prampolini and Antonio Vergnanini, the cooperative movement in
Reggio Emilia soon grew to be the most powerful in all of
Italy. The whole province of Reggio Emilia, in fact, came
to be known as "la provincia cooperativa." See Mario
Franceschelli, "Appunti sulle origini del movimento cooperativo italiano," Cooperazione ravennate, 1 (Dec.,
1952), 25.

[6]According to Sergio Nardi, it was Costa who had inspired the founding of the famous Associazione Generale
degli Operai Braccianti of Ravenna ("Il movimento cooperativo ravennate...," p. 408).

[7]Maria Pasolini, Una famiglia di mezzadri romagnoli
nel comune di Ravenna (Bologna: Tip. Fava e Garagnani,
1891), p. 8.

[8]Giovanni Zibordi, Un cavaliere dell'ideale (Milan:
Avanti!, 1916), p. 11. This, however, is not universally
true. According to Alessandro Schiavi, the most significant contributions to the socialist movement were made by
Malatesta, Baldini, Turati, and Costa. Costa's contribution consisted in "the transition from anarchism to legalitarian socialism, and his awakening, organizing, and educating propaganda...." See letter to Baldini, Feb. 16,
1942, quoted by Aldo Berselli, "Profilo di Nullo Baldini,"

Nullo Baldini nella storia della cooperazione, p. 152.

[9] Michels, *Il proletariato e la borghesia*, p. 176.

[10] In 1913 there were 8,420 socialists among the 8,655 registered voters in Imola, according to Lorenzo Bedeschi, "Il comportamento religioso in Emilia-Romagna," *Studi storici*, 10 (1969), 391.

[11] *A Farewell to Arms* (New York: Scribner's, 1929), p. 208.

[12] Mazzini, *Imola d'una volta*, I, 101.

[13] *Il Cuneo* (Cesena), Feb. 5, 1910. Romeo Galli also recalled the first speech he had heard Costa make: "It was delirium for the youngsters, a marvel for those who were older...." See *Corriere padana* (Padua), Aug. 5, 1952.

[14] *Socialismo popolare*, Dec. 4, 1892.

[15] He has been described as "a great apostle of the peasant masses," by Nardi, "Il movimento cooperativo ravennate...," p. 395.

[16] Giorgio Candeloro, *Storia dell'Italia moderna*, VI (Milan: Feltrinelli, 1970), 365. By 1892 even the Milanesi had to acknowledge that Reggio Emilia had become the heart of the socialist movement in Italy. See *Critica sociale*, Sept. 16, 1892.

[17] According to Zangheri, "Costa was the only socialist leader who was completely trusted by /Giuseppe/ Massarenti, the recognized head of the workers of Molinella." See "Andrea Costa e le lotte contadine del suo tempo," p. 27. Nullo Baldini, like Massarenti, saw in Costa his "master" and "inspirator," according to Enrico Bassi, "Nullo Baldini e Giuseppe Massarenti," *Figure del primo socialismo italiano* (Turin: Radiotelevisione Italiana, 1951), p. 55. It was also Costa who encouraged Marabini, who organized the peasantry in Imola, to extend his propaganda to the countryside. See Marabini, *Prime lotte socialiste*, p. 203. Siliprandi, the most important of the peasant leaders of Mantua, continually cited Marx, Lassalle, Garibaldi, and Costa in his articles in *La Favilla*. See Hostetter, "Lotta di classe...," p. 59.

[18] Letter of Aug. 17, 1877, B.C.I., no. 25, quoted in *La Lotta*, Jan. 22, 1911.

[19]Guido Ceccaroni, La Difesa (Florence), Jan. 22, 1910. At the time of Costa's death in 1910, La Giustizia, Prampolini's newspaper, commented: "We in the province of Reggio owe a special debt to Andrea Costa: because it was he who after 1886 began to promote that propaganda in our countryside which led to the rise and development of the Partito dei Lavoratori." See La Giustizia (Reggio Emilia), Jan. 29, 1910.

[20]Il proletariato e la borghesia, p. 277.

[21]Quoted in Sempre avanti! (Rome), Jan. 31, 1910. The conservatives, too, saw the social problem primarily in terms of morality. "The so-called social question," wrote one of them, "has always seemed to me...a moral question. It is moral education especially which is urgently needed by the lower classes." See Girolamo Boccardo, "Socialismo contemporaneo," Nuova antologia, 35 (Oct., 1891), 643. These conservatives, however, differed radically from Costa because they chose to view the social question only in terms of a moral problem.

[22]Quoted in La Provincia maceratese (Macerata), Jan. 26, 1910.

[23]"Annotazioni autobiografiche...," p. 319.

[24]Elements of a religious nature, of an intense laical religiosity, had permeated socialist...preaching in Italy ....This fact stands out very clearly in all the documents of early Italian socialism...." See Gaetano Arfé, Storia del socialismo italiano (1892-1926) (Turin: Einaudi, 1965), p. 19.

[25]The same thing, though to a lesser extent, may be said of Marxism in France. "What passed for Marxism in the 1880's, when Jules Guesde, Paul Lafargue, Charles Longuet, and Gabriel Deville began to popularize the new doctrine, was at best an approximation and at worst a caricature." See George Lichtheim, Marxism in Modern France (New York: Columbia Univ. Press, 1966), p. 9. Even Turati and the Milanesi had a limited understanding of the German philosophy. See Arfé, Storia del socialismo italiano, p. 11.

[26]"In the Romagna the modern orientation of socialism was not that which was best suited to the temperament of the population...Marxist principles did not respond to their nature, to their temperament," writes Angiolini, So-

cialismo e socialisti in Italia, p. 224.

[27]Avanti!, Aug. 13, 1882. This view of socialism was shared by Costa's followers in the Romagna. According to Gaetano Zirardini, for example, "Our resistance...is nothing more than the eternal human and social struggle so artistically and poetically symbolized in Prometheus, so humanly personified in Christ." See Il Sole, Mar. 29-30, 1884.

[28]Costa would always maintain that socialism signified the salvation of all classes, not just the proletariat. See his pamphlet, I diritti dell'operaio.

[29]"Sogni e programmi politici di Andrea Costa," p. 501. According to Rampazzi, p. 504, Costa was especially influenced by the "socialismo risorgimentale" of men like Ferrari and Pisacane, a socialism which derived primarily from the French thought of the early nineteenth century.

[30]For Malon's ideas, and those of his school, see Nenah Elinor Fry, "Integral Socialism and the Third Republic (1883-1914)," Diss. Yale 1964.

[31]"Andrea Costa," his friend Enrico Ferri wrote in 1910, "was above all a sentimentalist. His thought, nurtured by good literary and sociological studies, especially during the many months he spent in prison, was sometimes characterized, it is true, by scientific discipline; but his brain was conditioned for the most part by his heart." See Il Messaggero, Jan. 20, 1910.

[32]Judging from the composition of the gathering's organizing commission, it is apparent that the Romagnols had resolved their differences. The commission included Balducci, Brunelli, Ghirardini, and Mario Carrara, all of whom sympathized with Turati's ideas; it also included Costa and his leading supporters: Baldini, Marabini, Massarenti, and Gaetano Zirardini. See Il Moto, July 30, 1893.

[33]Other members of the Executive Commission of the Romagnol Federation elected at Imola: Baldini, Balducci, Brunelli, Carrara, Ghirardini, Marabini, Massarenti, Zirardini, Paolo Armaldi, Francesco Liverani, Giuseppe Magnani, Olindo Malagoli, and Angelo Negri (subprefect of Faenza to the prefect of Forlì, Dec. 27, 1893, A.S.F., Gab. Pref., vol. 157, fasc. 65).

[34]Cortesi, La costituzione del partito socialista

italiano, p. 234.

[35]Critica sociale, Feb. 1, 1910, reproduced in Filippo Turati, Uomini della cultura, ed. Alessandro Schiavi (Bari: Laterza, 1949), p. 78. In the party, Costa--who was always elected to preside over the organization's various national congresses--played an important role as a mediator between the major factions which arose within its ranks. The tolerance he displayed in performing this function earned him the esteem of all wings of the Italian Socialist Party. At his death in 1910, for example, the syndicalists glorified Costa as "master of all the struggles, a master good and great, a gentle master...." See La Propaganda (Naples), Jan. 22-23, 1910. Benito Mussolini, who belonged to the maximalist wing of the party, also had words of praise for his fellow Romagnol: "One of our great family is dead: one whom we might consider our father....The life of Andrea Costa is an example.... behold the...virility of this man. Understand him and bow down before him!" See La Lotta di classe (Forlì), Jan. 22, 1910.